SWALLOWS & MARTINS

An Identification Guide and Handbook

SWALLOWS & MARTINS

An Identification Guide and Handbook

ANGELA TURNER

AND CHRIS ROSE

Houghton Mifflin Company
Boston 1989

Printed in the Netherlands

CONTENTS

ACKNOWLEDGEMENTS

Throughout my swallow studies and the preparation of this book I have been helped by many swallow-watchers and others who have patiently answered my queries, allowed me to see unpublished information, manuscripts and reprints, provided stimulating discussion, or commented on drafts of various chapters or species accounts. I extend my sincere thanks for their help and time to:

D R Aspinwall, N Baldaccini, G F Ball, B Beasley, M D Beecher, E Bitterbaum, P St J B Bowen, M N Brown, R J Brown, D M Bryant, E H Burtt, Jr, R W Butler, R R Cohen, N J Collar, F de Lope Rebollo, E C Dickinson, P O Dunn, A Dyrcz, R Earlé, G Edwards, C Feare, J Fjeldså, C J Hails, M L Hebblethwaite, S Holloway, C E Hopla, D J T Hussell, G Jones, N Krabbe, P E Lederle, M Lentino, M P Lombardo, K-H Loske, J E Loye, S Madge, G Malacarne, E O Minot, A P Møller, E S Morton, P Park, T A Parker III, N Redman, J V Remsen, R J Robertson, K-L Schuchmann, W Serle, W M Shields, M L Snell, D W Snow, A Stattersfield, M J Tarburton, D R Waugh, D R Wells, D Wiggins, M Wilson.

The staff of the British Museum (Natural History) at Tring, particularly G Cowles, P Colston and M Walters, and B McGowan of the Royal Scottish Museum, C Fisher of the Merseyside County Museum, E Philip of Maidstone Museum, W Brotherton of the Scottish Ornithologists' Club Library and L Birch of the Alexander Library at the Edward Grey Institute have been of great help in providing study facilities for Chris Rose and myself; and J Remsen of the Louisiana Zoological Museum kindly loaned us skins.

Finally, Chris Rose and I thank the editor of this series, Chris Perrins, and David Christie, Jo Hemmings, Carolyn Burch, Darina Williams, and Linda McVinnie at Christopher Helm for getting the book off the ground.

INTRODUCTION

Swallows and martins form the family Hirundinidae within the order Passeriformes. They are familiar birds throughout the world, often nesting in close association with people, even inside their homes. They are known to many as harbingers of spring and as symbols of good luck. As a family they are easy to identify, but the family includes many closely related and similar species. This book is designed as a guide to the different species and to their biology.

Following the introduction, the first seven chapters provide an overall picture of the family. These are followed by plates, distribution maps and accounts of all the species, each account being a summary of the species' identification and biology. The plates and accounts are largely in taxonomic order, but in some cases this is altered so that, for example, species from the same geographical area are grouped together. A few species have been intensively studied, particularly in recent years, but many are still poorly known; hence the topic coverage varies from species to species. Mean lengths only are given, as this is not a useful measurement biologically but is a general guide to size. Measurements (range and mean) are given, in millimetres, of the nominate race and from prepared skins, unless otherwise specified (measurements of live birds are usually a few per cent greater than those taken from skins): wing length is the flattened chord; tail length is from the shaft root to the tip of the longest pair of feathers; fork length is the difference between the lengths of the central and the longest tail feathers; bill length is from the tip to the skull (the naso-frontal suture); tarsus length is from the 'knee joint' at the back of the leg to the joint between the tarsus and the middle toe. Weights are in grams. Egg measurements are given in mm (mean and range) and the mean egg weight in grams (some egg weights are calibrated values); these measurements are largely from Schönwetter (1979).

The literature on hirundines as a whole is too large, comprising several thousand papers, notes, reports and books, to give as a comprehensive bibliography in a book such as this. Instead, I have referred to regional guides, atlases, summaries or key papers where possible.

The Plates
The plates show the nominate form unless otherwise stated. Important or diagnostic features are mentioned in the captions on the facing pages.

The Maps
The maps show breeding and non-breeding distributions; more details are given in the species accounts. The movements of hirundines are often complex and many species move locally after breeding; in addition, both breeding and non-breeding ranges are often still poorly known. Hence the maps should be taken as a general guide only. Conventions used in the maps are as follows.

Yellow: Regular breeding areas; sporadic nesting areas are mentioned in the text where appropriate.

Green: Areas where regular breeding occurs and where individuals occur in the non-breeding season.

Blue: Areas where individuals are regularly present outside the breeding season. Individuals may be seen on migration between the areas coloured yellow and blue. Migration routes, where known, are discussed in the species accounts.

SWALLOWS & MARTINS

An Identification Guide and Handbook

MORPHOLOGY AND PLUMAGE

Swallows and martins are instantly recognisable by their slender, streamlined bodies, long, pointed wings and small bills: all adaptations for hunting insects on the wing. Because of their highly specialised lifestyles all the species are rather similar to each other, often differing only slightly in size or in details of plumage.

The family Hirundinidae is characterised by: the syrinx having more or less complete bronchial rings; a slender body and short neck; long, pointed wings with ten primaries, the outermost being extremely reduced; a short, compressed bill with a wide gape; a broad palate, and a broad tongue tapering to a short, bifid tip; loral feathers which are directed forwards; the presence (on some species) of a few rictal bristles; short tarsi and small, weak feet suited to perching rather than walking, although the claws are strong on burrowing and cliff-nesting species; the front toes are more or less united at the base; the tarsi are sharply ridged at the rear; the tarsi and toes are sometimes partly or fully feathered; and the tail has twelve feathers and is often forked, with the outermost feathers sometimes elongated to form streamers. In two genera, *Stelgidopteryx* and *Psalidoprocne*, there are serrations (a series of barbules) on the outer edge of the outer primaries. The sexes are similar in size and usually in plumage, although females may have shorter streamers. Juveniles are similar to adults, but duller, with short outer tail feathers.

The subfamily Pseudochelidoninae (genus *Pseudochelidon*) is intermediate in some respects between other hirundines and other passerine birds. Its members possess a large syrinx and half bronchial rings with a large internal membrane running the length of the bronchial tubes (Lowe 1938). In addition, they have a stout bill and large feet, which is unusual for aerial feeders. Their musculature is also intermediate, with some reduction in the leg muscles, but not so much as in other swallows (Gaunt 1969). Within the subfamily Hirundininae itself, the genera are morphologically quite similar.

The Hirundine Genera The White-thighed Swallow (*Neochelidon*) is a very small, sooty-brown hirundine with a small bill, proportionately short tail with a shallow fork, and a small foot with long white tibial feathers.

The Tawny-headed Swallow and American rough-winged swallows (*Alopochelidon* and *Stelgidopteryx*) are very similar genera, but the latter is characterised by recurved barbs on the outer web of the outer primary of the male and a stouter bill. The function of these barbs is unknown, but they may be used to produce a noise during displays (Lunk 1962). In both genera, the tail is short and almost square. The upperparts are dull grey-brown, but the Tawny-headed Swallow has tawny or rusty coloration on the head. The underparts are paler.

Tree swallows (*Tachycineta*) have a short tail, with a variable depth of fork. The upperparts are glossy or matt blue, green, violet, bronzy-green or coppery, sometimes with a white rump; and the underparts are completely white.

The South American *Notiochelidon* swallows are small hirundines with a short, deep bill. The tail is short and shallowly forked. The upperparts and undertail-coverts are glossy blue or sooty, and the rest of the underparts are white or sooty-grey.

In the White-banded and Black-collared Swallows (*Atticora*), the tail is very long and deeply forked. The upperparts are glossy blue-black, and the underparts are blue-black with a white breast-band or white with a blue-black band.

The American martins (*Progne*) are large (wing more than 115 mm) and have a stout bill and strongly decurved culmen. The tail is short and shallowly forked. These swallows are unusual in showing clear sexual dimorphism in plumage. In four of the five species, the adult males are glossy blue-black, sometimes with white on the underparts, whereas the females are mostly much duller, greyer birds.

Sand martins (*Riparia*) are small to medium-sized hirundines with a relatively small, conical bill, long claws and a short, shallowly forked or square, tail. The plumage is dull brown above and paler below, sometimes with a breast-band.

The African roughwings (*Psalidoprocne*) are small and have markedly long wings and tails and a characteristic series of barbs on the outer web of the outer primary of the male. The function of these barbs is not clear, but they may produce or contribute to the noise made by the birds when displaying (Brosset and Erard 1986). The tail varies from deeply forked to square. The coloration is generally uniform on the upperparts and underparts, ranging from dull brown to black or brown with a blue, green or purplish gloss.

The White-backed Swallow (*Cheramoeca*) is a medium-sized swallow which has largely metallic blue-black underparts and lower back, but has a white head, upper chest and upper back. The tail is deeply forked.

The Grey-rumped Swallow (*Pseudhirundo*) is a rather small hirundine which has a small bill and a metallic blue back, but a brown head and a grey-brown rump; the underparts are dull white. The tail is deeply forked.

The two species of African martin (*Phedina*) are medium-sized, largely grey-brown hirundines with extensively streaked plumage and almost square tails.

Swallows of the genus *Hirundo* range in size from small to large. The bill is small. The tail is long, sometimes with a deep fork and with the outer tail feathers elongated to form streamers. The upperparts are mainly metallic blue-black, often with rufous on the forehead or rump (sometimes on both); the underparts mostly vary from white to rufous, sometimes with streaking, a breast-band or a rufous throat. The inner webs of the rectrices often have white patches of varying size. This genus includes several distinctive groups: the crag martins have a non-glossy brown plumage; barn swallows are metallic blue above and white/buffy/rufous below, often with a breast-band and rufous on the forehead/throat; pearl-breasted swallows are small, with blue upperparts, white underparts and no rufous feathers; mosque swallows have a rufous rump, a plain head and rufous undertail-coverts; red-rumped swallows have a rufous rump and blue undertail-coverts; striped swallows have a rufous head and streaked undersides; and cliff swallows also have some rufous in the plumage, the rump is buffy or rufous, and the iridescent feathers of the mantle have pale edges.

House martins (*Delichon*) are medium-sized, chunky, bull-headed hirundines with a short tail, short, thick bill and feathered toes and tarsi. The upperparts are blue-black with a white rump; the underparts are white.

General Features

Hirundines are mostly small birds, ranging in length from 10 cm (4") to about 24 cm (9½") and in weight some fivefold from less than 10 g (0.3 oz) to over 60 g (2.1 oz), but are typically about 15 cm (6") long, weighing some 20 g (0.7 oz). The largest are the New World martins *Progne*, and there are several very small species such as the White-thighed Swallow in South America and the Grey-rumped Swallow and rough-winged swallows of Africa.

The bill is small, broad and flat, adapted for taking insects in flight. The jaw muscles are strong, and adapted partly for snapping at flying insects and partly for burrowing, or manipulating building materials (Gaunt 1965). The protractor muscles are large so that the mouth can be opened wide. In this, hirundines differ from swifts, which have weaker jaw muscles and are adapted to take softer-bodied, weak-flying insects (Morioka 1974). The hirundine's bill and jaw muscles are suitable for both snapping at prey and slashing at a substrate. In the sand martins, *Riparia*, however, the bill is further modified for burrowing (Gaunt 1965); it is relatively smaller and more conical compared with that of other swallows, so that stresses suffered during digging are reduced and slashing movements in any direction are facilitated. Bill shape also varies with the type of prey taken. In Britain, species feeding on larger prey have stouter bills (Waugh 1978). Hirundines also have forwardly directed loral feathers which act as a lens shade, a feature associated with partial forward vision, an important aid to catching moving prey (Beecher 1953).

Many hirundine species have a deeply forked tail with more or less elongated outer tail feathers. This makes the bird more manoeuvrable (i.e. increasing its ability to brake and turn) and better able to catch faster-flying insects. Species with the more deeply forked tails can fly more slowly and catch more mobile types of insect than the more square-tailed species (Waugh 1978). Long outer tail feathers, however, are also a sexual ornament; they are often much longer on males than on females. Female Barn Swallows thus choose mates partly on the basis of tail length (Møller 1988a, in press).

The legs and feet are relatively weak as they are not designed for habitual walking or running, although swallows can walk and run when necessary. The gait is usually a shuffling mincing walk or a brief run, sometimes with the aid of the wings. The muscles of the legs are reduced in size, number and complexity compared with those of other passerines (Gaunt 1969).

The hirundine plumage is typically dark glossy blue or green above and with paler, often white or rufous, underparts which are sometimes streaked to varying degrees. The rump and forehead are also sometimes pale or of a contrasting colour to the rest of the upperparts, and some species have a breast-band of blue or brown. Many species have white patches on the tail feathers or on the wings. In some hirundines, mainly species that burrow in river banks or live in dry or mountainous areas, such as sand martins or crag martins, the plumage is brown without any gloss, but the upperparts still tend to be darker than the underparts. Hirundines from dry areas, such as the northern races of the Rock Martin, tend to be paler than those from wetter areas. Forest species (such as the Forest Cliff Swallow), on the other hand, tend to be uniformly dark, a possible adaptation to humid conditions (Gloger's rule). The male and female are usually alike, though the female has shorter outer tail feathers when these are elongated in the male. In a few species, especially the *Progne* martins, the female is also duller.

The usually bright plumage with patches of contrasting white or red on the head and throat, white patches in the wings or tail and contrasting rump has probably evolved for social reasons, being used for courtship and threat displays: for example, the male Barn Swallow spreads his tail to show off the white patches during courtship. Coloration probably also serves to identify a particular species. This is necessary if breeding birds are to recognise others of their own species and so to avoid mating with the wrong species. Thus each species within the barn swallow superspecies has a distinctive facial and frontal (throat and upper breast) pattern (plates

15 and 16). The length of the tail also often varies between closely related species, perhaps contributing to a species' distinctive appearance.

Hirundine nestlings are altricial and hatch naked with a few downy feathers and with their eyes closed. The eyes open after four or five days. A denser coat of down develops after about a week, and the nestlings can then start to maintain their own body temperature (Marsh 1979, 1980). The juvenile is usually duller than the adults, with shorter outer tail feathers and sometimes with pale edges to some of the feathers, but is otherwise similar; in a few species, such as the Tree Swallow, first-years are also distinguishable by being brownish.

Moult

Hirundines typically undergo a single, complete, post-nuptial moult (Palmer 1972; Kasparek 1981). Some species also have an inconspicuous and partial second moult, but, except in house martins, this does not involve a change in appearance. In migratory species, such as the Barn Swallow, the moult usually starts on the wintering grounds. Some species, such as the Sand Martin, however, start on the breeding grounds with the mantle, scapulars, tail-coverts, tail and tertials, but the moult is then suspended until after the migration and it continues on the wintering grounds; only a few per cent of birds replace any of their primaries before migration (Mead 1980). In Purple Martins, the moult starts during migration but is suspended while they migrate over the Gulf and Central America (Niles 1972). Moult sometimes overlaps with breeding, especially for individuals breeding late in the season. In some cases, breeding and moult overlap extensively, for example in non-migratory Southern Martins (Eisenmann 1959), in Nepal House Martins (Stresemann and Stresemann 1969) and in Crag Martins (Cramp 1988). The moult is usually slow and protracted because of the need for the bird to fly efficiently at all times in order to feed.

The sequence of moult follows the typical passerine pattern (Palmer 1972; Kasparek 1981). The primaries are renewed descendently from one to nine, and the secondaries ascendently from one to six. Moult of the rectrices starts from the centre and proceeds outward in pairs. Tertial moult starts with the central feather, and the distal feather is dropped last.

CLASSIFICATION

Their unique adaptations as aerial insectivores and their distinctive syrinx (see page 1) make the swallow and martin family, the Hirundinidae, a well-defined group in the oscine Passeriformes (the songbirds). Morphologically, they appear not to have any close living relatives. Early naturalists mistakenly thought that they and the swifts were related because of the similarities in shape and feeding habits (e.g. Forster 1817), but towards the end of the nineteenth century when the last monograph on swallows and martins was written they were recognised as a separate family (Sharpe and Wyatt 1885–1894). Swifts in fact are not close relatives at all; they look similar only because of their similar, aerial, lifestyle.

Taxonomists in the present century (Mayr and Greenway 1956; Storer 1971; Voous 1977) have usually placed the swallows and martins at the beginning of the sequence of Oscines, adjacent to the flycatchers (Muscicapidae), the larks (Alaudidae), the pipits and wagtails (Motacillidae), the cuckoo-shrikes (Campephagidae) or the drongos (Dicruridae), but they have also been placed near the white-eyes (Zosteropidae), the waxwings (Bombycillidae), the starlings (Sturnidae) or the Old World warblers (Sylviidae). Recently, however, a comparison of the DNA of hirundines with that of other groups suggests that they are part of a superfamily which includes the nuthatches (Sittidae), the treecreepers and wrens (Troglodytidae), the titmice (Paridae), the long-tailed tits (Aegithalidae), the kinglets (Regulidae), the bulbuls (Pycnonotidae), the African warblers (Cisticolidae), the white-eyes and the Old World warblers and babblers (Sylviidae) (Sibley and Ahlquist 1982, 1985). Hirundines diverged from this group about 50 million years ago, early in its evolutionary history, and now differ in many ways.

There are two distinctive groups of hirundines: the river martins (subfamily Pseudochelidoninae) and other swallows and martins (subfamily Hirundininae). The river martins are very aberrant hirundines, in particular having more robust legs and feet and a large, stout bill. When the African River Martin was first discovered, it was not even considered to be a swallow: Hartlaub (1861) placed it with the rollers (Coraciidae), and later authors either created a new family for it or placed it with the wood-swallows (Artamidae). After a thorough comparison of its anatomy with that of hirundines and wood-swallows, however, Lowe (1938) concluded that the river martin was closest to the Hirundinidae, but was sufficiently dissimilar to be placed in a separate subfamily. The White-eyed River Martin, discovered only relatively recently, is similar to the African species and is placed in the same subfamily (Kitti 1968). The river martins are most likely to be an early offshoot from the main hirundine lineage. They occur as two localised and widely separated, apparently relict populations in Africa and Thailand, suggesting that they are the remains of an old group of species.

The classification of swallows and martins into genera has changed a great deal over the past century. (There is, incidentally, no real difference between 'swallows' and 'martins', although the term 'martin' usually refers to a hirundine with a squarish rather than a forked tail. The names are, however, used interchangeably in some cases: thus the Sand Martin of the Old World is known as the Bank Swallow in North America.) The earliest naturalists tended to put everything, even swifts, into the one genus *Hirundo*. Gradually, other genera were described. In their monograph, Sharpe and Wyatt (1885–1894) placed the swallows and martins into twelve genera. Earlier this century the number had grown to 26, including many containing only one or a few species. Such a classification tends to obscure evolutionary relationships and implies that there are substantial differences between the species in different genera. This may not be so, and more recently several genera have been merged, but there is still some debate about which are distinct and useful genera. A major problem in trying to classify hirundines is that they are greatly constrained morphologically by their adaptations for feeding on aerial insects, and so the various species often differ in only minor details of relative size and coloration, feathering on the tarsus, the degree of adhesion of the toes, the shape of the nostrils and the outline of the tail, features which often vary within as well as between species. These characters have been used to classify hirundines but their usefulness is uncertain. Ecological and behavioural differences, such as the type of nest used (Mayr and Bond 1943; Brooke 1972, 1974; Voous 1977), as well as biochemical ones (Sibley and Ahlquist 1982), may be more useful in separating genera, but unfortunately the majority of species are poorly known in these respects.

Within genera, some species are clearly more closely related to each other than to other species, thus forming what is termed a superspecies. Several superspecies (for example, the Purple, Grey-breasted, Snowy-bellied and Southern Martins in the New World) can be seen among the swallows and martins, with the member species replacing each other geographically (see below; Hall and Moreau 1970).

Some species of swallows are not clearly defined; and some authorities raise various subspecies to the level of species. Thus Peters (1960) recognised eleven species of African roughwing, instead of the five suggested by Benson (1961) and recognised here. Subspecies are morphologically and geographically distinct forms of a species, differing for example in the coloration of the underparts or rump; they can interbreed but rarely have the opportunity to do so. Different species rarely interbreed, even when they occur in the same area. However, it can be difficult to tell whether two geographically isolated populations are distinct species or just subspecies. A large number of subspecies exists among the swallows and martins. Some of these may be incipient species, still evolving distinct characteristics (Hall and Moreau 1970).

Subfamily Pseudochelidoninae

There are only two species in this subfamily. They are usually both considered to belong to the genus *Pseudochelidon*. Kitti (1968) originally placed them in this one genus since they share similarities in plumage, bill, feet and syringeal structure (see page 1). The White-eyed River Martin *P. sirintarae*, however, has a longer, flatter and wider bill and a less marked ridge between the nasal apertures than the African River Martin *P. eurystomina*. Brooke (1972) therefore suggested that they have quite different feeding ecologies; on the basis of this and of their isolated distributions, he created a new genus *Eurochelidon* for the White-eyed River Martin. Zusi (1978), however, retained the latter species in the genus *Pseudochelidon* on the basis of further measurements revealing a smaller average difference in bill size than was originally thought. The differences in plumage characters between the two species are those typical of congeneric species of hirundine and, without adequate knowledge of their feeding and breeding biology, there seems little justification for putting the river martins into separate genera.

Subfamily Hirundininae

Three New World genera have only one or two representatives: *Neochelidon* (the White-thighed Swallow), *Alopochelidon* (the Tawny-headed Swallow) and *Stelgidopteryx* (the rough-winged swallows). They resemble each other in morphology, coloration and nesting behaviour, all using natural or disused cavities and burrows, and only rarely excavating burrows themselves. They are clearly closely related, although the roughwings differ in having a series of barbules on the outer web of the outer primary. *Alopochelidon* is sometimes merged with *Stelgidopteryx* (e.g. Short 1975). These three genera appear to be the most distantly related of American swallows to the genus *Hirundo*, diverging some 15 million years ago (Sibley and Ahlquist 1982).

The difficulties of determining whether populations are separate species or subspecies is well illustrated by the roughwings. Throughout North and South America the roughwings vary clinally in colour and size. It is difficult to identify distinct populations as they grade into one another. They were considered first to comprise several separate species (Ridgway 1904), and later to be monotypic but with many races (Griscom 1929; Mayr and Short 1970). It was not until, relatively recently, two populations of roughwings, pale-rumped and dark-rumped, were reported breeding in the same area (Skutch 1960) that they were recognised as at least two distinct forms. Stiles (1981), in a re-analysis of specimens from Central America, concluded that two species of roughwings were breeding in Costa Rica without hybridising.

The tree swallow genus *Tachycineta* includes eight similar species, but it is sometimes split, with the Tree Swallow *T. bicolor*, White-rumped Swallow *T. leucorrhoa*, Chilean Swallow *T. leucopyga*, White-winged Swallow *T. albiventer* and Mangrove Swallow *T. albilinea* being placed in a separate genus, *Iridoprocne*. Two of the tree swallows, the Bahama and Golden Swallows *T. cyaneoviridis* and *T. euchrysea*, with restricted ranges on the Bahama Islands and Jamaica respectively, closely resemble the other tree swallows in plumage and behaviour but are sometimes placed in monotypic genera, *Callichelidon* and *Kalochelidon*, respectively, a classification based, however, only on trivial points such as the degree of feathering on the nasal operculum (Ridgway 1904). All these old genera are now usually merged (AOU 1983). Within the genus, the Chilean, White-rumped, White-winged and Mangrove Swallows, all with white rumps, form a distinctive group (Brooke 1974). The two former and the two latter species each form a superspecies. All the species of *Tachycineta* use natural or disused cavities for nest sites.

Four small montane swallows are included in the genus *Notiochelidon*, but they have sometimes been placed in other genera: the Brown-bellied Swallow *N. murina* in a monotypic genus *Orochelidon*, and the Blue-and-white Swallow *N. cyanoleuca* and the Pale-footed Swallow *N. flavipes* in *Pygochelidon* (e.g. Ridgway 1904; Hellmayr 1935; AOU 1983). The Blue-and-white Swallow is also occasionally placed in the genus *Atticora*. All four species have similar build and plumage, with glossy upperparts and dark undertail-coverts, and use natural cavities for nest sites. Separation into other genera is based on trivial points: thus *Orochelidon* is based on details such as the relative proportion of wings and tail and the degree of adhesion between the toes, which are not of generic significance. Nowadays, the genus *Atticora* usually includes just two distinctive species, the Black-collared Swallow *A. melanoleuca* and the White-banded Swallow *A. fasciata*, with a striking glossy blue-black and white plumage and long, deeply forked tail. These are poorly known species, however, requiring additional study to ascertain their affinities. The Black-collared Swallow has sometimes been placed in a separate genus, *Diplochelidon*. *Notiochelidon* diverged from the *Hirundo* lineage some 12.5 million years ago (Sibley and Ahlquist 1982).

The American martins, genus *Progne*, are the largest of the hirundines. They diverged from the *Hirundo* lineage some 11.5 million years ago (Sibley and Ahlquist 1982). Four of the species, the Purple Martin *P. subis*, the Grey-breasted Martin *P. chalybea*, the Snowy-bellied Martin *P. dominicensis* and the Southern Martin *P. modesta*, are closely allied and form at least a superspecies (if not a single species); they replace one another geographically. There is, however, disagreement about which forms are races and which are species, the races of the Southern and Snowy-bellied Martins sometimes being given specific status (AOU 1983) (see also pages 123–133). The Brown-chested Martin *P. tapera* differs in some minor ways from the other four *Progne* species and has sometimes been allocated a genus of its own, *Phaeoprogne*. In contrast to the other martins, the Brown-chested has similar sexes, lacks a glossy plumage, and has a more slender bill, a less deeply forked tail with broader plumes, weaker feet and more extensive feathering on the inner side of the upper tarsus. These, however, are relatively minor differences and, in order to maintain their obviously close relationships, I prefer to keep all five species in the same genus.

The sand martins, genus *Riparia*, are a group of four very similar species that have specialised in making their own burrows for nesting in. They probably originated in the Old World: three species, the Brown-throated Sand Martin *R. paludicola*, the Banded Martin *R. cincta* and the Congo Sand Martin *R. congica*, occur in the Old World only, but one, the Sand Martin or Bank Swallow *R. riparia*, is widespread in both the Old and the New Worlds. According to DNA analysis, they are most closely allied to the American martins (Sibley and Ahlquist 1982), but they differ markedly in their nesting behaviour as none of the American martins makes burrows.

The Old World genus *Psalidoprocne* (the African rough-winged swallows, also known as saw-winged swallows) contains eleven very similar forms, some of which are probably incipient species: i.e. they are likely to be evolving into distinct species (Hall and Moreau 1970). The various roughwings differ mainly in slight details of plumage, but more knowledge of their behaviour and ecology is needed before the specific or subspecific identity of some can be confirmed. Here, following Benson (1961), I recognise five species and retain the others as subspecies. The Cameroon Mountain Roughwing *P. fuliginosa* and the White-headed Roughwing *P. albiceps* form a superspecies characterised by a shallowly forked tail with broader outer tail feathers. The Black Roughwing *P. pristoptera* and the Fanti Roughwing *P. obscura* form a separate group with very deeply forked tail. The Square-tailed Roughwing *P. nitens* is probably not closely related to the other roughwings. The genus itself is distinctive, as these swallows have a series of minute barbules on the outer edge of the outer primary. Their relationships with other hirundines are unclear. The American roughwings have similar serrations on the wings and similar nesting habits, but differ in other respects, particularly in plumage and tail shape (pages 1–2).

The Grey-rumped Swallow has often been included in the genus *Hirundo* on the basis of its coloration, but its nesting habits are quite unlike those of typical *Hirundo* swallows as it does not build a mud nest; it also has a weaker, smaller bill. It is therefore best kept in the separate genus *Pseudhirundo* (Roberts 1922; Brooke 1972). It is monotypic, although the race *andrewi*, considered by Hall and Moreau (1970) to be a subspecies, is sometimes raised to specific level (Williams 1966; Brooke 1972). The monotypic genus *Cheramoeca*, the White-backed Swallow, is similar to *Pseudhirundo* in basic coloration, build and nesting habits, and these genera may be related.

The African martins, genus *Phedina*, have a disjunct distribution, with the Mascarene Martin *P. borbonica* in Madagascar and the Mascarene Islands and the Congo Martin *P. brazzae* in the lower Congo Basin, and neither builds a mud nest. They appear to be relicts of an early radiation of swallows and may be members of separate genera. Wolters (1971) created the genus *Phedinopsis* for *brazzae*, with which Brooke (1972) concurred. The striped plumage suggests a relationship with the genus *Hirundo*.

The most specialised and recent genus, *Hirundo*, comprises the largest number of species (34). These have often been split into several genera, the main ones being *Ptyonoprogne* (the crag martins), *Petrochelidon* (the cliff swallows) and *Cecropis* (the red-rumped, mosque and striped swallows, i.e. Red-rumped, Striated, Mosque, Rufous-chested, Lesser and Greater Striped Swallows) (e.g. Brooke 1972; Voous 1977), although other, sometimes monotypic genera have been suggested. Each group is distinctive: thus, typically, members of the crag martin superspecies are uniformly coloured, members of the cliff swallow superspecies mostly have a rufous or buffy rump and squarish tail, and red-rumped, mosque and striped swallows have a rufous rump and deeply forked tail. However, they are all similar to the Barn Swallow, the most typical *Hirundo*, in making mud nests and often in certain colour patterns such as white tail patches and buffy or rufous forehead or throat. Moreover, the American Cliff and Cave Swallows both hybridise with the Barn Swallow at a low but stable level where the species nest in proximity to one another (Martin 1980). One would not expect to see such hybridisation between members of different genera. In addition, comparison of their DNA indicates that the American Cliff Swallow is probably closely related to the Barn Swallow (Sibley and Ahlquist 1982). There are, thus, good reasons for including cliff swallows in the genus *Hirundo*. The red-rumped, mosque and striped swallows are also probably no more different from the barn swallows than are the cliff swallows. The crag martins differ primarily in lacking a glossy plumage and so are often retained in the genus *Ptyonoprogne* (Voous 1977). This difference is not, however, sufficient to warrant excluding them from the genus *Hirundo*, which they resemble in other respects such as their tail pattern, egg colour and nest type (Brooke 1972). The affinities of two 'cliff' swallows, *andecola* and *fuliginosa*, are still unclear, however: *andecola* may be related to the *Stelgidopteryx* group, and *fuliginosa* may belong to another *Hirundo* lineage (Earlé 1987e, pers. comm.). Apart from cliff swallows and crag martins, superspecies in the *Hirundo* genus include the barn swallows themselves (Barn, Red-chested, Angolan, Pacific, Welcome, White-throated and Ethiopian Swallows); Wire-tailed and White-throated Blue Swallows; Pied-winged, White-tailed and Pearl-breasted Swallows; Blue and Black-and-rufous Swallows; Lesser and Greater Striped Swallows; Mosque and Rufous-chested Swallows; and Red-rumped and Striated Swallows. The species that make open mud nests (such as crag and barn swallows) are probably the most primitive members of this genus, and those that enclose their nests (red-rumped and cliff swallows) the most derived.

The house martins, genus *Delichon*, are similar in colour pattern and nesting habits to the cliff swallows, but they differ in having feathered tarsi and their nests lack an extended opening. They are clearly a specialised offshoot of the cliff swallow-barn swallow lineage, and, indeed, there have been many cases of House Martins and Barn Swallows hybridising (Menzel 1984). The number of hybrids reported suggests that these two species are members of the same genus and are as closely related as are cliff and barn swallows. Wolters (1952) suggested merging the two genera. A comparison of their DNA and proteins with those of barn and cliff swallows is needed to confirm their relationships, and a change of genus before such a study is completed would be premature.

The following classification follows probable evolutionary relationships but does not necessarily indicate a linear sequence between genera or between species. For common names, I have retained the most frequently used local name, except where this might be confusing or not representative of the species as a whole. For example, the species *Hirundo rustica* is known in Britain simply as 'the Swallow'; in this case I have used the American name, Barn Swallow, which is being increasingly adopted.

FAMILY HIRUNDINIDAE
Subfamily Pseudochelidoninae: river martins

Genus *Pseudochelidon*
Pseudochelidon eurystomina — African River Martin
Pseudochelidon sirintarae — White-eyed River Martin

Subfamily Hirundininae

Genus *Neochelidon*
Neochelidon tibialis — White-thighed Swallow

Genus *Alopochelidon*
Alopochelidon fucata — Tawny-headed Swallow

Genus *Stelgidopteryx*
Stelgidopteryx ruficollis — Southern Rough-winged Swallow
Stelgidopteryx serripennis — Northern Rough-winged Swallow

Genus *Tachycineta*
Tachycineta bicolor — Tree Swallow
Tachycineta albilinea — Mangrove Swallow
Tachycineta albiventer — White-winged Swallow
Tachycineta leucorrhoa — White-rumped Swallow
Tachycineta leucopyga — Chilean Swallow
Tachycineta thalassina — Violet-green Swallow
Tachycineta cyaneoviridis — Bahama Swallow
Tachycineta euchrysea — Golden Swallow

Genus *Notiochelidon*
Notiochelidon murina — Brown-bellied Swallow
Notiochelidon cyanoleuca — Blue-and-white Swallow
Notiochelidon flavipes — Pale-footed Swallow
Notiochelidon pileata — Black-capped Swallow

Genus *Atticora*
Atticora fasciata — White-banded Swallow
Atticora melanoleuca — Black-collared Swallow

Genus *Progne*
Progne tapera — Brown-chested Martin
Progne subis — Purple Martin
Progne dominicensis — Snowy-bellied Martin
Progne chalybea — Grey-breasted Martin
Progne modesta — Southern Martin

Genus *Riparia*
Riparia paludicola — Brown-throated Sand Martin
Riparia congica — Congo Sand Martin
Riparia riparia — Sand Martin
Riparia cincta — Banded Martin

Genus *Psalidoprocne*
Psalidoprocne fuliginosa — Cameroon Mountain Rough-winged Swallow
Psalidoprocne albiceps — White-headed Rough-winged Swallow
Psalidoprocne pristoptera — Black Rough-winged Swallow
Psalidoprocne obscura — Fanti Rough-winged Swallow
Psalidoprocne nitens — Square-tailed Rough-winged Swallow

Genus *Cheramoeca*
Cheramoeca leucosternus — White-backed Swallow

Genus *Pseudhirundo*
Pseudhirundo griseopyga — Grey-rumped Swallow

Genus *Phedina*
Phedina borbonica   Mascarene Martin
Phedina brazzae   Congo Martin

Genus *Hirundo*
CRAG MARTINS
Hirundo rupestris   Crag Martin
Hirundo fuligula   Rock Martin
Hirundo concolor   Dusky Crag Martin
BARN SWALLOWS
Hirundo rustica   Barn Swallow
Hirundo lucida   Red-chested Swallow
Hirundo angolensis   Angolan Swallow
Hirundo tahitica   Pacific Swallow
Hirundo neoxena   Welcome Swallow
Hirundo albigularis   White-throated Swallow
Hirundo aethiopica   Ethiopian Swallow
WIRE-TAILED SWALLOW GROUP
Hirundo smithii   Wire-tailed Swallow
Hirundo nigrita   White-throated Blue Swallow
PEARL-BREASTED SWALLOW GROUP
Hirundo leucosoma   Pied-winged Swallow
Hirundo megaensis   White-tailed Swallow
Hirundo dimidiata   Pearl-breasted Swallow
BLUE SWALLOW GROUP
Hirundo atrocaerulea   Blue Swallow
Hirundo nigrorufa   Black-and-rufous Swallow
STRIPED SWALLOWS
Hirundo cucullata   Greater Striped Swallow
Hirundo abyssinica   Lesser Striped Swallow
MOSQUE SWALLOWS
Hirundo semirufa   Rufous-chested Swallow
Hirundo senegalensis   Mosque Swallow
RED-RUMPED SWALLOWS
Hirundo daurica   Red-rumped Swallow
Hirundo striolata   Striated Swallow
CLIFF SWALLOWS
Hirundo preussi   Preuss's Cliff Swallow
Hirundo rufigula   Angolan Cliff Swallow
Hirundo andecola   Andean Cliff Swallow
Hirundo nigricans   Tree Martin
Hirundo spilodera   South African Cliff Swallow
Hirundo perdita   Red Sea Swallow
Hirundo pyrrhonota   Cliff Swallow
Hirundo fulva   Cave Swallow
Hirundo fluvicola   Indian Cliff Swallow
Hirundo ariel   Fairy Martin
Hirundo fuliginosa   Forest Cliff Swallow

Genus *Delichon*
Delichon urbica   House Martin
Delichon dasypus   Asian House Martin
Delichon nipalensis   Nepal House Martin

DISTRIBUTION AND MIGRATION

Distribution

Swallows and martins are cosmopolitan. Although absent from the high Arctic and Antarctica, they breed on every continent and on many islands. Many species are confined to smaller areas, but two, the Barn Swallow and the Sand Martin, have colonised both sides of the Atlantic.

Africa is the richest continent for swallows: 29 species breed only there, while others either breed there and in Europe or Asia or visit Africa during the non-breeding season. This is probably the place where swallows originated. Nine species breed only in Europe and Asia, with a further four breeding in Africa as well, while Australasia has only four endemic species. The family is also poorly represented in North America, with five exclusive species; but it has diversified in South and Central America, where there are 19 breeding species in addition to northern visitors in the non-breeding season. Another two species are confined to Caribbean islands. Two species breed in Europe, Asia and North America.

The ranges of the different species vary widely, from the cosmopolitan Barn Swallow to the African River Martin (confined to the Congo River) and the Golden Swallow (confined to Jamaica and Hispaniola). The difference in extent of the present-day ranges is probably due to several factors, such as isolation during the history of a species, replacement by similar species and the species' habitat requirements.

Hirundines probably spread from Africa to the rest of the world at an early stage in their evolution when they were just hole nesters. The distribution of the hole-nesting genera must once have been more continuous, but has now become disjunct, perhaps because of changes in climate and vegetation; the extent of rainforest in Africa, for example, has varied considerably in the past 3 million years, at times stretching across the continent and separating northern and southern populations of open-country species (Moreau 1972; Livingstone 1975). Thus, isolated and even widely separated populations occur of what were once more widespread swallows. The river martins are found in Central Africa and in Thailand; the African martins have representatives in Central Africa and Madagascar; and the Grey-rumped Swallow of Africa and the White-backed Swallow of Australia are probably also relicts of a once widespread group. Within Africa, related species have also become isolated, as for example the White-tailed Swallow in southern Ethiopia, separated from the closely related Pearl-breasted Swallow in southern Africa and the Pied-winged Swallow in West Africa.

Many species are replacement species: that is two or more closely related species occur in adjacent geographical areas, such as the Northern and Southern Rough-winged Swallows, and the European and Asian House Martins. Often, it is not clear whether the two forms are in fact separate species or just races of a single species. If the ranges overlap without the two forms hybridising then they are clearly good species, but their exact breeding ranges are often not known well enough to determine this, and a small amount of hybridisation can be expected anyway between closely related species.

In the New World, hole-nesting swallows evolved into several genera: *Progne*, *Tachycineta*, *Notiochelidon*, *Neochelidon*, *Alopochelidon*, *Stelgidopteryx* and *Atticora*, each with only one or a few representatives. *Progne* and *Tachycineta* are the largest genera, with five and eight species respectively, replacing one another geographically from Canada to Tierra del Fuego. *Notiochelidon* includes four species in different areas and at different altitudes. *Stelgidopteryx* has a northern and a southern form, *Atticora* contains two Amazonian species, and *Neochelidon* and *Alopochelidon* each have a single South American representative.

In the Old World, the few hole nesters are mainly relict species, but one genus, *Riparia*, with four species, which dig their own burrows, has spread through Europe, Asia and North America. The genus *Psalidoprocne* is widespread throughout Africa and contains five species with many races which may be incipient species. The most successful genus, though, is *Hirundo*, with 34 species, mostly African but with some in Europe, Asia and the New World. Within this genus, nest construction has become more specialised, from simple open cups to closed nests with entrance tunnels. The cliff swallow group, in particular, with some of the most elaborate nests and the most colonial way of life, is represented by different species throughout Africa, Asia, Australia and North and South America. In Europe and northern Asia, the cliff swallows are replaced by the three species of *Delichon*, a close ally of *Hirundo*.

Though swallows and martins are widespread, on a local scale their distribution can be patchy because of their habitat requirements. They have evolved as hunters of insects on the wing, so they need a habitat with a good supply of insects and with open areas in which to manoeuvre. They also need suitable breeding sites. Originally these would have been mainly disused holes in trees and river banks, or crevices in cliffs and caves. When some species evolved the ability to build a mud nest or dig their own burrows they would have been rather less constrained, but they still needed overhanging boughs or rocks under which to build their nest or suitable banks to burrow into. Typical habitats include forested rivers, wooded savanna, deep gorges or sea-coasts with cliffs and caves, with different species specialising on different habitats and altitudes, from the Forest Cliff Swallow in lowland-forest clearings in Central Africa to the Nepal House Martin on the slopes of the Himalayas. During the non-breeding seasons, swallows and martins are less restricted to certain habitats, feeding over a wider range of altitudes and open areas.

The different genera differ substantially in their natural habitat requirements for breeding. The African River Martin needs sand-banks along forested rivers. *Tachycineta* is typical of areas of open water and coasts, mainly in the lowlands but with one upland specialist, the Violet-green Swallow. *Notiochelidon* specialises in upland areas where cliffs and banks are available for nesting. *Atticora* prefers forested lowland rivers. *Neochelidon* is also a forest species, frequenting clearings. *Alopochelidon* and *Stelgidopteryx* are less specialised and frequent a variety of open areas. *Progne* is also catholic in its habitat preferences, which range from cliffs in the Galapagos and pine ridges in the West Indies to the pampas and llanos of South America. *Riparia* is typically a lowland riverine group, needing river banks in which to burrow. *Cheramoeca*, *Pseudhirundo*, *Psalidoprocne* and *Phedina* also frequent rivers with suitable banks but use cliffs as well. *Hirundo* has species in every habitat from rainforest to desert, from sea-coasts to uplands, but the true upland specialists are the *Delichon* species.

When hirundines started using human structures and earthworks to build on or in, however, they became less restricted to a particular habitat and were able to expand their ranges into areas where previously they would not have found nest sites. Not all species took advantage of this; some (River and Congo Martins, Congo Sand Martins, Square-tailed Roughwings, Black-collared, White-banded, White-thighed, Black-and-rufous and White-tailed Swallows) still use only natural sites, and others such as the Blue Swallow and White-throated Blue Swallow (Snell 1979; Brosset and Erard 1986) are still experimenting with the new structures. Some, however, have exploited humans to the full. Barn Swallows are now typical farmland birds rather than a mainly coastal and cave-dwelling species. House Martins have perhaps gone furthest, changing from cliffs to towns and cities, and even nesting in the Docklands in the heart of London.

Range expansions have followed the change in habitat and the increasing availability of artificial nest sites: examples include the Barn Swallow in the southeastern United States (Robbins *et al.* 1986) and the Ethiopian Swallow in East Africa (Grant and Lewis 1984), perhaps sometimes aided by changes in climate (e.g. Red-rumped Swallow: de Lope Rebollo 1981).

Migrations

Many hirundines undertake regular migrations to and from wintering and breeding areas; in some cases, movements are local and even irregular. In addition to these, there is characteristically a dispersal of juveniles away from their natal site to other, often local, sites, where they breed the following season.

Hirundines breeding in temperate regions migrate regularly from north to south or vice versa to warmer areas for the non-breeding season. This may involve a long migration across the tropics: thus, Barn Swallows breeding in northern Europe migrate to southern Africa. Others travel less far, just enough to avoid the harshest conditions: thus, Tree Swallows migrate from North America only down to Central America and Crag Martins from southern Europe to northern Africa (AOU 1983; Cramp 1988). Certain species include both migratory and resident populations: northern populations of the Chilean Swallow are resident, while southern ones migrate north to winter (Johnson 1967). Hirundines breeding in North America winter in Central and South America, those breeding in Europe generally winter in Africa, and those breeding in Central and eastern Asia generally winter in southern and southeastern Asia, but there is considerable overlap. South American and Australian species migrate within their respective continents. Records suggest that swallows are faithful both to their breeding and to their wintering sites (Cramp 1988).

In Africa, hirundines often migrate with the rains, but the movements can be complex and are often poorly understood. Several species, such as the African River Martin, breed in areas that are flooded for part of the year and they then move elsewhere (Chapin 1953). Other species follow the rains to breed at the start of the wet season, when insects are most abundant: thus, the Banded Martin is a wet-season breeding visitor to Nigeria. Some African species vacate only part of their range: the Rufous-chested Swallow in Nigeria, for example, moves out of the southern part of its range in the wet season. Yet other species, such as the Grey-rumped Swallow, are nomadic, opportunistic breeders, sporadically appearing in and disappearing from parts of their range (Elgood *et al.* 1973).

Many species are resident but make some local movements after breeding, often deserting the breeding sites and sometimes moving to lower altitudes (for example, Rock Martins in South Africa: Maclean 1985) or to other areas where they can roost in flocks at night and disperse to feed during the day. Other species stay in the same area all year: Grey-breasted Martins in Trinidad, for example, remain close to the nest site when not breeding (Bitterbaum 1986).

Of those species migrating regularly, the long-distance migrant Barn Swallow, Sand Martin and House Martin are the best studied. Unlike many migrants, hirundines travel by day in small, loose groups, feeding as they go, often at low altitudes. There are, however, some areas such as the Alps and Sahara that they must cross without feeding, so they do have some fat reserves, although not as much as some long-distance migrants (Lyuleeva 1973). Some species can also become torpid in cold weather, thereby reducing their food requirements (Lyuleeva 1973). Even so, they can be severely affected if they encounter bad weather (Bruderer 1979).

Hirundines migrate primarily to avoid prolonged harsh weather, when their insect food becomes unavailable. There are few records of hirundines in winter at northerly latitudes, though Tree Swallows survive better than most by eating vegetable matter such as berries. By migrating to these northern areas to breed, on the other hand, they can take advantage of the plentiful supply of insects present during summer (Hails 1982). Barn Swallows arrive at their breeding sites as the abundance of insects is increasing, and they leave as it drops (Waugh 1978). A changing food supply probably governs the movements of most other hirundines as well. Long-distance migrations may thus have evolved by some individuals moving from areas with unpredictable food supplies (for example, in arid savanna in Africa) to more temperate northerly areas with a more abundant and predictable food supply for part of the year (Alerstam and Enckell 1979; Gauthreaux 1982).

FOOD, FORAGING AND COMPETITION

Diet

Insects are the mainstay of swallow life. The ecology and behaviour of swallows are intertwined with the distribution and abundance of insects. Species that feed on relatively large, dispersed insects are generally fairly solitary or nest in loose groups, whereas the colonial species often feed on small, swarming insects, benefiting from the increased foraging efficiency of the colony (Brown 1988). In addition, the timing of breeding coincides with the time when insects are most abundant locally (Waugh 1978).

Nearly all the food of swallows consists of insects caught in flight. Only one species eats a substantial amount of plant food: the Tree Swallow includes some seeds and berries, mainly the bayberry, in its diet (Beal 1918), but then only early in the breeding season or in bad weather when insect food is scarce. Greater and Lesser Striped Swallows have also been recorded eating fruits (Broekhuysen 1960; McLean 1988) and plant material occasionally turns up in the diet of other swallows (Beal 1918; Cramp 1988), but these are rare occurrences, not important components of the diet.

Not all insects are eaten equally. Different swallow species select different types of prey, this selection being based mainly on the size and mobility of the insect rather than on its taxonomic group. The mobility of the insect is important because a large fast-flying insect will be more difficult to catch than a large slow-flying one. Unfortunately, the diets of the majority of species are either unknown or poorly known; many swallows are simply recorded as eating 'insects' or 'flies', but detailed analyses have not been made. So far as is known, however, few hirundines regularly catch the largest insects such as dragonflies and butterflies, although many do so occasionally; those that do, the American martins, are the largest of the hirundines. Equally, few hirundines specialise on tiny insects such as greenfly; the House Martin is one of the few known to do so (Bryant 1973). The rest take varying proportions of medium-sized insects such as flies, beetles, mayflies, parasitic wasps and ants. All species, however, have a varied diet: even the dragonfly and butterfly specialists eat some smaller insects such as termites, ants and beetles (Beal 1918; Turner 1983; Dyrcz 1984), and there is no clear relationship between the size of the bird and the size of its prey. In bad weather, large flying insects are often scarce, hence hirundines commonly resort to taking small insects at such times (Turner 1980, 1984).

Although hirundines base their choice of food largely on its size, they do have some likes and dislikes of particular types of insects. Thus, in Britain, Barn Swallows take few dungflies, even when these are abundant (Turner 1980); they also usually avoid stinging insects such as wasps, and they catch few bees (those they do catch are usually stingless drones).

Despite their predilection for insects, swallows and martins occasionally eat other types of small prey. These are mostly spiders, which sometimes drift in the air and so can be caught by an aerial feeder. Some invertebrates such as sand flies and sand hoppers are eaten by swallows perching on the ground or on vegetation (Cramp 1988). There is also even a record of a Barn Swallow catching a stickleback (Gasterosteidae) (Cramp 1988)! Grit is also commonly ingested.

The diet can vary over the year, either because of local changes in insect abundance or because the hirundines move out of one area into another where the insects are different. Some types of insect are available for only a short period. Swarms of emerging or mating insects form at certain times of the year and are then exploited by swallows, but this food source may not last long. Termites and winged ants are particularly important prey for tropical hirundines, but they swarm and are available only when it rains. Swallows and martins that migrate between temperate and tropical areas change their diet quite radically. Barn Swallows eat mostly flies in Britain, but change to beetles and ants when they are in Africa (Waugh 1978). Diets also vary between different races or populations of the same species, probably mainly because the available insects are different: thus, the British Sand Martin eats more flies and fewer beetles and plant bugs than the North American Bank Swallow (Waugh 1979).

Nestling hirundines are often fed insects different from those eaten by the adults (Waugh 1978). Adults may catch small insects for themselves, but carry large items to the nestlings. Young nestlings are also given fewer hard-bodied insects such as beetles.

Feeding Behaviour   Swallows and martins feed in a variety of habitats but they concentrate their efforts wherever insects are plentiful, especially where swarms of insects occur. Few feed within forests, where flying insects are scarce and manoeuvring is difficult for the bird. Open ground, forest edge or open water are preferred. Any good source of insects, however transient, is exploited, including those provided by savanna fires and moving animals and tractors which disturb insects from the vegetation or ground. Welcome Swallows have even been recorded catching moths attracted to lights at night (Hobbs 1966).

Most insects are caught while the bird is flying in the open, but other techniques are also used. Hirundines sometimes brush past vegetation, which may disturb insects enough to make them fly or, in the case of caterpillars, cause them to dangle by threads from the vegetation, making it easy for the swallow to catch them (Turner 1981). They also occasionally hover in front of vegetation, and will even perch on vegetation and the ground, and pick up insects, spiders or crustaceans. Skimming over water also allows them to pick insects from the water's surface. Such techniques are rare, however, and usually occur only in bad weather when insects are not flying. Bad weather also often localises insects, perhaps in the lee of a shelterbelt or over a sheltered stretch of river, forcing the hirundines to concentrate in these areas. In the non-breeding season, when they are not pressed for time, swallows and martins often use a flycatcher technique, sallying out from a perch to catch a single insect and bringing it back to the perch to eat.

When breeding, swallows and martins feed close to the nest, especially when they have nestlings to look after, but species vary in this. Some, such as the Barn Swallow, concentrate their hunting to within a couple of hundred metres of the nest; others, such as the House Martin, feeding on more localised insects, may have to hunt several kilometres away (Bryant and Turner 1982).

Many species, including the Barn Swallow, are solitary hunters, although they sometimes feed in loose groups. A few, such as the Cliff Swallow, feed in flocks. Again, this is related to the type of insects caught: solitary hunters go after widely dispersed prey, whereas flock feeders tend to hunt localised, swarming prey.

Swallows and martins actively hunt insects; they do not just trawl for them while in flight. When hunting for their nestlings, they usually catch several insects at a time; these are compressed into a bolus, which is carried in the throat back to the nest. If the insects are large, only one or a few will be carried, but when the insects are small a bolus can contain more than a hundred (Turner 1980). The size of the bolus brought back also depends on how far away the parent collected the prey; Sand Martins and House Martins bring back more food when they have to travel further from the nest, although Barn Swallows do not (Bryant and Turner 1982).

Competition between Species

There are many similar species of hirundine and many have overlapping population ranges. They could thus potentially compete with one another. They also share the air space with other aerial feeders such as swifts and bats, and with birds such as flycatchers and bee-eaters that fly out from a perch to catch flying insects. They avoid competition in several ways, by using different geographical ranges, habitats, nest sites, breeding seasons, or food.

Closely similar species often replace each other geographically and may breed in the same areas only at the borders of their ranges: thus, Northern and Southern Rough-winged Swallows breed together only in Costa Rica, at their southern and northern limits, respectively (Stiles 1981).

Where two species do breed in the same area, they usually differ in some other way. In any community of aerial feeders, the different species usually feed at different sites and on different prey. Thus, in Britain, Barn Swallows feed on large, fast-flying insects, and hunt low (7–8 m on average) over the ground or water; Sand Martins feed on smaller insects at mid level (15 m) over open ground; House Martins feed on small insects at mid to high levels (22 m), again over open ground; while the fourth aerial feeder in this community, the Swift *Apus apus*, feeds on very small, weak-flying insects, high up (29 m) above both open ground and vegetation (Bryant 1973; Waugh 1978). When they do use the same air space, they avoid competition by increasing the difference in the size of prey they take (Waugh 1978).

Similar species also often avoid nesting together. The British hirundines and Swift use different nest sites: Barn Swallows keep to rural areas, nesting inside buildings; Sand Martins breed along rivers or in quarries; House Martins are both rural and urban dwellers, nesting on the outside of buildings; and the Swift nests in towns, inside buildings. Time is also important in separating species: swifts and swallows use the air space during the day, and are replaced by bats at night.

When the British hirundines migrate to Africa they would appear to face even more competition from the many resident species, several of which are breeding at that time and so have high food requirements. Hirundines in Africa, however, are segregated in many ways, including through altitude and habitat. Thus, the Red-breasted Swallow frequents more open country than the similar Mosque Swallow, and the African Rock Martin is confined to areas with gorges and cliffs (Benson *et al.* 1971). When several species do feed together, they adopt different feeding stations. In Malawi, the African swifts and the House Martin feed at high levels (55 m), Mosque Swallows and migrant and Brown-throated Sand Martins feed at mid levels (14–25 m), and the Lesser Striped, Grey-rumped, Wire-tailed and Barn Swallows feed low over the ground (6–8 m: Waugh 1978). Some species, especially the Wire-tailed Swallow, also concentrate on feeding over water whereas others, such as the

Grey-rumped Swallow, will feed over vegetation and open ground. The various species also differ in size, bill shape and manoeuvrability and so are likely to hunt different types of insects (Waugh 1978). Thus, the larger African Banded Martin may take larger prey than the smaller migrant Sand Martin. Such observations suggest that competition between the different species is minimised.

Elsewhere, other communities are segregated in similar ways. When Barn Swallows and Pacific Swallows are both present in Malaysia, the former feeds at higher levels (28 m) and catches smaller insects, mainly winged ants and parasitic Hymenoptera, than the Pacific Swallow (12 m), which catches more flies (Waugh and Hails 1983). In North and South America, the different species are segregated mainly geographically, by habitat and by altitude. There are several similar species, such as those of the tree swallow group, that replace one another in different areas and so do not compete. New World species also differ in their feeding habitat and their choice of food, from the dragonfly and butterfly specialists in the *Progne* group to specialists on small insects such as the cliff swallow group.

The increasing use of artificial structures as nest sites, however, is breaking down barriers between species and subspecies, extending their geographical ranges, increasing population sizes and perhaps increasing competition between them. Cave Swallows, for example, have spread into the USA, where they use the same breeding sites as Barn Swallows (Martin 1981); and long-term increases in migrant hirundine populations may have led to increased competition on the wintering grounds with resident species (Waugh 1978).

BEHAVIOUR

Although the behaviour of most species of hirundine is very poorly known, a few have been the focus of many detailed studies. Gilbert White's view of swallows presenting 'an instructive pattern of unwearied industry and affection' (White 1789) has become somewhat marred by the knowledge that they commit infanticide and rape, that males are promiscuous and that some females dump their eggs in others' nests, leaving the victim to rear the chick.

Social Organisation
For a male to breed successfully he must first acquire a nest site. This becomes his and his mate's territory, which is guarded against intruders. The size of the territory depends on how close together the individuals nest. In a highly colonial species such as the Cliff Swallow, whose nests abut one another, it is just the nest itself (Brown 1985a); in contrast, the Tree Swallow, which nests in loose groups, defends an area of about 15 m radius (Robertson and Gibbs 1982). Some species are more solitary nesters: Blue Swallows usually nest at least 0.8 km (½ mile) from each other, though they do not defend this large area as a territory (Snell 1969).

Because their insect prey is patchily distributed, hirundines often feed in flocks at sites where insects are concentrated, usually in the vicinity of the nest sites. The bickering at the nests is replaced by greater tolerance when feeding. The less colonial, more solitary species may, however, feed alone. Pairs of Mangrove Swallows, for example, keep to their own exclusive feeding areas (Dyrcz 1984) and Crag Martins feed largely within a defended area along a cliff face (Strahm 1963). The territory itself, however, is usually too small to provide an important place to feed.

Sociosexual Behaviour
In non-migratory populations, a mated pair may stay close to the nest all year, and gradually become more aggressive to intruders as the breeding season approaches (Bitterbaum 1986). In migratory populations (for example of the Barn Swallow, Sand Martin and House Martin: von Vietinghoff-Riesch 1955; Glutz von Blotzheim and Bauer 1985; Cramp 1988), the male usually arrives and selects a nest site first. Experienced breeders will often return to the same site, and usually the same nest, sometimes depending on whether or not they were successful the previous year, and they return early in the season. First-year breeders often return to a site near where they hatched and usually have to prepare a new nest. The male defends the site against other males trying to take it over, and he attempts to attract a female. Once they have paired, the female may participate in defending the site, but the male may then also guard his mate from other males wanting to copulate with her. Throughout the breeding season the nest must be defended against other individuals. These latter visitors may simply be gaining information about possible future breeding sites, but they may also be trying to copulate with the resident female or to kill the young nestlings and evict the residents, so obtaining a nest site (Lombardo 1986a; Crook and Shields 1987). Some of these visitors, for example in Tree Swallows, may be 'floaters', birds which have not yet obtained a nest site. Both males and, in Tree Swallows, females may kill nestlings; by doing so they may greatly improve their chances of breeding (Robertson and Stutchbury 1988).

Displays
Displays play an important role in site advertisement and defence.

20

In general they have not been well documented, but those of the New World martins have been studied in detail (Bitterbaum 1986). Male hirundines advertise the site to potential intruders and to potential mates by singing at the nest site. New World martins and Sand Martins (Kuhnen 1985) have an elaborate Advertising (or Claiming-Reclaiming) display accompanied by song: the male leaves the nest site, flys in a circle above it, returns, often repeatedly entering and emerging, and finally sits in the entrance, continuing to sing. Mud-nest builders generally cling to their prospective nest site and sing from there or fly above the site and sing.

Aggressive displays vary in intensity. In the low-intensity Head Forward Thrust of the New World martins, the wings and sometimes the tail are flicked or quivered, the body is held horizontally, and the plumage is sleeked though the crest and cheek feathers may be raised; the bill is pointed at the opponent. In the high-intensity version of this display, the wing- and tail-flicking cease and the head and neck may be extended. This display may end in the aggressor Bill Snapping and Lunging at its opponent. If the opponent does not retreat, a fight may ensue in which the birds peck and pull each other's feathers. Fights often take place in the air: the combatants grapple with each other and may fall to the ground still fighting. Individuals sometimes get killed in these fights. Although details vary between species, ruffling of the head and neck feathers and quivering of the wings are common elements of hirundine threat displays.

Gaping is a similar display to the Head Forward Thrust, but the bill is opened and the neck extended. Birds gape at others approaching the territory, whether intruders or their own mates.

High-Up displays are used by birds that have been disturbed, or are moving away from another bird or retreating after an agonistic encounter. The Withdraw High-Up involves the bird turning away from another with the head and body feathers erect; the head is held up and the bill directed away from the other bird. The Alert High-Up is a response to a more distant alarming stimulus: the head is raised and directed towards the stimulus, the plumage is sleeked, though the crest feathers are raised, and the wings and tail are flicked.

Pairing and copulation displays are usually brief. When attracting a mate, a male often leads the female back to the nest or may gradually allow a female to alight near him instead of threatening her. Before copulation, males often display by flying, quivering the wings and spreading the tail; the female quivers her wings and allows the male to mount. Copulation often takes place inside the nest.

The plumage is an important element in the displays. Patches of contrasting colour on the forehead and throat are displayed when the male is singing and when the birds threaten each other. Raising crest feathers or ruffling head and neck feathers enhances this visual display. The throat patch may be particularly conspicuous when the bird is sitting in a dark nest-hole. The tail is often patterned and this is displayed when the bird spreads its tail, during courtship, for example. Tail-coverts are also visible during tail-spreading. Wing and rump patches may similarly be enhanced by wing-quivering and tail-flicking. Parts of the plumage can also signal non-aggression. The New World martins have a patch of white on the anterior flank that is normally concealed; when the birds are loafing and preening, however, this patch is displayed, inhibiting attack and allowing the martins to maintain close contact. The dull, brownish plumage of young birds and of first-years in some species such as the Tree Swallow probably also acts as a signal of subordinate status (Stutchbury and Robertson 1987c).

Vocalisations

Song and other calls are also important, although the songs of hirundines are usually just a simple twittering. The song itself is used to advertise the territory and in courtship and may deter intruders such as males seeking extra-pair copulations (A.P. Møller, pers. comm.). The male usually sings while the female is building the nest and again before a second clutch is laid. Hirundines vary in how vocal they are and in the number of calls they have, and it is difficult to generalise. In addition, the calls of the majority of species are very poorly documented. The main types of call, apart from song, however, are: (1) a call used by birds when excited and during agonistic encounters; (2) a repeated short contact call, used to maintain contact with others of the species (members of a pair may also use a nest-relief call); (3) a short, soft call, used during courtship and often when withdrawing from another bird; (4) a harsh alarm call, uttered when a predator is present (there are sometimes low-intensity and high-intensity variants of this call); (5) a call used to assemble fledglings; and (6) a begging call uttered by the young.

Defence of Nest and Mate

Males not only defend their nest but also often guard their mate during her fertile period. Although hirundines form monogamous pairs, the males are promiscuous and attempt to mate, sometimes forcibly, with other females. In Sand Martins, for example, males follow their mates when they leave the burrow (Beecher and Beecher 1979): chases can often be seen, with males trying to inter-cept and mate with an unguarded female. Males also attempt these extra-pair copulations at sites where the birds congregate, for example where Cliff Swallows gather mud for their nests: birds at these congregations often flutter their wings, perhaps to prevent males alighting and copulating with them (Butler 1982b). Not all hirundines guard their mates; in some species such as the Cliff Swallow, it is more important for the nest to be guarded and so it is rarely left unattended (Brown 1985a).

Throughout the breeding season the nest is also defended against predators. A pair of birds will call an alarm and mob potential predators, and, in a colony or group, other birds will join in. Each pair, however, concentrates its mobbing at its own nest site, the male mobbing more intensely than the female (Shields 1984).

Nest-building to Fledging

For many hole-nesting species the nest site is simply a cavity, and nest-building consists of gathering vegetable fibres and feathers to make a soft pad on which the eggs are laid. For burrowing species or mud-nest builders, the process is more complex. A burrow or mud nest can take a week or more to build, and then a pad of vegetation or a lining is added. The burrow is dug by slashing with the bill and kicking out the sand with the feet. It often slopes upwards to prevent rain from entering, and it ends in an enlarged chamber where the nest is placed. A mud nest is made up of hundreds of mud pellets, sometimes mixed with dry grass or straw, to strengthen the structure; Blue and Black-and-rufous Swallows, however, are unusual in collecting the mud and grass together. It is usually started on some sort of projection where the bird can grip the substrate when it begins to build, and is usually close to a ceiling or overhang. First a nest base is made, then, from inside the nest, the birds add pellets in rows vertically and laterally to form a cup. In many species the nest is left as an open cup, but some, such as cliff swallows, red-rumped swallows and house martins, extend it up to the overhang or completely enclose it, leaving a small entrance hole at the top or building an entrance tunnel. The shape of the nest can vary, however, depending on where it is built. Species such as the South African Cliff Swallow which usually make enclosed nests will also nest in crevices and then just use mud to make the entrance smaller and to form a tunnel; in some cases, such as the Asian House Martin, the nest is even left open at the top (Durnev et al. 1983; Earlé 1985b).

Nests are often built several metres apart, but the highly colonial species build theirs abutting each other. Nests that are close together usually have entrances facing away from each other to reduce interactions between neighbours.

When the lining of the nest is added, the male often brings feathers or green leaves, which may be a preliminary to courtship (Morton 1987). Once the nest is completed the female lays her eggs, usually at one-day intervals. During this period some females dump one or more of their eggs in the nests of other females, leaving them to hatch and rear the nestlings. Cliff Swallows will even carry their own eggs to deposit them in others' nests (Brown and Brown 1988). This parasitism is well known only in the American and South African Cliff Swallows (Earlé 1985c; Brown and Brown 1989) and the European race of the Barn Swallow (Møller 1987a), but it probably occurs also among species such as Tree Swallows nesting in groups where the opportunity arises (Lombardo 1988). Parents appear not to recognise their own eggs and they accept the alien one.

Incubation starts when the penultimate egg is laid. When only the female incubates she remains on the eggs for periods of about 20 minutes, leaving them for shorter periods in order to feed. In cold weather, the female remains incubating for longer, but if the weather is very bad she may temporarily desert the nest (Turner 1980). In hot weather, the female often perches away from the eggs, and in the tropics less time is spent incubating (Moreau 1939a, b, 1940; Hails 1984). Where both parents incubate, the eggs are covered nearly 100% of the time. Nest change-over is rapid; the partners often call to each other as one enters the nest.

When the chicks hatch, the egg-shells are dropped over the side of the nest or out of the burrow. The chicks are brooded for several days. When the chicks are very young the faecal pellets may be eaten by the parents; later they are removed by the parents and dropped some distance away, but when the chicks are big enough they defaecate over the edge of the nest or burrow. The parents catch food for the chicks for much of the day, though there are often peaks of feeding in the early morning and late afternoon. The food is brought to the nest as a compact bolus, usually of several items; each chick normally receives a whole bolus, but it is sometimes divided between chicks. Usually several boluses are brought to each chick in an hour, but feeds are less frequent in cool, wet weather when it is more difficult for the parents to find food (Turner 1983a, b, 1984). In burrows and nests with entrance tunnels, the chicks come to the entrance to be fed when they are capable of doing so.

The chicks often fledge over a period of several days, returning to the nest to roost. After they have fledged, they continue to be fed for a while by the parents, sometimes in flight. Barn Swallow fledglings, for example, are fed for another two weeks. In some colonial species, such as Cliff Swallows and Sand Martins, the fledglings are left in a communal crèche while the parents forage; the parents return to and feed only their own offspring. In other species, such as the more solitary Barn Swallow and North American Rough-winged Swallows, each pair of birds leaves its own brood in a separate place. Associated with this difference in behaviour is a difference in the parents' ability to recognise their offspring (Beecher *et al.* 1986). While swallows cannot recognise their own eggs or nestlings, the Cliff Swallow and Sand Martin can identify their fledglings at least by their calls, which are individually distinctive, and possibly by variations in plumage as well. They need to do this because fledglings often land in neighbouring nest sites and must also be singled out in the crèche. The Barn Swallow and the North American Rough-winged Swallow, however, cannot recognise their own brood.

Post-breeding and Roosting Behaviour

First-brood fledglings may stay around the nest site for some time, and have occasionally been recorded helping to feed their parents' second brood (Bryant 1975). They may also indulge in playful burrowing or mud-gathering. Eventually, however, they disperse, often visiting other local nest sites, before joining pre-migratory flocks. Outside the breeding season, even solitary species will form flocks when feeding and, especially, roosting. Some of these flocks may contain hundreds or thousands of birds, sometimes of more than one species.

Outside the breeding season, before migration, roosts often form in reedbeds, tall grasses, crops such as maize or low bushes. Trees are less often used. Roosts also sometimes form on wires or buildings in towns. Before alighting at the roost site, swallows often assemble in large, spiralling flocks overhead, bunching and performing spectacular aerial manoeuvres. In cold weather, communal roosting in sheltered sites such as burrows or buildings also occurs, for example in the Black-capped Swallow (Skutch 1960). During the breeding season, the adults generally roost in the burrow or nest until the nestlings are well grown, when they will roost nearby.

Maintenance Behaviour and Energetics

The final category of behaviour that should be mentioned is that of body care and maintenance. Preening to keep the feathers in good condition is particularly important for birds that hunt in flight. Feather care also involves scratching and bathing. Hirundines bathe while flying, repeatedly dipping into and rising out of the water; they will also bathe in dew and spray from waterfalls, and will dust-bathe and mud-bathe. The function of sun-bathing is not known, but it may also be involved in feather care (Simmons 1987). Hirundines are known to sun-bathe or to expose parts of their body to the sun. House Martins adopt a spread-eagled posture, exposing the rump, and Barn Swallows also stretch or raise the wing, exposing the upper- or underside. This may be partly to allow the bird to warm itself; hirundines often sun themselves on warm surfaces on cool or windy days. At the other extreme, in hot weather, the tropical Pacific Swallow and the American Cliff Swallow drop their legs while in flight to enhance the loss of heat (Butler 1982; Bryant 1983).

Temperature regulation and energy conservation are important aspects of the biology of hirundines, for hunting flying insects is potentially costly in energy terms and yet their food supply is often unpredictable and in short supply. Hirundines thus often glide to save energy, instead of using expensive flapping flight, and do so particularly in cool weather when it is difficult to find food. Their streamlined shape and long wings also help to keep down the energy costs of flight, which are relatively much lower than in non-aerial-feeding birds (49–73% lower than other birds of similar size: Hails 1979). In very bad weather, some species can save energy by becoming hypothermic or torpid and huddling together; examples include Sand Martins (Mead 1970), White-backed Swallows (Congreve 1972), and House Martins (Prinzinger and Siedle 1988). In the House Martin, at least, energy expenditure is lower when food is scarce than when it is abundant, and also lower for large individuals than for small ones (Bryant and Westerterp 1983a).

BREEDING BIOLOGY

Swallows are typically monogamous, with both members of the pair to some extent looking after the brood (although females often do most of the nest-building and incubation). Males, however, are often promiscuous, actively seeking copulations with females other than their mate. This behaviour is most often seen in the highly colonial species such as the Sand Martin (Beecher and Beecher 1979) and Cliff Swallow (Brown 1985a), as well as species such as the Barn Swallow which nest in loose groups (Møller 1985; Crook and Shields 1987). Rarely, males have two mates; thus, Purple Martins are sometimes able to defend two adjacent nest sites and so attract two females, one nesting at each site (Brown 1979a).

Many species, among most of the genera, nest solitarily or in small loose groups depending on the availability of nest sites, particularly if pre-existing holes are used. Where nest sites are locally abundant, large groups of tens of nests sometimes develop, particularly in the genus *Hirundo* (for example, Barn Swallows on farms). However, these nests are not usually built close together and these species are not truly colonial. In a few species, notably in the genera *Pseudochelidon* (African River Martin), *Riparia* (sand martins), *Cheramoeca* (White-backed Swallow), *Hirundo* (the cliff swallow group) and *Delichon* (house martins), pairs nest close together in large colonies which sometimes contain hundreds or thousands of nests.

The Cliff Swallow colony, and probably those of other highly colonial species as well, acts as an information centre, allowing birds to follow successful foragers to sources of food and enhancing foraging efficiency (Brown 1986, 1988a). Individuals of non-colonial species such as the Barn Swallow do not use a breeding group in this way, but forage independently (Hebblethwaite and Shields, in press). The colonial species generally feed on small, patchily distributed insects, and sometimes have to travel far from the colony to find them, so they benefit substantially from the information centre. Solitary breeders, on the other hand, generally feed on larger, more widely dispersed insects, close to the nest, and so would benefit less from being in a colony. Colonies provide other benefits such as detection of and defence against predators (Hoogland and Sherman 1976), and certain individuals benefit from increased opportunities to copulate with females or to lay their eggs in other nests, but there are also costs such as a high incidence of ectoparasitism and interference from other birds in the colony (Brown 1985a; Møller 1987b; Shields and Crook 1987; Shields *et al.* 1988; Morton *et al.* ms).

Breeding is dependent on a good supply of insects for food and so is usually seasonal, starting when insect abundance is increasing: in the spring in temperate regions, and often at the beginning of the rains in tropical regions (Waugh 1978). Species that nest along river banks, however, such as the African River Martin, avoid the rains when their nest sites might be flooded (Chapin 1953). Breeding ceases as the insect supply decreases or when flooding is likely. In highly colonial species such as the cliff swallows, breeding is synchronised, most eggs being laid within a period of a couple of weeks (Brown and Brown 1987).

Nests Many swallows nest in holes, either in trees or in cliffs and river banks, often also using holes in artificial structures such as walls or nestboxes. Many hole nesters (*Tachycineta, Progne, Atticora, Alopochelidon, Neochelidon, Stelgidopteryx, Notiochelidon, Psalidoprocne* and *Phedina*) use already existing sites such as old woodpecker holes in trees or crevices in cliffs, or disused burrows in banks. *Stelgidopteryx* and *Psalidoprocne* occasionally dig their own or modify pre-existing burrows. A few (*Pseudochelidon, Cheramoeca, Pseudhirundo, Riparia*), however, predominantly make their own burrows, although *Cheramoeca* and *Pseudhirundo* will also use pre-existing ones. The largest genus of swallows, *Hirundo*, and the closely related genus *Delichon* instead make their own cavity by building a nest of mud which they attach to a cliff, cave roof, tree or artificial structure such as a bridge or house eaves.

These mud nests are often open bowls, but the red-rumped, mosque and striped swallows build a retort-shaped nest with a tunnel entrance and the cliff swallows and house martins build a closed bowl-shaped nest with a small entrance hole or spout. One species of *Hirundo*, the Tree Martin, has reverted to usually just using holes in trees, but it continues to use mud, in this case to make the entrance hole smaller, and it sometimes makes an open mud nest (Bell 1979). Mud is also used by the hole-nesting Purple Martin to shelter the nest cup itself (Allen and Nice 1952). Often both male and female build the nest, but the female may do the major part, especially when the lining is constructed. Males sometimes contribute feathers or green leaves.

The nest cup, placed inside a hole, at the end of a burrow or as a lining in a mud nest, is made out of fibrous material such as dry grass, pieces of bark, moss and hair — whatever is available locally. There is usually a lining of feathers, often white ones.

The nest is often re-used for later broods, both in the same year and in subsequent years, though not necessarily by the birds who first built it. Birds that use old mud nests repair them, often adding mud to the rim so that the nest can become very large after several years. Burrows, however, are not often re-used; Sand Martins, for example, usually move to new burrows for their second broods (Cowley 1983). Nest sites, not just the nests themselves, are often traditional and used by birds in successive years, unless they are damaged, for example by erosion. In some cases, however, such as the Cliff Swallow, nest sites are switched between years, perhaps to avoid parasites in the old nests such as the Swallow Bug *Oeciacus vicarius* (Sikes and Arnold 1984; Brown 1985; Loye ms).

Eggs and Incubation The eggs of hirundines are usually white, as is typical of hole-nesting birds where camouflage is not necessary (Schönwetter 1979). Many species of *Hirundo*, which often have open nests, have eggs that are white with reddish or grey/purple spots and freckles, often concentrated at the larger end. A few *Hirundo* species, the pied-winged and mosque swallow groups, have white eggs, and the striped and red-rumped swallow groups only occasionally have spotted eggs. Some species with enclosed nests, such as the cliff swallows, still have spotted eggs rather than white ones, showing their close relationship with the open-nesting barn swallow group. The Mascarene Martin also has brown-spotted eggs.

Four or five eggs, but sometimes six or seven, rarely eight, are typical of clutches of many temperate species; two or three are more normal for many tropical ones. There is typically a decline in clutch size from temperate to tropical latitudes. Several factors determine the size of clutch. Average clutch sizes generally decrease during the course of a breeding season: second or later clutches are smaller than first ones; and young birds, usually laying late in the season, also have smaller clutches than older birds, which usually breed earlier. The eggs are laid at daily intervals, but when food is scarce a female may defer laying for a day or more.

Clutch and brood sizes are probably determined by the number of young that the parents can support in a normal breeding season (Bryant and Westerterp 1983b; Turner 1983a). Insect abundance can be unpredictable even during summer, and too large a brood could not be fed adequately if food were scarce for a few days. In tropical regions there are fewer daylight hours in which to feed nestlings, and insects are not so abundant as in temperate latitudes (Hails 1982), so fewer nestlings can be reared. In many species two broods are often reared, at least by the older members of the population, and some individuals attempt three broods.

Incubation periods (from last egg laid to first hatched) are typically 14–16 days (range 11–20) but are sometimes extended in bad weather. The role of the sexes during incubation is not known in detail for many species. In solitarily nesting species it appears to be often only the female that incubates, whereas in the montane swallows *Notiochelidon* and in highly colonial species (cliff swallows, sand martins and house martins) the male also incubates, although he does less than his mate. A scarce or unpredictable food supply may be the evolutionary selection pressure behind this extra paternal care. The roles can vary, however, even between different populations of the same species: American Barn Swallow males incubate to a small extent, European Barn Swallow males not at all (Turner 1980; Ball 1983).

Nestlings

The eggs usually hatch asynchronously over a couple of days, so that nestlings within a brood may be of slightly different sizes. This probably spreads out the period of peak food requirements and makes it easier for the parents to collect sufficient food, but it can also be a consequence of variable food abundance during laying (Bryant 1978). Hatching success is usually high, so brood sizes are similar to clutch sizes. In the House Martin, at least, eggs vary in quality, and egg quality in turn depends on food abundance when the female is producing them (Bryant 1978). Low-quality eggs give rise to runt nestlings that are less likely to survive. Both parents feed the nestlings, often taking a more or less equal share. Feeding rates vary, but each chick is often fed several times an hour. The nestlings' food requirements are low for the first few days but then rapidly increase.

For the first week or so, the nestlings have only a little down and are unable to maintain a high body temperature, so the female (or sometimes both parents) broods them for much of the time. When the nestlings are older and can control their own temperature, the parents spend most of their time bringing food to them. The nestling's weight rapidly peaks but then drops again before the nestling fledges; the loss in weight is due to a loss of water (Ricklefs 1968). Hirundine nestlings have large fat reserves, the size of these depending on the predictability of the food supply. Thus, the House Martin, feeding on small insects at high levels, has the largest reserves of the three British swallow species and the Barn Swallow, feeding on large prey low down, has the smallest reserves (Turner and Bryant 1979). The tropical Pacific Swallow has relatively low reserves, probably because of a more stable food supply (Bryant and Hails 1983). House Martin nestlings are also able to become torpid in bad weather and their growth is flexible, varying with weather and food conditions (Bryant 1975, 1978b; Prinzinger and Siedle 1988). Hirundine nestlings therefore are able to survive up to a few days of food scarcity.

Nevertheless, nestlings do die of starvation, especially during prolonged bad weather. In those species that have been intensively studied, cold, wet weather, leading to food scarcity, is often recorded as a source of mortality, but its impact is very variable between years and between populations: Chapman (1935, 1955) recorded mortalities of nestling Tree Swallows of as high as 44% and as low as 6% in different years. Nestlings also suffer from the attentions of ectoparasites such as blood-sucking bugs, fleas and hippoboscid flies (Büttiker 1969; Summers 1975; Loye and Hopla

1983; Earlé 1985a). They can lose weight and die when ectoparasite numbers are high. In a study of Cliff Swallows, swallow bugs (*Oeciacus vicarius*) reduced survivorship by up to 50% (Brown and Brown 1986). High parasite levels can cause parents to desert eggs and nestlings (Møller 1987a; Moss and Camin 1970; J E Loye ms).

Predation is not often recorded as a major cause of loss of eggs or of nestlings, though it is likely to be more severe in the tropics than in temperate areas. Hirundines nesting in holes, burrows or mud nests attached to vertical surfaces are fairly well protected from many predators. Some nests are lost through erosion of nest sites or flooding, and old mud nests, re-used for many years, may fall down. Competitors for nests, such as starlings and sparrows, sometimes throw out eggs and young chicks, and a few young chicks are killed by conspecifics.

The nestling period is usually about three weeks (range 17–30 days), although it can be lengthened during bad weather when food is scarce. The large New World martins and the House Martin, which has a particularly unpredictable food supply, have the longest nestling periods of about a month; whereas the Barn Swallow and the tropical Pacific and Welcome Swallows, with a relatively stable food supply, fledge in under three weeks.

Fledging success can be high but is variable. In temperate species, often 60-80% of eggs laid produce fledged young, but the percentage can be much lower in a bad season. There have been few studies of tropical species, and these have been mainly short-term ones, but they indicate a greater loss both of clutches and of broods (e.g. Dyrcz 1984). Hails (1984) thus recorded a fledging success (from eggs laid) of only 38% for Pacific Swallows.

Mortality

Mortality rates of adults of temperate-zone species are also variable but are often about 60–70%. First-year birds are less likely to survive than older ones: in a study of Sand Martins, first-years had a mortality rate of 77% and older birds 60% (Mead 1979b). Most deaths occur outside the breeding season and are probably most commonly due to bad weather and droughts and concomitant scarce food supplies, particularly on migration. Some individuals, particularly young birds, are caught by predators such as Eleonora's Falcon *Falco eleonorae*, which specialises in hunting migrating birds. To some extent, there is a trade-off between mortality and breeding: thus, House Martins that rear a single brood in a year are more likely to survive to breed the following year than double-brooded birds (Bryant 1979).

Age Factors and Fidelity

Hirundines usually first breed when they are one year old, and then breed for only one or a few seasons before dying. There are, however, a few exceptional records of individuals reaching eight or more years, and one Barn Swallow died when nearly 16 (Rydzewski 1978). Rarely, some birds do not breed until they are two years old, as is sometimes the case with Tree Swallows and male Barn Swallows (Chapman 1955; Crook and Shields 1977; Møller 1988b). The young birds are usually the last to arrive at the nest site at the beginning of the breeding season; they lay late and have small clutches. Adults usually return to their previous nest site each year and may pair up with their previous mate. First-years, however, seem more likely to disperse to neighbouring areas. In non-migratory species such as the Grey-breasted Martin in Trinidad, the members of the pair remain together during the non-breeding season (Bitterbaum 1986).

POPULATION SIZES AND CONSERVATION

Population Sizes

Hirundine populations range from extremely abundant to rare and endangered, from widespread over whole continents to localised to a single site. Population sizes and densities, however, are poorly known and have been estimated for only a few populations. Barn Swallows are one of the most common with, for example, 500,000 to 1 million pairs in Britain (Sharrock 1976), although numbers have declined recently (Marchant 1984). The population density depends largely on the species' breeding dispersion, as many species will congregate where nest sites are available but will be absent from large areas without nest sites. Outside the breeding season, species may congregate to form large flocks and roosts, sometimes of millions of individuals.

The most successful and widespread species are those that extensively use artificial structures for nest sites. At one time hirundines would have been relatively rare, occurring mainly along coasts and in mountainous areas where caves and cliffs were available for nest sites, or else in clearings in forests and open woodland or savanna where they could nest in holes in trees, in termite mounds or along river banks. Populations would probably have been greatest during cool, wet periods of geological history when forests were most widespread (Benson et al. 1971; Moreau 1972).

Some species have probably long been associated with humans, nesting in native huts, under eaves of houses or in holes in walls. But it is the larger, more modern structures that have helped populations to take off: bridges, road culverts, farms and large-scale suburban and urban developments have provided extensive areas for nests, often in regions previously unoccupied by hirundines. Quarrying and road-cutting have also provided large artificial banks for burrowing species. In addition, nestboxes are put up on a large scale in some areas for particular species, such as in North America for the Purple Martin and Tree Swallow (Erskine 1979; Robbins et al. 1986).

Many species still nest predominantly in natural sites, occasionally using a human artefact when available. Others use both extensively. A few have discarded the cave-, cliff- and tree-dwelling habit almost completely, preferring artificial sites: records of some species such as Barn Swallows and House Martins in natural sites are now rare. Their populations must have increased considerably since the days of cave and cliff nesting, and now number millions of pairs (Cramp 1988). In some cases species have extended their range (see page 14).

Rare Species

Several species are rare or even endangered. These are mainly island or relict species with small geographical ranges, often nesting largely in natural sites that are rapidly disappearing because of human activity. Other species are so poorly known that their status is uncertain. The rarest species are the White-eyed River Martin and the Jamaican race of the Golden Swallow, both of which are probably close to extinction (King 1981; Collar and Andrew 1988). The former is known only from a few individuals at a winter roosting site, and the latter's population has decreased to a few individuals. The Blue Swallow in Africa is also rare and populations are declining (Brooke 1984). The status of the Bahama Swallow is uncertain

(Collar and Andrew 1988), as is that of the Red Sea Swallow, known only from a single specimen and a few possible sightings. Populations of some species, such as the Cameroon Mountain Rough-winged Swallow and the White-tailed Swallow in Ethiopia, are naturally small and localised but are under no immediate threat (Collar and Stuart 1985). Any disturbance of the populations, however, such as changes in land use, could threaten them. None of the rare species has been well studied, which makes it difficult to introduce effective conservation measures.

Population Declines

Populations are subject to several causes of mortality. Hirundines are affected a great deal by the weather. Many species need wet mud to build their nest, and rain is necessary if insects are to be abundant; but cold, wet weather also prevents them from feeding, can disrupt egg-laying and incubation and can lead to nestlings and adults starving and even to local population declines. Large-scale mortality has been recorded in or after a period of bad weather, both during the breeding season and on migration, particularly when crossing inhospitable areas such as the Alps (Graber *et al.* 1972; Bruderer 1979). Rain also swells rivers, flooding nests along banks (and eroding nest sites). On the other hand, if the weather is too hot and dry, chicks may overheat.

More extensive changes in the climate can have dramatic effects on populations. Thus Sand Martin numbers recently crashed in Britain following the drought in the Sahel region of Africa (Mead 1984), and cyclones have badly hit populations of the Mascarene Martin (Cheke 1987b).

Predators and parasites also cause some mortality but do not usually affect whole populations (see pages 28–29). As the nest sites are relatively secure, predation on eggs and chicks is not often a problem and is generally low. However, colonies are sometimes badly affected or even wiped out by parasites (Burgerjon 1964) or predators (Earlé 1985a).

Competition

Hirundines also suffer competition for nest sites, from other hole-users, or from sparrows and starlings taking over mud nests. This has sometimes been a severe problem, especially when these latter species were first introduced by humans into North America. House Sparrows *Passer domesticus* and Starlings *Sturnus vulgaris* have often been blamed for local declines in swallow and martin populations (Robbins *et al.* 1986), and Starling competitors are thought to be the main cause of the decline in the Jamaican Golden Swallow (King 1981).

Hirundines and Humans

The impact of humans is sometimes beneficial and sometimes deleterious to swallows and martins. The main benefit has been the provision of nest sites, but in addition, in many parts of the world, swallows, particularly the Barn Swallow, are welcomed by humans and are even symbols of good luck (Tate 1981). Superstitions have grown up, such as that, if a farmer destroys a swallow's nest, his cows will give bloody milk. Even in ancient Rome, swallows nesting on a house were thought to bring good fortune. The arrival of the first Barn Swallow is a sign of the coming of spring throughout Europe, and is often associated with particular Saints' days. In China, ledges were erected to encourage swallows to nest and so bring good luck, and in Japan house swallows were also believed to bring good fortune. In parts of Africa, swallows and martins are thought to be sent by the tribe's ancestors to comfort those still living. Swallows and martins are encouraged for more pragmatic reasons as well. American Indians and slaves in the southern states of the USA used to hang up gourds for Purple Martins to nest in, as these birds are effective at warning about, and mobbing, predators of livestock (Bent 1942). Thus, hirundines have long been given some measure of protection and often also encouragement to breed around farms and other buildings, although nests on houses or in garages and large roosts of hirundines on buildings are sometimes regarded as a nuisance because of the accumulation of faeces below them.

Human Persecution

There has been little direct persecution of swallows by humans. Nests are sometimes removed and roosts dispersed where they are considered to be a nuisance, and some species are shot or trapped (hirundines are one of many types of migrant bird hunted in southern Europe). The African River Martin, however, is the only species that is deliberately caught for food (Chapin 1954). The adverse effects of humans on hirundine populations are usually indirect, such as the introduction of nest competitors, pollution and changes in land use.

Pollution

Pollution can be a severe problem. Pesticides may be responsible for reducing insect numbers, and local spillages on farms can contaminate mud collected by swallows and martins for their nests. They have been implicated in both local and widespread declines, for example in farmyard colonies of House Martins and of Barn Swallows in Israel (Oliver 1975; Paz 1987). Air pollution has affected some populations, particularly of urban species such as the House Martin. In Europe, this species is known to be rare or absent in areas heavily polluted by fluoride, sulphur dioxide, fly ash, cement dust or nitrogen oxide (e.g. Newman 1979). Smoke and other urban pollutants in Britain also deter House Martins from nesting: in the first decades of the twentieth century they were absent from polluted areas such as Inner London and Manchester; since the Clean Air Act of 1957 in Britain, however, House Martins have returned to urban areas and are now nesting even in the heart of London (Cramp and Gooders 1967; Tatner 1978).

Land use

Land management or development has caused the loss of many suitable nesting areas, especially for species reliant on holes in trees or open ground. Changes in land use, particularly afforestation, have caused the decline in Blue Swallow populations by eliminating suitable nesting areas (Collar and Stuart 1985). The loss of natural nesting sites is sometimes alleviated by the increased availability of artificial ones, as has happened with the Tree Swallow (Erskine 1979). Some species, however, such as the Blue Swallow, have not taken to artificial sites or have done so only to a very limited extent, and so are more threatened by changes in their habitat. Changes in farming practices have an effect as well. In Denmark, for example, cutbacks in beef and milk production have led to decreases in Barn Swallow populations as this species nests preferentially on farms with cattle (Møller 1983).

PLATES 1–24

PLATE 1: RIVER MARTINS

Stocky, large-headed martins.

1 African River Martin *Pseudochelidon eurystomina* Text page 85

Congo Basin. Forested rivers, coastal savanna. Adult is blue-black or purple-black, with green sheen on back. Large red bill, red eye, pink eye-ring and large brownish-pink feet are diagnostic. Square tail. In flight, note brown underwing-coverts. Juvenile (not shown) is dull sooty-brown.

2 White-eyed River Martin *Pseudochelidon sirintarae* Text page 86

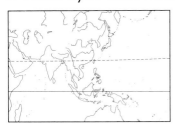

Known only from its wintering site in Thailand.

a ADULT: Black, with blue-green sheen and green gloss on back; silvery rump. Broad greeny-yellow bill, white eye and eye-ring and elongated tail feathers are distinctive.

b JUVENILE: Browner. No tail racquets.

1

2b

2a

Dull brown swallows with square or barely forked tails.

3 White-thighed Swallow *Neochelidon tibialis*   **Text page 88**

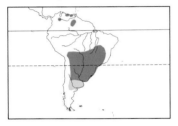

Panama to Brazil. Forests, low secondary growth, villages.

a ADULT: Small. Upperparts very dark, with paler rump and underparts; white thighs may be visible when perched. Northern race *minima* is depicted; nominate race is paler brownish-black, with slight green sheen. Juvenile (not shown) as adult, but with pale feather margins.

b Note conspicuous dusky undertail-coverts in flight.

4 Tawny-headed Swallow *Alopochelidon fucata*   **Text page 89**

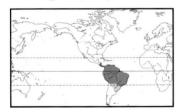

Northern and central South America. Open areas, often near water, foothills and mountains. Adult's white abdomen and undertail-coverts contrast with grey-brown upperparts and dark crown; tawny-rufous head merging into tawny-buff on sides of head, throat and breast diagnostic. The rump is as dark as the back, but has more extensive pale feather edges. Juvenile (not shown) as adult, but the tawny-rufous is replaced by yellowish-fawn.

5 Southern Rough-winged Swallow   **Text page 91**
Stelgidopteryx ruficollis

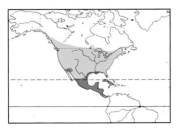

Central and South America to northern Argentina. Open and semi-open country, especially near water. Adult mainly grey-brown, merging into yellow on centre of abdomen; cinnamon-buff throat. In area of overlap with Northern Roughwing, paler rump is diagnostic. Juvenile (not shown) as adult, but has duller throat and pale edges to feathers on back.

6 Northern Rough-winged Swallow   **Text page 93**
Stelgidopteryx serripennis

North and Central America. Open country, often near water.

a ADULT: Similar to Southern Roughwing, but has a duller throat and in area of overlap the race *fulvipennis* has a darker rump.

b In flight, note absence of breast-band and long wings (cf. Sand Martin, plate 9).

c JUVENILE: As adult, but with cinnamon edges to feathers on upperparts.

3a

3b

4

6a

6b

6c

5

Mainly metallic blue or green, with white underparts.

7 Tree Swallow *Tachycineta bicolor*

Text page 97

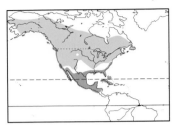

North America. Open and wooded country, often near water.

a ADULT MALE: Blue-green upperparts contrast with pure white underparts.

b FIRST-YEAR FEMALE: Females are duller, changing with age from brown to blue.

c In flight, note blue-green rump, white undertail-coverts and grey-brown underwing-coverts.

d JUVENILE: Dingier than adult, with brown upperparts and whitish underparts; greyish breast-band.

8 Mangrove Swallow *Tachycineta albilinea*

Text page 101

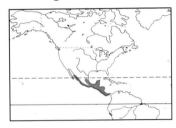

Mexico and Central America; possible race in Peru. Open country near water. Adult's head and back blue-green, but the rump, like the underparts, is white; white supraloral stripe is distinctive when visible. Broad white tips to inner secondaries in fresh plumage. Brown uppertail-coverts. Juvenile (not shown) is grey-brown above, with underparts washed grey-brown.

9 White-winged Swallow *Tachycineta albiventer*

Text page 103

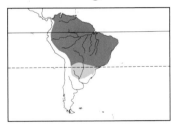

Northern and central South America. Open country, especially near large open expanses of water. Adult's glossy blue-green head and back contrast with white rump and uppertail-coverts and underparts; the white wing patch is diagnostic. Juvenile (not shown) is duller and browner than adult, with dusky breast and less white in wing.

10 Violet-green Swallow *Tachycineta thalassina*

Text page 104

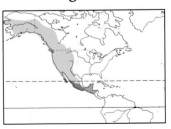

Western North America and Mexico. Open, wooded and forested country, human habitation. Adult has non-glossy, velvety green upperparts, with violet-blue rump; white of underparts extends above eye, and also forms distinctive white patches either side of rump. Females are duller and browner. Juvenile (not shown) is duller and browner than adult, with brown wash on chest.

Mainly metallic blue or green, with white underparts.

11 White-rumped Swallow *Tachycineta leucorrhoa*   Text page 106

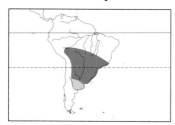

Central South America. Open country near water, open woodland, human habitation. Adult has blue-green upperparts with distinctive white streaks above lores; white rump. Juvenile (not shown) is duller and browner than adult, with dusky breast.

12 Chilean Swallow *Tachycineta leucopyga*   Text page 108

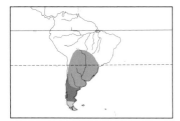

Southern South America. Open country near water, open woodland, human habitation. Adult has deep blue rather than blue-green upperparts, and lacks white above lores; white rump. Juvenile (not shown) is duller and browner than adult.

13 Bahama Swallow *Tachycineta cyaneoviridis*   Text page 109

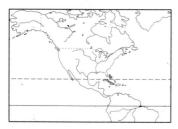

Northern Bahama Islands. Pine woodland, open country, human habitation.

a ADULT: Dark green upperparts, less glossy than other tree swallows, with a more bluish-green rump and bluish wings. Tail is strongly forked. Female is duller, with less pure white underparts. Juvenile (not shown) is duller and browner than adult male and has less deeply forked tail.

b Note forked tail, blue wings and green back in flight.

14 Golden Swallow *Tachycineta euchrysea*   Text page 110

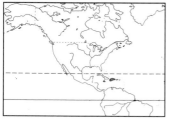

West Indies. Open hilly country.

a ADULT: Highly iridescent bronzy-green to coppery-bronze upperparts, extending down to ear-coverts, cheeks and chin. Tail is forked. Females duller, with chest mottled grey-brown. Juvenile (not shown) is duller and browner than adult, with chest mottled grey-brown and sides of head dusky grey.

b Note forked tail and iridescent green upperparts in flight.

11

12

13a

13b

14a

14b

15 Brown-bellied Swallow *Notiochelidon murina*   **Text page 112**

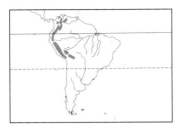

Upper elevations in Andes. Grassland and paramo, human habitation. Adult's upperparts have slight green-blue sheen. Often looks black in the field. Dark underparts distinguish it from other members of the genus. Juvenile (not shown) is duller than adult; underparts mostly greyish-white, throat dark brown.

16 Pale-footed Swallow *Notiochelidon flavipes*   **Text page 113**

Mid elevations in Andes. Cloud and elfin forest. Adult's pale rufous throat is distinctive. The sides of the body are dark, contrasting with the white breast and abdomen. Juvenile (not shown) has pale edges to undertail-coverts.

17 Black-capped Swallow *Notiochelidon pileata*   **Text page 114**

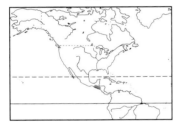

Guatemala, Chiapas, El Salvador. Montane grassland and woodland, human habitation. Adult's dark head and brown upperparts contrast with white underparts; the malar region, chin and throat are flecked brown, and the sides are grey-brown. Juvenile (not shown) has browner head than adult's, and chin and throat are more buffy; pale feather edges on rump and secondaries.

18 Blue-and-white Swallow *Notiochelidon cyanoleuca*   **Text page 116**

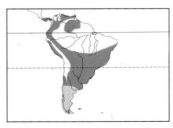

Mid elevations in the Andes. Open country, forest clearings, often near water; human habitation.

a ADULT: Contrasting blue upperparts and whitish underparts; pale throat and sides. Dark undertail-coverts (cf. tree swallows, plates 3,4).

b JUVENILE: Duller and browner; pale tips to rump feathers. Tail less forked.

15

16

17

18a

18b

PLATE 6: AMAZONIAN SWALLOWS

Riverine swallows with deeply forked tails.

19 White-banded Swallow *Atticora fasciata* Text page 118

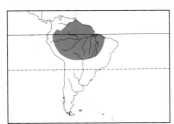

Northern South America. Forested rivers.

a ADULT: Blue-black; white breast-band.

b JUVENILE: Duller, with dusky underparts, and pale-edged secondaries, wing-coverts and underparts; shorter outer tail feathers.

20 Black-collared Swallow *Atticora melanoleuca* Text page 120

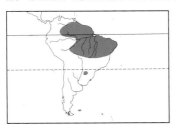

Northern South America. Forested rivers.

a ADULT: Blue-black upperparts; white underparts, with dark breast-band.

b JUVENILE: Mouse-brown upperparts, dirty white underparts; shorter outer tail feathers.

19a

19b

20a

20b

Large hirundines with slightly forked tails; wing shape reminiscent of starling *Sturnus*.

21 Brown-chested Martin *Progne tapera*   Text page 121

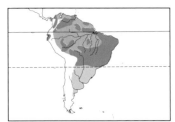

Northern and central South America. Open country near water, human habitation. Adult has dull brown upperparts, and white underparts broken by an indistinct brown breastband. Juvenile (not shown) as adult, but sides of throat greybrown and tail squarer.

22 Purple Martin *Progne subis*   Text page 123

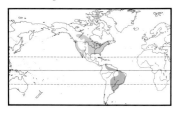

North America and Mexico. Open and semi-open country, especially near water; human habitation.

a   ADULT MALE: Blue-black.

b   FEMALE: Duller, with sooty-grey forehead, grey neck and greyish underparts.

c   JUVENILE: Grey-brown above and on chin and throat; grey-white below.

21

22b

22a

22c

PLATE 8: NEW WORLD MARTINS II

Large hirundines with slightly forked tails; wing shape reminiscent of starling *Sturnus*.

23 Grey-breasted Martin *Progne chalybea* Text page 126

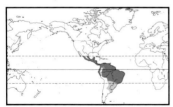

Central America and northern South America. Open country, especially near water; open woodland, human habitation.

a ADULT MALE: Grey-white underparts; some brown on chin and throat. Resembles female Purple Martin (plate 7), but has whiter undertail-coverts and blue forehead. Female is duller, with browner forehead and paler chin and throat. Juvenile (not shown) is duller, with sooty-grey upperparts.

b Note brownish throat and grey-white undertail-coverts in flight.

24 Snowy-bellied Martin *Progne dominicensis* Text page 129

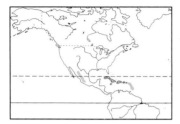

Mexico, Cuba, West Indies. Open and semi-open country, especially near water, human habitation.

a ADULT MALE: More sharply defined white lower breast and belly than on other New World martins. Female is duller, with brown forehead. Juvenile (not shown) as adult female, but duller.

b Note blue throat and white undertail-coverts in flight. More blue-black on flanks than Grey-breasted Martin.

25 Southern Martin *Progne modesta* Text page 131

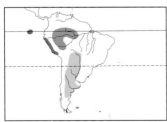

Galapagos, Peru, southern South America. Open and semi-open country, human habitation.

a ADULT MALE: All dark blue. Smaller than Purple Martin (plate 7). Female is duller, but has dark underparts (unlike females of other *Progne* species). Juvenile (not shown) as adult female, but duller.

b Looks wholly dark in flight.

23a

23b

25a

25b

24a

24b

PLATE 9: SAND MARTINS

Dull brown upperparts; no white in tail (cf. crag martins, plate 14). The tail is almost square or slightly forked.

26 Brown-throated Sand Martin *Riparia paludicola*   Text page 133

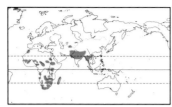

Africa, India, southern Asia. Closely associated with water. Adult has grey throat and breast, merging into white abdomen; no indication of a breast-band. Juvenile (not shown) shows buffy feather edges, especially on rump and wings; the underparts are sandy-buff or rufescent-buff.

27 Sand Martin (Bank Swallow) *Riparia riparia*   Text page 136

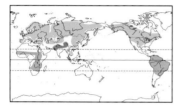

North America, Europe, Asia. Closely associated with water.

a ADULT: White throat; well-demarcated brown breast-band.

b JUVENILE: Pale feather edges, especially on rump and wings.

28 Banded Martin *Riparia cincta*   Text page 140

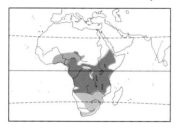

Africa south of the Sahara. Open country, often near water. Adult is a large martin with broad brown breast-band; white streak on side of head is diagnostic. Square tail. Juvenile (not shown) has rufous to cream feather edges and a pale breast-band.

29 Congo Sand Martin *Riparia congica*   Text page 143

Congo Basin. Forested rivers. Adult's underparts are white, apart from light brown upper breast; no impression of a distinct breast-band. Juvenile (not shown) has pale feather edges, especially on rump and wings.

Dark, mostly long-tailed, forest swallows.

30 Cameroon Mountain Rough-winged Swallow
Psalidoprocne fuliginosa

Text page 143

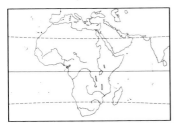

Cameroon Mountain and Fernando Po. Forests and cultivation. Adult is entirely matt brown, with a forked tail. Juvenile (not shown) is lighter brown than the adult.

31 White-headed Rough-winged Swallow
Psalidoprocne albiceps

Text page 144

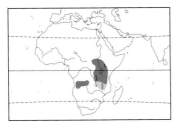

East Africa, Angola, southern Zaire. Wooded savanna and forest.

a ADULT MALE: Brownish-black with a slight green gloss (usually looks black in the field); white crown and throat.

b FEMALE: Has only the throat white, but may have some white feathers in crown.

c White throat and crown distinctive in flight.

d JUVENILE: Brownish-black, with ashy-brown throat.

30

31c

31a

31b

31d

PLATE 11: AFRICAN ROUGH-WINGED SWALLOWS II

Dark, mostly long-tailed, forest swallows.

32 Black Rough-winged Swallow

Psalidoprocne pristoptera

Text page 146

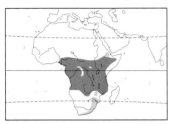

Africa south of the Sahara. Forest and woodland, wooded savanna, montane grassland.

a ADULT: Black with a blue sheen (looks black in the field). Juvenile (not shown) is duller and browner than the adult, with duskier underwing-coverts.

b On nominate race, white underwing-coverts are conspicuous from below in flight.

33 Fanti Rough-winged Swallow *Psalidoprocne obscura*   Text page 149

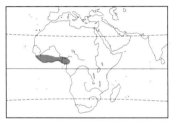

West Africa. Savanna and forest.

a ADULT: Dark, with a dark oily-green or bluish gloss. The tail is distinctively long and deeply forked; female has shorter outer tail feathers than male.

b JUVENILE: Brown, with little gloss; much shorter outer tail feathers.

34 Square-tailed Rough-winged Swallow

Psalidoprocne nitens

Text page 150

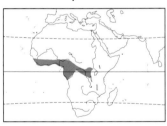

West Africa. Forests.

a ADULT: Dark, with green gloss; the chin, throat and cheeks are grey-brown, without any gloss. Juvenile (not shown) is duller dark brown than adult.

b Note square tail in flight.

32a

32b

33b

33a

34b

34a

PLATE 12: WHITE-BACKED AND GREY-RUMPED SWALLOWS

35 White-backed Swallow *Cheramoeca leucosternus*   Text page 151

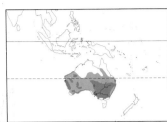

Australia. Open country, especially near water.

a ADULT: White crown, mantle, throat and upper chest contrasting with dark back and abdomen are diagnostic. Tail deeply forked.

b Note deeply forked tail in flight.

c JUVENILE: Duller and browner than adult, and white areas are more buffy; tail less deeply forked.

36 Grey-rumped Swallow *Pseudhirundo griseopyga*   Text page 153

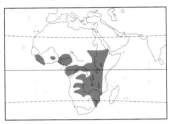

Africa south of the Sahara. Open grassland, especially near water.

a ADULT: Brown head and rump contrasting with blue back and white underparts are distinctive. Juvenile (not shown) is glossy like adult but browner, and feathers have buffy edges; short outer tail feathers.

b Pale rump and crown distinctive in flight.

35b

35a

35c

36b

36a

37 Mascarene Martin *Phedina borbonica*   **Text page 155**

Mascarene Islands. Open and semi-open country.

a ADULT: Sooty-brown upperparts are finely streaked; whiter underparts are more thickly streaked. Juvenile (not shown) has broad white tips to inner secondaries.

b Streaking on underparts is distinctive in flight.

38 Congo Martin *Phedina brazzae*   **Text page 157**

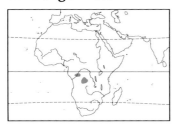

Congo Basin. Forested rivers.

a ADULT: Grey-brown upperparts indistinctly streaked; the white underparts are heavily streaked, and the breast has a brownish wash (less brown on flanks). Juvenile (not shown) has diffuse striping on underparts and rufous edges on back and wings.

b Streaking on white underparts is distinctive in flight.

37a

37b

38b

38a

PLATE 14: CRAG MARTINS

Dull brown birds of high elevations. Square tail with white patches. No breast-band (cf. sand martins, plate 9).

39 Crag Martin *Hirundo rupestris*   Text page 158

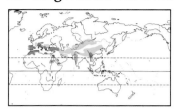

Southern Europe and Asia. Mountains.

a ADULT: Ashy-brown, with dusky speckles on throat.

b Note white in tail and absence of breast-band. Tail square.

c JUVENILE: Rufous feather edges.

40 Rock Martin *Hirundo fuligula*   Text page 160

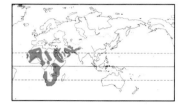

Africa and western Asia. Mountains, human habitation. Adult is earth-brown above, with rufous wash to underparts. Northern races are paler and greyer. Juvenile (not shown) has pale feather edges.

41 Dusky Crag Martin *Hirundo concolor*   Text page 163

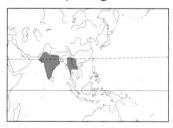

India to southeastern Asia. Mountains, human habitation. Adult is darker than other crag martins, and has pale rufous chin and throat; rest of underparts smoky-brown, darkening posteriorly. Juvenile (not shown) has rufous-grey feather edges and a paler throat.

39a

39c

39b

40

41

PLATE 15: BARN SWALLOWS I

Distinctive rufous-chestnut on forehead and often on throat; blue upperparts and pale underparts. Tail has white patches.

42 Barn Swallow *Hirundo rustica*

Text page 164

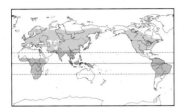

North America, Europe, Asia. Open country, especially near water; human habitation.

a ADULT: Chestnut forehead and throat, blue band below throat, and long tail streamers are diagnostic. Females have shorter streamers.

b ADULT race *erythrogaster* (North America): Chestnut underparts, broken breast-band.

c ADULT race *rustica*: In flight, note long streamers and complete breast-band.

d JUVENILE: Duller and browner, with rufous areas paler; outer tail feathers are short.

43 Red-chested Swallow *Hirundo lucida*

Text page 169

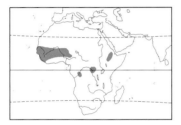

Africa in north tropics. Open country, especially near water; human habitation.

a ADULT: Short outer tail feathers and narrow blue breast-band. Juvenile (not shown) is duller and browner, with rufous areas paler.

b In flight, note more extensive white in tail, narrower breast-band and shorter streamers compared with Barn Swallow.

44 Angolan Swallow *Hirundo angolensis*

Text page 170

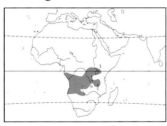

Equatorial Africa. Open country, forest clearings, human habitation.

a ADULT: Breast-band more or less broken; lower underparts ashy-brown; tail streamers short. Juvenile (not shown) duller and browner, with rufous areas paler; shorter outer tail feathers.

b In flight, note more extensive white in tail, broken breast-band and darker underparts compared with Barn Swallow.

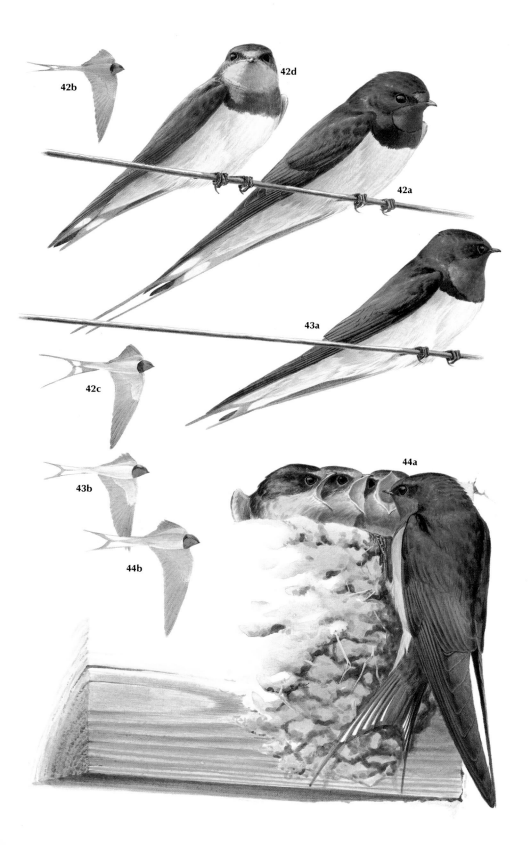

Distinctive rufous-chestnut on forehead and often on throat; blue upperparts and usually pale underparts. Tail usually has white patches.

45 Pacific Swallow *Hirundo tahitica*

Text page 172

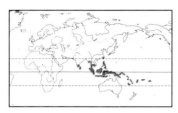

India, southeastern Asia, Pacific islands. Sea-coasts, open and forested country, human habitation.

a ADULT: Dusky underparts, no breast-band and only moderately forked tail. Juvenile (not shown) is duller and browner, with rufous areas paler; short outer tail feathers.

b ADULT

46 Welcome Swallow *Hirundo neoxena*

Text page 174

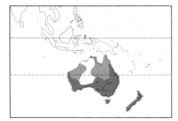

Australia and New Zealand. Open country, coasts, often near water; human habitation.

a ADULT: Dirty grey underparts and no breast-band. Juvenile (not shown) is duller and browner, with rufous areas paler; shorter outer tail feathers.

b Note deeply forked tail in flight.

47 White-throated Swallow *Hirundo albigularis*

Text page 177

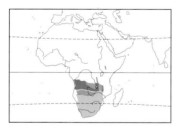

Southern Africa. Open country, especially near water; human habitation.

a ADULT: Chin and throat white, not rufous; band below throat tapers towards centre and is often broken. Rest of underparts smoky-grey. Juvenile (not shown) is duller and browner, with rufous areas paler; shorter outer tail feathers.

b Note deeply forked tail in flight (female has shorter outer tail feathers).

48 Ethiopian Swallow *Hirundo aethiopica*

Text page 179

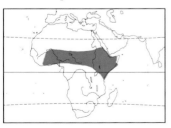

Central Africa. Open country, woodland, forest clearings, human habitation.

a ADULT: Buffy-white chin and throat; breast-band is reduced to patches on each side of breast. Underparts white.

b JUVENILE: Duller and browner, with rufous areas paler; shorter outer tail feathers.

45a

45b

46a

46b

47a

47b

48a

48b

49 Wire-tailed Swallow *Hirundo smithii*   **Text page 181**

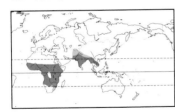

Africa and southern Asia. Open country near water, human habitation.

a ADULT: Combination of blue upperparts, creamy-white underparts and rufous-chestnut crown, together with very long outer tail feathers, is distinctive. Females have shorter outer tail feathers than males.

b From below, note creamy-white underwing-coverts and blue on flanks.

c JUVENILE: Duller and browner; shorter outer tail feathers.

50 White-throated Blue Swallow *Hirundo nigrita*   **Text page 183**

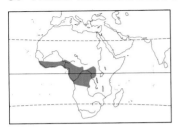

West and Central Africa. Forested streams and rivers. Adult is completely blue, with a distinctive white throat spot; white tail patches are visible when tail is spread. The tail is square. Juvenile (not shown) is duller and browner, with less white in tail and on throat.

49b

49c

49a

50

PLATE 18: PEARL-BREASTED SWALLOW GROUP

Blue-and-white swallows, lacking rufous.

51 Pied-winged Swallow *Hirundo leucosoma*   **Text page 185**

West Africa. Open country, human habitation.

a ADULT: Conspicuous, large white wing patch distinguishes this species from other swallows in its range. Juvenile (not shown) is duller and browner, with short outer tail feathers.

b From below, note white underparts; glossy blue on each side of breast.

52 White-tailed Swallow *Hirundo megaensis*   **Text page 186**

Ethiopia. Open grassland.

a ADULT: Blue upperparts and white underparts. Females have shorter outer tail feathers. Juvenile (not shown) is duller, with less white in the tail; short outer tail feathers.

b The largely white tail is conspicuous, especially in flight.

53 Pearl-breasted Swallow *Hirundo dimidiata*   **Text page 187**

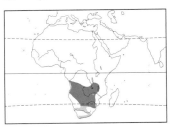

Southern Africa. Scrub and woodland, human habitation.

a ADULT: Pure blue upperparts contrast with dirty white underparts. Females have shorter outer tail feathers than males.

b In flight, note absence of white in tail.

c JUVENILE: Duller, with shorter outer tail feathers.

49b

49c

49a

50

PLATE 18: PEARL-BREASTED SWALLOW GROUP

Blue-and-white swallows, lacking rufous.

51 Pied-winged Swallow *Hirundo leucosoma* Text page 185

West Africa. Open country, human habitation.

a ADULT: Conspicuous, large white wing patch distinguishes this species from other swallows in its range. Juvenile (not shown) is duller and browner, with short outer tail feathers.

b From below, note white underparts; glossy blue on each side of breast.

52 White-tailed Swallow *Hirundo megaensis* Text page 186

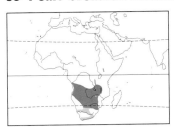

Ethiopia. Open grassland.

a ADULT: Blue upperparts and white underparts. Females have shorter outer tail feathers. Juvenile (not shown) is duller, with less white in the tail; short outer tail feathers.

b The largely white tail is conspicuous, especially in flight.

53 Pearl-breasted Swallow *Hirundo dimidiata* Text page 187

Southern Africa. Scrub and woodland, human habitation.

a ADULT: Pure blue upperparts contrast with dirty white underparts. Females have shorter outer tail feathers than males.

b In flight, note absence of white in tail.

c JUVENILE: Duller, with shorter outer tail feathers.

51a

51b

52b

52a

53b

53a

53c

54 Blue Swallow *Hirundo atrocaerulea*   Text page 188

Southern and eastern Africa. Open grassland. Adult is pure blue, with very long and slender tail streamers, latter shorter on females than on males. Juvenile (not shown) is sooty-black, with a brownish throat; short outer tail feathers.

55 Black-and-rufous Swallow *Hirundo nigrorufa*   Text page 191

Angola, Zaire, Zambia. Open grassland, especially near water. Adult has violet-blue upperparts contrasting with rufous-brown underparts. Females are paler below than males. Juvenile (not shown) is duller and browner above and paler below; short outer tail feathers.

56 Greater Striped Swallow *Hirundo cucullata*   Text page 192

Southern Africa. Open country, human habitation.

a ADULT: Chestnut crown, pale rufous rump; the buffy, narrowly streaked underparts are the most distinctive feature. Females have shorter outer tail feathers than males. Juvenile (not shown) is duller, with blacker crown and shorter outer tail feathers; shows tawny tips to inner secondaries and wing-coverts. Where the species overlaps with Lesser Striped Swallow, latter is smaller, with paler, more boldly streaked underparts and a darker rump.

b In flight, note pale rump and dark crown.

57 Lesser Striped Swallow *Hirundo abyssinica*   Text page 194

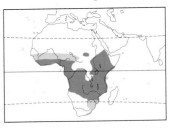

Africa south of the Sahara. Woodland, less often in open grassland; human habitation.

a ADULT: Rump is same colour as the crown; underparts white, with bold profuse streaks. Females have shorter outer tail feathers.

b In flight, note rufous crown and rump.

c JUVENILE: Duller, with blacker crown and shorter outer tail feathers; shows tawny tips to inner secondaries and wing-coverts.

Rufous rump.

58 Rufous-chested Swallow *Hirundo semirufa*   Text page 197

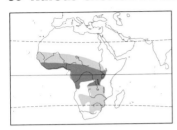

Africa south of the Sahara. Open grassland, open woodland, human habitation.

a ADULT: Rufous sides of neck and underparts; blue-black lores, cheeks and ear-coverts. Juvenile (not shown) is duller and browner, with paler underparts, shorter outer tail feathers and buffy tips to inner secondaries.

b From below, buffy underwing-coverts distinguish it from Red-rumped Swallow.

59 Mosque Swallow *Hirundo senegalensis*   Text page 199

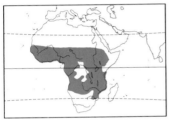

Africa south of the Sahara. Open woodland, cultivation; less often near human habitation.

a ADULT: Large. Distinctive rufous collar, cream chin and throat and rufous breast and abdomen. Has paler cheeks, is larger and has less deeply forked tail than the similar Rufous-chested Swallow. Juvenile (not shown) is duller and browner, with a less distinct collar, rufous areas paler and outer tail feathers shorter; some rufous tips to inner secondaries and wing- and tail-coverts.

b From below, note pale underwing-coverts and rufous undertail-coverts.

60 Red-rumped Swallow *Hirundo daurica*   Text page 201

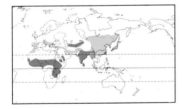

Southern Europe, Asia, Africa. Open, especially hilly country; human habitation.

a ADULT: Broad chestnut collar; faint narrow streaks on rump and underparts. Race *rufula* is depicted.

b From below, rufous underwing-coverts and black undertail-coverts are diagnostic, especially in Africa, where the races have little or no streaking (cf. Mosque Swallow and Rufous-chested Swallow).

c JUVENILE: Duller and browner, with rufous areas paler; buffy tips on wings and uppertail-coverts. Short outer tail feathers.

61 Striated Swallow *Hirundo striolata*   Text page 205

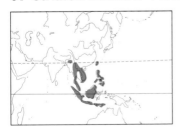

Southeastern Asia. Open country, cultivation, human habitation. Adult has heavily streaked underparts; rufous neck-collar is poorly defined and often absent. Juvenile (not shown) is duller and browner, with rufous areas paler; buff feather tips on wings, short outer tail feathers.

59a

59b

58a

58b

60a

60b

61

60c

PLATE 21: CLIFF SWALLOWS I

Usually some rufous on head; buffy or rufous rump; white streaks on back.

62 Preuss's Cliff Swallow *Hirundo preussi*

Text page 206

West Africa. Open grassland, near cliffs and rivers.

a ADULT: Buffy rump; pale buffy-rufous underparts; patch of rufous-chestnut behind eye.

b In flight, note squarish tail.

c JUVENILE: Duller and browner, with rufous areas paler; grey-brown marks on throat and breast.

63 Angolan Cliff Swallow *Hirundo rufigula*

Text page 208

Angola, Zaire, Zambia. Open country, near cliffs and rivers. Adult has deep rufous throat, lacks rufous behind eye; rump is rufous, not buffy. Juvenile (not shown) is duller, with rufous areas paler.

66 South African Cliff Swallow *Hirundo spilodera*
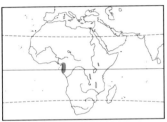

Text page 212

South Africa. Open country, especially flat grassland and savanna. Adult has pale rufous rump; underparts vary from pale rufous to whitish, with variable amount of black and rufous speckling on throat and breast. Tail square, without any white patches. Juvenile (not shown) is duller, with rufous areas paler.

71 Forest Cliff Swallow *Hirundo fuliginosa*

Text page 225

Cameroon, equatorial Guinea, Gabon. Forests, human habitation. Adult is wholly dark brown, with rufous tinge to chin and throat (fainter on females than on males). In the field, appears very similar to Square-tailed Rough-winged Swallow (plate 11), but has deeper fork to tail. Juvenile (not shown) as adult, but with less rufous on throat.

62b

62a

62c

66

63

71

PLATE 22: CLIFF SWALLOWS II

Usually some rufous on head; buffy or rufous rump; white streaks on back.

67 Cliff Swallow *Hirundo pyrrhonota*

Text page 216

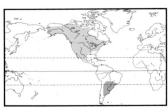

North America and Mexico. Open country, mountains, human habitation.

a ADULT: Pale forehead and rump, dark rufous and black throat.

b In flight, pale rump and square tail are distinctive.

c JUVENILE: Duller and browner, with pale throat and dark forehead; pale margins on upperparts.

64 Andean Cliff Swallow *Hirundo andecola*

Text page 209

High elevations in the Andes. Open country, human habitation.

a ADULT: Grey-brown underparts, whitish in centre of abdomen; dull blue gloss to head and mantle. Juvenile (not shown) is duller and browner, with rufous-brown rump, buffy tips on wing-coverts and white tips on inner secondaries.

b In flight, note brown rump and square tail.

68 Cave Swallow *Hirundo fulva*

Text page 219

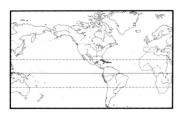

North America, Mexico, Greater Antilles, Ecuador, Peru. Open country, near water and cliffs; human habitation.

a ADULT: Dark chestnut forehead; cinnamon-buff throat, with grey-brown neck and collar. Juvenile (not shown) is duller and browner, with cinnamon margins to inner secondaries and uppertail-coverts.

b In flight, note cinnamon-rufous rump.

67a

67b

67c

64b

64a

68b

68a

PLATE 23: CLIFF SWALLOWS III

Usually some rufous on head; buffy or rufous rump; white streaks on back.

69 Indian Cliff Swallow *Hirundo fluvicola*

Text page 222

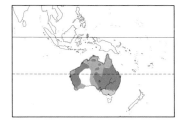

Afghanistan, Pakistan, India. Open mountainous country, human habitation.

a ADULT: Dull chestnut forehead and crown and pale brown rump; buffy-white, streaked underparts, streaking heaviest on face and upper breast.

b JUVENILE: Duller and browner, with pale edges to feathers; fainter streaks on underparts.

70 Fairy Martin *Hirundo ariel*

Text page 223

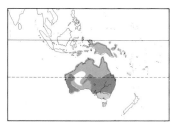

Australia. Open country, open woodland, often near water. Adult has dark rufous forehead and crown and dull white underparts and rump. Juvenile (not shown) is duller and browner, with buffy-white feather edges.

65 Tree Martin *Hirundo nigricans*

Text page 210

Australia, Timor. Open woodland, human habitation. Adult has rufous forehead and blackish crown, white (sometimes buffy) rump and white underparts. Juvenile (not shown) is duller and browner, with paler forehead and underparts and pale fringes on back and wings.

69a

69b

70

65

PLATE 24: HOUSE MARTINS

White rump and underparts; blue back.

72 House Martin *Delichon urbica*

Text page 226

Europe, North Africa, Asia. Open country, cliffs, human habitation.

a ADULT: Conspicuous white rump and pure white underparts.

b Note white underwing-coverts.

c JUVENILE: Duller; grey-brown freckling on underparts.

73 Asian House Martin *Delichon dasypus*

Text page 230

Central and eastern Asia. Open mountainous country, human habitation.

a ADULT: The white on throat and undertail-coverts is washed with grey. Juvenile (not shown) is duller, with grey-white underparts.

b Underwing-coverts are grey-brown.

74 Nepal House Martin *Delichon nipalensis*

Text page 232

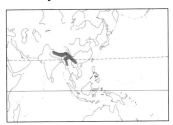

South-central Asia. Mountain river valleys, wooded ridges.

a ADULT: Black throat; dark terminal bands on uppertail-coverts. Juvenile (not shown) is duller, with buffy underparts.

b In flight, note black undertail-coverts and squarer tail than other house martins.

72a

72b

72a

73b

73a

72c

74a

74b

SYSTEMATIC
SECTION

1 AFRICAN RIVER MARTIN

Plate 1

Pseudochelidon eurystomina Hartlaub

Pseudochelidon eurystomina Hartlaub, 1861, J. für Orn., 9, p. 12: Gabon.

FIELD CHARACTERS The African River Martin is a very distinctive medium-sized swallow, and a highly vocal and gregarious one. Its most obvious features are its large orange-red bill, red eyes and entirely black plumage. It is unlike any other hirundine in its restricted range in Gabon and the River Congo. Indeed, it looks rather unlike a swallow at all, having a relatively large head, bill and feet. It breeds in large colonies and also occurs in groups in the non-breeding season. The flight is rapid.

HABITAT This species breeds on sandbars along forested rivers, on islands with sandy shores in the rivers and on beach ridges in coastal savanna. It can also be seen more widely over rivers and adjacent forests on both the breeding and wintering grounds, and on migration.

DISTRIBUTION AND STATUS The African River Martin is confined to a small area of West Africa, breeding mainly on the middle Congo River between Lukolela and Basoko, especially near Mbandaka and the west of Kisangani, and the lower Ubangi River (Chapin 1954). Nesting has also recently been reported in the coastal savannas of Gabon near Gamba (H. Morand and P.D. Alexander-Marrack, unpublished data), but it is not known if this involves a separate population or birds that have already bred along the River Congo earlier in the year. The exact distribution is thus not clear, and the species may well breed on other tributaries of the Congo such as the Kasai, and perhaps on other poorly explored rivers in this part of Africa. Equally, the population size is unknown, but it appears to be a common if local breeding bird. Flocks of several hundred have been seen, and large numbers are seen on migration in Gabon (Erard 1981). Chapin (1954) estimated the total numbers to be in excess of 100,000 and reported that the local people caught them in large quantities to eat.

MIGRATION The martins leave their main breeding sites in April when the waters of the Congo rise, flooding the nest sites. From June onwards, they arrive in the coastal regions of southern Gabon and the Congo from the mouth of the Nyanga to that of the Kwilu-Niari, about 960 km (600 miles) from their breeding range on the River Congo (Chapin 1953, 1954). Both small and large flocks pass through northeastern Gabon between June and the beginning of September, flying towards the coast. The martins return to the breeding grounds along the Congo when the water level falls in December–January. Large numbers pass through northeastern Gabon between the end of December and the beginning of March (Brosset and Erard 1977, 1986; Erard 1981), presumably on their way back to the breeding grounds.

FOOD AND BEHAVIOUR The flight is rapid and energetic, with brief periods of gliding. River martins are usually seen in flocks in flight. In Gabon, Brosset and Erard (1977) recorded them perching on an airfield, on utility wires, on roofs of houses, in bushes and at the tops of tall trees. On the breeding grounds, however, they rarely perch anywhere but on the ground, where their gait is a walk or shuffle; they also bathe in the sand (Chapin 1954). They have been seen feeding, far from the colony, high over the forest, and on the wintering grounds they are known to feed over rivers and adjacent forest. The diet, analysed from stomach contents, includes mainly winged ants, but also small Lepidoptera, largely butterflies of the family Lycaenidae, and a few bugs (Hemiptera and Homoptera), small beetles and dipteran flies (Chapin 1953).

This species is highly gregarious when breeding, as well as on migration and on the wintering grounds (Chapin 1954; Brosset and Erard 1977, 1986). Large numbers, up to about 800, breed together, with as many as four tunnels per m^2. They also dig tunnels for overnight roosting in the non-breeding season. On migration they are usually seen in small groups. Brosset and Erard (1977) recorded aerial displays consisting of chases between pairs or trios, with the birds hovering and singing intermittently. Displays were also seen on the ground: in these the bird's body would be held horizontally, the tips of the wings drooping, the wings held slightly open, the head horizontal, and the neck stretched vertically. The birds involved would run parallel to one another, then face and move laterally away from one another, while singing. In another display, one bird would stretch vertically, approach another bird and start to dig the ground with its beak. Unfortunately, the contexts of the displays and the sexes of the birds involved were not known. The displays may be aggressive in nature or be part of the species' breeding behaviour; they were however, described for migrants in northeastern Gabon returning to breed, rather than for birds actually on the breeding grounds.

BREEDING The breeding grounds on the Congo are occupied from mid December to April, when the river is low and the sandbars are exposed, but not during July and August, when the water level is again low. Eggs and nestlings have been found in February and March (Chapin 1954). In Gabon, nesting has been reported at the end of October in the early rainy season (H. Morand and P.D. Alexander-Marrack, unpublished data). The nest holes, dug into sandbars, are about 1 m to nearly 2 m long, descending obliquely and ending in a rounded pocket some 50 cm below the surface (Chapin 1954). In the only known breeding site in Gabon, the river martins nest together with the Rosy Bee-eater *Merops malimbicus* (H. Morand and P.D. Alexander-Marrack, unpublished data). A few twigs and leaves and seedpods such as those of the copal tree serve as a scant nest. The eggs are white and unspotted, numbering two to four in a clutch; they measure 21.9–26.0 × 16.4–18.2 mm (Chapin 1953, 1954). The incubation and nestling periods are unknown. Both parents have been caught in the nest with the nestlings, suggesting that the male participates in their care.

VOICE Chapin (1954) noted several calls, all brief and unmusical, given by members of flocks, variously described as 'kee-r-r', 'chee-chee-chee', 'kee-k-k', 'peep'. They call together, 'cheer-cheer-cheer', when they fly up as a flock, and they are very vocal on migration, uttering piercing gull-like calls (Erard 1981). Chapin did not record a territorial or courtship song, but Brosset and Erard (1977) noted a jingling noise, heard during displays, which they called a song.

DESCRIPTION The adult has a largely blue-black or purple-black plumage. The head is purple-black; the lores and ear-coverts are velvety black. The crown sometimes has a dark oily-green sheen, but the head usually contrasts strongly with the back, mantle, scapulars and rump, which are tinged with green and slightly lustrous. The upperwing-coverts are non-glossy black, tinged green, and the uppertail-coverts are purplish-black with a green gloss. The underparts are mainly purple-black, but the underwing-coverts and axillaries are sooty-brown. The primaries and secondaries are black. The wings are long, extending beyond the tail. The tail is black, square, and the shafts of the feathers, especially those of the middle pair, project beyond the barbed portions. The short, broad bill is a conspicuous orange-red, with a yellow tip. The iris is red, and there is a pink eye-ring. The legs and feet are brownish-pink. The sexes are alike. The juvenile is a dull sooty-brown, rather darker above and a more greyish-brown below. The moult probably takes place soon after arrival on the non-breeding grounds, having largely finished by October (Chapin 1954).

Measurements Length 14 cm (5½"). Wing 118–130 (mean 122); tail (square) 45–53 (mean 48); bill 11–14.3 (mean 13.1); tarsus 14–15 (mean 14.5).

2 WHITE-EYED RIVER MARTIN   Plate 1
Pseudochelidon sirintarae Kitti

Pseudochelidon sirintarae Kitti, 1968, Thai natn. scient. Pap., Fauna Ser. No. 1. Holotype from Bung Boraphet, Amphoe Muang, Nakhon Sawan Province, central Thailand.

FIELD CHARACTERS This is a distinctive medium-sized swallow, having a black plumage with a blue-green gloss, silvery rump and long tail racquets, white eyes and a large bill and feet, unlike any other hirundine in its range. It is known only from a lake in Thailand where it winters.

HABITAT At night in winter it roosts in a reed-filled part of a shallow, marshy reservoir, but its breeding and winter daytime habitats are unknown. Immatures have been recorded perching in trees (Sophason and Dobias 1984).

DISTRIBUTION AND POPULATION This species was discovered in a winter roost of swallows and other migrants in a reservoir, Bung Boraphet, in central Thailand in January 1968 (Kitti 1968). Since then, it has been caught at this site between November and February. In the first few years after its discovery, over 100 individuals were caught but soon died in captivity (Sophason and Dobias 1984). The local people catch birds at the lake for sale in the local markets for food or for release by devout Buddhists; White-eyed River Martins have been seen in the market, but they have rarely been observed in the wild. A few, both adults and juveniles, were seen in 1972, 1977 and in 1980. None has been reliably reported since then (Sophason and Dobias 1984), despite an intensive search by staff of the Association for the Conservation of Wildlife (Thailand) in the winter of 1980/81. However, one was reputedly trapped by a local in 1986 (Ogle 1986). Its breeding range is a mystery, but, if its habits resemble those of its nearest relative, the African River Martin (1), it probably nests along one of the Thai or Chinese rivers. In 1969, Kitti looked for them on the Nan, Wang and Yom Rivers in northern Thailand but failed to find any evidence of them (Kitti 1969), although, since his expedition was in May and June, he may have missed the season when the birds would be breeding. Southwestern China, in the valleys of the Salween, Mekong and Chang Jiang Rivers, is another possible breeding area. There has been speculation that the species breeds in China (Dickinson 1986), but at present this seems unfounded (Parkes 1987).

The population size is unknown but must be very small, and the species may be on the verge of extinction. Very few have been found despite many thousands of other birds being caught at the lake. The large numbers of Barn Swallows have also declined at this roost owing to the harvesting of reeds and disturbance by illegal bird-trapping. The White-eyed River Martin is recorded as 'status indeterminate' in the Red Data Book, as endangered in the ICBP World Conservation Priorities, and it is listed in Appendix 2 of the 1973 Convention on International Trade in Endangered Species of Wild Fauna and Flora (King 1981). In Thailand, it is legally protected from capture or hunting.

MIGRATION White-eyed River Martins are clearly migratory, but the details of their movements are unknown. They have been seen at their winter roost site only between November and February, although local people claim to have seen them from October onwards.

FOOD AND BEHAVIOUR Its flight has been described as graceful and buoyant (King and Kanwanich 1978), and it is said not to use perches when caged. The stomach of one specimen contained the remains of a beetle (Kitti 1968); otherwise nothing is known of its feeding habits.

BREEDING Its breeding habits are also a mystery. It is possible that it uses holes in sandbanks, as the African River Martin does. If it nests along Thai rivers, it probably does so in March and April, before the monsoons increase the water levels enough to flood the potential nest sites (King and Kanwanich 1978).

VOICE The calls have not been recorded. This seems to be a silent bird on its wintering grounds.

DESCRIPTION The White-eyed River Martin is largely black with a blue-green gloss and a silvery-white rump. The plumage is strikingly silky. The lores are velvety black, but lack the gloss of the rest of the head. The mantle, back and scapulars are paler than the head and have a green gloss. The chin is velvety black, and the rest of the underparts are black with a blue-green gloss; the axillaries and underwing-coverts are light brown. The upper- and undertail-coverts are also black with a green gloss; they are very long, nearly reaching the tips of the rectrices. The long, narrow wings are black, but the remiges are pale brown along the inner webs. The rounded tail is black with a green gloss, each feather being tipped with pale brown; the shafts of the feathers project beyond the vanes. The two central tail feathers are elongated, forming long, narrow racquets which are expanded slightly at the tips. The bill is broad, bright greeny-yellow and has a black decurved tip to the upper mandible. The eyes and the margins of the lids are white, giving the appearance of a white eye-ring. The flesh-coloured legs, feet and claws are large and robust. The sexes are similar. The juvenile is similar to the adult, but lacks the tail racquets and has a wood-brown head and chin; the underwing is brownish-buff rather than light brown. Juveniles taken in January and February were in body moult (Kitti 1968).

Measurements Length 18 cm (7″). Wing 112–116 (mean 114.5); tail 92–128 (mean 106.8); racquets 49–85; bill 20–21; tarsus 10–12 (mean 11.3).

3 WHITE-THIGHED SWALLOW
Neochelidon tibialis (Cassin)

Plate 2

Petrochelidon (?) *tibialis* Cassin, 1853, Proc. Acad. Sci. Phil., 6, sig. 53, p. 370: 'probably South America'. Hellmayr, 1935, suggests vicinity of Rio de Janeiro as type locality.

Neochelidon tibialis minima Chapman, 1924, Juntas de Tananá, Rio San Juan (Chocó), Colombia.

Neochelidon tibialis griseiventris Chapman, 1924, Candamo (Puno), Peru.

FIELD CHARACTERS This is the only small, all-dark forest swallow in its range. It is sympatric with the Southern Rough-winged Swallow (5), but differs in being smaller and darker. It also resembles the Brown-bellied Swallow (15), but has a pale rump and brownish-black back and occurs at lower elevations. The white thighs are not always visible but may be seen when the bird is perched. Its bat-like erratic flight is also distinctive. It is usually seen in small groups.

HABITAT This is a swallow of humid tropical forests, feeding in small forest openings and clearings, along forest rivers, in low secondary growth, overgrown gardens, roadsides, streams, around villages and in more open terrain with scattered trees (Hilty and Brown 1986; Parker and Remsen 1987). It is often seen feeding in the clearings around huts and farms in forested areas. In southeastern Brazil it ranges up to 500 m (1640 ft), in primary and old secondary forest (Scott and Brooke 1985). In Colombia it frequents forested humid or wet lowlands or hills up to 1000 m (3300 ft) (Hilty and Brown 1986). In Venezuela it inhabits rainforest and scrub from 300 up to 900 m (980–2950 ft) (de Schauensee and Phelps 1978). Wetmore *et al.* (1984) recorded it as occurring up to 1250 m (4100 ft) in Panama.

DISTRIBUTION AND POPULATION The range is split between a southern population in southeastern Brazil and a northern one which breeds from Panama south to Colombia, Ecuador, Peru and western Brazil. The exact limits of the distribution are poorly known, however, as this species is generally rare and has not often been seen or collected. The gap between the two populations may thus be less than supposed. The southern, nominate, race *tibialis* occurs in southeastern Brazil in the states of Espirito Santo (Santa Leopoldina) and Rio de Janeiro (Cantagallo); it has also reputedly been recorded from the Rio Tapajos (Zimmer 1955), and, recently, in the state of São Paulo along the eastern coastal escarpments and at the Varjao do Guaratuba northeast of Bertioga (Willis and Oniki 1985). To the north, *minima* occurs in Panama (Canal Zone; Darién), Colombia in the tropical zone of the Pacific coast and the middle Magdalena valley south to El Centro southwest of Bucaramanga, and western Ecuador south to Chimbo. The third race, *griseiventris*, occurs in southern Colombia (Morelia; Macarena Mts, western Caqueta; southeastern Nariño and Vaupés), southeastern Venezuela (Cerro Auyán-tepui; Cerro Paurai-tepui; Alto Paragua; Amazonas along the upper Rio Orinoco and east of Cerro Duida), eastern Ecuador, eastern Peru in the departments of Junín, Cusco, Puno and Madre de Dios, and western Brazil on the upper Juruá (Igarapé Grande). The species (presumably this last race) has also recently been seen near Cobya in northern Bolivia (Parker and Remsen 1987).

White-thighed Swallows are not often seen and they seem to be generally rare, although they are numerous in some localities. They are uncommon to fairly common in southeast Brazil (Scott and Brooke 1985) and locally fairly common in Colombia (Hilty and Brown 1986). Wetmore *et al.* (1984) found them common locally in Panama. They may have benefited from clearings in the forest created by humans.

MIGRATION Little is known of any migratory movements made by this species, but it occurs in the upper Anchicayá valley at 1000 m in Colombia only in April and July–November, outside the breeding season (Hilty and Brown 1986). It may thus make some local movements after breeding. In Panama it is resident (Wetmore *et al.* 1984).

FOOD AND BEHAVIOUR White-thighed Swallows are usually seen in pairs or small groups, flying low, about 1 m (3 ft) above the ground, with a buoyant, erratic, bat-like flight, usually in circles, near a waterfall or river. They also sometimes feed above the forest canopy, hawking for insects. They often perch together on low to high bare twigs or branches, but remain separate from groups of larger swallows. Like other swallows, they bathe by dipping to the surface of open water. The diet includes tiny beetles, bugs and Hymenoptera (Wetmore *et al.* 1984). Prey are usually caught in the air, but during heavy rain these swallows also glean insects from the undersides of leaves (KL Schuchmann, pers. comm.).

BREEDING The limits of the breeding season are poorly known. Birds in breeding condition have been recorded in Colombia from March to May, and a copulation was observed in January (Hilty and Brown 1986). In Panama, a fledgling being fed by parents was seen in September, but nesting birds have been seen in February and pairs guarding tree holes between early April and June (Wetmore *et al.* 1984). Nests are built in natural and disused cavities, such as woodpecker holes in trees, disused burrows in banks or natural tree and bank cavities (Wetmore *et al.* 1984). Sites close to human habitation are used, but not artificial structures themselves. The nest is a pad of dry grass (Sclater and Salvin 1879). No information is available on the eggs or nestlings.

VOICE These swallows call constantly while foraging (KL Schuchmann, pers. comm.). This call is a soft 'zeet-zeet' . It has a broad frequency range, which may be an adaptation to a noisy riverine environment (KL Schuchmann, pers. comm.).

DESCRIPTION The upperparts from the forehead to the back, and the scapulars, are sooty-black or brownish-black with a slight olive-green sheen. The lores are velvety black; the ear-coverts and sides of the neck are dark brown, and the cheeks are grey-brown. The rump and uppertail-coverts are a sooty grey-brown, slightly paler than the back, and with pale edges to the feathers. The underparts, including the underwing-coverts and axillaries, are mostly sooty grey-brown like the rump. The undertail-coverts are blackish-brown. The wings and tail are brownish-black and the tail is slightly forked. The greater upperwing-coverts and tertials have slightly lighter tips. When in fresh plumage, the upperparts appear blacker and the underparts darker brown. The bill, eyes, legs and feet are dark brown; the lower leg bears a tuft of white feathers. The sexes are alike. The juvenile is very similar to the adult, but the feathers of the underparts have faint pale edges. Wetmore *et al.* (1984) recorded that specimens collected between January and April were in body moult, which suggests that breeding and moulting overlap to some extent.

Measurements Length 12 cm (4¾"). Wing 89–96. (*minima*) Wing 81–89 (mean 85); tail 36–47 (mean 41.5); fork 7–11 (mean 9.3); bill 7.1–10.3 (mean 8.0); tarsus 9–11 (mean 9.7). Weight 9.5.

RACES The northern race, *minima*, is the tiniest. Its entire body is dark chocolate-brown, with a slightly paler rump and underparts, which have a grey tinge. There is some variation in the colour of the bare parts: one male from Panama had a black bill and fuscous-black legs and feet, while a female had the maxilla and tip of the mandible black, the base of the mandible fuscous-black and the legs and feet fuscous-brown (Wetmore *et al.* 1984). The race *griseiventris* is mouse-grey below, not so brown as the other races, and is more metallic above with a dark green sheen on the brownish-black mantle; it has a paler mouse-grey or ashy-grey rump and underparts than *minima* and is larger (wing 89–98).

4 TAWNY-HEADED SWALLOW

Alopochelidon fucata (Temminck)

Plate 2

Hirundo fucata Temminck, 1822, Pl. col., livr. 27, pl. 161, fig. 1: Brazil. Vicinity of the city of São Paulo suggested as the type locality by Pinto, 1944, Aves do Brasil, pt. 2, p. 316.

FIELD CHARACTERS The Tawny-headed Swallow is a small and dully coloured hirundine with a dark crown and tawny-rufous forehead, eyebrow and neck. It is similar to the rough-winged swallows (5,6), but is smaller, with conspicuously tawny head markings, a blacker cap and a darker rump. Like roughwings, it seems to be a rather quiet, solitary species of open country.

HABITAT This swallow frequents open areas in the tropical and subtropical zones, especially near ponds and marshes and along streams in forest clearings, and it also occurs in the pampas of Argentina. It can be found in lowland areas and at elevations of up to 1600 m (5200 ft) (Fjeldså and Krabbe 1989).

DISTRIBUTION AND POPULATION The range is disjunct, there being a northern population in Venezuela and northern Brazil and a southern one south of the Amazonian Basin (Fjeldså and Krabbe 1989). The species breeds in Venezuela in the mountains of the north coast from El Valle to Cumaná and in the mountains of eastern Bolivar; in extreme northern Brazil in the Territory of Rio Branco (opposite Santa Elena, Venezuela), and southern Brazil in the states of Mato Grosso, Minas Gerais, São Paulo and Rio Grande do Sul (plus a sight record from Rio de Janeiro: Mitchell 1957); in eastern Peru (Urubamba Cañon; in Bolivia in the departments of Cochabamba and Tarija; Paraguay; Uruguay; and in northern Argentina south to the provinces of Mendoza, Cordoba, Santa Fé, Entre Rios and Buenos Aires. In Colombia it is known only from a few specimens from the foothills at La Colorada on the Rio Casanare, Arauca, but whether the species is resident here or a migrant is uncertain (Hilty and Brown 1986).

Nowhere are Tawny-headed Swallows very numerous, although large flocks are occasionally seen in the non-breeding season; few measures of abundance are available, however. Belton (1985) noted that this species was uncommon in southeastern Brazil, occurring mainly along the coast, in the central lowlands and in the west. Its breeding distribution is probably largely limited by the availability of natural banks for nest sites, as it rarely uses artificial sites.

MIGRATION Only the southern population appears to migrate (Pereyra 1969; Belton 1985). Where it winters is not well known,

but the southernmost birds may move into the northern part of the breeding range. In the Rio Grande do Sul in Brazil it is present all year around, but is more common in the late autumn and winter, suggesting an influx of non-breeding birds (Belton 1985). Further south it is absent in the winter, from April to July.

FOOD AND BEHAVIOUR Tawny-headed Swallows are usually seen in pairs or small groups, but large flocks, including one of over 100 individuals, have been recorded outside the breeding season. They fly low and swoop frequently. They are seldom seen with other swallows. Insects are caught in flight and include curculionids and other beetles, flies and Hymenoptera (Olrog 1965). The species is not very gregarious, and pairs usually nest alone or in small scattered groups (Dinelli 1924).

BREEDING The southern population breeds from September to November; the northern population possibly breeds in May and June, as specimens collected at this time had enlarged gonads (Zimmer 1955). Details of the breeding biology of Tawny-headed Swallows are sparse. Nests are built mainly in holes along sandy river banks. Dry and wet ditches and other watercourses are also used. The holes used are 1 m or more long, with an enlarged chamber at the far end where the nest is placed (Dinelli 1924; Belton 1985). Both members of the pair make the nest. It is not known whether these swallows dig their own tunnels or use vacant burrows of other species; they may do both, or they may just enlarge and adapt existing tunnels. The nest itself is a loose construction of grass, straws and feathers (Dinelli 1924). In Argentina the clutch size is four or five (Pereyra 1969). The eggs are white and measure 17.7–12.7 mm (17–19 × 12–13.9; weight 1.5).

VOICE The calls have not been recorded.

DESCRIPTION Tawny-headed Swallows are small and rather dull, apart from the rich tawny-rufous head. The forehead, eyebrow and broad nuchal collar are deep tawny-rufous, merging into cinnamon-buff on the ear-coverts, sides of the head, the chin, throat and breast. The crown is largely brownish-black, but the feathers have tawny-rufous edges. The extent of the tawny colour, however, is variable. The lores are blackish. The rest of the upperparts, including the lesser and median wing-coverts, are uniformly grey-brown, the feathers having pale edges, which are especially marked on the rump and upper-tail-coverts and are also present on the greater wing-coverts and tertials. The underwing-coverts and axillaries are grey-brown. The abdomen and flanks are dull white or buffy-white, and the undertail-coverts are a purer white. The sides are light grey-brown. The wings and tail are dark brown, and the tail is almost square. The bill is black, the eyes are brown, and the legs and feet are reddish-grey to black. The sexes are alike. The juvenile is similar to the adult, but the tawny-rufous on the feather margins is replaced by a yellowish-fawn colour.

Measurements Length 12 cm (4¾"). Wing 91–109 (mean 100.1); tail (square) 39–49

(mean 44); bill 6.6–8.1 (mean 7.6); tarsus 9.8–10.8 (mean 10.5). Weight 13–15.

RACES There is no marked geographical variation. Southern specimens tend to have a duskier cap and less distinct margins to the feathers of the crown and they tend to be slightly larger (wing 95–109) than those from the north coastal range of Venezuela (wing 91–96). Individuals from the Roraima region have at one time been considered to be a separate subspecies on the basis of supposedly small size and paler plumage. Individuals of both northern and southern populations, however, overlap in characters and size, and those from the Roraima region do not differ overall from southern specimens, so there are probably no separate subspecies (Zimmer 1955).

5 SOUTHERN ROUGH-WINGED SWALLOW   Plate 2
Stelgidopteryx ruficollis (Vieillot)

Hirundo ruficollis Vieillot, 1817, Nouv. Dict. Hist. Nat., 14, p. 523: Brazil.

Stelgidopteryx ruficollis decolor Griscom, 1929, Divalá, Chiriqui, Pacific slope of Panama.

Stelgidopteryx ruficollis uropygialis (Lawrence), 1863, Isthmus of Panama = near Lion Hill *fide* Zimmer 1955.

Stelgidopteryx ruficollis aequalis Bangs, 1901, Santa Marta, Colombia.

FIELD CHARACTERS Southern Rough-winged Swallows are small, dull swallows. They closely resemble the Northern species (6), but where the two overlap Southern Roughwings can be distinguished by the paler rump and brighter throat; they also tend to have a larger bill, longer wings and more yellowish underparts. In South America they could be confused with Tawny-headed Swallows (4), but the latter have a dark rump, blackish-brown crown and a tawny-rufous eyebrow and collar. Like the Northern species, they are generally silent, solitary, open-country birds.

HABITAT Roughwings can be found in a variety of open and semi-open areas, especially near waterbodies, such as savanna in Surinam, llanos in Venezuela, forest clearings, rivers with steep banks and montane areas in Central America (Fjeldså and Krabbe 1989). They range from sea level to over 2000 m (6600 ft), and a few have been recorded up to 3600 m (11,800 ft) in Colombia (Hilty and Brown 1986).

DISTRIBUTION AND POPULATION Southern Roughwings have an extensive range in Central and South America, slightly overlapping that of the Northern Rough-winged Swallow (Stiles 1981; Fjeldså and Krabbe 1989). In the area of overlap in the central highlands of Costa Rica, *uropygialis* and the race *fulvipennis* of the Northern Roughwing breed together locally, although the former is mainly a lowland race and *fulvipennis* is mainly a montane form. The race *decolor*, however, is still problematic: specimens are very variable and resemble an intergradation between *uropygialis* and the nominate race of the Northern Roughwing; thus, they may point to a hybrid zone between the Northern and Southern forms (Wetmore *et al.* 1984).

The nominate race *ruficollis* occurs in southeastern Colombia, eastern Ecuador, eastern Peru, probably southeastern Bolivar in Venezuela, the Guianas, Brazil, eastern and southern Bolivia, Paraguay, Uruguay, and northern Argentina as far south as the Buenos Aires region. The race *decolor* occurs on the Pacific coast of Costa Rica and Panama, from the eastern shore of the Gulf of Nicoya to western Veraguas. The race *uropygialis* occurs in the Caribbean lowlands of Central America, from Honduras and southeastern Nicaragua to Darién, and south also in the Pacific lowlands of eastern Panama; in Colombia on the Pacific coast, in the western Andes, the upper Cauca valley, and the central Andes; in western Ecuador; and in northwestern Peru. Specimens from northwestern Peru are intermediate between *uropygialis* and *ruficollis*. The fourth race, *aequalis*, occurs in northern Colombia, in Venezuela east to the Orinoco delta and south to Territorio de Amazonas and northern Bolivar, and in Trinidad. Specimens from Mount Roraima and Auyán-tepui in Venezuela share characteristics of three races: *ruficollis*, *uropygialis* and *aequalis*.

Southern Roughwings are common in some parts of their range where suitable nesting sites are available, but are often sparsely or locally distributed, occurring mainly along rivers or in forest clearings. As yet they have benefited little from the presence of artificial nest sites.

MIGRATION Southern populations are migratory (Pereyra 1969). Thus, in Rio Grande do Sul, Brazil, roughwings are largely absent between mid February and mid August (Belton 1985). Migrant *ruficollis* from the south have been recorded in northern South America, including Surinam and Colombia, in the austral winter, but the full extent of their wintering range is not clear. Northern forms are resident.

FOOD AND BEHAVIOUR The flight is slow and wavering, rather bat-like, with shallow wingbeats. These swallows forage alone or in small groups, usually flying low over the ground and, especially, water. Small flies, and flies of the family Muscidae, beetles, bugs, and Hymenoptera, including winged ants and wasps, have been recorded in the diet (Freeman 1922; Moojen et al. 1941). Hymenoptera predominate in the diet in Costa Rica (Hespenheide 1975). Southern Roughwings breed in single pairs or in small, scattered groups, depending on the availability of nest sites, but after the breeding season they will form large flocks. Resident birds may stay in pairs and remain near the nest site for most of the year (Skutch 1981). At the beginning of the breeding season, a lot of chasing can be seen around the nest sites as males defend territories (as in the Northern Roughwing (Skutch 1981)).

BREEDING Breeding has been recorded from April to June in Surinam, with birds in breeding condition from February; late March to June in Panama; and April to June in Costa Rica and Trinidad (Haverschmidt 1968; Wetmore et al. 1984). A copulation was seen in October in Brazil (Belton 1985). In Colombia, birds in breeding condition have been taken in January–March, and nesting has been recorded from February to July (Hilty and Brown 1986). Only one brood is raised each season; replacement clutches may be laid if the first is lost, but these are in different burrows (Skutch 1981). The breeding biology of the Southern Roughwing is not so well known as that of the Northern form, but is apparently very similar. For nest sites, it uses natural cavities or old burrows dug by other species (such as the Swallow-wing *Chelidoptera tenebrosa* or Blue-crowned Motmot *Momotus momota*) in sandy banks, quarries or road cuttings (Skutch 1981). Unlike the Northern species, the Southern Roughwing appears nearly always to nest in natural situations. Although already existing burrows are generally used, Hilty and Brown (1986) noted that one was seen digging a burrow in Colombia, which roughwings also sometimes do in Panama (Wetmore et al. 1984).

The nest itself is made of fibrous material such as dry grass, leaves, straw, stems and feathers. The eggs are pure white and measure 19.7 × 13.5 mm (18.1–21.6 × 12.3–14.7; weight 1.87). The clutch size is four to six eggs in Central America, three to six in Trinidad, three or four in northern South America and three to five in southern parts of the range (Pereyra 1969; ffrench 1980; Skutch 1981; Hilty and Brown 1986). The eggs are laid at intervals of one or occasionally two days. Only the female incubates. The incubation period is 15–18 days and the nestling period 18–21 days (Skutch 1981). Both parents feed the nestlings. The fledglings do not usually return to the burrow but move to a nearby perch, where their parents feed them. The parents and fledglings may go to separate communal roost sites, but during the day each family remains together near the nest site. The fledglings are fed for several days, and one family was fed for at least 25 days after fledging (Skutch 1981).

VOICE Southern Roughwings have few vocalisations, and these are similar to those of the Northern species. Stiles (1981) described the calls of *uropygialis* as being lower-pitched, more rolling and less harsh than those of the Northern Roughwing (race *fulvipennis*). The repertoire includes twitterings and harsh buzzy or grating notes which are used during chases at the nest site and may be a territorial call (Skutch 1981).

DESCRIPTION Southern Roughwings have dull, rather dark grey-brown upperparts, including the lesser and median wing-coverts, slightly darker on the crown than on the mantle, back and rump, while the rump is scarcely paler than the mantle and back; the feathers of the rump and outer uppertail-coverts have very slightly pale edges. The lores are dark brown and the ear-coverts dark grey-brown. The throat is cinnamon-buff. The underwing-coverts, breast and sides are dark grey-brown, fading to a yellowish-white on the centre of the abdomen. The undertail-coverts are white. The wings and tail are blackish-brown, and the tail is square. The tertials, inner secondaries and greater wing-coverts have pale edges. The eyes are dark brown, the bill and legs and feet are black. The sexes are alike, but the female is slightly smaller. As in the Northern Roughwing, there is a series of barbs on the outer web of the outer primary, more marked on the male than on the female. Juveniles are similar to adults, but the feathers of the mantle, back, tertials and wing-coverts have extensive pale edges and the throat is duller. The moult takes place after the breeding season.

Measurements Length 13 cm (5"). Wing of male 104–114 (mean 109), of female 94–104 (mean 100.4); tail (square) of male 47–56 (mean 52.6), of female 47–52 (mean 48.7); bill 9.3–10.8 (mean 9.9); tarsus 10–11 (mean 10.7). Weight 14–18 (mean 15.2).

RACES There is a clinal variation in coloration, with the darkest form (*ruficollis*) in the south of the range and a paler form

(*decolor*) on the drier Pacific side of Central America than on the wetter Atlantic side. Throughout Central and South America the races intergrade with each other, confusing their demarcation, and the species is sometimes considered monotypic. The race *decolor*, in particular, is variable and may not be distinct from *uropygialis* (Wetmore et al. 1984). The Central American race *decolor* has medium to fairly dark upperparts, the tertials are edged with pale grey, the throat is pale cinnamon, the breast and sides are pale grey-brown with dark shaft streaks to the feathers, the abdomen is white with a yellowish tinge, the undertail-coverts are white with dark shaft streaks and usually dusky tips to the central feathers (sometimes with dusky subterminal spots), and the rump is pale greyish, not contrasting strongly with the back (wing of male 100–111, of female 94–103). The race *uropygialis* is darker than *decolor*, but has a whitish rump contrasting strongly with the back and tail, the tertials are edged with white, the throat is cinnamon-rufous or pale rufous, the breast and sides are a darker grey-brown and the abdomen is more yellowish; the undertail-coverts are sometimes tipped with black (wing of male 104–115, of female 95–104). This race is rather paler below than *ruficollis*. The fourth race, *aequalis*, has brown upperparts, a tawny-buff throat, the breast and sides are pale greyish, the abdomen is whitish with a yellow tinge, and the longest undertail-coverts have dusky tips; it has lighter upperparts, a lighter throat and a more whitish rump than *ruficollis* (wing 100–115). Bangs and Penard (1918) named another race, *cacabatus*, from Surinam, with a range in southeastern Bolivar in Venezuela, the Guianas and possibly Brazil north of the Amazon. Zimmer (1955) suggested that this race should be merged in *ruficollis*, and Haverschmidt (1982) concluded that the description of it was based on migrants of *ruficollis* and that the race was not valid.

6 NORTHERN ROUGH-WINGED SWALLOW   Plate 2
Stelgidopteryx serripennis (Audubon)

Hirundo serripennis Audubon, 1838, Orn. Biogr., 4, p. 593: Charleston, South Carolina.

Stelgidopteryx serripennis psammochrous Griscom, 1929, near Oposura, Sonora.

Stelgidopteryx serripennis fulvipennis (Sclater), 1859, Jalapa, Veracruz.

Stelgidopteryx serripennis ridgwayi Nelson, 1901, Chichén Itzá, Yucatan.

Stelgidopteryx serripennis stuarti Brodkorb, 1942, Finca Panzamalá, Alta Verapaz, Guatemala.

FIELD CHARACTERS This is a small, dull grey-brown swallow with a pale rump. It closely resembles the American Bank Swallow (Sand Martin, 27), but it is larger, lacks the latter's well-defined breast-band, and has a greyish rather than a white throat. Some juvenile Tree Swallows (7) also resemble roughwings, but the former also have a whiter throat and dull grey upperparts. Roughwings are rather silent, solitary, open-country swallows.

HABITAT The preferred habitat is open areas with waterbodies where there are banks or roadside cuttings in which to nest. Roughwings breed over a wide altitudinal range, with nests recorded at up to 2000 m (6600 ft) (E. von Siebold Dingle in Bent 1942).

DISTRIBUTION AND POPULATION
Northern Roughwings have an extensive breeding range, from southeastern Alaska and southern Canada through the United States and Central America as far as Costa Rica (AOU 1983; Phillips 1986). The nominate race *serripennis* breeds in southeastern Alaska and southern Canada south to northern California, western and northern Nevada, northern Utah, northern New Mexico, northern Arizona, eastern Texas, the Gulf States and southwestern and south-central Florida. The race *psammochrous* breeds along the southwestern boundary of the United States, from southern California (south of the Tehachapi Mountains and San Bernardino County) to southern Texas, and south through the northern coastal plains and the arid interior of Mexico to Baja California, Oaxaca and Tamaulipas. The extreme northern part of Arizona and the extreme southern part of Utah may be an area of intergradation between the races *serripennis* and *psammochrous* (Behle 1985), and *psammochrous* and *fulvipennis* intergrade in Guerrero (Brodkorb 1942). The third race, *fulvipennis*, breeds in the lowlands and middle altitudes of Mexico (except northern Yucatan) and in Central America from Oaxaca and Veracruz south to the central highlands of Costa Rica. Two other, dark, races, sometimes designated as a separate species, occur in Central America. One, *ridgwayi*, is confined to the Yucatan peninsula. The other, *stuarti*, occurs from southern Veracruz, Oaxaca and Chiapas to Belize and Guatemala.

Throughout its breeding and wintering ranges, the Northern Roughwing is a generally common or fairly common swallow, although locally distributed depending on the availability of suitable areas for nesting. In Guatemala, however, it is uncommon when breeding but is fairly common in winter (Land 1970). In Alaska it is still rare, both as a migrant and as a breeding bird (Kessel and Gibson 1978). The breeding range has expanded in the north in the past several decades, and the population is increasing in the eastern and central regions of the United States (Robbins *et al.* 1986). In New England, roughwings were rare visitors in the last century but now breed there regularly. In the Montreal region of Canada, they were not recorded until 1947 but now occur in small numbers (Ouellet 1970). In Florida, too, roughwings are spreading through the peninsula, using artificial structures such as canal banks and quarries for nesting (Robertson and Kushlan 1974). The greatest population densities are in the Sonoran desert, Idaho, California and Alabama (Robbins *et al.* 1986). In general, humans have probably had little impact on roughwing populations as this species does not nest in artificial structures to a great extent. In some areas, however, particularly on the edge of the range, such structures have contributed to its spread (Erskine 1979).

MIGRATION The North American *serripennis* winters mainly in Mexico and Central America to Panama, but also in the southwestern United States, the Gulf Coast and southern Florida (casually in South Carolina) (AOU 1983; Phillips 1986). The Central American *psammochrous* winters in the southern part of its breeding range and south to central Panama, moving south in September or early October and north in late February; southern populations may be resident. The race *fulvipennis* is mostly resident but makes some local post-breeding movements, altitudinally and geographically (for example, in Costa Rica), and some winter as far as western and central Panama; in El Salvador it makes vertical migrations from the mountains and foothills to the coastal lagoons in winter (Dickey and van Rossem 1938). The other races, *ridgwayi* and *stuarti*, are resident. Migrant Northern Roughwings have been recorded in the northwestern

Bahama Islands, Cuba, Jamaica and the Cayman and Swan Islands, Socorro Island and the Virgin Islands, and a few are seen regularly in the West Indies in winter. There are also casual records of the species from northern Alaska and southern Yukon.

FORAGING AND FOOD The flight of roughwings is stronger and involves less twisting and turning than that of the Bank Swallow. Foraging birds fly low over the ground near their nest site, feeding over open ground but especially over water; in bad weather they feed particularly close to the ground. They generally fly and perch in small groups. Flies make up a third of the diet, but ants and other, parasitic, Hymenoptera are also taken in large numbers. Beetles and plant bugs each comprise about 15% of the diet; most bugs are taken in the autumn. Moths, caterpillars, dragonflies, mayflies, spiders and grasshoppers are eaten to a lesser extent (Beal 1918). The nestlings' diet includes hoverflies and other Diptera, and Hymenoptera (Lunk 1962). Roughwings have also been seen feeding on the ground, scavenging dead midges and feeding on larvae in dead fish (Sealy 1983; Hobson and Sealy 1987).

BEHAVIOUR Roughwings nest solitarily or in small, scattered groups, depending on the availability of nest sites. Even where they nest in groups, the burrows are often a few metres apart, but may be closer together where nest sites are scarce (Lunk 1962). They often nest on the periphery of Bank Swallow colonies, with just a few pairs per colony. In Canada in general, group sizes average only four, but in British Columbia the average is 15 (Erskine 1979). After the breeding season; large flocks form and roost together in marshes, mangrove islands and sugar-cane fields. In bad weather, several roughwings may roost together in a burrow (Lunk 1962). Males tend to arrive at the breeding sites before the females and establish a small territory around a nest site. Chases and fights are frequent. Males threaten others by gaping and uttering the territorial call. There is no clear pair-formation behaviour, but males chase females in a leisurely manner and display by spreading their white undertail-coverts, and males also often raise their crown feathers in display; the birds return to the same site each year (Lunk 1962).

BREEDING The breeding season extends from about the beginning of May to the middle of July, with eggs being laid towards the end of May or beginning of June (E. von Siebold Dingle in Bent 1942). Egg-laying starts earlier in the south than in the northern part of the range; the race *fulvipennis* in Costa Rica lays from mid April to mid May (Skutch 1960). Only one brood is reared, but pairs will re-lay if their first attempt fails (Lunk 1962). Roughwings nest in any suitable cavities, such as crevices in caves, old burrows in banks of sand, clay or gravel, gutters, drainpipes, and holes in walls, bridges and culverts. One nest was built on a buttress in a steamboat; and there are records of nests in cinder and slag dumps and sawdust piles (E. von Siebold Dingle in Bent 1942; Lunk 1962). Holes in trees are rarely used, and holes in buildings are less commonly used than natural cavities and disused burrows dug by other species such as Bank Swallows. In Canada, nearly three-quarters of nests are in natural sites (Erskine 1979). There are very few reports of roughwings digging their own burrows (E. von Siebold Dingle in Bent 1942), and in Lunk's (1962) study they were only seen kicking sand out of already existing burrows. The nest itself is made of a variety of fibrous material, including dry grass, corn leaves and husks, stems and rootlets, twigs, moss, straw, pine needles and seaweed, according to what is available (Lunk 1962). Green material is added towards the end of nest-building or later when the eggs are laid. The lining is usually of grass, not feathers. Dung is also sometimes added to the nest. The female collects the material and makes the nest, accompanied by her mate. Building usually takes six or seven days but may be delayed by cool or wet weather, and building activity is usually sporadic. The nest may be placed 1 m or so along a burrow, but not usually at the back of long burrows such as those dug by kingfishers.

The eggs are white and rather elongate. Those of the race *serripennis* measure 18.8 × 13.2 mm (16.5–21.0 × 12.2–15.0; weight 1.78); Skutch (1960) gave measurements of Guatemalan eggs as 19.8 × 13.6 mm. Clutches often differ in the size and shape of the eggs. The clutch size is four to eight, usually five to seven eggs, with an average of six in Lunk's study. There is a slight decline in clutch size from north to south, with the race *fulvipennis* laying five or fewer eggs and averaging 4.7 (Skutch 1960). The eggs are laid on successive days early in the morning, but days are occasionally missed, probably because of bad weather. Only the female incubates and broods the young (Lunk 1962); the male rarely enters the nest, but perches near the nest while his mate is incubating. The female incubates for periods of up to half an hour, leaving the eggs for a shorter period to feed. Males roost away from the burrow. The incubation period is 16 days; Skutch (1960) gave the incubation period of *fulvipennis* as 16–18 days, rather longer than for *serripennis*. The eggs hatch somewhat asynchronously. Both sexes feed the young, which come forward in the burrow to meet their parents as they near fledging. The nestling period is 18–21 days, the younger members of the brood leaving at an earlier age than their older siblings. They do not generally return to the burrow once they have fledged, but families keep together for a short period while the fledglings are still fed by their parents. The parents do not recognise their offspring, at least not by voice (Beecher *et al.* 1986). The fledging success is generally high: Blake (1953) reported 68% of eggs producing fledglings and Lunk (1962) 61%. The main causes of nest failure in Lunk's study were predation by weasels, or losses through erosion of the nest site.

VOICE Roughwings are generally silent, and there are few calls apart from a subdued 'brrt', chirps uttered during chases and a harsh alarm call. The male also has a territorial call consisting of a series of rapid, short notes.

DESCRIPTION On the Northern Roughwing, the upperparts, including the ear-coverts, the sides of the head and neck and the lesser and median wing-coverts are grey-brown. The lores are dark grey-brown. The rump appears slightly paler, as the feathers have pale edges. The chin, throat, breast, sides and flanks are pale grey-brown, the chin and throat being palest; in fresh plumage, the throat has a buff tinge. The rest of the underparts, including the undertail-coverts, are white. On some individuals, the shafts of the longer undertail-coverts are darkened subterminally; occasionally this dark area forms a spot. The underwing-coverts and axillaries are light grey-brown, the marginal coverts with pale tips. The wings are dark grey-brown, and the tertials, secondaries and greater wing-coverts have pale grey edges. The tail is dark grey-brown and square. The eyes are brown, the bill is black, and the legs and feet

blackish. The sexes are alike, although males have slightly longer wings and tail and longer and broader undertail-coverts. These swallows are called roughwings from the series of fine recurved hooklets on the outer web of the outer primary, these being more distinct on the male. Juveniles of the race *serripennis* have a tawny or pale cinnamon wash on the upperparts, the wing-coverts have cinnamon edges, the tertials and secondaries have dull buff margins and the chin, throat and breast have a paler cinnamon wash; the hooklets on the outer primaries are absent or nearly so. Some first-years also have weakly developed serrations. The moult takes place after the breeding season.

Measurements Length 13 cm (5"). Wing of male 104–118 (mean 110.7), of female 99–115 (mean 104); tail (square) of male 47–55 (mean 50.4), of female 43–53 (mean 47.5); bill 9.3–10.6 (mean 10.2); tarsus 10.3–11.7 (mean 11.2). Weight 10.3–18.3 (mean 15.9).

RACES The race *fulvipennis* is darker than *serripennis*, particularly on the crown, and the shafts of the undertail-coverts are darkened subterminally (the spots so formed tend to be darker and larger); the chin and throat are tinged rufous or buff (wing of male 105–117, of female 99–109). Individuals from the north tend to be larger than southern ones. The race *psammochrous* is paler above and below than *serripennis*, particularly on the crown and rump (wing of male 105–112, of female 100–107). The race *ridgwayi* is larger than *serripennis*, darker above but with paler anterior underparts, and the longest undertail-coverts are extensively dusky towards the tips (wing of male 116–122, of female 104–108). The race *stuarti* is very dark, the throat is tinged rufous, and the undertail-coverts also have blackish tips (wing 105–115). Further work is needed to judge whether the races *stuarti* and *ridgwayi* constitute a separate species; they appear to overlap geographically with the race *fulvipennis*, but it is not known whether they are separated ecologically or if they interbreed. A fifth race, *aphractus*, with a greyish throat and dark upperparts, has been described from the western Great Basin region of the United States, but it is not a well-defined race in colour or size (Miller 1941). None of the known races is as clearly defined as in some other species of swallow. Rather, there is a cline in coloration from *serripennis* to *fulvipennis*, and a tendency for pale birds to occur in the southwestern United States and north-western Mexico; there is also a cline in size, wing length increasing towards the northwest and size increasing slightly from north to south (Stiles 1981).

7 TREE SWALLOW
Tachycineta bicolor (Vieillot)
Alternative name: White-bellied Swallow

Plate 3

Hirundo bicolor Vieillot, 1808, Ois. Amer. Sept. 1 (1807), p. 61, pl. 31: centre of the United States; New York.

FIELD CHARACTERS This is a small swallow with blue-green upperparts and only a slightly forked tail. It differs from other American swallows, except the Violet-green Swallow (10), in having both a dark rump and immaculate white underparts. The white cheek patch, however, does not extend above the eye as on Violet-greens. Juveniles are superficially similar to rough-winged swallows (5,6), but are more chunky, have a white throat and are gener-ally whiter on the breast and abdomen; they differ from juvenile Violet-green Swallows in that the brownish-grey upperparts are more sharply cut off from the white under-parts, and from Bank Swallows (Sand Martins, 27) in having a less distinct brown breast-band. They are often seen alone or in small groups, but they will breed in large, loose groups and will form large flocks when not breeding.

HABITAT Tree Swallows breed in a variety of habitats, but generally in open or wood-ed areas, often but not necessarily near water. Formerly they would have required trees for nesting, but the provision of nest-boxes, especially in prairie regions, has allowed them to spread into other habitats.

DISTRIBUTION AND POPULATION The Tree Swallow has an extensive breeding range in North America, from north-central Alaska, across Canada as far north as the tree limit, south as far as the upland areas of Tennessee in the east and north-central New Mexico in California in the west and Kansas in the centre of the range (AOU 1983). It breeds casually further south to northern Louisiana and Mississippi. Within this range, however, it is sometimes locally distributed, depending on the availability of suitable nest sites. It is a very common species. The Canadian population alone may number a million pairs (Erskine 1979).

In recent years it has increased throughout the continent, particularly in the north-eastern states, the Great Lakes states and Canada, but there has been a decrease in Massachusetts and New Jersey (Robbins *et al.* 1986). The provision of nestboxes has increased the availability of nest sites, but there has also been some loss of natural sites through deforestation; in some areas, the Tree Swallow is dependent on nest-boxes (Holroyd 1975). Most mortality is probably due to the weather, as cold wet weather reduces insect availability and thus can lead to both adults and nestlings star-ving (Christy 1940; Chapman 1955; DuBowy and Moore 1985). There is also competition for nest sites, especially with Starlings (Holroyd 1975) and House Spar-rows, which may have contributed to local declines (Graber *et al.* 1972).

MIGRATION The winter range extends from southern California, southwestern Arizona, northern Mexico, the Gulf Coast and southeastern Virginia, south to southern Baja California, Honduras, where it is very abundant in winter, Nicaragua, Costa Rica, northwestern Panama and the West Indies (mainly the northern Bahamas and Cuba, but also Jamaica, Grand Cayman, Hispan-iola and Puerto Rico). The migration routes east of the Rockies are along the east coast to Central America for east coast and Great Lakes birds; the Mississippi Basin to the Gulf Coast and Central America for Canadian prairie and mid-west birds; and along the Rockies to Mexico for populations from the eastern Rockies (Butler 1988). It occasion-ally winters further north, as far as Long Island and Massachusetts (Bull 1974). It is an irregular winter visitor south of Honduras, on the Pacific slope of Central America, but there are several records from South America, mainly in Colombia, Venezuela, Guyana and Trinidad. There are also supposed sightings of individuals along the western South American coast as far south as Salta, Argentina (Gochfeld et al. 1980). It occurs casually or accidentally in northern Alaska, St Lawrence Island, the Bering Sea and Greenland.

FORAGING AND FOOD The flight is a mixture of rapid flying and gliding. When feeding, the birds characteristically fly in a straight path, suddenly turning to one side or down to catch an insect, then resume a straight path (Burtt, pers. comm.). They have occasionally been seen to feed in bayberry bushes and on the ground in severe weather, when flying insects are likely to be scarce (Chapman 1955; Erskine 1984; Hobson and Sealy 1987), and also occasionally hover to pick insects from vegetation. Normally, however, they feed aerially, usually within a few kilometres of the nest site when feeding nestlings, sometimes further (Kuerzi 1941). They feed over grass and water, both high and low, crisscrossing the feeding area, alone or in flocks. Sometimes large flocks gather at abundant sources of food such as swarming ants or emerging mayflies (Bent 1942). Beal (1918) analysed the stomach contents of 343 individuals from throughout North America: unusually for swallows, 80 (23%) of the stomachs contained vegetation, mostly bayberries *Myrica carolinensis*; these were taken throughout the summer, but probably only during inclement weather when flying insects were temporarily unavailable. Chapman (1955) recorded breeding Tree Swallows eating bayberries during a period of cold weather, and Eaton (cited by Tyler in Bent 1942) recorded swallows feeding on seeds on a frozen pond. Elliott (1939) examined faeces of Tree Swallows wintering on Long Island and found that they had fed on Crustacea, water boatmen, spiders, sedge, bayberry and smartweed seed. Berries and seeds may be particularly important to this swallow because it arrives early on the breeding grounds, when temperatures are still low and insects scarce, and it moults early and leaves late for its wintering grounds. In cold weather, the birds will also cluster together in roosts to conserve heat (Weatherhead et al. 1985) and may even become torpid (Stake and Stake 1983). In Beal's study, craneflies, horseflies, robberflies, hoverflies and houseflies made up 40% of the diet, 14% were beetles, mainly scarabeids, and 6% were ants; the diet also included some hemipteran bugs, moths, grasshoppers, dragonflies, mayflies and spiders. In a later study at one site in Ontario (Quinney and Ankney 1985), nestlings were fed 44% nematoceran flies, 30% other flies and 21% plant bugs; at another site, they were fed 90% nematocerans, and only 9% of the diet was made up of other flies and plant bugs. The adults select medium-sized prey, generally 4–6 mm long, from what is available.

SOCIAL ORGANISATION The Tree Swallow nests in single pairs or in groups, depending on the availability of nest sites. It is one of the most aggressive of swallows, and defends a relatively large area of about 15 m radius around the nest (Robertson and Gibbs 1982). Pairs avoid nesting close to each other in space and time. If extra boxes are present within the defended area, they, too, are incidentally defended. Outside the breeding season, Tree Swallows will form small or large flocks, sometimes containing thousands of individuals.

SOCIOSEXUAL BEHAVIOUR Males defend a nest site as soon as they arrive at their breeding grounds; they perch near the nest hole and call frequently, probably both to deter intruders and to attract a mate (Robertson, pers. comm.). If suitable nest sites are scarce, there can be intense competition between individuals to acquire one, and fights have often been recorded: these sometimes take place in mid air, with the birds gripping each other and often falling to the ground still locked together; there are cases of Tree Swallows killing each other in fights. Tree Swallows, especially males, may also kill and throw out nestlings in occupied nests, if the resident male is missing or displaced, in attempts to acquire a nest site (Robertson and Stutchbury 1988). Pairs defend the site by chasing intruders and by 'hole-perching': by perching on the hole they effectively block the entrance, and their conspicuous white breast may serve as a keep-out signal (Robertson, pers. comm.). There is generally a shortage of males with nest sites, which leads to competition between the females (Leffelaar and Robertson 1985): intruding females have been known to evict resident females and mate with the resident male. Most matings are monogamous, but males are sometimes polygynous (Quinney 1983). Unlike several other hirundines, but like the Cliff Swallow (67), the male Tree Swallow does not guard his mate before and during the laying period; this may be because there is little likelihood of cuckoldry and because both members of a pair are needed to defend the territory (Leffelaar and Robertson 1986). Extra-pair copulations do occasionally occur, however (Lombardo 1986a).

There is a 'floating' population of females, and probably some males, which do not obtain a mate until late in the season (Stutchbury and Robertson 1985, 1987a). The majority of these are first-years. They intrude briefly on the territories of established pairs and take over any vacant boxes they find. Late in the season intrusions are less frequent; the intruder may then be gaining information about nest sites for the next breeding season (Lombardo 1987). The brown plumage of these first-years may suppress aggression from the established pairs at nestboxes by indicating to the territorial male that the intruder is a female and to the resident female that the intruder is subordinate (Stutchbury and Robertson 1985, 1987b, c).

Courtship can start with a male attacking an unfamiliar female; wing-fluttering flight by a female can elicit attack and appears to be a courtship invitation. Courting males can also adopt a vertical display posture, with tail slightly spread and raised, wings slightly drooped and flicked; this stimulates the female to fly up and over to him as if to land on his back; the male flies up to avoid the female and the display is repeated. The male then typically flies to the nest site, utters a nest advertisement call and the female enters to examine the site. The pair bond starts to develop long before copulation takes place. In the copulation display, the male hovers above the female, darts down, uttering aggression calls, and makes cloacal contact while holding her neck feathers with his bill; the male stands on the female's slightly outstretched wings; the sequence is then repeated (Kuerzi 1941; R. R. Cohen, pers. comm.).

The adults tend to return to the same nest cavity, or nearby, to breed if they bred there successfully the previous year; most unsuccessful females do not return to the same area; and males are more likely than females to return; first-years disperse more widely, breeding mostly within 30 km of the natal nest site in one population and 80–100 km in another (Cohen 1981, pers. comm.; Houston and Houston 1987).

BREEDING This is the first swallow, apart from the Violet-greens, to arrive on its breeding grounds in the spring, with females arriving with or soon after the males. The early arrivals do not breed as soon as they pair and obtain a nest site (Stutchbury and Robertson 1987d); they appear to wait until the weather is favourable and they synchronise their laying with that of other pairs in the vicinity. Eggs have been recorded from the end of April to the end of June in the south of the range, and from early May to mid June in the North (Bent 1942; Robertson, pers. comm.). Although replacement clutches are laid, true second broods are very rare. Burtt (pers. comm.) recorded 1–2% in central Ohio, all double-brooded females being among the first ten birds to lay in the spring. Intraspecific parasitism has been recorded but is probably rare: Lombardo (1988) recorded seven cases out of 120 nests.

The typical natural nest site is in a cavity, such as an old woodpecker hole, in a tree stump or dead tree limb in or near water, but Tree Swallows nowadays often use nestboxes. Erskine (1979) estimated that in Canada some 14% of pairs use tree holes and 81% use nestboxes (though the percentage using tree holes may have been underestimated: Robertson, pers. comm.), but the use of boxes varies: in British Columbia, for example, 46% use natural holes. Rarely, cavities in buildings and fence posts (even once a fire hydrant) are used (Bent 1942). The nest takes anything from a few days to a few weeks to build, depending on the weather. The female does nearly all the work of collecting material and building the nest, although the male collects feathers for the lining. The nest is a hollowed-out pad up to 3 cm (1⅖") deep, made of dry grasses and/or pine needles, sometimes with a few thicker stems and twigs, lined with generally white feathers. Females continue to add feathers during incubation, but old birds start with more than sub-adults (Burtt, pers. comm.)

The clutch size is three to seven (occasionally eight) eggs, but usually five or six. The eggs are pure white, but are pinkish-white when first laid. They measure 19.0 × 13.3 mm (16.8–21.4 × 12.2–14; weight 1.76). Yearling females do not lay so early as some older females, and early in the season they lay smaller clutches (Stutchbury and Robertson, in press). The clutch size decreases during the season for both yearling and older females. Eggs are laid at daily intervals, but there is sometimes a gap of a few days between eggs during inclement weather. The incubation period is about 14 days. The female alone incubates, but the male has been known to sit on the eggs in bad weather and in one case successfully incubated a clutch when his mate had died (Kuerzi 1941). Weydemeyer (1934) reported that the male sometimes brings food to his mate while she is incubating, but this is not generally the case. When she is off the eggs he enters the nest hole and guards the entrance. The eggs hatch synchronously but in poor weather may hatch asynchronously, leading to a weight hierarchy among the young. The earliest to hatch reaches a higher weight and is more likely to fledge (Zach 1982). The female alone broods the nestlings for the first few days although the male may do so, as in very cold weather, but both male and female feed them, bringing about equal amounts of food. (Leffelaar and Robertson 1986). The nestlings are fed about once every three minutes (Quinney 1986). The nestling period is about 19 or 20 days. The fledglings do not usually return to the nest, and they receive little extra care from their parents.

Nesting success is variable, depending largely on the food supply, but averages 76% of eggs laid producing fledged young (Butler 1988). Some nests are destroyed by predators, but another serious factor is the weather, high mortality following wet and cold weather when insects are scarce. Chapman (1935, 1955) recorded an average of 25% mortality of nestlings over 15 years in poor feeding habitat, but this varied greatly from 44% in one year to 6% in the subsequent year; Kuerzi (1941) recorded a nestling mortality of only 2% over five years in a habitat with a better food supply. Pesticide contamination has been reported (Shaw 1983). Most individuals breed for two to four seasons, living on average 2.7 years, but the longevity record is eleven years for a female (Hussell 1982; Butler 1988). The mortality rate is about 61% for adults but higher (79%) for first-years (Chapman 1955; Houston and Houston 1987; Butler 1988). Adult female mortality during bad weather may be biased towards yearlings (Lombardo 1986). Late-hatching young are less likely to return the following year.

VOICE The song consists of three fairly long, descending notes ending in a liquid warble and repeated over and over; the male also twitters before copulating; and there is an alarm call that is a short, sharp note, repeated several times (Kuerzi 1941).

DESCRIPTION The adult male is a glossy metallic blue with greenish reflections on the upperparts, including the sides of the head, the lesser wing-coverts and inner secondaries. The median wing-coverts are duller black with steel-blue or greenish margins. The lores are black and the ear-coverts are blue-black. The underparts are pure white, except for the axillaries and underwing-coverts which are grey-brown. The wings and tail are sooty-black with a faint green sheen; the tail is slightly forked. The bill is black, the eyes are dark brown and the legs and feet are pale brown. The adult female is similar to but often somewhat duller than the male, and the plumage changes with age (Hussell 1983a): females with dusky grey-brown upperparts are predominantly one year old, but some are two years old; blue-backed females are two or more years old; a few one- and two-year-old females are intermediate between brown and blue. Older females often differ from males in having a brownish forehead, a less pure and glossy blue back, and/or a greyish wash on the breast and a shorter wing (Cohen 1984; Stutchbury and Robertson 1987a). Tree Swallows are unusual among passerines in that the yearling female rather than the yearling male has a sub-adult plumage. The juvenile is also a dull grey-brown above, without the iridescent blue feathers of the adult, and often has a greyish wash on the breast; the wings and tail are slaty-brown with slight greenish reflections, and the secondaries and tertials are edged with pale grey-white. Juveniles moult in August–October into the adult/sub-adult plumage. Adults start to moult in August, after breeding and before they migrate. In autumn and winter the male's plumage is greener than in spring, and the tertials are white-tipped but the tips wear away before spring.

Measurements Length 13 cm (5"). Wing of male 114–125 (mean 119.3), of female 110–121 (mean 115.3); tail 48–60 (mean 54.2); fork 7–12 (mean 8.7); bill 8.2–11.2 (mean 9.7); tarsus 11.1–14.4 (mean 12.7). Weight 15.6–25.4 (mean 20.1).

8 MANGROVE SWALLOW

Plate 3

Tachycineta albilinea (Lawrence)

Petrochelidon albilinea Lawrence, 1863, Ann. Lyc. Nat. Hist. New York, 8, no. 1, p. 2: New Granada = line of Panama R.R.

Tachycineta albilinea stolzmanni (Philippi), 1902, Chepen [Department of Libertad], Peru.

FIELD CHARACTERS The Mangrove Swallow is a small hirundine with a green-blue back, white rump, a white line above the lores and white underparts. It resembles the White-winged Swallow (9), but the latter has more white on the inner webs of the outer rectrices, the bases of its mantle feathers are always white (never grey), it lacks the white supraloral streak, and it has a white breast and a relatively shorter, broader bill. Mangrove Swallows are closely associated with water and are usually seen alone or in small groups.

HABITAT This swallow favours not only mangroves but also other areas of water, such as rivers, lakes, ponds and marshes, and sometimes coastal beaches and meadows. In Honduras, it frequents wet grassy savannas in the coastal pine ridges, and large rivers on the coast and inland (Russell 1964). In Panama, it occurs around the Panama Canal, Gatún Lake and bays on the coast (Wetmore *et al.* 1984). It is mainly a coastal and lowland species and is rarely seen far from water.

DISTRIBUTION AND POPULATION The breeding range is restricted to Mexico and Central America and possibly Peru (AOU 1983). The species occurs in the coastal parts of Mexico and Central America, from central Sonora, and southern Tamaulipas (Tampico) on the Gulf of Mexico, south through Central America, the Yucatan and neighbouring islands, to Panama as far as Colón and eastern Darién, including Isla Coiba in the south. There is a possible race (*stolzmanni*) in coastal Peru. It is generally described as common, for example on the coast of Honduras (Russell 1964) and of Panama, and along the Sonoran coast (Russell and Lamm 1978), or fairly common, for example in Guatemala (Land 1970, and frequent on the coast of Peru (Parker *et al.* 1982). It tends to be rarer inland. In some areas, such as El Salvador, however, numbers appear to have been reduced in the past few decades, perhaps because of the loss of trees or the application of pesticides (Phillips 1986).

MIGRATION This swallow appears to be resident throughout its range, although there are probably some post-breeding movements. Thus, in Sonora, numbers are low between mid summer and mid March, and in Nayarit numbers increase over winter (Phillips 1986). However, there are a few unsubstantiated reports from Colombia, suggesting more extensive movements (Gochfeld *et al.* 1980).

FOOD AND BEHAVIOUR The flight is rapid and direct, interspersed with some gliding. Mangrove Swallows usually feed low over waterbodies and bays but at times 30 m (100 ft) or more up (Ricklefs 1971). They sometimes feed over marshes and meadows. Non-breeding swallows feed in small groups and often perch on branches or telegraph wires, but when breeding they feed alone or in pairs. In Ricklef's study, one pair had a feeding area of about 500 m^2 (600 sq. yds): food for the nestlings was caught close to the nest, food for the adults was caught more than 200 m away. Most foraging is done early in the morning or late in the afternoon, nestlings being fed mostly just after dawn and before dusk, possibly to avoid exposure to the sun during the hottest part of the day (Ricklefs 1971). Mangrove Swallows feed on unusually large prey for their size. Dyrcz (1984) studied the diet of two broods of nestlings over six days in Panama and found that they were fed mainly dragonflies (26%), Lepidoptera (26%), flies of the family Sarcophagidae (21%) and bees (Apidae) (15%); a few other Diptera and Hymenoptera, especially winged ants, were taken. The average prey was 16 mm long. The stomachs of two adults contained flying ants, other Hymenoptera, beetles, bugs and a fly (Hespenheide, in Ricklefs 1971), suggesting that adults feed on smaller prey than they catch for the nestlings. Like the related Tree Swallow (7), the Mangrove Swallow is very aggressive, and nests are well spaced out: Dyrcz (1984) found that the nests were several hundred metres apart. Breeding birds attack both conspecific and other species of swallows close to the nest. Foraging areas are not defended, but two neighbouring pairs in Dyrcz's study used exclusive areas.

BREEDING Breeding records are generally from between March/April and June/July in Mexico and northern parts of Central America (Russell 1964; Russell and Lamm 1978; Wendelken and Martin 1986); in Panama it breeds in the dry season, laying from January to April and feeding nestlings through July (Ricklefs 1971). Two broods are commonly reared in a season. Like Tree Swallows, Mangrove Swallows nest in cavities, usually in stumps or trees that are partially submerged in lakes and rivers; they also sometimes use abandoned woodpecker and other holes in trees, such as in open areas of pine ridges in Honduras (Russell 1964). The nest site is often low, but above flood level. This species also readily uses nestboxes; other artificial structures are rarely used but Wetmore *et al.* (1984), for example, recorded a nest in a cavity in one of the pilings of a wharf. The nest, which is several centimetres deep, is made of loosely arranged grass, fine stems and moss mixed with a few leaves and sticks and is lined with feathers. The eggs are white and measure 17.3 × 12.8 mm (15.7–18.7 × 12.3–13.3; weight 1.64). The clutch size is three to five eggs. The incubation period at one nest studied by Dyrcz (1984) was 17 days (last egg to last chick). Hatching is asynchronous. The nestling period is 23–27 days. Both parents feed the nestlings, averaging 17 visits an hour. Dyrcz's study nests were not very successful, five being lost to termites, predators and nest-site competitors (Grey-breasted Martins, 23).

VOICE The song is a soft trill, and there is a short sharp alarm note.

DESCRIPTION The Mangrove Swallow is a small member of the tree swallow group. The forehead, crown, hindneck, mantle, back, scapulars and lesser and median wing-coverts are steel-blue with a green-blue gloss; the tail-coverts are browner than the rest of the upperparts, often with whitish or greyish margins. The plumage is greenest when fresh, becoming more blue with wear. The lores are black, with a narrow white line above and a narrow black line below them. The ear-coverts are blue-black. The feathers of the lower hindneck have white bases or, sometimes, an indistinct white line, but this is not readily seen in the field. The rump is white, with finely marked dusky shaft lines. The underparts, including the undertail- and wing-coverts and axillaries, are white, sometimes with fine shaft streaks. The breast and sides have a pale grey wash. The wings are black, with a faint green gloss; the tertials, inner secondaries and inner greater wing-coverts are edged with white in fresh plumage. The tail is black and only slightly forked. The bill is black, the eyes are brown and the legs and feet blackish. The sexes are alike. Juveniles have dull black lores, bordered above by a narrow white line, and a white rump, the rest of the upperparts being a drab grey, sometimes with a faint green gloss; the white underparts are washed with grey-brown, and the outer underwing-coverts are banded with dull grey.

Measurements Length 11 cm (4¼"). Wing of male 92–105 (mean 97.5), of female 92–99 (mean 94.7); tail 39–47 (mean 42); fork 3–7 (mean 5.0); bill 9.9–11.8 (mean 11.0); tarsus 9.5–11.5 (mean 11.0). Weight 10–16 (mean 13.9).

RACES There is no clear geographical variation over most of the range. A separate race, *stolzmanni*, has been described from the coast of Peru in the Department of Libertad, but its status is doubtful. Stolzmann collected four or five specimens, of which the type specimen was lost from the Warsaw Museum in the First World War. Hellmayr (1935) concluded that it was conspecific with *albilinea*, but it has also been regarded as a distinct species. The lack of other records of Mangrove Swallows between Panama and Peru make it doubtful that this is just a race of the Mangrove Swallow (Wetmore *et al.* 1984). The type of *stolzmanni* lacked the white supraloral streak (like *T. albiventer*), but the breast was washed with grey as on *albilinea*; it also had a smaller bill, grey instead of white bases to the feathers of the back, and greyer underside compared with the nominate race. Another race, *rhizophorae*, with supposedly more white on the head, has been described from Sonora, but the birds from this area do not vary consistently from those elsewhere (Wetmore *et al.* 1984).

9 WHITE-WINGED SWALLOW
Tachycineta albiventer (Boddaert)

Plate 3

Hirundo albiventer Boddaert, 1783, Tab. Pl. enlum., p. 32: Cayenne, ex Daubenton, pl. 546, fig. 2.

FIELD CHARACTERS This species is a medium-sized hirundine with green-blue upperparts, a white rump and underparts, and a conspicuous white wing patch. It closely resembles the Mangrove Swallow (8) of Central America, but it has a much broader area of white on the wings, whiter rather than grey bases to the mantle feathers, no white supraloral streak, a whiter breast, and a relatively longer, narrower bill. It is usually solitary, and frequents open expanses of water.

HABITAT The normal habitat is open, wet, lowland areas, especially in mangroves and on sandy beaches on the coast and along rivers, reservoirs and other waterbodies inland, but this swallow can also be seen in flooded llanos and dry savanna and it penetrates into forests along rivers. Although it usually feeds over water or wetlands, grassy airstrips and pastures away from water are also acceptable feeding areas. Sewage ponds are also frequented (Schmitt *et al.* 1986). This species is widely sympatric with the White-banded Swallow (19), with which it is often seen, but it typically prefers more open expanses of water, usually keeping away from vegetation, river banks and forests.

DISTRIBUTION AND POPULATION The White-winged Swallow has a wide range in South America (but not the Pacific slope), from the Magdalena valley in northern Colombia east through Venezuela, Trinidad and the Guianas, south through eastern Ecuador, eastern Peru and the greater part of Brazil to Bolivia, Paraguay and northern Argentina (gobernaciones of Chaco and Misiones, casually to northern Santa Fé Province and Paraná). Although population sizes are unknown, it is a generally common and widespread species. It has been reported to be common in Colombia and Ecuador (Chapman 1917a, b; Hilty and Brown 1986), quite common in Surinam (Haverschmidt 1968), and fairly common in French Guiana (Tostain 1979).

MIGRATION It is resident in much of its range, but is migratory in the extreme south. From Argentina to Brazil it is present only as a breeding bird, from mid September to mid April (Pereyra 1969; Belton 1985). The winter range of the southern population is not well known, but is presumably in the northern part of the breeding range in the Guianas, Venezuela and Colombia.

FOOD AND BEHAVIOUR The White-winged Swallow is generally a solitary hunter, but will feed in small groups. It hawks low over the water or ground, less often over waterside vegetation, with a direct flapping flight, rather than gliding, and often perches on stakes in the water and on overhanging branches. Several types of insect have been recorded in the diet, including brachyceran flies, tabanid flies, proctotrupid Hymenoptera, curculionid beetles and Lepidoptera (Haverschmidt 1968). White-winged Swallows, like the rest of the tree swallow group, are aggressive to other breeding pairs and nest solitarily, although dispersed groups may form if nest holes are available.

BREEDING Breeding has been recorded in January and February in the Macarena Mountains, upper Magdalena valley and the mouth of the Rio Cauca; and from February to April in the Orinoco region of Venezuela (Hilty and Brown 1986). In Trinidad, the breeding season is from April to August (ffrench 1980), while one nest was seen in August in French Guiana (Tostain 1979). In southern parts of the range, breeding takes place September–April, but precise dates are not known (Pereyra 1969; Belton 1985). The nest is built in a hole or crevice in a variety of sites, usually a few metres above water, including in crevices between rocks, in tree stumps, cliffs, eaves of houses and pipes; old holes made by woodpeckers are often used. Nests have even been recorded on board ferry boats which regularly crossed rivers in French Guiana and Brazil (Tostain 1979; Belton 1985). The nest itself is made of dry grass and rootlets and lined with feathers of a variety of species and sometimes of a variety of colours. The clutch size is three to six eggs in Trinidad (ffrench 1980), usually four or five in the Orinoco region (Cherrie 1916). The eggs are pure white and measure 19.2 ×

13.7 mm (17–20 × 13–14.6; weight 1.9). Incubation and nestling periods are not known.

VOICE The song is a trilled 'zweeed', and there is a short harsh alarm call.

DESCRIPTION This medium-sized swallow is a glossy green-blue on the forehead, crown, mantle, back, scapulars and lesser and median wing-coverts, although old birds are more blue than green; the mantle is greener than the head. The lores are black and the ear-coverts are blue-black. The feathers on the mantle have white bases, but these are not usually visible. The rump, uppertail-coverts, underwing-coverts, axillaries, chin, throat, breast and abdomen are white, sometimes with fine shaft streaks. The flanks are greyer. Both the tail, which is slightly forked, and the wings are black, with a slight blue-green sheen; the outer tail

feathers have some white on the basal part of the inner web. The most distinctive feature is a very conspicuous white wing patch formed by the broad white margins of the greater wing-coverts and the tertials and secondaries, the margins being broadest on the innermost feathers. However, the white area is sometimes reduced by abrasion to narrow margins along the feathers. The sexes are similar, but the female has less white on the wings. The eyes are dark brown, and the bill and legs are black. There is no geographical variation. Juveniles are much duller and browner than adults, with greyer underparts, duskier breast and less white in the wings.

Measurements Length 14 cm (5½"). Wing 100–108 (mean 104); tail 42–51 (mean 46.4); fork 6–10 (mean 8.0); bill 10.2–13.2 (mean 11.8); tarsus 10.4–12.3 (mean 11.3). Weight 14–17.

10 VIOLET-GREEN SWALLOW   Plate 3
Tachycineta thalassina (Swainson)

Hirundo thalassinus Swainson, 1827, Philos. Mag., n.s., 1, p. 366: Real del Monte, Hidalgo, Mexico.

Tachycineta thalassina lepida Mearns, 1902, Campbell's ranch in the Laguna Mts, 20 miles north of Campo, San Diego County, California.

Tachycineta thalassina brachyptera Brewster, 1902, Sierra de la Laguna, Baja California.

FIELD CHARACTERS This species is a small swallow with matt green rather than glossy upperparts, a violet-blue tinge to the rump, and pure white underparts. Females are markedly duller. It is very similar to the Tree Swallow (7), which it largely replaces in western North America, but differs in having a matt plumage, conspicuous white patches on the sides of the rump, and the white on the head is more extensive, reaching to above the eye. It is usually seen in open woodland or in suburbs, alone or in small groups.

HABITAT The Violet-green Swallow occurs most frequently in the highlands, in open coniferous, deciduous or mixed forest or woodland, and is commonly seen around human habitation. It feeds in open country, over water or over the forest canopy. In the northern part of the range it frequently breeds at low altitudes, but in the southern parts, such as Arizona and Utah, it is more common in montane forests at high elevations.

DISTRIBUTION AND POPULATION The breeding range extends over the western side of North America, from central Alaska and western Canada south to the Mexican highlands (AOU 1983). The nominate race *thalassina* has a restricted range, breeding on the Mexican plateau region from southern Chihuahua south to Oaxaca. The race *brachyptera* also has a limited range, in the mountains of central and southern Baja California, and the coastal plain of southern Sonora, possibly south to Sinaloa. The third race, *lepida*, is the most widespread, breeding in central Alaska and southern Canada south to central Baja California, southern Arizona, southern New Mexico, western Texas, coastal Sonora, northern Chihuahua and Coahuila. The races *thalassina* and *lepida* intergrade in Coahuila, those from the south being nearer *thalassina* and those from the north nearer *lepida*: these hybrids have a greener back than *thalassina* and are larger than *lepida* (Urban 1959).

Throughout most of the range these

swallows are common breeding birds, but they are most abundant in the Los Angeles ranges. In Texas, however, they are common migrants but uncommon summer residents (Lane 1978). Large numbers are also seen on passage and in the wintering areas (e.g. Phillips *et al.* 1964; Linsdale 1936; Hayward *et al.* 1976). The population as a whole appears to be stable but is increasing in the Northern Plains States (Robbins *et al.* 1986). Locally in Mexico, however, numbers have decreased in the past few decades (Phillips 1986). The species has probably benefited from additional nesting sites provided by humans, but may have suffered from competition for nest sites with the introduced House Sparrow and Starling, while some natural nest sites may have been lost through deforestation (Erskine 1979).

MIGRATION Violet-green Swallows migrate early in spring, arriving in the northern breeding grounds in April, but also leaving early in July (Bent 1942). Further south, they leave in August–September. The main wintering sites extend from southern Baja California and central Mexico south to Guatemala, El Salvador and Honduras, although there are winter records from Sonora, Chihuahua and Coahuila (AOU 1983); individuals recorded in winter further north, in Arizona, Texas, California and New Mexico, are probably late or early migrants. This swallow is a common winter visitor to the interior highlands of Honduras from 300 to 1600 m (980–5200 ft) (Monroe 1968), and to the highlands of Guatemala (Land 1970), but is less common in the lowlands. It is a rare migrant to Panama (Wetmore *et al.* 1984), but it occasionally winters as far south as Costa Rica. It has been recorded once in South America, in Colombia in January 1983 (two birds seen flying with swifts: Hilty and Brown 1986). There are casual records from the Aleutian Islands east to southern Manitoba, North Dakota, Missouri and central Texas, and a few sight records from Minnesota, Nova Scotia, New Hampshire, Oklahoma and Florida. There are a few spring records in Kansas (Johnston 1965) and a doubtful record from Yucatan (Parkes 1970). The race *thalassina* remains in Mexico for the winter, possibly migrating to lower altitudes. The race *brachyptera* winters in the lowlands of southern Baja California and Sinaloa, and possibly in southern Sonora; it

has also been recorded in Arizona in July (Phillips *et al.* 1964).

FOOD AND BEHAVIOUR Violet-greens feed at various heights, but often at greater heights than other swallows do. The flight is rapid and direct but includes some gliding. They feed in small groups or loose flocks, skimming low over fields or water or circling high above the ground. They have also been seen foraging on the ground on accumulations of insects such as midges, and mayflies (Erskine 1984; Hobson and Sealy 1987). In a study of stomach contents, a third of the diet consisted of hemipteran bugs, mainly leafhoppers and leafbugs; flies made up another 29%, and Hymenoptera, mainly flying ants, wasps and bees, another 23%; beetles and a few moths were also eaten (Beal 1918).

These swallows will nest solitarily but groups have been recorded where nest sites are numerous. Bent (1942) cited instances of 20 pairs nesting in a single dead pine tree in Colorado and of colonies of 100 or more pairs nesting in crevices in granite or lava cliffs in Washington and of six to 50 pairs in Alaska. In British Columbia, many of the natural sites are groups on cliffs (Erskine 1979). Brown (1983), however, found that they usually nest in single pairs in the Chiricahua Mountains in Arizona, and large groups have not been reported recently. Outside the breeding season, they will form large flocks.

BREEDING Eggs have been recorded from the beginning of May to the beginning of July in southern areas; breeding starts towards the end of May in the northern part of the range (Bent 1942). Only one brood is usually reared per season, although Gullion (1947) stated that two were reared in Oregon. Nests are built in cavities and crevices of cliffs, woodpecker holes, natural cavities in trees, crevices in the walls and roofs of buildings, birdboxes, piled lumber, etc. There are also reports of Violet-green Swallows using the old nests of Cliff Swallows (67) and the burrows of Bank Swallows (Sand Martins, 27) (Bent 1942). In Canada, more than half the nest sites used are in boxes or buildings rather than natural sites (Erskine 1979). The race *brachyptera* nests in holes in the giant cacti of the coasts of northwestern Mexico.

The nest is woven of fine fibres such as dry grass, horsehair, straw and fine twigs and is lined with feathers; feathers are sometimes added during the laying period. Usually eggs are laid at daily intervals. The usual clutch size is four to six eggs, but seven have been recorded; clutches of two or three are usual in the area occupied by *brachyptera*. The eggs are pure white. There may be some regional variation in egg size: in the north they measure 18.7 × 13.1 mm (16.3–20.8 × 12.2–13.7; weight 1.68), whereas those of *brachyptera* measure 17.3 × 12.9 mm (16.8–18.3 × 12–13.5). The incubation period is about 14 or 15 days, and hatching is asynchronous. The fledging period is about 23 days (Edson 1943). The fledglings remain near the nest for a few days while they are fed by their parents. The female seems to do most of the nest-building, all of the incubation and much of the feeding during the nestling period (Combellack 1954). Occasionally, a second female has been reported at a nest (Shirling 1935).

VOICE The calls are of two types (Brown 1983). 'Chee-chee' calls, of one or two syllables, appear to be contact calls, and are usually uttered when two or more swallows are together, for example when they are foraging or chasing each other or other species; adults also use this call when flying to and from nesting sites, and juveniles still dependent on their parents also use it. Twitter calls are usually a single syllable and associated with courtship and the establishment of territories; they are given in flight while the adult is investigating holes and when competitors are chased from holes. Apart from chee-chee calls, established pairs are largely silent.

DESCRIPTION On the adult male, the forehead, crown, back of the neck and the mantle and back are matt green, with a violet tinge to the mantle, nape and rear crown; the head, however, is more olive than the rest of the upperparts. The lores are grey. The scapulars and lesser and median wing-coverts are purplish-green. The median part of the rump and the uppertail-coverts are dark green, sometimes with a violet-blue tinge. The sides of the head and the underparts, including the undertail-coverts, are pure white; the white extends over the sides of the rump (seen as distinctive white patches in flight), and over the cheeks up to the eye. The axillaries and underwing-coverts are pale grey, the latter being whitish on the edge of the wing. The primaries, secondaries, greater wing-coverts and tail are black with a bluish or purplish sheen; the tail is only slightly forked. In fresh plumage, the tertials sometimes have narrow white tips. The bill is black, and the eyes and legs and feet are dark brown. The female is similar to the male but rather duller, with dull bronzy-green or bronzy-purple upperparts, dull green rump and tail-coverts and a greyer foreneck, side of head, upper hindneck, upper breast and scapulars; her wings are also slightly shorter. The juvenile is a grey-brown above, with a faint bronzy sheen on the back; the underparts are white, but the breast, especially on the sides, often has a brown tinge. The moult occurs mainly on the breeding grounds.

Measurements Length 12–13 cm (4¾–5"). Wing of male 115–129 (mean 122.5), of female 110–116 (mean 114.2); tail 45–55 (mean 49.4); fork 5–10 (mean 8.4); bill 8.7–9.8 (mean 9.4); tarsus 10.9–12 (mean 11.5). Weight (*lepida*) 14–16.

RACES The nominate race is the largest and has a distinct violet sheen to the plumage. The other races are somewhat smaller and have a greener mantle and bluish-green rump and uppertail-coverts. The race *lepida* is intermediate in size (wing 105–125), while *brachyptera* is the smallest of the three (wing 99–109).

11 WHITE-RUMPED SWALLOW

Plate 4

Tachycineta leucorrhoa (Vieillot)
Alternative name: White-browed Swallow

Hirundo leucorrhoa Vieillot, 1817, Nouv. Dict. Hist. Nat., 14, p. 519: Paraguay.

FIELD CHARACTERS This swallow is small, with a blue-green mantle, white rump and white underparts and a white supraloral streak. It is very similar to the Chilean Swallow (12), but is larger, blue-green rather than deep blue, and can be easily distinguished by the presence of white streaks on the face. It is closely associated with water and usually nests solitarily.

HABITAT The White-rumped Swallow breeds near lagoons, marshes and other bodies of water, and feeds over water, pastures and open areas in woodlands. It is not usually associated with large towns, but can be seen in inhabited areas and frequently uses buildings as nest sites.

DISTRIBUTION AND POPULATION This swallow's known breeding range is in south-central South America, from northern Bolivia, Paraguay, southern Brazil and Uruguay southwards to northern Argentina (Tucumán and Buenos Aires). The exact breeding limits, however, are unclear: the species has been recorded (possibly as a migrant or winter visitor) as far north as southeastern Peru (Cosnipatá), Mato Grosso (Villa Bela) and Minas Gerais (Lagoa Santa); it has also been recorded in São Paulo and the state of Rio de Janeiro, but its status there is not clear. Its breeding range appears to overlap that of the closely related Chilean Swallow in northern Argentina. Wetmore (1926) described it as common in Paraguay and Uruguay; it is also a common swallow in Argentina. Scott and Brooke (1982) found it generally rare in southeastern Brazil, but Belton (1985) has recorded it in large numbers in winter.

MIGRATION White-rumped Swallows are migratory, but only partially so in the north of their range. In Argentina, this is the last swallow to leave in the autumn, going in February and March, but some remain all winter in Buenos Aires (Sclater and Hudson 1888; Pereyra 1969). They return in September and October. In Brazil it is present all year, but there are fewer during the winter in the southeast, when they are mostly seen along the coast (Belton 1985).

FOOD AND BEHAVIOUR The flight is fast, like that of Tree Swallows (7), the birds often skimming low over the ground. White-rumped Swallows have been seen following humans on horseback and are attracted to humans and animals that are disturbing insects. They feed on a variety of insects, including carabid, elaterid, lamelicornid, curculionid and chrysomelid beetles, flying ants, dipteran flies, acridid Orthoptera and Lepidoptera (e.g. Marelli 1919; Araveno 1928; Zotta 1936). Sclater and Hudson (1888) described these birds as very aggressive; chases and fights at nest sites are frequent. The fights can be protracted: Hudson described the birds as clutching

each other and falling to the ground 20 times an hour. When attracting females, the males perch by their cavities and display by raising their wings. The birds breed as isolated pairs, not tolerating close neighbours. After the breeding season, however, they will form large flocks of hundreds of individuals, often with other species of swallow.

BREEDING In Brazil, these swallows breed from at least October to December; individuals have been seen carrying nesting material in October and feeding nestlings in November and December (Belton 1985). Males collected in February and May were not in breeding condition, while juveniles are commonly seen at this time. In Argentina, breeding takes place between October and February (Daguerre 1922). The nests are built in cavities, such as pipes or narrow tubes, holes in walls under overhanging tiles or thatch, in roofs, or in trees, or in the abandoned nests of *Anumbius acuticaudatus* (Sclater and Hudson 1888; Daguerre 1922). Isolated buildings are often used; buildings in towns are used less frequently. The nest is large but loosely constructed, being made of straw and other fine fibres, and lined with feathers and horsehair. The clutch size in Argentina is five to seven eggs (Pereyra 1969). The eggs are white and measure 19.6 × 13.7 mm (17.8–21 × 12.9–14.2; weight 1.9). Incubation and nestling periods are not known.

VOICE The calls are similar to those of the Tree Swallow. Wetmore (1926) described the song as a broken warble. Sclater and Hudson (1888) described it as beginning with 'long soft, tremulous notes, followed by others shorter and more hurried, and sinking to a murmur', and they noted that the birds sing in flight at dawn. There is a short, harsh alarm note.

DESCRIPTION The White-rumped Swallow is a small hirundine. The forehead, crown and nape are deep glossy blue-green, with pure white streaks above the lores which usually meet above the bill. The lores are black, and the ear-coverts are black with a blue-green gloss. The rest of the upperparts, including the scapulars and lesser and median wing-coverts, are mostly a glossy blue-green, the greater wing-coverts are duller with a green wash, while the rump, shorter uppertail-coverts and the underparts are pure white, though the rump has some fine shaft streaks. The white extends onto the sides of the neck. The longer uppertail-coverts are dusky blue-green, sometimes with whitish fringes. The sides have a slight brown wash. The primaries, secondaries and the slightly forked tail are black with a green wash. The inner secondaries, tertials and greater wing-coverts often have broad white tips which give the wings a ladder-like effect when the bird is perched, but these abrade with age. The legs, feet and bill are black, and the eyes are brown. The sexes are alike. The juvenile is duller and browner and has a dusky breast, but has the distinctive facial markings.

Measurements Length 13 cm (5"). Wing 111–122 (mean 115.7); tail 49–57 (mean 51.4); fork 5–8 (mean 6.6); bill 10.2–12.2 (mean 11.1); tarsus 11.5–13.2 (mean 12.2). Weight 17–21 (mean 19).

12 CHILEAN SWALLOW
Tachycineta leucopyga (Meyen)

Plate 4

Hirundo leucopyga 'Lichtenstein' Meyen, 1834, Nova Acta Acad. Caes. Leop. Carol., 16, suppl. i, p. 73, pl. 10, fig. 2: Santiago de Chile.

This species may be only subspecifically distinct from the White-rumped Swallow (11), with which it forms a superspecies, but their ranges apparently overlap in northern Argentina, suggesting that they are full species.

FIELD CHARACTERS Chilean Swallows are small, blue swallows with a white rump and white underparts. They differ from the White-rumped Swallow in being smaller, with a relatively smaller bill, in having a bluer sheen to the plumage and darker underwing-coverts, and in lacking the white streaks above the eye. This species is often seen near water, and is usually alone or in small groups.

HABITAT The preferred habitats are open or semi-open areas near water, such as rivers, lakes, reservoirs, marshes, lagoons and coastal areas. It also frequents forest edges, clearings, scrub, coastal forest, open forest and woodland. It is sometimes seen in villages and towns, and occasionally over dry slopes and steppes.

DISTRIBUTION AND POPULATION The breeding range is restricted to southern South America, from the province of Atacamo, Chile, in the west and from the Rio Negro (possibly further north) in the east, south to the Magellan Straits and Tierra del Fuego (Johnson 1967). Information on population levels is sparse. It is reported to be common in the southern forested part of Tierra del Fuego, and in the northwest, but scarcer in the north (Humphrey et al. 1970; Adams and Templeton 1979). It is the most abundant swallow in Chile (Johnson 1967). It frequently takes advantage of artificial nesting sites, which may have allowed the population to expand.

MIGRATION This swallow is resident in the northern part of its range and migratory in the southern part. In Tierra del Fuego it is present from October to February (Humphrey et al. 1970). In Chile, the northern birds are resident but the southern ones migrate north to winter from the south-central provinces northward (Johnson 1967). In Argentina, these swallows winter north to Mendoza, Tucumán, Santa Fé and Buenos Aires Provinces; the breeding and wintering ranges in Argentina are not clearly defined. There are also winter records from Bolivia (Schulenberg and Remsen 1982; Schmitt et al. 1986), Paraguay (Johnson 1967) and Peru (Parker et al. 1982), and there have been casual records in the Falkland Islands. In southeastern Brazil, Chilean Swallows are uncommon winter visitors, from mid May to mid September (Belton 1985).

FOOD AND BEHAVIOUR Chilean Swallows fly fast and low over the ground. They are usually solitary feeders, but can sometimes be seen in small groups. The diet includes a variety of flying insects, such as beetles, dipteran flies, ants, reduviid bugs and other Hemiptera (Zotta 1936, 1940). They usually nest singly, but will also nest in loose groups if suitable nest sites are clumped. After breeding, they form small flocks of tens of individuals, and in winter will also associate in loose flocks with other hirundines such as White-rumped Swallows (e.g. Belton 1985).

BREEDING Two or three broods a year are raised in Chile, where the breeding season is from September to February (Johnson 1967). In Tierra del Fuego it breeds between October and February (Humphrey *et al.* 1970). The nest, a pad of grass lined with feathers, is built in crevices in the eaves and walls of houses and in holes in trees, particularly old woodpecker holes; urban as well as rural sites are used. In Chile, the clutch size is from four to six eggs (Johnson 1967). The eggs are pure white and measure 20.2 × 13.8 mm (17.8–21 × 13–14.3; weight 2.03). Details of incubation and the nestling period are not known.

VOICE The song has been described as consisting of three or four high-pitched gurgles followed by lower guttural sounds (Humphrey *et al.* 1970).

DESCRIPTION The upperparts of this small swallow, including the scapulars and lesser and median wing-coverts, are mostly a deep metallic ultramarine-blue; the greater wing-coverts are duller, with a blue wash. The lores are black, and the ear-coverts are black with a blue gloss. There are occasionally a few white feathers over the bill and lores. The rump, shorter uppertail-coverts and underparts are immaculate white, but with a brown wash on the sides. The white extends onto the sides of the neck. The feathers of the rump occasionally have a dark subterminal shaft spot. The longer uppertail-coverts are blackish with glossy blue margins. The lower breast feathers have dusky marks at the base. The axillaries and underwing-coverts are light grey-brown; the longest undertail-coverts occasionally have a blackish subterminal spot and dark shaft. The tail, primaries and secondaries are brownish-black. The tertials and inner secondaries have white apical edges which abrade with age. The tail is slightly more forked than on the White-rumped Swallow. The legs and bill are black, and the eyes are dark brown. The sexes are alike. The juvenile is similar to the adult, but is duller and browner with only a slight gloss on the mantle and lesser wing-coverts; the longer uppertail-coverts are blackish with white tips; it often has a narrow white line above the lores.

Measurements Length 12 cm (4¾") Wing 105–117 (mean 110.3); tail 47–57 (mean 52.9); fork 5–10 (mean 7.1); bill 9.6–11.1 (mean 10.2); tarsus 10.6–12.5 (mean 11.1). Weight 15–20 (mean 17).

13 BAHAMA SWALLOW
Tachycineta cyaneoviridis (Bryant)

Plate 4

Hirundo cyaneoviridis Bryant, 1859, Proc. Boston Soc. Nat. Hist., 7, sig. 8, p. 111: Nassau, New Providence, Bahama Islands.

FIELD CHARACTERS Bahama Swallows are medium-sized hirundines with green upperparts, blue wings and tail and white underparts. This species is similar to the Tree Swallow (7). The adult can be distinguished from this and other similar species by its deeply forked tail; the juveniles of the Tree and Bahama Swallows are more similar, but the juvenile Bahama looks greyer on the back and head and has less brown on the breast. It is a rather solitary, woodland swallow.

HABITAT The typical breeding habitat of this species is pine woodland, but it also occurs locally in towns and around other human habitation. It feeds in open and partly open areas, such as woodland clearings, marshes, open fields, about cliffs and along the coast (Riley 1905).

DISTRIBUTION AND POPULATION This species breeds only in the northern Bahama Islands (Grand Bahama, Great Abaco, Andros and New Providence) (AOU 1983). It favours islands with pine trees for breeding, spreading to other islands after breeding. Throughout the Bahamas these swallows seem to be uncommon breeding birds; even collectors in the last century found them so (Bent 1942). Bryant (1859) noted about 40–50 swallows at one site at Nassau, and Maynard (1896) estimated the population on New Providence to be about 50. They are still rare on New Providence (Brudenell-Bruce 1975), occurring regularly at only two sites: at one of these, a small group has regularly nested on a hotel (Bahama Swallows have been present there since at least 1859); at the other, there has regularly been a flock of about 20 birds, which may nest in the nearby pine woods. The status is uncertain, but it is not yet so rare as to be thought endangered (Collar and Andrew 1988). One estimate of population size gave a figure of 6.8 birds per km² (2.6 per sq. mile) (Emlen 1977).

MIGRATION The northern islands are vacated to some extent from November to March (Paterson 1972). On New Providence, breeding birds are present between April and the end of July (Brudenell-Bruce 1975). Wintering birds can be found throughout the Bahama Islands and in eastern Cuba (AOU 1983; Buden 1987). There are also records of migrants in the lower Florida Keys and on Dry Tortugas, with casual records in southern Florida as far north as Tarpon Springs (AOU 1983).

FOOD AND BEHAVIOUR Bahama Swallows usually feed high up, often gliding; but they have also been seen feeding low over the ground, flying rapidly and darting after insects (Emlen 1977). According to Todd and Worthington (1911), they are most active in the evenings and in cloudy weather, perching during the hottest part of the day. Examination of stomach contents has revealed almost entirely dipteran flies, mostly minute ones, with some beetles (Cory 1890; Bent 1942). Pairs breed solitarily or in small loose groups, but they will form small flocks, particularly when not breeding.

BREEDING The breeding season appears to be between April and July. Bryant (1859) did not find any individuals in breeding condition up to the end of April. Details of the breeding biology of this swallow are sparse. The nests are built in holes, such as old woodpecker holes in trees or rarely other sites such as woodpiles. They are also sometimes made in holes in buildings, such as under the eaves. Todd and Worthington (1911) recorded nests 15 m (50 ft) or more up in cavities in dead pines. The clutch size is three, and the eggs are pure white. The incubation and nestling periods are not known.

VOICE The call is a metallic 'chep' or 'chi-chep'.

DESCRIPTION The adult Bahama Swallow is medium-sized, with dull metallic dark green forehead, crown, neck, mantle, back and scapulars. The lesser and median wing-coverts, rump and uppertail-coverts are a more bluish-green. The greater wing-coverts and tertials are dusky green-blue with lighter margins. The lores are dusky. The ear-coverts, sides of the head and neck below the eye, the axillaries, underwing-coverts and underparts are pure white. The primaries, secondaries and strongly forked tail are dark greenish-blue with lighter margins; the outer tail feathers sometimes have narrow whitish margins. The bill is black, the eyes are brown and the legs and feet dark brown. The sexes are alike, but the female is somewhat duller and the underparts are a less pure white, with some slaty-brown beneath the eye, on the ear-coverts, across the breast and on the sides of the breast; she also has a shorter fork to the tail. There is no geographical variation. The juvenile is a dull brown above with a green sheen, the green most pronounced on the mantle and wing-coverts; the head, upper margin of the ear-coverts and uppertail-coverts are more sooty-brown, and the sides of the head, ear-coverts and underparts are white, with a patch of sooty-brown on the sides of the upper breast; the tail is less deeply forked than the adult's. The juvenile male more closely resembles the adult female.

Measurements Length 15 cm (6"). Wing of male 113–120 (mean 115.5), of female 105–117 (mean 109); tail of male 66–73 (mean 68), of female 59–69 (mean 63); fork of male 25–31 (mean 27.1), of female 19–24 (mean 21); bill 10.3–10.9 (mean 10.6); tarsus 11–12 (mean 11.7). Weight 16.3–19.5 (mean 17.5).

14 GOLDEN SWALLOW

Plate 4

Tachycineta euchrysea (Gosse)

Hirundo euchrysea Gosse, 1847, Birds of Jamaica, p. 68: higher mountains in the centre of Jamaica.

Tachycineta euchrysea sclateri (Cory), 1884, Santo Domingo.

FIELD CHARACTERS The Golden Swallow is small, with a distinctive iridescent, bronzy plumage, unlike that of any other swallow. It occurs in hilly, open country or montane forest, usually alone or in small groups.

HABITAT The preferred habitat is in the hills of the interiors of the islands, usually open country. The birds are seen less frequently in forested country. They are occasionally seen over towns. In Jamaica they used to breed in moist high montane forest, but became restricted to dry, wooded limestone hills and are now known from only a single site (King 1981; Bond 1985).

DISTRIBUTION AND POPULATION The Golden Swallow is confined to the West Indies. The nominate race *euchrysea* is locally distributed in Jamaica. The race *sclateri* is locally distributed in the mountains of Hispaniola. Bond (1928) recorded the species as common in the mountains of Haiti. March (1863) stated that it was uncommon and local in Jamaica. The race *sclateri* is still local but not uncommon in Hispaniola, but *euchrysea* is very rare and may be critically endangered. The latter used to be more widely distributed in the interior of Jamaica, but had decreased by 1936 (Bond 1936) and is now restricted to the vicinity of Ram Goat Cave in the Cockpit Country (King 1981); the population size is not known, but few individuals have been seen recently, and then only on rare occasions, although twelve were seen in June 1969 (King 1981). Hurricane Gilbert, which struck Jamaica in September 1988, may have reduced numbers still further. Its decline may be due largely to competition for nest sites from the introduced Starling (King 1981). It is protected by law, but management such as the provision of nest-boxes is needed. It may already be close to extinction.

MIGRATION Both races are year-round residents, although they may move down to the lowlands after breeding. They have thus been recorded as more abundant at La Vega in late summer than in May (Wetmore and Swales 1931).

FOOD AND BEHAVIOUR Little is known of the behaviour of this species. It flies singly or in small groups, often low over the ground, darting after insects. One stomach that was dissected contained parasitic wasps of the family Ichneumonidae (Osburn 1869). Pairs nest alone or in small groups.

BREEDING The breeding season is in June–July in Jamaica, and breeding has also been recorded in April on Haiti (Osburn 1869; Wetmore and Lincoln 1933; Bond 1943). The nests are usually built in old woodpecker and other holes in dead pines, high above the ground. March (1863) recorded a number of pairs in a building in Jamaica, and Osburn (1869) recorded a nest in a cave; nests are also often placed in the eaves of buildings, under tiles or in thatch (Wetmore and Lincoln 1933). The nest is made of fine vegetable fibres such as cotton, silk and pappus (e.g. of the plant families Compositae and Tillandsiae), but with the seeds broken off, and is lined with silk, cotton and feathers, including green parrot feathers (Osburn 1869). The diameter of one nest was about 12 cm (5") and the depth about 5 cm (2"). The clutch size is three, and the eggs are white. Incubation and nestling periods are not known.

VOICE The call is a soft, repeated two notes, 'tchee-weet', with little variation in tone (Wetmore and Swales 1931).

DESCRIPTION This small swallow is a golden version of the Tree Swallow (7). The plumage is strongly iridescent even for a swallow. The adult male has glossy bronze upperparts, including the sides of the head, chin and malar region. The lores and ear-coverts are duller. The forehead, crown and nape are bronzy-green, while the mantle, back, rump, uppertail-coverts and scapulars are golden or coppery-bronze. The lesser and median-wing coverts are coppery-bronze. The greater and primary wing-coverts are dusky bronze-green, the feathers of the greater coverts and tertials having golden-bronze margins. The underparts are immaculate white, but the sides and flanks are streaked with dusky bronze. The axillaries and underwing-coverts are dusky with broad bronzy-green margins. The primaries, secondaries and the slightly forked tail are also dusky bronze-green. The bill is black, the eyes and the legs and feet are dark brown. The female is similar, but the breast and sometimes the throat and undertail-coverts are mottled with grey-brown. The juvenile's plumage is less glossy, the breast is more extensively mottled with grey-brown, and the sides of the head are dusky grey.

Measurements Length 12 cm (4¾"). Wing 102–113 (mean 106.8); tail 50–57 (mean 53.6); fork 9.5–12 (mean 10.7); bill 8.5–9.6

(mean 9.1); tarsus 9.5–11.2 (mean 10.4).

RACES The race *sclateri* has longer wings (108–119) and a smaller bill (7.5–8.3) than the nominate race, and the tail is also more deeply forked (13–20). The plumage is less golden, the forehead and uppertail-coverts are blue-green, and the wings and tail are blue-black.

15 BROWN-BELLIED SWALLOW   Plate 5
Notiochelidon murina (Cassin)

Petrochelidon murina Cassin, 1853, Proc. Acad. Sci., Phil., 6, sig. 53, p. 370: Ecuador.

Notiochelidon murina meridensis (Zimmer and Phelps), 1947, Llano Rucio, 2500 m, Mérida, Venezuela.

Notiochelidon murina cyanodorsalis (Carriker), 1935, Hichuloma, 10,700 ft, Yungas R.R., La Paz, Bolivia.

FIELD CHARACTERS This species is the only large, dark swallow that is commonly seen in the high Andes, so it is unlikely to be confused with other species. In the field it often looks black all over, as the gloss is not readily seen. It most closely resembles the White-thighed Swallow (3), but the latter can be identified by its pale rump and brownish-black back. Brown-bellied Swallows are typical of open country at high elevations, often alone or in small groups.

HABITAT Brown-bellied Swallows have specialised habitat requirements and can be found only in open areas at high elevations, 2100–4300 m (6930–13,200 ft), mostly up to the tree line, near crags and cliffs in the humid subtropical and temperate zones and also, to a lesser extent, in the paramo of the Andes up to 3800 m (12,500 ft) (Fjeldså et al., in press). They tend to replace the similar Blue-and-white Swallow (18) altitudinally. They forage in open country such as grassland and cultivated fields in the mountains, montane shrub, elfin forest and *Polylepis* woods, especially near bodies of water, and they are frequently seen around human habitation.

DISTRIBUTION AND POPULATION These are typically swallows of the high Andes, breeding in the mountains of Colombia, Venezuela, Peru and Bolivia (Fjeldså et al., in press). The nominate race *murina* occurs in the upper subtropical and temperate zones of Colombia in the Santa Marta Mountains, the Perija Mountains and all three Andean ranges, chiefly at between 2100 and 3750 m (6930–12,360 ft), and in the temperate zone of the Andes in Ecuador and Peru south to Arequipa and Cuzco. The race *meridensis* occurs in the upper subtropical, temperate and paramo zones of the Andes in western Venezuela, in the states of Mérida and Trujillo. The third race, *cyanodorsalis*, is known only from the Cordillera in western Bolivia, but may also occur in the adjacent puno in Peru.

Despite its restricted range, this swallow is relatively abundant. Chapman (1917a, b) recorded the nominate race *murina* as common. Hilty and Brown (1986) described it as the common swallow of the temperate zone of Colombia, it is common in the humid subtropical, humid temperate, paramo and montane scrub zones in Peru (Parker et al. 1982), and I found the Venezuelan race to be abundant in the subtropical and paramo zones in Mérida.

MIGRATION None of the subspecies is known to migrate.

FOOD AND BEHAVIOUR Little is known of the behaviour or breeding biology of these swallows. They are not highly gregarious, either when feeding or when breeding. In Venezuela in the paramo zone I found them hawking insects in flight, either in small, loose groups, in pairs, or alone, flying lower and in a more direct manner than the Blue-and-white Swallow. Most of the time they use flapping flight when foraging, but occasionally glide as well. Pairs often nest alone, but may nest in small, loose groups where suitable nest sites are clumped.

BREEDING Individuals in breeding condition have been recorded from January to August in the central and eastern Andes, and adults have been seen building nests in September and October (Hilty and Brown 1986). Juveniles have been recorded from June to August (Fjeldså and Krabbe 1989).

The nests are simple pads constructed of dry grass or moss, and are placed in a variety of sites such as crevices in caves and cliffs, holes in road cuttings, and under the eaves of buildings. The eggs are pure white and the clutch size is two or three. The eggs measure 18.3 × 13.3 mm (17.8−19 × 13.2−13.4; weight 1.7). Incubation and nestling periods are not known.

VOICE Brown-bellied Swallows are usually quiet and are less vocal than other swallows, but like Blue-and-white Swallows they have a weak buzzy song, a harsh alarm note and a chirp-like contact call 'tjrip, tjrip-tjrip-tjrip'. The calls are more intense and prolonged at dusk (Fjeldså *et al.*, in press).

DESCRIPTION This is a medium-sized, dark swallow. The whole of the upperparts, including the scapulars, are uniformly blackish, with a greenish-blue gloss which is most prominent on the mantle. The head is dullest, and the lores and ear-coverts are dull blue-black. The underparts from the throat to the abdomen are a uniform sooty-grey-brown. The underwing-coverts and axillaries are grey-brown. The undertail-coverts are black, being darkest at the tips. The wings and tail are dark brown, with slight gloss on the lesser and median coverts, and the tail is moderately forked. The bill is black, the eyes are brown and the

legs and feet are blackish-brown. The sexes are alike, but the female is rather duller. The juvenile is duller than the adult, being sooty-brown above and greyish-white below, with a dark brown throat; it has a slight greeny gloss on the mantle, the feathers of the rump have narrow, faint pale tips, and the undertail-coverts are dusky; the tail is less forked than on the adult.

Measurements Length 14 cm (5½"). Wing 105−116 (mean 111.6); tail 52−67 (mean 58.9); fork 11−22 (mean 17.4); bill 9.1−10.2 (mean 9.5); tarsus 10.8−11.5 (mean 11.2).

RACES There are three races. There is some variation in colour in the nominate race, with specimens from northern Peru being greenest on the upperparts and palest below. Those from the Bogotá region are paler below than Ecuadorian ones. The variation in plumage is not, however, sufficiently marked and consistent for additional subspecies to be recognised. The Venezuelan race *meridensis* has a blue gloss on the upperparts, the underparts are smoky grey-brown, the throat is a paler grey-brown, and the undertail-coverts are tipped with metallic dark blue; the female is duller and has brown undertail-coverts. The Bolivian race *cyanodorsalis* has a stronger steel-blue gloss on the upperparts.

16 PALE-FOOTED SWALLOW

Plate 5

Notiochelidon flavipes (Chapman)
Alternative name: Cloud-forest Swallow

Pygochelidon flavipes Chapman, 1922, Am. Mus. Novit., no. 30, p. 8: Maraynioc, 3250 m, Junin, Peru.

FIELD CHARACTERS This small swallow has glossy blue upperparts and white underparts, with dark underwing- and undertail-coverts. It resembles the Blue-and-white Swallow (18), but it is somewhat smaller and has blacker sides and a pale rufous throat. It can be distinguished from immature Blue-and-white Swallows by the blue upperparts, darker throat and duskier sides and flanks. In coloration, Pale-footed Swallows are intermediate between Blue-and-white Swallows, which have pure white underparts, and Brown-bellied Swallows, which are grey-brown below.

HABITAT Forest, forest glades and forest

edge at 2800 to 3600 m (9200−11,870 ft) seem to be the preferred habitat for this swallow; it has been seen once as far as the tree line at 3260 m (10,760 ft) in southern Peru. The Pale-footed Swallow occupies altitudes intermediate between those of the Blue-and-white Swallow and the Brown-bellied Swallow. It is usually found in humid upper cloud forest and elfin forest just above the altitudinal range of the Blue-and-white Swallow and in more closed, forested areas than the latter, and at lower elevations than the upland grassland habitat of the Brown-bellied Swallow. It may, however, occasionally be seen flying with either of these species (Parker and O'Neill 1980). It is occasionally seen at lower altitudes in bad weather, but rarely as far down as 200 m (660 ft) (Fjeldså *et al.*, in press).

DISTRIBUTION AND POPULATION The known range of this swallow is very restricted. It occurs in Peru and in the central Andes of Colombia (the western slope near Manizales — Laguneta at 3000 m, Caldas; and the adjacent eastern slope near Ibagué — Toche, 2200 m, Tolima), in Nariño near the Ecuador/Colombia boundary (La Victoria, 2000 m), and in Venezuela in Merida and the Paramo de Tamé. However, it apparently ranges fairly continuously from the central Andes of Colombia, eastern Ecuador (where it has been seen in the Sangay area) and central Peru (one specimen is known from the Department of Huánuco in the Carpish Mountains), to northern Bolivia; and also in Venezuela, where it has been recorded only since 1985, although it may well have been missed previously (Lentino 1988; Fjeldså *et al.*, in press). There are no indications that it migrates.

Pale-footed Swallows are apparently uncommon and locally distributed. In Colombia, the species is known only from three specimens from the central Andes of Colombia, and a sight record of two at the southwestern entrance to Puracé in February 1984 (Hilty and Brown 1986). In Peru, it is locally more common from 2685 to 2980 m (8850–9810 ft) (upper Urubamba valley, southern Peru: Parker and O'Neill 1980). It may, however, be more common and widespread than is thought, as it can easily be mistaken for a Blue-and-white Swallow and so may often have been overlooked.

BEHAVIOUR Small flocks of 10–15, occasionally up to 50, Pale-footed Swallows have been recorded (Parker and Rowlett 1984). The flight is rapid and direct (more so than that of the Blue-and-white Swallow). Individuals have been recorded over forest canopy and in open parts of the forest,

perching on dead branches of tall trees. Its diet is not known.

BREEDING One male collected by Parker and O'Neill (1980) between July and September had enlarged testes and a brood patch, but two other males and a female were not in breeding condition. No details of the behaviour, diet or breeding biology of this species are known. It probably nests in cavities, as does its close relative the Blue-and-white Swallow, but using those in trees in the forest. The fact that one male collected by Parker and O'Neill had a brood patch indicates that both sexes probably incubate the eggs, as with the other members of this genus.

VOICE The call is a musical 'threeep' and a buzzy 'bzeet' (Parker and O'Neill 1980).

DESCRIPTION The Pale-footed Swallow is a small hirundine with a steel-blue gloss on the blackish upperparts, including the scapulars. The forehead, crown and nape, and the sides of the head, are glossy blue; the ear-coverts and lores are duller. The throat is pale rufous; the breast and abdomen are white; and the sides and flanks are sooty-brown. The underwing-coverts and axillaries are blackish-brown. The undertail-coverts are a dark steel-blue. The wings and the forked tail are blackish-brown, with a slight gloss on the lesser and median coverts. The eyes are dark brown, the bill is black with a pink mouth lining, and the legs and feet are pinkish-flesh. The sexes are similar, but a male specimen from Colombia had darker, glossier upperparts and a more deeply coloured throat than the female specimens (Zimmer 1955). There is no indication of geographical variation in plumage. The juvenile has not been · described, but an immature male had pale edges to the undertail-coverts (Lentino 1988).

Measurements Length 12 cm (4¾"). Wing 90–92 (mean 90.7); tail 47–51 (mean 49); fork 11–12 (mean 11.5); bill 9; tarsus 9–11 (mean 10). Weight 8.8–12 (mean 10.6).

17 BLACK-CAPPED SWALLOW
Notiochelidon pileata (Gould)
Alternative name: Coban Swallow

Plate 5

Atticora pileata Gould, 1858, Proc. Zool. Soc. Lond., pt. 26, p. 355: Guatemala.

FIELD CHARACTERS In the field, the combination of brown upperparts, black under-

tail-coverts and black head, together with the small size of this bird, is distinctive. It is an upland bird, usually seen alone or in small groups in woodland or cultivation.

HABITAT This is a specialised montane species, being recorded primarily in the interior highlands between 750 and 2650 m (2465–8740 ft) (Skutch 1960). It frequents woodland edge, and open woodland, cultivated areas, villages and towns.

DISTRIBUTION AND POPULATION Black-capped Swallows have a restricted range in northern Central America, occurring only in the highlands of Guatemala and adjoining parts of Chiapas (Triunfo; Volcan Tacaná) and El Salvador (Los Esesmiles), and on the Honduran border, to the north of the range of the other members of this genus. They are common in the highlands of Guatemala, ranging down into the subtropics (Land 1970). Skutch (1960) described it as common in the towns of the highlands and as abundant on the Sierra de Tecpán in Guatemala.

MIGRATION Black-capped Swallows make relatively short-distance movements. They can be found in Guatemala all year (Land 1970), but Marshall (1943) recorded it as a summer visitor to El Salvador, arriving in the second week of March. It also ranges into the mountains of Honduras in the non-breeding season: one specimen was collected and five others were seen in January 1963 at 1860 m (6100 ft) and 1920 m (6320 ft), northeast of La Esperanza (Monroe 1968). At one breeding site in northwestern Guatemala, the birds departed after breeding, leaving by the beginning of September (Baepler 1962).

BEHAVIOUR The flight is quick and fluttering, including many periods of gliding, with infrequent wingbeats, but also periods of flapping flight (Marshall 1943). Black-capped Swallows are usually seen singly or in small groups. Wetmore (1941) found 30 roosting in a hole in a bank in November, and Skutch (1960) also noted small groups roosting together in burrows after the breeding season between October and December at an elevation of 9000 m (30,000 ft) in a bank by a highway; the roosting site found by Skutch was a considerable altitudinal distance from areas where these birds were feeding during the day. The swallows roost for long periods, well into the daylight hours when the temperature is low. Several hundred were seen in a large dead pine at the head of a canyon at 2600 m (8570 ft) in El Salvador (Marshall 1943). They feed alone or in small groups, low over fields, bare ridges and knolls, clearings and landslides in forested areas. At one site, they fed within a few hundred metres of the nests (Baepler 1962). Their diet is not known. This species breeds in solitary pairs or small, loose groups.

BREEDING These swallows are known to breed from April to July in Guatemala, peaking in June (Skutch 1960; Baepler 1962). In Chiapas, however, breeding has been recorded from February to April before the rains, probably to avoid flooding of the nests (Wagner 1951). Few details are known about the breeding biology of this swallow. The nests are built in holes and crevices in rock faces, caves, river banks, road cuttings, cliffs and buildings. Dearborn and Cory (1907) recorded them using burrows in a bank by the roadside in April and nesting in the walls of a cathedral at Tecpán: they stated that the birds were drilling holes themselves, but other accounts describe these swallows as using natural cavities or burrows dug by other species. Amadon and Eckelberry (1955) recorded them using holes in a road cutting in May. Skutch (1960) noted that they use the vacant burrows of motmots in roadside banks but do not dispossess the original owners. Dead pine needles, twigs and dry leaves, and sometimes feathers, are used to make the nest; green leaves are also collected (Skutch 1960), and Baepler (1962) recorded mud being used. Both sexes build the nest, which is placed far back at the end of a burrow, and both sleep together while the nest is being built. One nest took five days to make (Skutch 1960).

The eggs are white and measure 16.6 × 12.8 mm (15.7–17.3 × 12.7–13.1; weight 1.42). The clutch size is four, the eggs being laid on successive days. According to Skutch (1960), the male does not sleep with the female during egg-laying and incubation, but does when the nestlings are being fed. Both parents feed the nestlings; one pair made 36 trips to a nest in one hour (Baepler 1962).

VOICE The song is a rolling 'bzeet' (Marshall 1943), and these swallows also utter a harsh chirp.

DESCRIPTION This is a small, dark swallow. The forehead, crown, hindneck and sides of the head and neck are glossy black with a faint blue sheen. The lores and ear-coverts are black. The mantle, back and scapulars are grey-brown, darker on the rump and sooty-black or sooty-brown on the upper-tail-coverts. The malar region, chin and throat are white, with sooty-brown flecks. The breast and abdomen are white. The sides of the breast, flanks, axillaries and underwing-coverts are grey-brown. The undertail-coverts are sooty-black or sooty-brown. The lesser wing-coverts are glossy brownish-black or black; the rest of the wings are brownish-black but more grey- or sooty-brown on the secondaries and inner-most wing-coverts. The tail is black or sooty-black and is moderately forked. The bill is black, and the eyes and legs and feet are brown. The sexes are alike. There is no geographical variation in plumage. The juvenile is browner and less glossy, with a brown head, a buffy chin and throat, and pale edges to the feathers on the rump and secondaries.

Measurements Length 12 cm (4¾"). Wing 93–97 (mean 95.5); tail 51–58 (mean 53.9); fork 15–20 (mean 16.8); bill 7.4–8.4 (mean 7.9); tarsus 10–11.6 (mean 10.8).

18 BLUE-AND-WHITE SWALLOW   Plate 5
Notiochelidon cyanoleuca (Vieillot)

Hirundo cyanoleuca Vieillot, 1817, Nouv. Dict. Hist. Nat., 14, p. 509: Paraguay.

Notiochelidon cyanoleuca peruviana (Chapman), 1922, Huaral, Lima, Peru.

Notiochelidon cyanoleuca patagonica (d'Orbigny and Lafresnaye), 1837, Patagonia.

FIELD CHARACTERS This is a small swallow with blue upperparts, dark underwing- and undertail-coverts and white throat, breast and abdomen. In the field, it most closely resembles the tree swallow group (7–14), but its contrasting white belly and dark undertail-coverts are distinctive. It also resembles the Pale-footed Swallow (16), but the adult Blue-and-white Swallow has a whiter throat and paler sides; the juvenile Blue-and-white is browner above and has a much paler throat. This is a swallow of middle elevations, in fairly open country, often seen alone or in small groups, but large flocks occur on migration.

HABITAT Throughout their range, Blue-and-white Swallows often breed in villages and towns, on farms and in forest clearings. It is a highland species in the northern parts of its range, occurring in the tropical and temperate zones up to about 4000 m (13,000 ft), but mostly in the subtropical zone in Central America. Further south, it also occurs in lowland areas such as the pampas of Argentina. In Tierra del Fuego, Blue-and-white Swallows are found mainly in the northern non-forested areas. The race *peruviana* prefers open lowland habitat.

DISTRIBUTION AND POPULATION The Blue-and-white Swallow has an extensive distribution from Central America south to Tierra del Fuego (Fjeldså and Krabbe 1989). The northern race *cyanoleuca* occurs in the foothills and highlands of Costa Rica, western Panama in the provinces of Chiriquí and Veraguas, Colombia in the upper tropical and lower temperate zones, the subtropical zone of Venezuela, Trinidad, Guyana, Ecuador, Peru, Bolivia, southern and eastern Brazil from the Mato Grosso (Chapada), eastern Pará (Benevides), Piaui and Pernambuco south to northwestern Argentina (Tucumán), Paraguay and Uruguay. The race *peruviana* is restricted to the coast of Peru from the Department of Libertad to the Department of Arequipa. The southern race *patagonica* breeds from the central provinces of Chile and central Argentina (probably north to La Rioja, Cordoba, southern Entre Rios and Buenos Aires) south to Tierra del Fuego.

The Peruvian race is common on the coast of Peru and up to 2500 m (8200 ft), and is abundant in Lima itself (Koepcke 1983). The southern race *patagonica* is widespread up to 4000 m (Johnson 1967). The two races *patagonica* and *cyanoleuca* meet in Tucumán in northwestern Argentina, but *cyanoleuca* is probably the resident breeder there. Skutch (1952) described this species as abundant in the central plateau and surrounding mountains in Costa Rica. It is also abundant in Panama, Colombia, Bolivia and Venezuela and is common in towns. It is probably benefiting from the spread of human habitation in tropical areas. There have, however, been local declines in the past: Wilson (1926) noted a decline in this species around Santa Fé, following the extermination of vizcachas *Lagostomus*, in whose burrows they nest.

MIGRATION The northern populations are resident, but *patagonica* has been recorded on migration or in winter to northern Chile, northern Argentina, Paraguay, Bolivia, eastern Peru, Colombia, Venezuela, Trinidad, the Guianas and Panama; exceptionally, it occurs further north, with records in Nicaragua and Chiapas, Mexico. In Chile, *patagonica* is present all year in the north but only from late August to March in central and southern parts of the country. On migration these swallows keep to the more elevated country. They arrive in Argentina and Uruguay in August–September and leave in January–March, migrating northwest along the Andes, then north across Bolivia and Peru, Ecuador, eastern Colombia and northern Venezuela as far as Panama (Zimmer 1955). A few individuals have been recorded on the western coast, in the lowlands of the Amazon valley, and from Paraguay and western Brazil.

FORAGING AND FOOD In fine weather, Blue-and-white Swallows feed mainly over open ground and around trees, usually 3–15 m (10–50 ft) above the ground, occasionally up to 25 m (80 ft), but in cloudy, wet weather they also feed extensively over water (Wolf 1976; Turner 1983b). Most of the time they use flapping flight, zigzagging to and fro with frequent wingbeats and gliding about a quarter of the time, rather more in cloudy weather. They frequently feed around livestock, catching the insects disturbed by them. They forage alone or in loose flocks. In the Andes of Venezuela (see Turner 1983b), the adults take mainly Hymenoptera (71% of the diet), especially winged ants and parasitic species, but small flies are also important in the diet in the non-breeding season (37%). A few beetles, plant bugs and moths are also eaten. Nestlings are fed a wider variety of prey, mainly small flies (27%), winged ants (22%), beetles (11%) and mayflies (15%); plant bugs, moths, termites and parasitic Hymenoptera are brought to the nestlings in smaller numbers. Nestlings receive larger prey items on average than the parents eat themselves. Elsewhere, a similar variety of insects is eaten. For example, Freeman (1922) found an ortalid fly, a chalcid wasp, a bug, a muscid fly, winged ants and small beetles in the stomachs of three individuals from Trinidad.

BEHAVIOUR Pairs probably usually remain together throughout the year in resident populations (Skutch 1960). They are highly territorial at the nest and chase and fight with intruders. They nest alone or in loose groups, depending on the availability of nest sites. After breeding, migrants will form flocks of tens or hundreds of individuals.

BREEDING In tropical areas, these swallows breed at the end of the dry season or at the beginning of the wet season, before the peak in rainfall (Turner 1983b; Fjeldså and Krabbe 1989). Most nesting activity thus occurs between January and June/July. In southeastern Colombia, however, three peaks in breeding have been recorded, in September–December, February–April and June to the beginning of August (Lehmann 1960). In temperate parts of South America they generally breed between October and February, the austral summer, although in Chile the breeding season is September–December; in Bolivia it is October–March. Two broods are apparently sometimes reared; two are usual in Chile, but one at high elevations (Skutch 1952; Johnson 1967). The nest is a pad of dry grass and feathers placed at the end of a burrow or in a crevice. Almost any cavity seems acceptable, be it an old hole in a tree, a disused burrow or crevice in a bank, ditch, sand dune or road cutting, crevices in cliffs or between rocks, in holes in walls, bridges, or wells, under eaves or beneath roof tiles, in thatched roofs or in the tops of lamp posts. Artificial structures are frequently used except by the race *patagonica*, which often uses holes dug by the Common Miner *Geositta cunicularia* in the burrows of the vizcacha (Johnson 1967). Both members of the pair build the nest.

The eggs are pure white and measure 17.2 × 12.5 mm (15.3–20 × 11.7–14; weight 1.4). However, they are larger in Chile (18.2 × 13.2: Johnson 1967). Clutch size varies geographically, from five or six eggs in Argentina, or three to six in Chile, to two to four in Costa Rica and Colombia and two or three in Venezuela. The eggs are laid at daily intervals, although there is sometimes a gap of a day between eggs. Both male and female incubate, leaving the eggs uncovered only in hot weather, and sleeping together at the nest. The incubation period is about 15 days. Both parents feed the young. Feeding rates average three per hour per nestling. The nestling period lasts 26 days, and the fledglings return to roost in or near the nest for several days more while the parents continue to bring food to them.

VOICE The song is a repeated weak and monotonous trilling. Hilty and Brown (1986) described it as a series of jumbled buzzes and squeaks. The song of the southern race is a short 'trip'. There is also a harsh alarm call. Members of a pair utter chirp-like contact calls of one or two syllables, particularly when relieving each other at the nest.

DESCRIPTION This is a small swallow. The forehead, crown, sides of the head and neck, scapulars, mantle, back, rump and uppertail-coverts are glossy steel-blue. The feathers of the mantle are spotted beneath the surface with white or pale grey. The ear-coverts and lores are a duller blue. The lesser and median wing-coverts are black with steel-blue margins; the greater coverts have less distinct margins. The underparts are white, with an extensive smoky-grey wash on the sides and flanks. The extreme sides of the breast are glossy black. There are often a few dusky spots along the centre of the chest which sometimes form a narrow collar. The undertail-coverts are black with steel-blue margins. The under-wing-coverts and axillaries are sooty-grey with a few narrow whitish tips. The primaries, secondaries and tail are greyish-black and the tail is only slightly forked. The

bill is black, the eyes are brown and the legs and feet are blackish-brown. The sexes are alike. The juvenile has dark grey-brown rather than blue upperparts, with a dull sooty-brown crown and back, and a slight gloss on the mantle; the wings and tail are blackish-brown, the chin and throat are white with a buff tinge, the breast-band and sides are smoky-grey with a buff tinge, the flanks have a slight buff tinge, the breast and abdomen are white, and the undertail-coverts are dull brown, sometimes with narrow white tips; the feathers of the rump have faint, narrow, pale tips. The tail is less forked than on the adult. Moult starts towards the end of the breeding season.
Measurements Length 12 cm (4¾"). Wing 88–102 (mean 94.2); tail 42–55 (mean 49.7); fork 7–15 (mean 10.6); bill 6–8 (mean 7); tarsus 9.1–11 (mean 10). Weight 9–13 (mean 10.5).

RACES The southern race *patagonica* is larger than the nominate race (wing 99–112) and has only the longer undertail-coverts black, the anterior ones being white; the sides are paler, and the under-wing-coverts are pale ashy-grey with silvery white tips (they are particularly pale on juveniles). The race *peruviana* has very little white on the undertail-coverts compared with *patagonica* (the basal series having some white at their base) and is smaller (wing up to 97); the underwing-coverts are blacker, and the brown tinge on the sides of the body is darker and more extensive.

19 WHITE-BANDED SWALLOW   Plate 6
Atticora fasciata (Gmelin)

Hirundo fasciata Gmelin, 1789, Syst. Nat., 1, pt. 2, p. 1022: Cayenne.

FIELD CHARACTERS White-banded Swallows are easily identified by the contrasting white breast-band on an otherwise pure blue-black plumage and the deeply forked tail, quite unlike other swallows. They are seen only along forested rivers, alone or in small groups.

HABITAT White-banded Swallows have a specialised habitat. They occur in the tropical zone, breeding along the upper reaches of forested rivers and feeding over water (clear or blackwater rivers) or in clearings, along the forest edge and in open grassy areas with bushes in the lowlands and

foothills. In the blackwater regions of Vaupés, the preferred habitat is rocky rapids and waterfalls on the larger rivers. They occur at altitudes of up to 1400 m (4600 ft) (Hilty and Brown 1986).

DISTRIBUTION AND POPULATION The range extends over northern South America, east of the Andes and generally south of the Orinoco, from western Meta and Vaupés south to Bolivia and Amazonian Brazil. White-banded Swallows are found in southeastern Colombia, southern Venezuela, the Guianas, eastern Ecuador, eastern Peru, northern Brazil south to the Rio

Juruá (Rio Eirú), Rio Purús (Bom Luguar), Rio Gi-Paraná (Maruins), Rio Guapore (Tres Barros), the Para region, and northern Bolivia in the departments of Beni and La Paz. There are no indications that this swallow migrates. These are uncommon or locally common swallows; they are rare or locally common on the larger, muddy rivers such as the Amazon (Hilty and Brown 1986). Naumberg (1930), however, described it as abundant in the Mato Grosso, and Haverschmidt (1968) also found it common on the forest-fringed rivers of the interior of Surinam. They are restricted to suitable natural habitat as they do not use artificial structures for nesting.

FOOD AND BEHAVIOUR These swallows are usually seen alone, in pairs or in small groups. They fly low and erratically, rapidly skimming and crisscrossing the water, but also sometimes fly above the forest. They are often seen perching on branches overhanging the river or on boulders or snags in the water, sometimes in the company of White-winged (9) or Black-collared Swallows (20). However, they keep closer to vegetation and rocks than the White-winged Swallow does. Small numbers flock together at dusk to roost. Their diet consists of insects caught in flight and includes bees, chalcid wasps, ants, sawflies, elaterid beetles, plant bugs and brachyceran flies (Haverschmidt 1968). Pairs breed alone or in small, loose groups.

BREEDING Little is known of the breeding biology of these swallows. They have been seen at holes in February and March, and a female about to lay was recorded in February in the Macarena Mountains (Hilty and Brown 1986). Haverschmidt (1968) recorded fledglings being fed by their parents in mid December in Surinam, and Niethammer (1956) recorded fledglings in Bolivia in September. White-banded Swallows are thought to dig their own burrows, but disused burrows made by other species may be used instead of or as well as their own ones. The nest is a simple pad of dry grass placed at the end of the burrow. The eggs are pure white, and clutches of four and five have been recorded. They measure 18.5 × 12.8 mm (17.1–19.7 × 12–13.5; weight 1.58). Incubation and nestling periods are not known.

VOICE The song is a fine buzzy 'z-z-z-z-ee-eep' (Snyder 1966). The alarm call is a sharp 'tschra'.

DESCRIPTION This is a medium-sized and strikingly plumaged swallow. The upperparts from the forehead and crown to the uppertail-coverts, including the scapulars and lesser and median wing-coverts, are glossy blue-black. The greater wing-coverts are duller. The lores and base of the forehead are velvety black and the ear-coverts blue-black. Apart from a conspicuous broad white band — which broadens at the sides — across the breast, the underparts are also glossy blue-black. The underwing-coverts and axillaries are blackish-brown. The edge of the wing is barred white. The thighs are white-feathered. The primaries, secondaries and tail are black with a slight blue sheen, and the tail is long and deeply forked. The eyes, bill and legs and feet are black. The sexes are alike. The juvenile is duller, with mostly matt black upperparts with very little gloss, dusky underparts and a whitish breast-band; the abdomen, lower flanks, underwing-coverts, axillaries and undertail-coverts are all browner than on the adult, and the greater wing-coverts, secondaries, tertials and the feathers on the underparts have pale edges; the outer tail feathers are also shorter than on the adult.

Measurements Length 15 cm (6"). Wing 92–108 (mean 101.3); tail 55–80 (mean 66.7); fork 20–40 (mean 31.5); bill 8.1–9.2 (mean 8.8); tarsus 10–11 (mean 10.5). Weight 12–16.

RACES There is a clinal decrease in size from the Guianas and Venezuela to Peru and southern Brazil: e.g. in Guyana the wing length is 101–109; in Venezuela 97–108; in eastern Ecuador and northeastern Peru 97–105; and in the rest of Peru and in southern Brazil 92–100. Hellmayr (1935) suggested that the birds north and south of the Amazon were distinct, the southern population being smaller with a less deeply forked tail, less purplish-blue upperparts and a somewhat wider white breast-band. The change in size, however, is gradual throughout the range, and there is a great deal of overlap in tail measurements of birds north and south of the Amazon, suggesting that there are no distinct races (Zimmer 1955).

20 BLACK-COLLARED SWALLOW   Plate 6
Atticora melanoleuca (Wied)

Hirundo melanoleuca Wied, 1820, Reise Brasilien, 1, p. 345: Rio Grande do Belmonte, Baia.

FIELD CHARACTERS Black-collared Swallows have blue-black upperparts, and white underparts with a blue-black breast-band. They superficially resemble Bank Swallows (Sand Martins, 27), but the adults are blue-black rather than brown and the tail of both adults and juveniles is conspicuously more deeply forked. They are also similar to juvenile Barn Swallows (42), but the latter are less pure white below and have a pale forehead. They frequent lowland forest rivers and are usually alone or in small groups.

HABITAT The preferred habitat is similar to that of the White-banded Swallow (19), but Black-collared Swallows are usually found closer to large lowland rivers, especially with rocky outcrops and waterfalls, and they prefer wider, more open stretches of water with protruding rocks than their congener. The species ranges to 250 m (820 ft) in Colombia and 300 m (980 ft) in Venezuela (de Schauensee and Phelps 1978; Hilty and Brown 1986).

DISTRIBUTION AND POPULATION Like the White-banded Swallow, this species is restricted to the Amazonian Basin, but the range is poorly known, especially in Brazil. It is found in the tropical zone of southeastern Colombia from eastern Vichada and Guainía south to Vaupés, southern Venezuela in western Amazonas, Bolivar along the Orinoco to Delta Amacuro and south to the lower Rio Caura and middle Rio Paragua, the Guianas, and northern and eastern Brazil east of the Rio Negro and the Rio Madeira, south to the Rio Guapore (Forte do Principe), Rio Roosevelt (Rio Branco), Rio Xingu, Rio Tocantins (Arumateua) and Bahia (Rio Belmonte). There are sightings in eastern Colombia at Maipures and Pto Inirida south to Mitú. The southernmost record of the species is at Iguazu in the extreme northeast of Argentina and it probably occurs between these two parts of its range. Black-collared Swallows are not known to migrate. There are no measures of abundance, but in Colombia and Surinam Black-collared Swallows are locally fairly common along the larger forested blackwater rivers, near rocky outcrops, rapids and waterfalls (Haverschmidt 1968; Hilty and Brown

1986). Naumberg (1930) also recorded them as common in Brazil. They occur only in natural habitat, as they do not nest on artificial structures.

FOOD AND BEHAVIOUR What little is known of this species' behaviour is again similar to that of the White-banded Swallow, but Black-collared Swallows often fly higher, gliding over rivers or adjacent forest, sometimes with other swallows. They do, however, also fly low, rapidly zigzagging over the water as they hawk for insects. They perch in small groups on rocks or sandbanks. Their diet includes beetles of the families Ipidae and Staphylinidae, Hymenoptera (mainly ants and chalcid wasps), plant bugs of the family Jassidae, and flies (Nematocera and Brachycera) (Haverschmidt 1968). They breed in single pairs or in loose groups.

BREEDING Breeding has been recorded from February to March in the Orinoco region (the dry season) (Cherrie 1916). Haverschmidt (1968) recorded a fledgling in mid August in Surinam. Details of the breeding biology of this swallow are sparse. It uses crevices in large rocks, usually about 2 m (6½ ft) above the water level, or holes in sandy river banks. The nest is a simple shallow cup made of dry grass and lined with only a few feathers. The eggs are pure white and the clutch size is three (Friedmann 1948). The eggs measure 18×12.8 mm ($17.1–19.5 \times 12.2–14$; weight 1.55).

VOICE No calls have been noted.

DESCRIPTION These small swallows have glossy blue-black upperparts, including the scapulars and sides of the head and neck. The wing-coverts are duller, with most gloss on the lesser and median coverts. The lores are velvety black and the ear-coverts are blue-black. The underparts are mostly immaculate white, but there is a narrow blue-black breast-band and the undertail-coverts are also blue-black. A few blue-black feathers sometimes extend from the breast-band down the breast, and the sides of the upper breast are blackish. The underwing-coverts and axillaries are blackish-brown, with some white near the edge of the wing. The primaries, secondaries and tail are blackish, the tail being long and forked. The eyes, bill, legs and feet are also black. The sexes are alike. There is no geographical variation. The juvenile is duller, with mouse-brown upperparts and breast-band, and dirty white underparts; the blue feathers of the adult plumage appear irregularly; the tail is less deeply forked than on the adult.

Measurements Length 14 cm (5½"). Wing 89–97 (mean 93); tail 72–82 (mean 77.6); fork 32–45 (mean 38); bill 7–8.5 (mean 7.9); tarsus 10.1–10.9 (mean 10.7). Weight 10–12.

21 BROWN-CHESTED MARTIN
Progne tapera (Linnaeus)

Plate 7

Hirundo tapera Linnaeus, 1766, Syst. Nat., ed. 12, 1, p. 345: America. Restricted to eastern Brazil by Berlepsch and Hartert, 1902, Novit. Zool., 9, p. 14, and to Pernambuco by Pinto, 1940, Rev. Mus. Paulista, 1, p. 270.

Progne tapera fusca (Vieillot), 1817, Paraguay.

FIELD CHARACTERS Brown-chested Martins are dull sandy-brown above, and white below with a brown breast-band. They are similar to Bank Swallows (Sand Martins, 27), but can be distinguished by their much larger size. This species is usually associated with water and is fairly solitary when breeding. Outside the breeding season it forms large flocks.

HABITAT This martin is often locally known as the River Martin, as it tends to breed near lakes and rivers in open country. The migrant race *fusca* is said to stay at low altitudes, being recorded up to about 400 m (1300 ft) in Venezuela, but in Colombia in the eastern Andes they have been recorded at over 3000 m (9900 ft) (Fjeldså and Krabbe 1986) and in Peru to 4000 m (13,000 ft) (Fjeldså and Krabbe 1989). The race *tapera* can be found from sea level up to over 1000 m (3300 ft), mainly in the humid tropical zone. I have seen it at 1600 m (5200 ft) in the Andes of Venezuela, and it has been recorded at the same altitude in Colombia (Hilty and Brown 1986). It forages over grassland, farms, open country with trees, clearings, river banks and savanna.

DISTRIBUTION AND POPULATION The Brown-chested Martin occurs over the northern part of South America, breeding from the Caribbean coast and Trinidad south to Paraguay, northern Argentina and Uruguay (Fjeldså and Krabbe 1989). The nominate race *tapera* occurs in Colombia along the Caribbean coast, the Magdalena valley and the region to the east of the eastern Andes, Venezuela, the Guianas, southern Ecuador, northern Peru and Brazil on the Rio Jurúa, Rio Purús, the Madeira, the Rio Beni extending into Bolivia, the lower Tapajozs, Xingu, Tocantins and Capim Rivers, south to Pernambuco, Bahia and Goiaz. The southern subspecies, *fusca*, breeds from eastern Bolivia (Santa Cruz), the Mato Grosso (north to Descalvados and Guiabá), southern Goiaz, Minas Gerais and Espirito Santo south to Paraguay, northern Argentina (La Rioja, Tucumán, Cordoba, Corrientes and Buenos Aires) and Uruguay. Specimens from the Matto Grosso are intermediate between the two races (Chapman 1929).

Population sizes are unknown, but the species is said to be common in south-eastern Brazil (Mitchell 1957; Belton 1985) and it is also common in the foothills of the Andes in Venezuela and fairly common in Colombia (Hilty and Brown 1976). Haverschmidt (1968) stated that it is less common in Surinam than is the Grey-breasted Martin (23). It may be limited to some extent by the availability of breeding sites. Its range has extended, for example, in southeastern Brazil, where the Rufous Hornero (*Furnarius rufus*), whose nests it uses, has also extended its range (Mitchell 1957). Large numbers are often seen in the wintering areas.

MIGRATION In the northern part of the range the species is sedentary, but *fusca* migrates north to winter from March to October or early November as far as northern and eastern Colombia, Venezuela, the Guianas, eastern Peru, northern Brazil and Panama and casually on the coast of southwestern Peru (Fjeldså and Krabbe 1989). It may have extended its wintering area in the past few decades as it has been

121

regularly reported from Panama only since the early 1950s, although numbers vary greatly from year to year, and it has been seen once in central Costa Rica (Wetmore et al. 1984). This species has also recently turned up in North America, in Massachusetts (Monomoy Island) in June 1983 (Peterson et al. 1986).

FORAGING AND FOOD Unlike the Purple Martin (22), Brown-chested Martins do not soar much, but sweep over the vegetation or fly slowly and weakly with shallow wing-beats around trees or over open ground. In dry weather they often fly within a few metres of the ground, hunting for dragonflies and other large insects over waterside vegetation. In wet weather they often fly higher, feeding on swarming termites and ants. They are weak flyers and often perch. Stomach contents of seven birds from Minas Gerais in Brazil included mainly small individuals of beetles (including weevils) and wasps, ants and plant bugs (Moojen et al. 1941). Haverschmidt (1968) noted dragonflies, beetles, bees, ants and Lepidoptera in the diet. In Venezuela, the adult diet consists mainly of termites, ants and dipteran flies, with fewer numbers of dragonflies, hemipteran bugs and beetles, although by weight dragonflies form an important part of the diet (Turner 1983). Termites and ants are caught mainly in wet weather. During their first two to three weeks, the nestlings are fed mainly dipteran flies (especially hoverflies), Hymenoptera (ants and bees) and small butterflies and moths, as well as lesser numbers of termites and hemipteran bugs (Turner 1983), but as they grow bigger they are brought an increasingly higher proportion of dragonflies. Their diet also depends on the weather: over 60% consists of dragonflies in dry weather, but less than 40% when it is raining.

BEHAVIOUR These swallows are not gregarious when breeding, but if nest sites are limited they will nest in close proximity to each other. Thus, at one particular site in Venezuela, they nested in bridges over streams along a main road: five bridges had a single nest, two had three nests and only one (with at least 16 apparently suitable holes) had four active nests. Each pair aggressively defends its nest hole from intruders, one of the birds usually sitting in the entrance to the hole. Intruders are lunged at, and a fight may ensue if the

intruder persists. The birds also display in flight, with wings held stiffly and decurved. In the non-breeding season Brown-chested Martins form large flocks, sometimes numbering hundreds or thousands of birds, often perching on buildings, trees and wires. Fraga (1979) reported the presence of 'helpers' at the nest: four or five adults attending and feeding two fledglings.

BREEDING In southern parts of the range such as Argentina and Brazil, the main breeding season is from November to March (Pereyra 1969). In Venezuela, pairs were breeding in April–June, while in Colombia birds in breeding condition have been collected in March and May (Hilty and Brown 1986). In areas where nests may be flooded, breeding takes place towards the end of the dry season to avoid high water levels. In many areas, such as the Argentine pampas, this swallow usually breeds in nests of horneros: a pair will evict the horneros if they still occupy the nest, fighting with them over several days, but the horneros are usually gone by the end of October, leaving their nests free for the martins (Sclater and Hudson 1888). The martins also nest in holes in buildings in towns, in trees and in bridges; in villages and towns they often use the local church. Holes in earth banks and termite nests are also used. The nest itself is a small pad of dry grass lined with feathers, placed at the back of the hole.

The eggs are white and measure 23.4 × 16.3 mm (21.2–24.2 × 15.6–16.6; weight 3.24). The clutch size in Venezuela averages four eggs (ranging from three to five) and is also four in Argentina (Pereyra 1969). The incubation period is 14–15 days. Only one member of the pair, presumably the female, incubates, while the other perches on a wire or branch nearby. The eggs are incubated for about 60% of the daylight hours for periods of two to 25 minutes in dry weather, but for up to 54 minutes in wet weather when hunting for insects is more difficult for the parent. The incubating parent feeds for periods of one to 18 minutes. The nestlings come to the entrance of the nest hole to be fed at about 18 days, and fledge at about four weeks of age. They are fed about three times an hour in dry weather, but less often when it is wet. Both the male and the female feed the chicks. In my study, losses were high: six of ten clutches were lost to predators or were flooded, and ten of 14 nestlings (71%) fledged. The fledglings stay as a family group for several days at least, perching near the nest.

VOICE The usual notes are harsh and guttural, with occasional series of gurgling sounds, usually rising and falling: 'djuit-djut' or 'dchri-dchrie-dchrruid'. Sclater and Hudson (1888) described this species as being very garrulous, with a bold song that ranges from harsh to silvery. It also has a 'chu-chu-chip' contact call, which is often uttered by birds in flocks.

DESCRIPTION The Brown-chested Martin is a rather dull member of the purple martin group. The upperparts, including the sides of the head and the wing-coverts, are a sandy-brown, the wing-coverts and inner secondaries and tertials being narrowly edged with white. There are extensive pale edges to the feathers of the upperparts. The lores and ear-coverts are brown. The chin, throat and abdomen are white, and there is an indistinct sandy-brown breast-band. The sides are brownish. The undertail-coverts are long and pure white and usually protrude from the sides. The wings and the slightly forked tail are also sandy-brown, but are darker than the back and head. The bill is black, the eyes are brown and the legs and feet are black. The sexes are alike. The juvenile resembles the adult, but has the sides of the throat grey-brown and has a slightly squarer tail.

Measurements Length 16 cm (6¼"). Wing of male 125–137 (mean 130), of female 117–127 (mean 124); tail 53–70 (mean 63.7); fork 12–16 (mean 13.7); bill 13.3–15.9 (mean 15); tarsus 12.9–15.1 (mean 14.2). Weight 29.9–40 (mean 36.1).

RACES The southern race *fusca* is slightly larger (wing of male 129–143, of female 127–140), has a more well-defined breast-band contrasting with a purer white throat, is darker on the sides and flanks and is slightly darker above, and has distinctive pear-shaped dusky marks down the centre of the lower breast and upper abdomen.

22 PURPLE MARTIN   Plate 7
Progne subis (Linnaeus)

Hirundo subis Linnaeus, 1758, Syst. Nat., ed. 10, 1, p. 192: Hudson Bay.

Progne subis hesperia Brewster, 1889, Sierra de la Laguna, Baja California.

Progne subis arboricola Behle, 1968, Payson Lakes, Utah.

FIELD CHARACTERS With their wholly steel-blue plumage, male Purple Martins are distinctive in most of their range, but are difficult to tell apart from the race *cryptoleuca* of the Snowy-bellied Martin (24); Purple Martins have a relatively shorter and less deeply forked tail. The females and young are duller and greyer, and are similar to Grey-breasted Martins (23). The former, however, have a greyer forehead, are paler on the sides of the neck and have darker, streaked underparts. Purple Martins are large, garrulous swallows, and often nest in groups around human habitation.

HABITAT The Purple Martin frequents a variety of open or semi-open habitats, especially near water, open woodland, farms or towns. Feeding sites are generally over open fields, crops and pastures, open water and marshes. The montane race *arboricola* frequents areas of coniferous forest, and the race *hesperia* breeds in deserts where there are saguaro or organ-pipe cacti.

DISTRIBUTION AND POPULATION This martin is widespread in North America, breeding from Canada to Mexico (AOU 1983). The nominate *subis* breeds throughout much of southern Canada, south through the eastern United States, west to Montana and central Texas, central parts of the Plains states, western Oklahoma, southern Florida and the highlands of central Mexico. The race *hesperia* replaces *subis* in Baja California, the lowlands of southern Arizona, western coastal Sonora and Tiburon Island. The race *arboricola* breeds in the western mountainous parts of North America.

These are generally common birds, reaching (probably artificially) high densities when they nest in martin houses. Their numbers have probably increased greatly since humans started to provide nest sites for them. Bartel (1959, cited in Graber *et al.* 1972) recorded urban densities of 13–29 birds per 100 acres at one site between 1936 and 1959, and Graber *et al.* (1972)

recorded up to 42 birds per 100 acres in southern Illinois. They are often locally distributed, however, and are absent from extensive areas. The species is affected severely by adverse weather: in 1966 the population in the Midwest crashed when spring temperatures remained below freezing (Graber *et al.* 1972), and declines have been reported after hurricanes. Purple Martins also suffer from competition with Starlings, House Sparrows and House Wrens (e.g. Brown 1981). Populations are increasing in eastern and central States (Robbins *et al.* 1986), but declines have been noted in the middle of the continent.

MIGRATION The nominate race *subis* migrates via Central America, the Florida Keys, Bahamas and Greater Antilles south to the Amazon Basin, southern and eastern Brazil, northern Bolivia and coastal northern Argentina. Their presence in Guiana and Surinam, however, is uncertain (Mees 1985). Migrants are most commonly seen along the coast and islands, rather than inland. It is present in the east Andes up to 4000 m (13,000 ft) from August to December, and in southern Venezuela from September to April; it has also been recorded from Ecuador. The races *hesperia* and *arboricola* have also been recorded on migration in Mexico and Central America; their winter range is unknown but may also be in Brazil and Bolivia. Purple Martins have been recorded casually north to the Pribilof Islands, Alaska, the central Yukon, northwestern Ontario and northern Nova Scotia. Individuals have appeared in Bermuda and the British Isles.

FORAGING AND FOOD Purple Martins alternate gliding in circles on outstretched wings for short periods with flapping flight. They appear not to be so manoeuvrable as smaller swallows and frequently use the tail when turning (Blake 1948). Groups forage loosely together, usually flying high, some 30–60 m (100–200 ft) above the ground. Beal's (1918) analysis of stomach contents revealed that the adults eat mainly Hymenoptera (some 23% of the diet), especially ants and wasps but also some drone bees. They also frequently eat flies, including calypterates and tipulids, hemipteran bugs, beetles, moths and butterflies and dragonflies. Other items in the diet include spiders, mayflies and grasshoppers. Johnston (1967) also recorded the diet from stomach analyses: he found that beetles were important prey throughout the summer, while flies formed two-thirds of the diet from April to June and Hymenoptera formed most of the diet in August; hemipteran bugs were also important prey in June. Brown (1981) recorded several cicadas being eaten. A study of the nestling diet in Alberta revealed that mainly dragonflies, butterflies and hoverflies were eaten (Walsh 1978). Although they usually feed on the wing, Purple Martins have been seen picking up ants and other insects on the ground (Bent 1942).

SOCIAL ORGANISATION Once a relatively solitary bird, the Purple Martin now frequently nests in groups owing to the provision by humans of high-density martin houses. The average group size in several studies has only six to eight, but large groups, even one of 250–300 pairs, have been reported (Allen and Nice 1952). In natural sites, the martins breed in single pairs or small groups, depending on the availability of holes. Up to 20 nests per tree have been recorded (Allen and Nice 1952). After the breeding season, they can form large flocks and roosts of sometimes several thousand individuals; one roost in Argentina contained about 5,000 birds.

SOCIOSEXUAL BEHAVIOUR Martins arrive early in spring, about two months before they start laying, perhaps because of competition between males for females and nesting opportunities (Rohwer and Niles 1977). The males return to the breeding sites before the females, and older birds before first-years. On arrival, males set up territories, and subsequently females visit them and choose a site and a male. Pairs become established after a few hours to a few days. A pair defends an area around the nest, which may include more than one 'room' in a bird house, but this area decreases during the breeding season. Males display and sing to proclaim possession of a territory. The Claiming-Reclaiming display involves flying from the nest, gliding around, re-entering the house, turning and singing in the entrance (Johnston and Hardy 1962). Aggressive behaviour involves Head Forward Thrust displays, Gaping, Bill-snapping, Lunging and physical fighting; the retreating bird uses a High-Up display (Bitterbaum 1986; see page 21). The male sometimes defends a larger area than the female, and a few males are polygynous. Copulations appear to take place mainly at night (Brown 1980), but extra-pair copulations are often attempted during the day (Brown 1978d). Males vary in the frequency with which they guard their mates from 0% to 100% while the mate is gathering nest material (Morton 1987). While guarding, they erect their bright crown feathers and call at and attack approaching males. Young males lack the bright violet-blue plumage of older males and resemble females: in this way, the young male may gain access to breeding and feeding areas and preferred perching sites without being attacked by dominant adult males (Rohwer and Niles 1979; Brown 1984).

BREEDING Breeding starts early, eggs being laid from April through to July, later in the north than in the south of the range (Bent 1942). Only one brood is usually reared, but pairs are occasionally double-brooded (Brown 1978b). Only rarely does the Purple Martin use natural tree holes and crevices in cliffs for nesting in the eastern parts of its range. Humans have long encouraged them, at first because of their use in chasing off predators, but later for aesthetic reasons. First native Indians and then slaves on the southern plantations would put out hollow gourds for the martins to nest in; nowadays nearly all martins nest in martin houses provided by humans, which may contain many individual nestboxes. A few have been recorded nesting in holes under eaves, in walls, or bridges. Western birds still use natural cavities in trees. In the deserts of the southwest, they use holes in saguaros, and the montane race uses old woodpecker holes in aspens, spruce and firs. The female collects most of the material for the nest, but the male collects green leaves, which may be part of a copulation display (Morton 1987). Other material, such as twigs, feathers, paper, straw, shreds of bark and string, is also used. Mud and sticks are used to make a mat or wall near the entrance, sloping towards the rear of the box, which may serve to shelter the nest. Fresh green leaves are added to the nest during incubation; these may be insecticidal or may provide moisture for the eggs.

The clutch ranges from two to eight eggs, averaging four to six; first-year birds lay smaller clutches. The eggs are pure matt white and measure 24.7 × 17.4 mm (23–27 × 15.9–20; weight 3.9). They are incubated for about 16 days by the female only. The male guards the nest while the female goes off to feed. The eggs often hatch asynchronously. Both parents feed the young, which fledge at about 28 days. The parents are unable to recognise their nestlings or fledglings (Brown 1979); they gather together their newly fledged young in areas around the nest site, on wires or other convenient perches, but the broods sometimes accidentally mix (Brown 1978c). The young return to the nest to roost for a few days after fledging, then congregate with the adults in large pre-migratory roosts which can number hundreds or thousands of individuals.

Estimates of fledging success vary from over 80% of the original clutch in Texas to about 30% in Michigan (Allen and Nice 1952; Brown 1978a). Nestling production is affected adversely by bad weather (and hence scarce food supplies) and nest parasites (e.g. Moss and Camin 1970). Most individuals breed for two or three seasons, but one lived to an age of eight years (Allen and Nice 1952).

VOICE This is a highly vocal swallow, which uses a variety of different calls (Brown 1984; Bitterbaum 1986). Females give 'choo' calls when leading their brood. Both sexes use the 'zwrack' call as an alarm, whereas mainly males use the 'hee-hee' call during territorial defence. 'Zweet' calls are used when the martins are alarmed or excited: for example if an intruder approaches a male's mate, the male gives this call. The most commonly used call is the 'cher', which is usually accompanied by flips or shakes of the body and wings; it is used in many contexts, including courtship and greetings between neighbours. 'Chortle' calls are given in similar situations but indicate a greater level of excitement. The male croak song is uttered during courtship and other sexual contexts, and the female uses a chortle song in the same situations. Around dawn, martins fly over the nest site, using a mixture of cher and chortle calls and croak and chortle songs. Males also have a subsong, uttered towards the end of the breeding season. Bitterbaum (1986) also recorded a rattle call used between mates when one approached too closely. Brown (1984) documented geographical variation in the structure of the calls: the montane and desert birds have similar calls, and both differ from the nominate race.

DESCRIPTION The Purple Martin is one of the few swallows with clear differences in plumage between age classes and between the sexes. The adult male is a uniform metallic violet/steel-blue, the feathers being sooty-grey at the base with glossy tips. The underwing-coverts and axillaries are dark sooty-grey. The lesser and median wing-coverts are also glossy violet-blue, but the rest of the wings and the tail are sooty-black with little gloss on the wings. The tail is moderately forked. There are concealed tufts of white feathers on the sides of the lower back and the upper margins of the sides. The bill is black, and the eyes and legs and feet are dark brown. Adult females are much duller, the dark bases of the feathers being more exposed. The forehead, and sometimes the fore part of the crown, is sooty-grey. The feathers of the forehead are greyish with dusky central spots. The lores are dusky, and the ear-coverts are dusky with a violet-blue sheen. The sides and back of the neck are greyish, the hindneck having an indistinct greyish band across it. The chin, throat, upper breast, sides and flanks are sooty-grey, but the feathers of the throat and upper breast have pale margins. The lower breast, abdomen and undertail-coverts are pale greyish-white with narrow sooty-grey streaks (the undertail-coverts are often sooty-grey with white on the margins of the feathers). The axillaries and underwing-coverts are dark sooty-grey, the coverts near the edge of the wing having white margins. Juvenile males and females resemble each other, but the female has more grey on the head. The juveniles are sooty- or greyish-brown above, with grey on the head and a grey nuchal band, and a faint greenish-blue gloss on the mantle, back, scapulars and rump; below, they are white with mouse-grey on the chin, throat, breast, sides and tibiae, while the feathers of the chin, breast and abdomen have narrow dusky shaft streaks. After the first moult, the male is

darker with more steel-blue on his upperparts but with grey chin, throat, breast and sides and a whitish abdomen; he closely resembles the adult female. The female is duller, with less gloss and whiter underparts; the feathers of the anterior underparts have whitish margins, and the rest of the underparts are whiter than on the male. The autumn moult starts in late July to August, after the breeding season but during the southward migration. It is interrupted while the martins migrate over the Gulf and Central America and is completed in the winter quarters (Niles 1972). First-year and older males complete the moult sooner than females, and juveniles do not moult their primaries until on the winter grounds.

Measurements Length 19 cm (7½"). Wing of male 134–153 (mean 145), of female 136–147 (mean 141.7); tail of male 65–78 (mean 74), of female 64–76 (mean 69); fork 14–21 (mean 17.9); bill 13.1–15.4 (mean 14.3); tarsus 15–15.9 (mean 15.4). Weight 48–64 (mean 56).

RACES Throughout the range, males are uniformly blue, but females in the southwestern deserts are paler than those in the east and in the mountains (Johnston 1966). Thus, the male of the race *hesperia* resembles male *subis*; but the female is paler than female *subis*, more extensively white below, with a greyish-white chin and throat, greyish-white margins to the chest feathers, more extensive greyish-white on the forehead, and a distinct greyish-white collar. Both sexes are smaller than *subis* (wing of male 132–147, of female 132–140). The race *arboricola* is the largest form (wing of male 146–157, of female 141–154), and, as those of *hesperia*, the females are whiter than *subis* on the forehead and underparts.

23 GREY-BREASTED MARTIN
Progne chalybea (Gmelin)
Alternative name: White-bellied Martin

Plate 8

Hirundo chalybea Gmelin, 1789, Syst. Nat., ed. 2, 1, p. 1026: Cayenne.

Progne chalybea macrorhamphus (Vieillot), 1817, Paraguay (*domestica* auct. occupied, Brooke 1974).

FIELD CHARACTERS This is a large swallow. The male has steel-blue upperparts, grey throat and breast and white abdomen. The female closely resembles the female Purple

Martin (22), but is whiter below and has a browner forehead. The juvenile resembles the Brown-chested Martin (21), but lacks the latter's breast-band. It frequents open or wooded lowland country, usually nesting alone or in loose groups.

HABITAT Grey-breasted Martins frequent lowland areas of open water, swamps and rivers, large clearings, forest clearings, lowland pine ridges, lowland woodland forest, coastal mangroves, savannas, and, especially, villages and towns. In Brazil, it is associated more with wooded areas than is the Brown-chested Martin (Belton 1985).

DISTRIBUTION AND POPULATION This species replaces the similar Purple Martin as the breeding representative of this super-species in Central America and northern South America, although *chalybea* may overlap the range of the race *sinaloae* of the Snowy-bellied Martin (24). The nominate race breeds in Mexico on both coastal slopes and on offshore islands, up to ca 1500 m (5000 ft), from Nayarit in the west and Tamaulipas in the east, south through Central America and northern South America in Colombia, Venezuela, Trinidad (but not Tobago) and the Guianas to western Ecuador and northwestern Peru on the Pacific coast and, east of the Andes, to eastern Peru, eastern Bolivia, northern Argentina and northern Brazil south of the Rio Negro and the Amazon. The southern race *macrorhamphus* breeds from eastern Bolivia and central and eastern Brazil south to Paraguay and northeastern Argentina and Uruguay. The two races intergrade in Brazil.

This is a common martin throughout most of its range, but it tends to be locally distributed and is absent from large areas of forest and other unsuitable habitat. It is most abundant in and around human habitation where artificial nest sites are plentiful. It has suffered some declines, though, particularly as a result of introduced House Sparrows taking over nest sites (e.g. Daguerre 1922) and the population on Trinidad is considered vulnerable.

MIGRATION Grey-breasted Martins winter in the northern parts of the breeding range, but their movements are poorly known. The nominate race seems to be partly migratory in the north. It is common in winter from Costa Rica and Panama south to northern Bolivia and central Brazil, but is less common at this time in the more northerly parts of the range, especially on the Caribbean slopes of Central America, north of Costa Rica. Wetmore *et al.* (1984) suggested that there are seasonal move-

ments of this species in Panama. In Honduras it makes erratic movements in autumn and winter (Russell 1964), and it is resident in Nicaragua (Howell 1972) and Trinidad (Bitterbaum 1986). Martins are partial migrants in southwestern Ecuador, being more common in January–June, when they are breeding (Marchant 1958). It is casual in southern Texas. The southern race migrates across the range of *chalybea* at least as far north as Venezuela, Surinam and Curaçao and perhaps in Central America (Eisenmann and Haverschmidt 1970). Around Buenos Aires and in Rio Grande do Sul it is present only during the breeding season (Sclater and Hudson 1888; Belton 1985), but further north some remain over winter (Mitchell 1957).

FORAGING AND FOOD Grey-breasted Martins glide about half the time they are in flight, interspersing gliding with fast flapping flight when chasing insects. When foraging, they fly mainly at medium heights, over open grassland, low vegetation and water, but also occasionally around trees. Three stomach contents of *macrorhamphus* in Brazil contained large flies, beetles, wasps and bees, heteropteran bugs and plant bugs (Moojen *et al.* 1941), and migrants in Surinam contained froghoppers, braconid Hymenoptera, ants and dragonflies (Eisenmann and Haverschmidt 1970). In stomachs of Argentinian birds, there were cassid and lamelicornid beetles, penta-tomid bugs, culicid flies, lacewings, Hymenoptera, moths and Orthoptera (Zotta 1936). Birds from Panama contained Diptera and Hymenoptera (Hallinan 1924). In northern Venezuela, I recorded half of the items in the diet of adults as Hymenoptera, mainly winged ants, with dragonflies, butterflies and termites each making up a tenth of the diet; flies, beetles, bugs and ant-lions were also taken. In a study of the nestlings' diet, about three-quarters of the prey items brought to the nest were winged ants, but the most important prey in terms of weight were dragonflies and butterflies (Dyrcz 1984); a few plant bugs and flies, especially hoverflies, were also taken. Hartley (1917) recorded flying ants, termites, ant-lions and dragonflies being brought to the nest. Grey-breasted Martins occasionally forage on the ground on locally abundant sources of insects (Slud 1964).

SOCIAL ORGANISATION These martins are territorial, defending a small area around the nest: fights between territory-owners and intruders are frequent. They nest singly or in loose groups, depending on the availability of nest sites. After breeding, they gather in pre-migratory flocks or communal roosts and will join groups of other martins. Flocks of several hundred birds have been recorded.

SOCIOSEXUAL BEHAVIOUR Grey-breasted Martins have several displays (Bitterbaum 1986; and see pages 20–21). The male defends his nest site against intruders. In agonistic encounters he uses the Head Forward Thrust display, with the feathers of the cheeks and crest raised, and sometimes Gapes. This can lead to the resident bird Lunging at the intruder, and a fight on the territory or in the air can ensue. Females also fight, but only at the time pairs are forming. The male uses the Claiming-Reclaiming display to advertise his territory and attract a female; he flies in a circle or a short direct flight from the nest, then re-enters, sits at the entrance and sings. During courtship the female utters a 'cree' call and quivers her wings before the male mounts. These birds also use the Gaping display between mates and the High-Up displays when alarmed. Where they are resident all year, the members of a pair stay together in the vicinity of their nest site (Bitterbaum 1986).

BREEDING In Central America and northernmost South America, the breeding season extends from March or April to June or July. In Panama it is apparently longer, from February to early August (Wetmore et al. 1984). In the southern parts of the range breeding has been recorded from September to December, although Mitchell (1957) reported that a pair was nesting in May in Brazil. Hartley (1917) stated that there were two broods a year in Guiana, but it seems unlikely that a pair would usually have time to rear two broods. Any available cavities such as old woodpecker holes in trees, cavities in cliffs, on corners of beams, under piers and jetties, under the eaves or in roofs of buildings, in drainpipes or in bird houses are used as nest sites. In savanna areas, martins use old arboreal termite nests. Like the Purple Martin, this species frequents towns and villages, breeding in churches, houses and other buildings. The nests are made of a few grass stems, sticks, straw, string, cloth or any other fibrous material. Like the Purple Martin, the Grey-breasted Martin brings green leaves to the nest (Dyrcz 1984). According to Sclater and Hudson (1888), the birds will use mud and straw to make an entrance hole smaller.

Estimates of clutch size vary. Sclater and Hudson (1888) and Hudson (1920) stated that five was usual in Argentina, but Pereyra (1969) noted two or three eggs per clutch. In northern South America and Central America, clutches contain two to four or five eggs. In Dyrcz's (1984) study, however, clutches consisted of two to four eggs, with a mean of 3.3. The eggs are white and measure 23.3 × 16.1 mm (21.4–26.3 × 15–17.1; weight 3.18). The incubation periods for three clutches in Panama were 16, 16 and 18 days respectively, and Hartley (1917) recorded periods of 15–16 days. The female alone incubates, but both parents feed the young. Hatching can be asynchronous. The nestling period is 25–28 days. The young of one brood remained near the nest for a few days after fledging (Dyrcz 1984). Hartley (1917) noted that the nestlings fledged at 22 days but returned to the nest for a few nights. They were fed by the parents for a week or more after fledging. At one nest, however, the young were 28 or more days old when they fledged.

VOICE Bitterbaum (1986) recorded several calls. The 'cheur' call is a contact call between members of a pair or a flock. A 'rattle' call is also heard between mates. The 'cree' is a staccato call uttered by the female during courtship and by birds retreating from an opponent. The 'zwat' is used during agonistic encounters. The 'zurr' is characteristic of aerial fights, but it is also used as an alarm call when a predator appears, whereas the 'krack' call is used mainly when mobbing predators. Territory-owners also utter a 'cluck' call when intruders appear. The song is a short warbling series of notes, and is heard when the male advertises his territory and when intruders appear.

DESCRIPTION The adult male is a large swallow with dark steel-blue or violaceous steel-blue upperparts, including the scapulars and lesser and median wing-coverts. The lores and sides of the head, chin, throat, breast, sides and outer parts of the flanks are grey-brown or sooty-grey, the chin and throat being paler. The feathers of the breast usually have greyish-white tips. On some there is a patch of steel-blue of varying size on the sides of the breast. The rest of the underparts are pure white. The longer undertail-coverts have dusky shafts. The axillaries and underwing-coverts are deep sooty-grey. The wings and tail are black with a faint blue gloss, and the tail is moderately forked. The bill is black, the eyes are brown and the legs and feet are blackish or dusky brown. The female is duller, with less steel-blue gloss, especially on the head, and has a paler grey chin and throat. The first-year male is like the adult female. Juveniles of both sexes are similar to adult females, but duller, with dark greyish-sooty upperparts and little if any gloss; the underparts are grey towards the front and white towards the rear; the inner webs of the outer tail feathers have a dull whitish or pale grey subterminal spot, and the sides and flanks sometimes have a pale brown tinge. The moult takes place after the breeding season north and south of the Equator,

although the relation between the two is unclear at the Equator (Eisenmann 1959).

Measurements Length 17 cm (6¾"). Wing of male 124–141 (mean 131.8), of female 118–137 (mean 130.4); tail of male 58–74 (mean 63.9), of female 54–69 (mean 62); fork of male 11.5–19.5 (mean 15.1), of female 9–16 (mean 12.7); bill 14–15.3 (mean 14.8); tarsus 14–15.4 (mean 14.5). Weight 33.5–50 (mean 41.5).

RACES The nominate race is smaller than the southern race *macrorhamphus* (wing of male 137–144, of female 135–142). The latter tend to have a paler throat and breast, and juvenile *macrorhamphus* have paler edgings on the breast. Nominate *chalybea* is occasionally melanistic, with a blue-black breast. Hybrids with the race *elegans* of the Southern Martin (25) and with *sinaloae*, a race of the Snowy-bellied Martin, have been recorded (Holt 1926).

24 SNOWY-BELLIED MARTIN
Progne dominicensis (Gmelin)
Alternative name: Caribbean Martin

Plate 8

Hirundo dominicensis Gmelin, 1789, Syst. Nat., 1, pt. 2, p. 1025: Hispaniola.

Progne dominicensis cryptoleuca Baird, 1865, Cuba and Florida Keys?; type from Remedios, Cuba.

Progne dominicensis sinaloae Nelson, 1898, Plomosas, Sinaloa.

The races of this species have been considered to be races of the Purple Martin (22) or separate species (Zimmer 1955; Bond 1971; AOU 1983). However, Snowy-bellied Martins breed sympatrically with Purple Martins in western Mexico so they are probably not conspecific (Davis and Miller 1962). Rather, races of the Snowy-bellied Martin are intermediate between Purple and Grey-breasted Martins (23). Thus *cryptoleuca* males resemble *subis* males but *cryptoleuca* females resemble *chalybea* females. The Mexican race, *sinaloae*, is certainly close to the West Indian *dominicensis* and these forms at least are most probably conspecific; and I believe *cryptoleuca* is sufficiently similar to be included in this species, too.

FIELD CHARACTERS This is a large swallow, the male having steel-blue upperparts and breast contrasting with a white abdomen and undertail-coverts. The female has more grey-brown in the plumage. They are very similar to other members of the *Progne* group, but they have a more sharply defined white belly. They are most like Grey-breasted Martins, but have more blue-black on the flanks. They generally frequent open country, and are fairly solitary swallows.

HABITAT The preferred habitat is open and semi-open situations, near water, sea-

coasts, cliffs or towns. The race *sinaloae* frequents pine oak associations and semi-open habitat in mountainous areas.

DISTRIBUTION AND POPULATION The breeding range of this martin is restricted to Mexico, Cuba and the West Indies (AOU 1983; Phillips 1986). The nominate race *dominicensis* breeds in the Greater Antilles in Jamaica, Hispaniola, Ile à Vache, Mona, Puerto Rico, Vieques, the Virgin Islands, Lesser Antilles (but not all of the islands in the Leeward group) and Tobago. It is absent from Cuba and the Isle of Pines, where it is replaced by the race *cryptoleuca*. The race *sinaloae* breeds on the western slopes of the Sierra Madre Occidental between about 700 and 2000 m (2300–6600 ft) in southwestern Chihuahua, eastern Sonora south through Sinaloa, northwestern Jalisco and northern Nayarit to central Michoacan. It occurs nearer the coast than the nominate race of the Purple Martin, and to the east and north of the race *hesperia* of the latter species and the nominate race of the Grey-breasted Martin.

MIGRATION The West Indies race *dominicensis* is absent from its breeding range in November and December, but its wintering range is not known; it presumably migrates to South America. There are casual or accidental records from the Bahamas and it is an uncommon transient in the Cayman Islands from April to May (Johnston *et al.* 1971). The winter range of *cryptoleuca* is also unknown, but it is absent from its breeding area from September to January; it is quite likely that it winters in Brazil; it occurs casually in southern Florida. The Mexican race *sinaloae* has been recorded on migration in Mexico, casually in northern Guatemala and accidentally in Bermuda; its wintering range is not known but is probably in northern or central South America. In the West Indies, Snowy-bellied Martins are generally common and widespread breeding birds; they have probably benefited from the presence of artificial nest sites. However, the population on Tobago is considered vulnerable.

FORAGING AND FOOD Snowy-bellied Martins often feed high up, but will forage low over fields and follow cattle to catch insects disturbed by them. The flight consists of periods of gliding alternated with gentle flapping. An analysis of twelve stomachs revealed a diet of 24% heteropteran bugs of the family Pentatomidae, 8% beetles, 26% flies, 33% Hymenoptera (mainly wasps and a few chalcids), and 8% dragonflies; these martins have also been seen to eat termites (February–May: Wetmore 1916). Danforth (1935b) recorded damselflies, a small coreid bug, bits of beetles and other insects in a stomach of *cryptoleuca*. In other studies of *dominicensis*, Danforth (1929, 1935a) recorded mainly Pentatomidae in one stomach; in three others, 35% hoverflies, 25% wasps, 19% carabids, a few bean-flea beetles *Ceratoma ruficornis* and a dragonfly; and, in a fifth, hydrophilid beetles and hemipteran bugs.

BEHAVIOUR Pairs nest singly or in loose groups. Thirty pairs have been recorded nesting in one brick chimney (Wetmore 1916). These birds use the typical martin displays (Bitterbaum 1986; and see pages 20–21). Males defend a territory and attack intruders using the Head Forward Thrust display, continuously flicking their wings and tail, Bill Snapping, Lunging and sometimes physically fighting. Birds retreating from an opponent use the High-Up display. The male advertises the territory with a Claiming-Reclaiming display, circling or performing a figure of eight or double lap over the nest before returning to the nest and singing from the entrance. Members of a pair use the Gaping display to each other.

BREEDING In Puerto Rico, these martins prepare for breeding in February but do not lay until May, while fledglings are still being fed in August (Wetmore 1916). In Hispaniola and the Lesser Antilles, the breeding season lasts from March to June (Bond 1943; Pinchon 1963). Nesting has been recorded in June and July in Tobago (ffrench 1980). Only one brood is raised. Cavities in trees, chimneys, belfries, houses and other buildings, hollow pipes, caves and cliffs are all used as nesting sites. Nests have also been recorded in drainage pipes and in cracks in an air-conditioning system of a hotel (Balat and Gonzalez 1982). In the West Indies, at least, many pairs nest in artificial rather than natural sites. The nest is made of fine fibres such as grass, silk, paper, twigs and leaves. The eggs are white and measure 23.9 × 16.4 mm (21.4–24.5 × 15.9–17; weight 3.24). The clutch size is four to six in the West Indies, but only two on Tobago (ffrench 1980).

VOICE The calls are similar to those of the Purple and Grey-breasted Martins (Bitterbaum 1986). The 'zwoot' is a contact call between members of a pair or flock mates. The 'kweet' is also a contact call but is often used during aggressive exchanges. The 'wheet' is used when a bird is alarmed, as when another martin flies near the territory. The 'croot' is uttered during courtship and by birds moving off. The 'peak' call is a high-pitched alarm call to predators, whereas the 'wrack' is used mainly when mobbing predators. The territorial song is a warbling, beginning and ending with a sharp or inflected syllable.

DESCRIPTION The adult male of this large swallow is mostly a uniform glossy steel-blue or violaceous steel-blue, including the scapulars and lesser and median wing-coverts, sides and flanks. The median part of the breast, the abdomen and the under-tail-coverts, however, are pure white, contrasting strongly with the rest of the plumage. The longer undertail-coverts sometimes have a central patch of dusky grey, and the lateral undertail-coverts some-times have dusky grey outer webs with white edges. The underwing-coverts and axillaries are grey-brown. The wings and tail are black with a bluish gloss, and the tail is moderately forked. The bill is black, the eyes are brown and the legs and feet are brownish-black. The adult female resem-bles the male, but the forehead is sooty-brown, the wings and tail have a greenish-blue gloss, the sides of the head and neck are grey-brown or sooty, the ear-coverts with a steel-blue gloss, the malar region, chin, throat, breast, sides, flanks, axillaries and underwing-coverts are sooty-grey or grey-brown, the chin and throat somewhat paler, and the breast feathers with pale grey tips. The first-year male is like the adult female. Juveniles of both sexes are also like the adult female, but have even less steel-blue gloss.

Measurements Length 17 cm (6¾"). Wing of male 134–149 (mean 143), of female 130–148 (mean 140); tail of male 66–79 (mean 72.8), of female 65–76 (mean 70.4); fork 14–22 (mean 18.7); bill 14.1–15.6 (mean 14.8); tarsus 13.5–15 (mean 14.3). Weight 38–42 (mean 40).

RACES Individuals of the race *sinaloae* are smaller (wing of male 132–144, of female 130–136) than *dominicensis* and have a broader, whiter abdominal area, contrasting more with the dark throat and upper breast, and purer white undertail-coverts, although these sometimes have shaft streaks. Males of the race *cryptoleuca* (wing 140–145) are like Purple Martin males, but there is a broad white band across the lower abdo-men (although this is always concealed) and the tail is relatively longer and more deeply forked. Female *cryptoleuca* are similar to but darker than female *dominicensis*, having sooty-brown upperparts with steel-blue margins to the feathers (except on the forehead and front of the crown), a green-ish-blue gloss on the wings and tail, grey-brown or sooty-grey from the sides of the head to the breast, sides and on the axil-laries and under wing-coverts, and white on the rest of the underparts; the undertail-coverts have dark shaft smudges, and there is usually some shaft streaking on the breast and sides.

25 SOUTHERN MARTIN
Progne modesta Gould

Plate 8

Hirundo concolor Gould, 1837, Proc. Zool. Soc. Lond., pt. 5, p. 22: Galápagos Archi-pelago; type from James Island. *Progne modesta* Gould, 1838, in Darwin, Zool. Voy. Beagle, pt. 3, pl. 5, new name for *concolor*.

Progne modesta elegans Baird, 1865, Rio Bermejo, Argentina.

Progne modesta murphyi Chapman, 1925, cliffs near Talara, coast of northwestern Peru.

All three races of this species have been elevated to specific status by some authors (AOU 1983), but they resemble each other closely and *murphyi* is intermediate between the other two races, suggesting that these are now isolated and diverging populations of a single, perhaps once widespread, species. Southern Martins are sympatric with a race of the Grey-breasted Martin (23), *macrorhamphus*, in the southern Chaco, suggesting that they are separate species, but hybrids between *elegans* and *macrorhamphus* have been reported from Cordoba (Eisenmann and Haverschmidt 1970; Short 1975), indicating a close relationship between these forms although not necessarily meaning that they are con-specific. Until more information is available, *elegans*, *murphyi* and *modesta* are probably best regarded as separate from other forms of *Progne*.

FIELD CHARACTERS Southern Martins are large swallows with a uniform steel-blue plumage. Females and juveniles are sooty-black above and brown below. They differ from the other *Progne* martins in being darker, with duskier underparts. They occur in open and partly wooded country, usually alone or in small groups.

HABITAT Southern Martins on the Galapagos Isles frequent a variety of habitats: forested areas, mountain tops up to 3200 ft (970 m), the shore and coastal lagoons; they feed low over the ground and around houses on Albemarle. The Peruvian race *murphyi* occurs around cliffs, fields and villages and lowland woodland. The race *elegans* frequents pampas, chaco scrub, dry forest and steppe, as well as human habitation, up to 2600 m (8600 ft).

DISTRIBUTION AND POPULATION This martin has a disjunct distribution on the Galapagos, in Peru and in southern South America (Harris 1975; Fjeldså and Krabbe 1989). The race *modesta* occurs on the central and southern islands of the Galapagos archipelago (James, Albemarle, Duncan, Daphne, Seymour, Indefatigable, Barrington, Chatham, Charles and Hood, Floreana and North Chatham). The most widespread race, *elegans*, breeds from the highlands of Bolivia (north to Cochabamba) and Paraguay south to western and central Argentina from southern Buenos Aires Province south to Chubut in northeastern Patagonia. In Peru, the third race, *murphyi*, is restricted to the coast south to the Department of Ica (Hacienda Ocucaje), rarely inland to 1800 m (5900 ft) in Arequipa. The Galapagos race is commonest on Albemarle, although it is not very common anywhere (Gifford 1919); Harris (1973) described it as occurring in small numbers, and it is rare on Hood, where it is not resident. In Peru, *murphyi* is also rare (Koepcke 1983). The race *elegans* is fairly common (Wetmore 1926; Fjeldså and Krabbe 1989).

MIGRATION Although the full extent of the wintering range is unknown, *elegans* has been recorded in winter in north and northwestern Brazil, eastern Peru, and as far north as Colombia, Surinam and Panama in small numbers; individuals have turned up in southern Florida and the Falkland Islands, and there are a few records of individuals wintering in Argentina (Guerra 1969; Phillips 1986; Fjeldså and Krabbe 1989). The Peruvian race occurs casually in northernmost Chile and numbers increase in southern Peru from January to April. The Galapagos race is not known to migrate (Swart 1931).

FOOD AND BEHAVIOUR The flight is slow and weak, consisting mainly of gliding. Southern Martins often feed high up, but will also skim over open ground, for example when chasing dragonflies. In the Galapagos Isles, adults have been seen feeding themselves and their nestlings on butterflies and moths (Gifford 1919; Beebe 1924). Two stomachs of *elegans* in Argentina contained Lepidoptera and Hymenoptera (Mnioidae, ants, Scolidae and ichneumonids), and one in Surinam contained large dragonflies (Eisenmann and Haverschmidt 1970). Pairs nest singly or in loose groups, depending on the availability of nest sites.

BREEDING Southern Martins of the race *elegans* are present in the breeding areas between August/September and February/March (Pereyra 1969). On the Galapagos, both birds in breeding condition and nests have been recorded in March (Gifford 1919). For nesting sites, the martins use crevices in cliffs, trees, holes under roofs or in walls, or holes made in river banks by other species such as the Burrowing Parrot *Conurus patachonicus* in Patagonia (Sclater and Hudson 1888; Hudson 1920). The nest is shallow, and is made of grass stems or twigs with a lining of a few feathers (Gifford 1919). On the Galapagos Isles, two clutches were of two and three eggs (Gifford 1919); in Argentina the clutch size is three (Pereyra 1969). The eggs are white and measure 22.9 × 15 mm (22.3–23.5 × 15; weight 2.7). Incubation and nestling periods are not known.

VOICE The calls are similar to those of Purple (22) and Grey-breasted Martins. There is a short warbling song; a short, harsh contact call; and a high-pitched alarm call.

DESCRIPTION The male is similar to the male Purple Martin, but is slightly smaller. It also lacks the concealed white patch of feathers on the sides and flanks. The upperparts, including the scapulars and lesser and median wing-coverts, as well as the underparts, are a uniform glossy dark violaceous steel-blue. The underwing-coverts and axillaries are dark sooty-grey. The wings and the slightly forked tail are black with a slight bluish or greenish gloss. The bill is black, the eyes are brown and the legs and feet are brownish-black or dusky brown. The female, which is somewhat smaller than the male, is sooty-black above and dusky brown below (sometimes the underparts have a few pale edgings); the mantle and scapulars are glossed with steel-blue, and the upper-tail-coverts sometimes have narrow pale terminal margins. Many adult females are uniformly dark below and are always darker than the females of other *Progne* species. Juveniles are also sooty-black above and dusky brown below; juvenile males sometimes have a few glossy blue feathers in their otherwise brownish plumage. The continental, migratory, race *elegans* moults after the breeding season, specimens in moult being taken north of the breeding range. The island race *modesta* moults during the breeding period, specimens being in moult between February and May and in breeding condition during March (Eisenmann 1959). **Measurements** Length 15 cm (6"). Wing of male 121–129 (mean 125), of female 115–125 (mean 121); tail of male 61–64 (mean 62.2), of female 55–61 (mean 59); fork 10–14 (mean 12); bill 13.6–14.5 (mean 13.9); tarsus 11–12 (mean 11.7).

RACES The race *murphyi* is larger than nominate *modesta* and is intermediate in colour between the race *elegans* and the race *subis* of Purple Martin: the male is more blue than *subis*, similar to *elegans*, but the female is nearer *subis*, with pale, unmargined underparts and grey-white undertail-coverts. The island race *modesta*, which is the smallest race, is the darkest of the *Progne* superspecies, the males being entirely blue without any white tufts of feathers, and the females being uniformly sooty-brown below. The most widespread race, *elegans*, is large (wing of male 138–143, of female 132–140): males have concealed white on the sides and flanks like *subis*, but duller undertail-coverts and more dusky underparts; female *elegans* have more extensively pale-margined underparts than the females of the other races.

26 BROWN-THROATED SAND MARTIN   Plate 9
Riparia paludicola (Vieillot)
Alternative names: Plain Sand Martin, African Sand Martin

Hirundo paludicola Vieillot, 1817, Nouv. Dict. Hist. Nat., 14, p. 511: South Africa.

Riparia paludicola mauritanica (Meade-Waldo), 1901, Wad Moorbei, Rehamra, Morocco.

Riparia paludicola paludibula (Rüppell), 1835, Gondar Province, Ethiopia (*minor* auct. occupied, Brooke 1975).

Riparia paludicola newtoni Bannerman, 1937, Bambulue, near Bamenda, Cameroons.

Riparia paludicola ducis Reichenow, 1908, western Ruanda.

Riparia paludicola cowani (Sharpe), 1882, Ankáfana Forest, Betsileo, Madagascar.

Riparia paludicola chinensis (Gray), 1830, no locality given, probably Taiwan.

FIELD CHARACTERS The Brown-throated Sand Martin is small, and brown above and grey-white below. It is similar to the Sand (27) and Banded Martins (28), but is smaller, has browner underparts and lacks a breast-band. It is smaller than the crag martins (39–41) and also differs in lacking any white tail patches. It is closely associated with water and is highly gregarious.

HABITAT These martins replace the Sand Martin at low latitudes and thus frequent warmer areas, but otherwise the two species occupy similar habitats. They are often seen at the same sites when the Sand Martin is on its wintering grounds. Brown-throated Sand Martins occur near rivers, streams, lakes, estuaries, sewage works, reedbeds, wetlands and ricefields, but also on grassland at high elevations. They occur over a wide altitudinal range, breeding both in the lowlands and in mountainous country, up to 3000 m (9900 ft) in East Africa and 4600 m (15,200 ft) in northern India.

DISTRIBUTION AND POPULATION This swallow has an extensive breeding range throughout Africa, India, and southern Asia as far as Taiwan and the Philippines, generally south of the range of the Sand Martin; where the two species overlap, the Brown-throated tends to breed at lower elevations. The nominate race occurs in southern Africa as far north as Angola, Zambia and southern Tanzania. Further north, the race *ducis* breeds in eastern Africa in Kenya and Tanzania. In Central and West Africa, the range of the race *paludibula* extends from Ethiopia to Senegal. Three races have restricted ranges: *mauritanica* occurs only in western Morocco (Oued Oum R'bia, Oued Tensift, Oued Sous, with a recent extension of its range near Rabat); *cowani* breeds only in Madagascar, in the east, from 500 to 1800 m (1640–5900 ft); and *newtoni* is found only at about 1100–1400 m (3600–4600 ft) in the mountains near Bamenda in Cameroon and probably the Mambila Plateau in Nigeria. The Asian race *chinensis* is separated from the rest of the species' breeding range by the Middle East region: it occurs in Afghanistan, Pakistan, northern India east to Assam and south to the Bombay region, Bangladesh, Burma, southern Yunnan (Szemao), northwestern Tonkin (Vietnam), Thailand, Laos, Taiwan, and Luzon in the Philippines. There is an isolated population in south-central USSR.

In many parts of its range the Brown-throated Sand Martin is a common breeding bird, but sometimes only locally so, depending on the availability of nest sites. It is generally common in eastern and South Africa and abundant in the valleys of the Vaal and Orange Rivers, but it is less common in Natal, and in Zambia it is most common in the Luangwa and middle Zambezi valleys (Clancey 1964; Benson *et al.* 1971). Milon *et al.* (1973) described the race *cowani* as fairly common in Madagascar. In the northern parts of its range in Africa it is also locally abundant (Urban and Brown 1971; Gore 1981). In Asia, too, it is common in some areas. It does not often nest in artificial sites, but benefits from vertical sand banks in quarries.

MIGRATION Brown-throated Sand Martins are partly or locally migratory, but their movement patterns are unclear (Mackworth-Praed and Grant 1963; Britton 1980). Post-breeding dispersal, particularly away from flooded breeding sites, appears to be the norm, rather than regular migrations. In southern Africa *paludicola* is resident but makes local movements, dispersing after the breeding season. The species is often present for most of the year, but numbers vary, falling in winter. Some long-distance movements are known. Two recoveries of ringed birds indicate movements of 92 km (57 miles) and 181 km (112 miles) (Tree and Earlé 1984). In Zimbabwe, on the Mashonaland highveld, two populations are present, one during the summer, the other during the winter (Tree and Earlé 1984). In northern parts of the range, *paludibula* is often locally absent for part of the year and

numbers also vary locally, suggesting some immigration: thus, in Borgu in Nigeria, it is absent in June and commonest from October to May (Elgood *et al.* 1973); it is a vagrant to the west coast. The races with restricted ranges appear to be resident but may also disperse locally after breeding (Etchécopar and Hüe 1967). In Asia, *chinensis* is known to make local movements between breeding and wintering sites (Ali and Ripley 1972), and the population in south-central USSR is also migratory (Dementev and Gladkov 1968).

FORAGING AND FOOD They generally feed over water, close to the colony when breeding (Serle 1943), at an average height of 14 m (45 ft) (Waugh 1978), though they also skim the surface for low-flying insects. Their flight is slow and fluttering and noticeably less agile than that of the Sand Martin (da Rosa Pinto and Lamm 1958). They often fly late in the evening compared with other swallows (Taylor 1942). The diet consists of small insects. In Asia they are known to eat flies such as mosquitoes and to visit grass fires to feed on the fleeing insects (Ali and Ripley 1972). In one stomach from an African bird, there were small insects such as gnats and also minute beetles (Bannerman 1939). Chapin (1953) found beetles and other insects in stomachs of birds from Zaire. They have also been recorded catching small dragonflies and grasshoppers (Taylor 1942; Maclean 1985).

SOCIAL ORGANISATION Like the Sand Martin, this species is gregarious both during and after breeding. It nests in groups of usually a few pairs but ranging up to several hundred pairs, and it sometimes nests solitarily (Belcher 1941; Clancey 1964; Mackworth-Praed and Grant 1963). The tunnels are dug close together. These martins occasionally share colonies with the Sand Martin. Flocks of more than 50 birds are commonly seen, as are mixed flocks with other hirundine species. It roosts in old breeding holes, or, in winter, in large flocks in reedbeds. Outside the breeding season, flocks can contain hundreds of individuals.

SOCIOSEXUAL BEHAVIOUR The breeding behaviour is probably similar to that of Sand Martins, although it has not been well documented. Broekhuysen and Stanford (1954) noted an apparent copulation on the ground in which the mounting bird first crouched with the head stretched low and forward, then nibbled the second bird's chest and anal feathers, and finally mounted while opening its wings and spreading its tail; an intruder was chased off after the (presumed) male adopted a crouched posture, which may have been a threat. An unsuccessful attempt to copulate in flight has been recorded (Taylor 1942).

BREEDING The breeding season is variable, probably depending on a combination of rainfall, food availability and the risk of nest sites being flooded. Breeding occurs in the dry season in the southern tropics and in the rains (from March to September) in East Africa (Brown and Britton 1980). In southern Africa breeding takes place in the dry season, varying locally (Maclean 1985). In Zimbabwe the peak is from June to September, whereas in the southwest Cape it is from August to February. In northern parts of its range, the peak season is December–February, but in Ethiopia breeding may be at almost any time of the year (Urban and Brown 1971). In Morocco, these martins nest from November–December to February or exceptionally to April (Cramp 1988); in Madagascar, from November to April (Rand 1936; Benson et al. 1976); and in Asia generally from October to February, rarely April and May (Dementev and Gladkov 1968; Ali and Ripley 1972). Tunnels are dug into sandbanks along rivers, by lakes, rain-courses, roads or in pits, old mine dumps or quarries. The tunnel is some 30–80 cm (1–2½ ft) long, often inclined upwards, and ends in an enlarged chamber where the nest, measuring some 11 × 3 cm (4¼ × 1¼ in), is loosely constructed. Occasionally, tunnels dug by other species are used, and one nest in a drainage pipe has been recorded (Tree and Earlé 1984). Both sexes excavate the tunnel, taking turns to dig. One tunnel took about 20 days to complete (Ou-u-kijo 1936). The nest is made of dry grass, hair and other fibres, and is lined with feathers. Serle (1943) described one nest with an outer layer of coarse grass and rootlets, an intermediate layer of rootlets, and an inner layer of feathers.

The eggs are white and ovate, measuring on average 17.2 × 12.3 mm (16.2–18.5 × 11.9–12.7; weight 1.36). The clutch size is usually two to four eggs throughout the range, averaging three, but it is three to five in Madagascar (Rand 1936) and five or six in Assam (Ali and Ripley 1972). Incubation lasts about 12 days and fledging about 20 days. Both sexes incubate and feed the young. The fledglings are dependent on their parents for several days (Oo-u-kijo 1936). One recaptured bird was at least five years old (Irwin 1981).

VOICE The song is a weak high-pitched twitter, often uttered in flight. There is also a harsh contact call, 'svee-svee'. A chittering 'skirr' and harsh weak sounds have been noted from members of *mauritanica* flocks (Cramp 1988), and *chinensis* also has a 'rit' call (Etchécopar and Hüe 1983).

DESCRIPTION This small swallow has olive-brown upperparts, including the crown, with pale fringes to the feathers. The lores are blackish. The chin, throat and breast are grey tinged with brown, becoming off-white on the abdomen and vent. The undertail-coverts and flanks are off-white streaked with grey-brown. The axillaries and under-wing-coverts are grey-brown. The wing-coverts and tertials have grey-brown margins, giving the edge of the wing a barred appearance. The primaries, second-aries, upperwing-coverts and tail feathers are dark brown; the tail is square. The eyes are brown, the bill is black and the legs and feet are brownish. The sexes are alike. Juveniles have buffy tips to the feathers of the upperparts, particularly the rump, buffy edges to the wing-coverts and secondaries, and a narrower margin to the inner prima-ries; the underparts have a sandy or rufes-cent-buff wash, and the feathers along the inner edge of the wing also have buffy tips. The moult starts after the breeding season (Cramp 1988).

Measurements Length 12 cm (4¾"). Wing 97–114 (mean 104.2); tail (square) 49–60 (mean 53.8); bill 7.3–8.8 (mean 8.2); tarsus 8.8–10.8 (mean 10). Weight 11–15 (mean 13.1).

RACES The various races differ in their depth of colour and size; the races from arid areas are paler than those from more humid areas. Even within a race, however, coloration may vary. Thus about one in ten *paludicola* has a brownish abdomen (Maclean 1985). The race *ducis* is the darkest, sometimes with a blackish crown; only its undertail-coverts are white (wing 92–102). In *paludibula*, the upperparts are darker than in *paludicola*; it is also a small race (wing 92–100). The race *newtoni* is darker brown than *paludibula*; the lower breast and abdomen are light brown rather than white, but whiter when freshly moulted. The race *mauritanica* is a small, pale race (wing 97–104); *cowani* is small (wing 87–95) and has a greyish underside with a pale

grey-white throat; and *chinensis* has a pale grey-brown throat and whitish abdomen and is small (wing 90–96).

27 SAND MARTIN   Plate 9
Riparia riparia (Linnaeus)
Alternative name: Bank Swallow (North America)

Hirundo riparia Linnaeus, 1758, Syst. Nat., ed. 10, p. 192: Sweden.

Riparia riparia ijimae (Lönnberg), 1908, Tretiya Padj, Sakjhalin.

Riparia riparia diluta (Sharpe and Wyatt), 1893, Badan River, near the Fortress of Chimkent.

Riparia riparia shelleyi (Sharpe), 1869, Dongola.

FIELD CHARACTERS The Sand Martin has brown upperparts, white underparts and a brown breast-band. It is superficially similar to several other swallow species in its wide range, particularly to juveniles, which are often browner than the adults with short outer tail feathers. The combination of a distinct breast-band and square tail, however, generally distinguishes it. In North America, the Northern Roughwing (6) and juvenile Tree Swallow (7) are most similar, but lack the distinct breast-band. In South America, the Brown-chested Martin (21) is also similar, but much larger. In Africa and Asia, it can be distinguished from the Brown-throated Sand Martin and the crag martin group (39–41) by its clear breast-band contrasting with white underparts. It differs from the Banded Martin (28) in being smaller and lacking any white on the forehead. It is often associated with water and is highly gregarious. The flight is fast.

HABITAT During breeding, Sand Martins frequent mainly riverine areas, lakes and coasts where vertical sand banks are available for nesting, but also use artificial sites such as sand quarries. When not breeding, they feed in open areas such as wetlands, grassland and farmland. They generally avoid built-up and forested areas, but will breed in villages and towns in the USSR (Dementev and Gladkov 1968). They occur across a wide altitudinal range, up to 4500 m (14,850 ft) in the Himalayas (Ali and Ripley 1972) but are typically lowland birds in Europe and North America.

DISTRIBUTION AND POPULATION The Sand Martin has one of the most extensive ranges of any swallow, breeding throughout most of North America, Europe and Asia, to

northern India, southeastern China and the northern islands off the Pacific coast (AOU 1983; Cramp 1988). The nominate race breeds throughout much of North America, except the southwest and Gulf Coast, Europe and locally in North Africa, the Near East to western Iran, Russia north of the Kirghiz Steppes and the Altai, east to Kolyma River, north to about 70°N. The boundaries between *riparia* and the races *ijimae* to the east and *diluta* to the south, however, are not well defined: *ijimae* breeds in northeastern Asia, including the Kamchatka peninsula and the Kurile Islands, south to the Amur River and Hokkaido; *diluta* breeds from the Kirghiz Steppes and the Altai Mountains to eastern Iran, Afghanistan, northern India and southeastern China. The race *shelleyi*, is confined to lower Egypt in the Wadi Natrun, the Delta, Faiyum and Suez Canal region.

The abundance of the species at the breeding grounds is variable from year to year because of the transient nature of the nest sites. In North America, where it is most abundant in Quebec, New Brunswick, the St Lawrence Plain and the eastern Great Lakes Plain and rare west of the coastal Pacific ranges, it has recently decreased in the eastern and central regions but has increased in the west (Robbins *et al.* 1986). Road-building and quarrying may have increased the number of available nest sites in formerly undeveloped or unsuitable breeding areas in some parts of the range, affecting the distribution or abundance of the species (Erskine 1979; Jones 1986a); many colonies are now in quarries and these are often larger than colonies in river banks. In Britain numbers have recently declined dramatically, which may be linked with a drought in the Sahel region of Africa; one colony in Scotland fell from over 900 pairs in 1982 to fewer than 200 in 1984 (Jones 1987a): this came after a decline in the late 1960s, again coinciding with climatic changes south of the Sahara; the population in 1984 was down to less than 10% of its mid 1960s level (Mead 1984), but is now apparently recovering. Marked declines in recent years have occurred in the Netherlands, Poland, Switzerland and Romania, and locally in East and West Germany and Sweden (Cramp 1988).

MIGRATION Sand Martins are migratory, wintering in South America, Africa, India and southeastern Asia. There are only occasional winter records of Sand Martins in the breeding range. In South America the winter range extends mainly east of the Andes, south to eastern Peru, Bolivia (where there are few records), Brazil, northern Argentina and Paraguay, with casual records in northern Chile; it has also recently been observed on the southeast coast of Brazil (Willis and Oniki 1985). In northern South America and Panama it is seen on migration, but some records may be of wintering birds as well. In North America, it migrates throughout the southern states, Central America, the West Indies and northern South America. It is irregular in Florida and transient in Arizona. It is casual or accidental in the Lesser Antilles, the Pribilof, western Aleutian and Commander Islands, Victoria and Melville Islands, northern Manitoba, Aldabra, Barbados and the Galapagos Islands. In South and Central America, it is often commoner as an autumn migrant than as a spring migrant.

There are winter records from throughout Africa, including Madagascar, but the main wintering sites for western and Siberian populations are the Sahel zone and eastern Africa south to Mozambique (Moreau 1962). The Siberian populations extend the furthest south in Africa, large numbers remaining until late May. Although once a scarce visitor, it is now fairly common in southern Africa, where numbers have been increasing since the 1950s (Maclean 1985). The pattern of winter distribution may be changing because of the Sahel drought (Tree 1986a).

The movements of European birds have been extensively studied (Cramp 1988). Early-fledged juveniles wander after leaving their natal colony, visiting other colonies and roosts, whereas adult movements are more directly south to the wintering range (Mead and Harrison 1979a). British and Irish birds migrate through western France, some then moving to the Mediterranean coast of Spain, others going inland to the Coto Doñana area; they cross into Morocco and reach the Sahel by October or early November (Mead and Harrison 1979b). Some birds remain together during the migration and appear to keep to traditional routes (Mead and Harrison 1979b). On the wintering grounds they are apparently nomadic. Many British birds appear to move east and return in spring by a more easterly route than the autumn one, via Tunisia, Italy and eastern France. They start to arrive in Britain in March, adults some three weeks before first-years and males before females (Mead and Harrison 1979a).

The winter range of *ijimae* is not well known, but includes Burma, Thailand and Indochina and it has been recorded as an uncommon winter migrant in India around Bombay, Bihar and Gujarat (Abdulali 1975). It winters in small numbers on the Malay peninsula south to Singapore, and there is one record for Borneo in 1883 (Smythies 1968). This race migrates through eastern China, some wintering in Kwangtung, and has been recorded in Honshu on migration; it is accidental in Alaska. The race *shelleyi* winters along the Red Sea coast, in the Sudan and in the Nile Valley from October to April. The race *diluta* migrates to Pakistan, India south to Bombay and Bihar, and Tonkin; it has been recorded in Egypt in March, April and September (Etchécopar and Hüe 1967) and in Syria on passage in spring (Meinertzhagen 1954), and is accidental in arctic America and Bermuda. In eastern Asia, northern breeders migrate to winter in southern China. The species is a vagrant to New Guinea (Beehler *et al.* 1986).

FORAGING AND FOOD The flight is fast, but involves more gliding and fewer twists and turns than that of the Barn Swallow (42); the wingbeats are shallow and rapid. During breeding the feeding sites are close to the colony, usually some 200 m away when young are being fed (Turner 1980), but this varies from site to site depending on the availability of good hunting areas; in Svensson's (1969) study, birds fed 6 km (3¾ miles) from the colony. They feed at an average height of 15 m (50 ft) (Waugh

1978) over open ground, but low over water in bad weather. They feed singly, in pairs or in flocks, the latter especially in bad weather when feeding on a localised source of prey. Most insects are caught in flight, but are occasionally taken on the ground or from the surface of water (Cramp 1988).

Sand Martins take a wide variety of insect prey (see Glutz von Blotzheim and Bauer 1985, and Cramp 1988 for a detailed list). In North America, in Beal's (1918) study, flies, mainly of the muscid and tipulid families, formed a quarter of the diet. Many beetles and winged ants were also taken, together making up a third of the diet. Mayflies were commonly taken in April, but not at other times. Some plant bugs and a very few crickets and grasshoppers, moths, dragon-flies and caterpillars were also taken. In New York State, Stoner (1936) found that beetles (mainly leaf and dung beetles and weevils) and flies (mainly muscids, crane-flies and hoverflies) each formed a third of the diet, and plant bugs another 18%; other bugs, parasitic Hymenoptera, damselflies, spiders, mayflies, stoneflies, lacewings and crickets were also taken. Adults ate more beetles and fewer flies and plant bugs than they brought to nestlings. In one study in Scotland, flies, mainly acalypterates, were more important, forming 70% of the diet; plant bugs, especially aphids, formed 13% and beetles 11% (Waugh 1979). In my study in Scotland (Turner 1980), nestlings were fed 30% mayflies, with flies (especially Nematocera) 37% and plant bugs 26% forming most of the rest; early in the breeding season, adults took mainly beetles, aphids and small flies (Turner 1982b). In the USSR flies and plant bugs also predominate (Pavlova 1962). Parents bring back 60 prey items per visit on average (Turner 1980).

SOCIAL ORGANISATION Sand Martins are highly colonial, with burrows often only 30 cm (1 ft) apart (Sieber 1980). Discrete colonies are difficult to demarcate but may contain thousands of burrows. The mean colony size, however, is smaller: for example, 42 in Canada and 38 in Britain (Erskine 1979; Morgan 1979; Cramp 1988). Most large colonies are at artificial sites, but some also occur along river banks (e.g. Loske 1983b). After breeding they will form flocks and roosts of hundreds or thousands of individuals (for details of flock and roosting behaviour, see Cramp 1988).

SOCIOSEXUAL BEHAVIOUR The behaviour and breeding biology of Sand Martins have been widely studied (e.g. Stoner 1936; Petersen 1955; Asbirk 1976; Hoogland and Sherman 1976; Sieber 1980; Turner 1980; Kuhnen 1985; and see Glutz von Blotzheim and Bauer 1985, and Cramp 1988). Older birds return to the nest sites before first-years, choosing burrows high on the face of the bank (Sieber 1980). Birds often return to the same site as in the previous year, especially if they bred successfully, while year-lings return to the natal or nearby areas (Freer 1977; Mead 1979a). They are not, however, so site-tenacious as other swallows with more stable nest sites (Freer 1977; Loske 1983a) and may move several kilometres away. One-year-old females are less faithful to a site than are one-year-old males (Persson 1978; Cowley 1979).

New burrows are usually dug each year. Subcolonies form on favoured sites; later birds settle in other areas. Pairs in subgroups are synchronised, but different subgroups are not necessarily so. Sites high up on the cliff face are preferred. The male claims an area and starts digging. When the tunnel is about 30 cm long, he attempts to attract a female. He performs an advertising (Claim-ing-Reclaiming) display from the burrow in which he sings, ruffles the head and throat feathers and vibrates his closed wings; when a female approaches he flies out, still singing (Kuhnen 1985). He also makes circl-ing flights around the burrow, returning each time to the nest hole, calling and either landing or hovering by the entrance to lure the female in. When other females come to the territory of a new pair, the resident female threatens by 'facing', spreading the neck feathers and bill-gaping. The male appeases the female by bristling head feathers and vibrating wings. A threat display is used against intruders: the resi-dent ruffles its neck feathers, utters the Excitement call, and may gape, peck at and chase or even fight with the intruder; fight-ing birds, locked together, sometimes fall to the ground (Petersen 1985; Sieber 1980). Males defend their mates from other males which chase them and attempt extra-pair copulations, forcing them back into the burrow if several males harass them (Beecher and Beecher 1979). Males both mate with one female and attempt to copu-late with other females that appear to be in their fertile period (Jones 1986b). Copu-lations may take place in the burrow, but have been seen only on the ground, on wires, at the bank face and in the air. The male sings while approaching the female, sometimes quivering his wings, then mounts and copulates with wings raised.

BREEDING The breeding season is chiefly May–August over much of the range, with northern birds laying earlier than southern ones (A.O. Gross in Bent 1942; Cramp 1988). In India the breeding season lasts from November to May, with most activity in February–April (Ali and Ripley 1972). Some birds have second broods, but not necessarily with the same partner or in the same nest; some females leave their first broods before they are fully fledged in order to start a second (Turner 1980; Cowley 1983). In the far north and east of the range, one brood is usual. For nest sites, a suitable vertical sandy bank, such as banks of rivers, lakes, road and railway cuttings in sand, sandstone, clay or gravel, and soft earth such as loess, sawdust mounds, sand and gravel quarries, coastal cliffs and dunes, even colliery slag heaps and rubbish tips and the faces of cut peat, are used. There have also been a few instances of Sand Martins using artificial cavities such as holes in walls (e.g. Hellyar 1927) and drainage holes in concrete banks (Cramp 1988). In Canada, only two out of five are in natural sites such as on sea-coasts, lake and river shores, the rest being in artificial sites (Erskine 1979). Although nest sites are re-used each year, new burrows are usually dug, perhaps because of the presence of parasites. Nest sites are also particularly subject to erosion. Sand Martins dig their own burrows, some 50–100 cm (20–40 in) long, sloping upwards and ending in a wider chamber in which the nest is placed. Dry grass, eelgrass, seaweed, pine needles, bamboo leaves or whatever is available locally are used for the base of the nest, which is lined with feathers. The length of the tunnel depends on how easily workable the substrate is. Digging time is variable, depending on the weather, but averages four or five days (Sieber 1980). Both male and female excavate and initially both often sleep in the burrow at night, but by the time nestlings are present often one or no partner sleeps in the nest.

The eggs are laid in the early morning at daily intervals. The clutch size is usually three to six eggs, averaging five, with occasional records of clutches of seven; the clutch size decreases from north to south (e.g. in Britain: Morgan 1979). The eggs are pure white and measure 17.5 × 12.6 mm (15.2–20.0 × 10.7–13.7; weight 1.43). Both sexes incubate, although the male does not develop an incubation patch and does only a third of the incubation (Turner 1980). Incubation starts with the penultimate egg, and the birds incubate for nearly 100% of the time; the incubation period averages 14 days but varies from 12 to 16 days. The nestling period is about 22 days (Turner and Bryant 1979). Both parents brood and feed the nestlings. When they are 10–12 days old, they run forward in the tunnel to meet the parents. Feeding trips by the parents average 5.2 minutes (Bryant and Turner 1982). Fledglings return to the burrow for four or five days after their first flight, sometimes landing in neighbouring burrows or perching on suitable twigs nearby. Fledglings stay in crèches, where parents come to feed them. Parents recognise their chicks' calls and vice versa, and siblings recognise each other, facilitating family cohesion (Beecher et al. 1981a, b; Beecher and Beecher 1983; Sieber 1985). Juveniles sometimes engage in digging shallow holes and incipient nest-building and brooding.

The fledging success is often high, about 70% of eggs laid (e.g. Asbirk 1976; Sieber 1980). Most nestling mortality is due to bad weather reducing the supply of insects and leading to starvation. Erosion and predators also sometimes destroy nests. Mortality can also be high on migration during the crossing of the Sahara (Ash 1969), or because of severe weather on the breeding grounds early in the season (Mead and Harrison 1979b). Survival rates vary from study to study, but are generally about 30–50% for adults (Freer 1977; Mead 1979b; Cramp 1988) and 20–40% for first-years. The majority thus live for only one or a few years, but there is a record of a nine-year-old bird (Petersen and Mueller 1979).

VOICE The territorial song which is used to repel intruders and to attract females is an unmusical twittering broken into phrases (Cramp 1988). There are also a mating song, which is a softer, more continuous twittering directed towards the partner, and an almost continuous chatter used by males guarding their females. The contact call is a harsh one- or two-syllable 'tschr', given perched or in flight and also by males finishing a

Circling Flight. Petersen (1955) observed a male uttering a single note to urge young to leave the nest. The Excitement call is a series of 'schrrp' sounds uttered during confrontations with conspecifics. Parents and young call to each other as the parents bring food. Parents have single- or double-note calls which are individually distinct as are the chicks' calls. There are two alarm calls: adults at a colony initially give a high-intensity repetitive call, then, in a flock, they give single lower-pitched calls. Alarm calls stimulate nestlings to retreat into the burrows (Windsor and Emlen 1975).

DESCRIPTION The upperparts are mousy grey-brown with paler edges to the feather tips in fresh plumage, and a more uniform brown when worn; the pale edges are broadest on the forehead, rump, uppertail-coverts and median and greater upperwing-coverts. The lores and feathers near the gape are pale grey-brown, and there is a black spot in front of the eye. The under-parts are white, except for a grey-brown breast-band, broadest at the sides, and a few brown-spotted feathers in the centre of the breast. The chin and throat have a buffy tinge in fresh plumage. The flanks are dark grey-brown. The underwing-coverts and axillaries are dark grey-brown, with pale fringes to the tips of the lesser coverts. The tail, flight feathers and greater upper primary coverts are blackish-brown with a faint olive tinge and green gloss; the outer-most primaries are the blackest. The tail feathers and secondaries have white outer edges and tips when fresh, and the tail is slightly forked. The eyes, legs and feet are dark brown, the bill black. Above the hind toe is a small tuft of feathers. The sexes are alike. Juveniles have cinnamon, rufous-cinnamon or creamy edges to the feathers of the upperparts, especially conspicuous on the forehead, rump, and wing- and tail-coverts; these have largely worn off after two to four months; there is a strong cinnamon or buffy wash from the chin to the chest, and a buffy or creamy tinge on the rest of the underparts. The extent and colour of the edges to the feathers and the wash on the underparts, however, are very variable. The body moult starts on the breeding grounds at the end of the breeding season, but few birds moult their primaries until after migrating (more do so in the south of the breeding range) (Cramp 1988).

Measurements Length 12 cm (4¼ in). Wing 103–111 (mean 107); tail 48–54 (mean 51); fork 7–13 (mean 9); bill 8.9–11.2 (mean 9.9); tarsus 9.6–11.5 (mean 10.5). Weight 11–19.5 (mean 13.5).

RACES The race *ijimae* (wing 97–111) is darker than the nominate form, with black-ish-brown upperparts, with more distinct pale edges to the rump and flight feathers, and a well-defined breast-band. The race *diluta* (wing 97–108) has pale, grey-brown upperparts and a blurred breast-band. The race *shelleyi* is small (wing 88–98) and pale, with a narrow, pale breast-band. The three populations of *ijimae*, *diluta* and *riparia* intergrade with one another where they meet, and the resulting intermediate forms have sometimes been considered to be separate races: e.g. *kolymensis*, where *riparia* and *ijimae* meet in eastern Siberia; *taczanowski*, where *ijimae* and *diluta* meet in Manchuria and Ussuri; and *stoetzneriana*, where *riparia* and *diluta* meet in western Siberia and northern Iran. The race *diluta* has also often been divided into several other races: *fohkienensis* (a small, dark form in central and southern China), *indica* (a small form with an ill-defined breast-band from the Punjab) and *tibetana* (a dark form from central Asia). There are intermediates between *ijimae* and *diluta* in northeastern China. Individuals in the Punjab, identified as *indica* by Ticehurst (Peters 1960), may be a separable race as they are in breeding condition at the time when individuals from the north are recorded in non-breeding condition (Abdulali 1975).

The southern populations of the species tend to be smaller than the northern but the difference is slight; the variation in size and colour is clinal. The low level of variation in the breeding range may be due to the high dispersal of adults (Loske 1983a).

28 BANDED MARTIN   Plate 9
Riparia cincta (Boddaert)
Alternative name: Banded Sand Martin

Hirundo cincta Boddaert, 1783, Tab. Pl. enlum., p. 45: Cape of Good Hope.

Riparia cincta erlangeri Reichenow, 1905, Ethiopia.

Riparia cincta suahelica van Someren, 1922, Escarpment, Kenya.

Riparia cincta parvula Amadon, 1954, Luluabourg, Kasai, Belgian Congo.

Riparia cincta xerica Clancey and Irwin, 1966, Angola.

FIELD CHARACTERS Banded Martins are brown above and white below, with a white stripe above the eye, black lores and eyebrows, and a broad brown breast-band. This is a distinctive martin in the field because of its large size and black and white head markings. It also has conspicuously long wings, a wide wingspan and a square tail compared with the other sand martins (26, 27, 29). It is a solitary martin, usually found near water. The flight is slow and erratic.

HABITAT Banded Martins are found in open country such as grassland, farmland and lightly bushed savannas. They are usually but not always near water, especially watercourses where banks are available for breeding. The race *parvula* occurs generally on grassy plains, *xerica* on drier areas such as the Kalahari sand plains, and *suahelica* occurs typically on montane and grassland areas up to 3000 m.

DISTRIBUTION AND POPULATION Banded Martins have an extensive range throughout much of Africa south of the Sahara. There are no validated records of breeding in West Africa, but there have been suggestions that they do breed in Nigeria (e.g. Bannerman 1939; Elgood *et al.* 1973). The nominate race breeds in southern Africa from Zimbabwe and Natal south to Cape Province, but not in the drier western part of the area. It is partly replaced in drier country by *xerica*, whose range extends across the Kalahari of northern Botswana and Namibia to Angola and western Zambia. To the northeast is the range occupied by *suahelica*: throughout much of Zambia and East Africa. The race *parvula* breeds in Zaire, Cameroon and northern Zambia. The race *erlangeri* occurs in Ethiopia and probably on the upper White Nile.

Banded Martins are generally locally distributed and uncommon to fairly common in southern and eastern Africa (Maclean 1985; Benson *et al.* 1971; Tree 1986b). In Ethiopia, the race *erlangeri* is frequently seen in the western, southeastern and Rift Valley areas, but less so elsewhere (Urban and Brown 1971). The race *parvula* is also uncommon. These martins usually nest in natural sites, and have not benefited from the presence of quarries or other artificial sites.

MIGRATION The various races seem to move north and south with the rains, those breeding furthest from the Equator migrating furthest north for the non-breeding season, and may also move from high to low altitudes (Aspinwall 1983). The overwintering areas, however, are poorly known. The southernmost race, *cincta*, regularly migrates to overwinter between May and August in the southern equatorial belt of Angola, Zaire, northern Mozambique, Zambia and Malawi, occasionally overwintering in Zimbabwe and Botswana; it migrates north through Zimbabwe in February–May, but the southern migration route is not known. It is also an uncommon migrant to West Africa between May and mid November, mainly in Nigeria and Cameroon and west to Ghana, but there are a few records as far west as the Gambia (Gore 1981; Grimes 1988). On the eastern side of Africa *cincta* probably does not migrate much further north than the Kasai and Malawi, as East African specimens are all of the race *suahelica* (Britton 1980). The latter race is generally resident but makes some movements, for example between Zimbabwe and Zambia (individuals passing north in Zambia in March–April may be of this race: Benson *et al.* 1973); *suahelica* is a visitor to Zimbabwe from September to mid April, but its movements in East Africa are not clear (Aspinwall 1983). Few birds of either race are present in Zambia in July and August. The race *parvula* is resident, but makes local movements after the breeding season; White (1961) mentioned a migratory form of *parvula* from Upemba. The race *erlangeri* also makes local post-breeding movements in Sudan and Ethiopia (Urban and Brown 1971), moving as far south as Moroto and Naivasha (Britton 1980). The race *xerica* winters to the north of its breeding range, occurring in Botswana in the rains, but its wintering grounds are not clearly known (Aspinwall 1983).

FOOD AND BEHAVIOUR Compared with the other sand martins, this is not a particularly sociable species. Individuals are often seen alone, in pairs or in small flocks. They feed low over pasture and grasslands, with a slow, deliberate, erratic flight, occasionally gliding and frequently resting. They perch in the open on bare twigs and wire fences (D.R. Aspinwall, pers. comm.). They feed on flies and other large insects, particularly beetles (Bannerman 1939), and they will also pick insects off grass inflorescences (Maclean 1985). Banded Martins do not nest colonially like other sand martins; they breed in single pairs or small groups. On migration, however, non-breeding birds sometimes form larger flocks, containing tens or hundreds of individuals.

BREEDING Breeding generally occurs in the rainy season, although in Zambia and the Kasai the main part of the season may be in advance of the rains (Benson *et al.* 1971). In southern Africa, breeding is from August to October in the southern Cape and usually November–March elsewhere (Maclean 1985). Further north, most breeding occurs in September–February in Zimbabwe (Irwin 1981), August–January in Zambia (Benson *et al.* 1973), February–November in East Africa (Brown and Britton 1980), August–November in Zaire (Lippens and Wille 1976), and May–August in Ethiopia (Urban and Brown 1971). Tunnels are usually dug in sandbanks, earth mounds or the roof of an aardvark burrow, but disused kingfisher or starling burrows are sometimes used. The tunnel is 60–90 cm (2–3 ft) deep, and ends in a round chamber, where the nest, an untidy pad made of straws, grass, rootlets and feathers, is placed. The feathers are often arranged so that the ends curl inwards over the eggs.

The eggs are white and elongate, measuring 22.1 × 15.0 mm (20.6–24 × 14.6–16.5; weight 2.79). The clutch size is usually three or four eggs in South Africa (Maclean 1985), three to five in East Africa (Brown and Britton 1980), and two to four (rarely five) in Zaire (Lippens and Wille 1976). The incubation and nestling periods are not known. It is likely that, as with the Sand Martin (27), both sexes share the tasks of tunnelling, nest-building, incubation and nestling-feeding. One male was carrying nesting material when shot (Rand *et al.* 1959). One recovery was of a bird at least four years old (Irwin 1981).

VOICE The vocalisations are a loud chattering call and a short 'chuk' (Maclean 1985). The song is a subdued squeaky warbling which sometimes ends in a trill.

DESCRIPTION This martin is a large hirundine and the largest of the sand martin group. The upperparts are earth-brown, darker on the crown and becoming paler towards the rump and uppertail-coverts, the feathers of the mantle, back, rump and uppertail-coverts having paler edges. There is a broad white stripe from the base of the stout bill to just above the eye. The lores and eyebrows are black. The ear-coverts are brown. The underparts are white, apart from a broad brown breast-band and a few brown feathers along the centre of the breast. The thighs are brown. The undertail-coverts are white. The axillaries and under-wing-coverts are white, the latter with faint brown marks along the edge of the wing, giving it a mottled appearance. The primaries, secondaries and upperwing-coverts are dark brown. The edge of the wing below the carpal joint is white. The tail is dark brown, the outer feathers edged with a narrow line of white and the others having buffy edges; it is square with rounded tips. The eyes are brown, the legs and feet are dark brownish or blackish, and the bill is triangular and black. The sexes are alike. Juveniles are similar to adults, but have a paler breast-band; the crown feathers have rufous-brown edges, the feathers of the mantle, back and scapulars have rufous tips and the wing-coverts and secondaries have golden-rufous tips, giving a mottled appearance to the upperparts; the feathers of the rump and uppertail-coverts are tipped with cream, and the terminal portions of the outer webs of the primaries have buff edges. The moult occurs after the breeding season (Grant and Mackworth-Praed 1942).

Measurements Length 17 cm (6¼ in). Wing 125–135 (mean 130); tail (square) 55–69 (mean 61.7); bill 11.6–13.5 (mean 12.4); tarsus 12–14.1 (mean 13.1). Weight 20–23.

RACES The nominate race is a pale form of the species. The race *erlangeri* is similar to *cincta*, but has a narrow breast-band and is larger (wing 135–146). The race *parvula* is also pale above, but has a dark breast-band and is smaller (wing 114–124). The race *suahelica* is the darkest form, with both the back and the breast-band being almost blackish-brown (wing 123–137). There is a cline in colour and size from *suahelica* to *cincta*, with an intermediate form, *xerica*, in the western part of the cline; *xerica* has a pale breast-band and pale mantle and back.

29 CONGO SAND MARTIN
Riparia congica (Reichenow)

Plate 9

Cotile congica Reichenow, 1887, J. für Orn., p. 300: Manyanga, Lower Congo, between Vivi and Stanley Pool.

Congo Sand Martins are closely related to, and may be derived from, the Sand Martin (27), perhaps from individuals failing to migrate (Hall and Moreau 1970).

FIELD CHARACTERS Congo Sand Martins are brown above and white below, with a brown but indistinct breast-band. They are very similar to the Sand Martin, but lack the tuft of feathers on the feet and do not have a clearly marked breast-band. In the field, however, the two species are difficult to distinguish. They are usually found near water and they nest in colonies along forested rivers.

HABITAT The habitat is very specialised. These sand martins are found only along forested stretches of river where suitable sandbanks are available for breeding.

DISTRIBUTION AND POPULATION The range of this martin is very restricted, extending only along three parts of the lower and middle Congo/Zaire River: between Boma and Kinshasa; along the middle stretches of the river north and south of Mbandaka and along the River Ubangi; and along the upper middle part of the river near Buta (Lippens and Wille 1976). It was first discovered on the Ubangi River only in 1952. Within this range these martins are fairly abundant (Chapin 1953), although only a few pairs have been seen on the Ubangi River. There is no indication of migratory and other movements. Numbers are constant throughout the year.

BEHAVIOUR The flight is similar to that of the Sand Martin. Congo Sand Martins forage mainly over the river, but will also feed some miles from it, in clearings and other open areas (Chapin 1953). They do not usually perch in trees. Their diet is not known. They feed in small groups and will join flocks of other hirundine species, particularly Sand Martins (Lynes 1938). They also nest colonially.

BREEDING Little is known of the breeding biology of these martins, although it is probably similar to that of the Sand Martin. They nest in sandy river banks, at low water, preferring steep faces as where the water has cut away the sand from islands or bars. Nesting activity has been recorded in February and March, when the water level of the river is low and the nests will not be flooded (Chapin 1953; Mackworth-Praed and Grant 1973). The nest is placed at the end of a tunnel dug by the birds themselves 1 m or so above the water.

VOICE The calls have not been recorded.

DESCRIPTION Congo Sand Martins are small, dull brown swallows. The upperparts are mouse-brown, the crown and wing-coverts darker than the rest. There is a blackish stripe from the front of the eye to the base of the upper mandible. The ear-coverts and lores are dark brown. The chin and throat are white, the upper breast is light brown and the lower breast and abdomen are white. The sides are light brown. There is no impression of a breast-band as on the Sand Martin. The undertail-coverts are white, the axillaries mouse-brown. The underwing-coverts are dark brown, the feathers tipped with white. The primaries and secondaries are brown, the tertials are paler, like the back, and have narrow white fringes. The tail is square and dark brown. The eyes are dark brown, the bill is black and the legs and feet are dusky brown. The sexes are alike. Juveniles have pale fringes to the feathers, especially on the back, wing-coverts, rump and uppertail-coverts.

Measurements Length 11 cm (4¼ in). Wing 88–98 (mean 92); tail (square) 40–50 (mean 46.3); bill 9–10; tarsus 6–8.

30 CAMEROON MOUNTAIN ROUGH-WINGED SWALLOW
Psalidoprocne fuliginosa Shelley

Plate 10

Psalidoprocne fuliginosa Shelley, 1887, Proc. Zool. Soc., p. 123: Cameroon Mountain.

FIELD CHARACTERS Cameroon Mountain Roughwings are readily identified by their wholly matt brown colour and forked tail, as well as by their localised distribution They are fairly solitary and their flight is leisurely.

HABITAT These roughwings were discovered at an altitude of 2700 m (8900 ft) on Cameroon Mountain. They are sometimes numerous at the tree line at 2400–2700 m. Serle (1965) recorded them from sea level to 2800 m (9200 ft); Stuart (1986) recorded them from 1 to 3000 m (3–9900 ft) on the southeastern slope, but only between 600 and 2900 m (1970–9550 ft) on the northern slope. They feed over pools, clearings, forests, forest edge, plantations, grassy slopes, forested gorges, farmland and villages, and perch on bare branches on the forest edge or in clearings. They are commonly seen in coffee plantations bordering montane forest down to 300 m (980 ft) on Fernando Po (Wells 1968).

DISTRIBUTION AND POPULATION This roughwing occurs over a very limited area, being confined to a tiny part of Cameroon on the island of Fernando Po (Bakaki, Clarence Peak, Santa Isabel) and Cameroon Mountain. There are sight records away from Mount Cameroon, in Nigeria on the Obudu Plateau and from montane areas of Cameroon (Elgood 1965, 1976), but these require confirmation. There are no records of any migratory movements being undertaken by this species. Although this roughwing has an extremely restricted distribution, it is apparently quite abundant. There are no measures of population size available, but Young (1946) described it as common between 750 and 2700 m (2470–8900 ft), and Serle (1965) and Basilio (1963) also recorded it as being a common bird. Collar and Stuart (1985) believe that it is under no immediate threat.

BEHAVIOUR The flight of these swallows is unhurried, with frequent swoops and glides. They sometimes pause in the air and then swoop vertically down. The birds are usually seen in pairs or small groups close to the ground or in clearings. One flock numbered over 50 individuals (Stuart 1986). They will also join flocks of other hirundines. The diet consists of flying insects but is not known in detail. They nest in isolated pairs, or in small groups of a few pairs where nest sites are plentiful.

BREEDING The limits of the breeding season are not clear but appear to be between at least October and March (Eisentraut 1956, 1963; Serle 1981). Eisentraut (1956) recorded nests with eggs at the beginning of March and in January, and birds carrying nest material in February. The nesting sites are rocky ledges, or crevices in lava cliffs and ravines. These birds will also occasionally use buildings; one nest was at the back of a hole 35 cm (14 in) deep in the brickwork of an outhouse (Eisentraut 1956). The nest is a small tightly woven pad of vegetation such as lichen and other plant fibres, with some moss underneath (Eisentraut 1956, 1963). Recorded nests have contained two eggs. The eggs are white and measure 18.8 × 12.2 mm. The incubation and fledging periods are not known.

VOICE The call is a whispered 'see-su' and a 'tchik-tchuk', both uttered in flight (Young 1946). Eisentraut (1956, 1963) also recorded a soft, melodious and repetitive call rendered as 'dju dju diob diob djuob djuob'.

DESCRIPTION This small swallow is the most drab of the African roughwings. It is a dull uniform chocolate-brown all over. The lores are almost black and the ear-coverts are dark brown. The undertail-coverts are chocolate-brown, the underwing-coverts and axillaries a paler more smoky-brown. The wings are a slightly darker brown than the rest of the body. The tail is plain chocolate-brown and is moderately forked. The adult male has tiny barbules along the outer web of the longest primary which the female lacks, but in other respects the sexes are identical. Juveniles are similar, but a lighter brown.

Measurements Length 12 cm (4¾ in). Wing 97–115 (mean 104.3); tail 53–69 (mean 63.8); fork 15–23 (mean 19.5); bill 6.9–8.9 (mean 7.8); tarsus 9.6–10.9 (mean 10.1). Weight 11–12.

31 WHITE-HEADED ROUGH-WINGED SWALLOW　　Plate 10
Psalidoprocne albiceps Sclater

Psalidoprocne albiceps Sclater, 1864, Proc. Zool. Soc. Lond., p. 108, pl. 14: Uzinza, Tabora district, Tanzania.

Psalidoprocne albiceps suffusa Ripley, 1960, Cacalo, Angola.

FIELD CHARACTERS The male is brownish-black, with a white head and throat. The female has less white on the head. They resemble the Black Roughwing (32), but the white head is very conspicuous and the tail is less deeply forked. This is a woodland swallow, usually seen in small groups. The flight is weak and fluttering. It is usually silent.

HABITAT The preferred habitat is wooded savanna, woodland, scrub and forest in upland regions rather than open areas. This roughwing often feeds in glades or at the forest edge or over bush and cultivation. In Zambia, it occurs in miombo woodland, also riparian, evergreen or moist montane forest to over 2000 m (6600 ft) (Benson *et al.* 1971). In Malawi, it occurs mainly at 1200–1500 m (3900–4950 ft), once at 2100 m (6930 ft), often in dense evergreen scrub and replacing the Black Roughwing in dry *Brachystegia* areas (Benson 1951, 1953). In East Africa, it is usually seen in forest clearings and glades, farmland and bushed grasslands (van Someren and van Someren 1949; Friedmann and Williams 1969; Britton 1980). In Zaire, it frequents open but wooded country and forest edge, including montane forest up to 2300 m (7600 ft) (Lippens and Wille 1976). The race *suffusa* was originally taken at 1400 m (4600 ft) in a forest clearing.

DISTRIBUTION AND POPULATION White-headed Roughwings have a disjunct and limited distribution in East Africa and Angola (Hall and Moreau 1970). The nominate race occurs on the upper White Nile south through the lake region of eastern Zaire, Uganda, western Kenya, western Tanzania to Zambia, Ruanda-Burundi and northern Malawi. The range of the race *suffusa* is mainly in northern Angola, but also locally in southern Zaire. This species is generally sparsely and locally distributed and is uncommon in Malawi, Kenya and Tanzania (Benson and Benson 1977; Britton 1980). It is more widespread and common in the Lake Victoria Basin, northwestern Tanzania and Uganda (Britton 1980). It uses mainly natural nest sites, and population sizes depend on their availability.

MIGRATION The movements of this swallow are poorly known. It seems to be mainly a partial migrant, and there are several records of birds wandering outside the usual range. In Zambia and Malawi, at least, it is migratory, being present as a breeding population in the Northern and Luapula Provinces and northern Malawi from October to April, sometimes as early as late September and as late as mid May (Benson *et al.* 1971; Benson and Benson 1977).

FOOD AND BEHAVIOUR The flight is slow and hesitant. It feeds low over bush or grassland and frequently perches (van Someren 1916). It usually feeds in small flocks. The diet is poorly known, but the stomachs of two specimens contained winged ants (Friedmann and Williams 1969) and Chapin (1953) recorded small beetles in the diet. It is a fairly social species, nesting in groups of several pairs. Chapin (1953) noted that during courtship the female is followed persistently by her mate, suggesting that the latter undertakes mate-guarding.

BREEDING In Zambia there are breeding records in January and December, though birds with active gonads have been recorded in October and November (Benson *et al.* 1971). In East Africa it breeds more or less only in the rains, in June and October in Uganda (Brown and Britton 1980). The White-headed Roughwing excavates tunnels some 60 cm (2 ft) long in the vertical banks of rivers, road cuttings, borrow pits and similar sites. A nest pad of *Usnea* lichen, or grass and feathers, is placed at the end of the tunnel. The tunnel is inclined upwards. The clutch size is two to four (van Someren 1916; Mackworth-Praed and Grant 1960; Lippens and Wille 1976). The eggs are white. One clutch of two measured 19 × 13 and 19.2 × 13 (Benson and Pitman 1957). Both male and female incubate, but the female takes longer spells of 20–30 minutes to the male's 15 minutes or less (van Someren and van Someren 1949). The incubation and fledging periods are not known.

VOICE The call is a weak twittering, but these swallows are often silent.

DESCRIPTION The male has a wholly dark brownish-black plumage with a slight oily-green gloss, apart from a white crown, forehead, sides of the head, chin and throat. A black line extends from the bill to the back of the head. The ear-coverts are dark brown. The underwing-coverts and axillaries are ashy-brown. The wings and the moderately forked tail are brownish-black. The bill is black and the eyes, legs and feet are dark brown. The sexes are alike, though the female has shorter outer tail feathers; only the throat is white and it has some brown feathers, she may also have some white feathers on the head. In addition, the male has a marked serration on the outer web of the first primary. Juveniles are nearly wholly brownish-black, but have an ashy-brown throat; white feathers appear irregularly on the head. The juvenile's tail is also less deeply forked than the adult's.

Measurements Length 13 cm (5"). Wing 96–110 (mean 102.9); tail of male 71–83 (mean 75.4), of female 60–68 (mean 65.4); fork of male 22–26 (mean 24), of female 15–20 (mean 18); bill 6.8–8.6 (mean 7.7); tarsus 9–10.1 (mean 9.6). Weight 11–12.

RACES The race *suffusa* differs from *albiceps* in being blacker and in having the underwing-coverts and axillaries pale creamy grey-brown, not brown; the ear-coverts are greyish rather than brown; the throat is greyer, with less white, and the white part of the crown is smaller.

32 BLACK ROUGH-WINGED SWALLOW   Plate 11
Psalidoprocne pristoptera (Rüppell)

Hirundo (Chelidon) pristoptera Rüppell, 1836, Neue Wirbelth., Vög., p. 105, pl. 39, fig. 2: Simen Province, Ethiopia.

Psalidoprocne pristoptera blanfordi Blundell and Lovat, 1899, Bilo, Ethiopia.

Psalidoprocne pristoptera oleaginea Neumann, 1904, Schubba in West Kafa, Ethiopia.

Psalidoprocne pristoptera antinorii Salvadori, 1884, Denz, Shoa.

Psalidoprocne pristoptera petiti Sharpe and Bouvier, 1876, Landana and Chinchoxo.

Psalidoprocne pristoptera ruwenzori Chapin, 1932, Kalongi, 6900 ft, Butahu Valley, West Ruwenzori.

Psalidoprocne pristoptera massaica Neumann, 1904, Kikuyu.

Psalidoprocne pristoptera holomelaena (Sundevall), 1850, Durban, Natal.

Psalidoprocne pristoptera reichenowi Neumann, 1904, Chinchoxo.

Psalidoprocne pristoptera orientalis Reichenow, 1889, Lewa, Dodoma District, Tanzania.

Psalidoprocne pristoptera mangbettorum Chapin, 1923, Medje, Ituri District, Belgian Congo.

Psalidoprocne pristoptera chalybea Reichenow, 1892, Victoria, Cameroons.

FIELD CHARACTERS Black Roughwings can be distinguished in the field by their wholly sooty-black appearance and their deeply forked tails. They frequent forest and woodland and are often seen in pairs or small flocks. The flight is weak and fluttering.

HABITAT The typical habitat is clearings in bush and forest, villages and forest edges, woodland, wooded savanna, grassy hills, tree-lined rivers and plantations. Richer, wetter habitats are preferred, and they are attracted to recently felled areas and to new rather than old plantations (Clancey 1969a). Several races frequent montane grassland and moorland. In Ethiopia roughwings are rarely seen below 1200 m (3900 ft) except in forested areas, although the race *oleaginea* occurs from 300 to 2400 m (980–7800 ft) (Urban and Brown 1971).

DISTRIBUTION AND POPULATION These roughwings occupy much of Africa south of the Sahara, except for the dry southwest and extreme west. The geographical limits of the different races are still not well known, however. Four races range over the northeast of Africa. The nominate *pristoptera* occurs in the highlands of Eritrea and northern parts of the western highlands of Ethiopia. The race *blanfordi* occurs in the western highlands to the north and northwest of Addis Ababa; *oleaginea* breeds in the Maji area in southwestern Ethiopia; and *antinorii* breeds in the mountainous central and southern parts of Ethiopia from Addis Ababa south to Lake Turkana. To the west, *petiti* occurs from the highlands of eastern Nigeria and the Cameroons and extreme western Zaire south to the lower Congo River, and *reichenowi* from the lower Congo and Cabinda south to Benguela in Angola and east to southeastern Zaire and Zambia. The race *mangbettorum* occurs in northeastern Zaire as far as the Congo-Nile divide. The race *chalybea* occupies the area between the ranges of *petiti* and *mangbettorum*; in northeastern Zaire it is replaced by *mangbettorum* between Buta and Titule. In East Africa, *ruwenzori* occurs in eastern Zaire and western Uganda on the slopes of Ruwenzori, south to Kigezi and Lake Kivu and northwestern Tanzania; *massaica* occurs in Kenya, mostly above 1500 m (4930 ft), south to the Uluguru and Usambara Mountains in Tanzania, and in northeastern Uganda; and *orientalis* occurs in southeastern Tanzania and south through northeastern Zambia and Zimbabwe, to Malawi and northern Mozambique (the type of this race was a wanderer from outside the breeding range). In southern Africa, *holomelaena* occurs from the Cape to Natal and Zululand, Swaziland, eastern and northern Transvaal, southern Mozambique, southern Zimbabwe and northern Botswana.

Throughout much of their range, Black Roughwings are often locally common or even abundant swallows, for example in northern Zambia and the Bamenda highlands (Serle 1965; Benson *et al.* 1971), Ethiopia (Urban and Brown 1987) and Mozambique (Jackson 1973b). They are probably restricted to areas with suitable natural nest sites, though they will use artificial sites such as road cuttings.

MIGRATION Over much of the range, this species is a local resident and partial migrant, and makes local movements after the breeding season, sometimes moving to lower altitudes. In Eritrea, the race *pristoptera* migrates further south into Ethiopia after breeding. In southern Africa the Black Roughwing is a breeding migrant, being present mainly from September to April in the southernmost part of the range, and from November to April in Zimbabwe (Maclean 1985). The wintering range of these birds is very poorly known but may be in the northern part of their range in Mozambique, where there is an influx of birds in the winter (Benson 1982). The race *holomelaena* has also been recorded in southern Malawi and southeastern Zimbabwe (Hanmer 1980). The race *reichenowi* also appears to leave Zambia in the

dry season (Aspinwall 1981). The races in central and east Africa are sedentary, making local movements (Lippens and Wille 1976; Britton 1980; Benson 1982). In West Africa, *petiti* is sedentary (Brosset and Erard 1986).

FOOD AND BEHAVIOUR The flight is weak, wavering and circular. Roughwings are often seen sailing over clearings or skimming along forest tracks or across clearings, usually staying close to the forest edge and low over the ground. They also frequently perch, using twigs and branches of high trees, or felled trees in clearings, particularly during the hottest part of the day. They feed in open places among trees, above the forest or over water, usually alone, in pairs or in small groups, at an average height of 7 m (23 ft) (Waugh 1978). They often skim the ground, fly up to the canopy, then swoop down again (Skead 1964). Feeding activity is greatest towards evening (Clancey 1964). When breeding, they do not feed near the nest sites (Moreau 1940). Small dipteran flies, Hymenoptera (including ants and ichneumonids) and small beetles (including wood-boring beetles) are known to be eaten (e.g. Moreau 1940; Chapin 1953; Germain *et al.* 1973). These roughwings nest in single pairs or occasionally in small groups, but often feed and perch in flocks, especially after the breeding season (Belcher 1941). Chapin (1953) noted an apparent display by a bird pursuing another in which the wings were moved stiffly and mostly held low.

BREEDING The breeding season varies geographically, usually being in the local wet season. In Ethiopia, *pristoptera* breeds in May–June, possibly March; *oleaginea* breeds in March; and *antinorii* in February, July and possibly August (Urban and Brown 1971). In West and Central Africa, roughwings breed mainly from April to June and in October–November (Lippens and Wille 1976). In East Africa there are records all year, with a peak in November and December (Britton and Brown 1980). In southern Africa, the main season is November–March (Maclean 1985). The Black Roughwing uses holes some 30–60 cm (1–2 ft) long in vertical banks of streams, between tree roots, in antbear warrens, in quarries, clay pits, low sandy cliffs along the shore, or roadside cuttings; one nest was in a hole in brickwork but the use of artificial structures is rare (Benson 1980). Natural holes are used, either crevices or holes dug by other species such as kingfishers (e.g. Martin and Broekhuysen 1961), but some burrows are dug by the birds themselves (Serle 1950b). These may take up to three weeks to dig. A nest made of moss, lichen, pine needles or dry grass is constructed at the end of the burrow. There are also records of nests in rock crevices and on ledges under over-hangs (Sharpe 1870; Priest 1935; Moreau 1940).

The clutch size is usually two, sometimes three eggs. The eggs are white and measure 18.6 × 12.8 mm (18.3–19.3 × 12.7–13; weight 1.6). Maclean (1985) gave the incubation period as about 14–15 days and the nestling period as at least 25 days, although Moreau (1940; see also Moreau and Moreau 1940) noted incubation periods of 18 or 19 days and fledging periods of 24–27 days. In Moreau's (1940) study of five nests, the eggs were usually covered for 31–66% of the time, with 28–62% of the incubation spells lasting longer than 15 minutes; the pattern of incubation suggests that only one parent usually incubates. Both parents feed the chicks, with intervals between feeds for broods of two being between eight and 15 minutes. The nestlings begin to leave the nest and come to the mouth of the hole a few days before fledging. In Moreau's study, the fledglings left the burrow independently of their parents.

VOICE This is said to be a very silent swallow. Priest (1935) recorded a shrill cry when birds were entering nest holes, and Bates (1930) recorded a low weeping note. The alarm call is a soft chirp, and the song is a low twittering. There is also a contact call, used for example by birds in flocks; this is a nasal call described as 'chirr chirrr cheeeu' for *holomelaena* and 'tseeu, tseeu tsee-ip' for *orientalis*, which race also has a whistling mewing call (Maclean 1985).

DESCRIPTION Black Roughwings are small, wholly black swallows, the plumage having a dark blue sheen above and below, including the scapulars and lesser and median wing-coverts. The greater wing-coverts, primaries, secondaries and tail are greenish-black, and the tail is strongly forked. The lores are black, the ear-coverts are blue. The underwing-coverts and axillaries are white. The bill is black, the eyes dark brown and the legs and feet blackish. There is a series of barbules on the outer web of the first primary. The sexes are similar, but females do not have the marked serration on the first primary and have shorter outer tail feathers. Juveniles are duller, more blackish-brown without any gloss or with a faint gloss on the crown and back, and with dusky white underwing-coverts.

Measurements Length 13 cm (5"). Wing 99–110 (mean 106.3); tail of male 67–82 (mean 73.8), of female 59–75 (mean 65.7); fork of male 26–32 (mean 28.3), of female 20–29 (mean 24.3); bill 6.7–8.2 (mean 7.1); tarsus 8–9.9 (mean 9). Weight 11–13 (mean 11.8).

RACES The numerous subspecies differ in small respects in size, the shape of the tail, the depth of the fork, the wing length, the shade of gloss on the plumage and the colour of the underwing-coverts (Benson 1961). Three races found in the northeast of Africa (the nominate race, *antinorii* and *blanfordi*) have broader and less attenuated outer tail feathers than other races and they all have white underwing-coverts. While *pristoptera* has a bluish sheen, *antinorii* is matt brown with a purplish sheen and *blanfordi* has a deep blue-green sheen. A fourth northeastern race, *oleaginea*, differs from these in having more attenuated outer tail feathers; it is brown with a green sheen and white underwing-coverts. These four races are all similar in size.

The other races, in central, eastern and southern Africa, have mostly a green gloss and differ primarily in the colour of the underwing-coverts and the length of the tail. In the race *mangbettorum* the underwing-coverts are white and the gloss is pronounced. It is similar to *oleaginea* but has a longer, more deeply forked tail (tail 79–93, fork 33–47). In *holomelaena*, *massaica* and *ruwenzori* the underwing-coverts are brown; and in *petiti*, *reichenowi*, *chalybea* and *orientalis* they are grey (greyish-white in *orientalis*). The race *massaica* is the largest of the races with brown underwing-coverts, and *ruwenzori* has the shortest, most shallowly forked tail (*massaica* wing 110–119, tail 85–99, fork 39–45; *holomelaena* wing 105–113, tail 82–90, fork 38–49; *ruwenzori* wing 107–114, tail 73–86, fork 28–35).

The race *orientalis* is the largest of the races with grey underwing-coverts, and *reichenowi* has the shortest tail (*orientalis* wing 105–112, tail 76–90, fork 37–48; *chalybea* wing 93–100, tail 85–94, fork 38–54; *reichenowi* wing 107–114, tail 73–85, fork 28–35). The race *petiti* is small (wing 98–105, tail 70–82, fork 25–35) and sooty-brown, with a slight purplish gloss and with underwing-coverts tinged grey.

Several other subspecies/species have been suggested, such as *kosteri* from Benguela, *percivali* from southern Malawi, Zimbabwe and Mozambique, and *bamingui* from the upper Shari River, but are not clearly distinguishable.

The various races are often treated as separate species, but they all seem to breed in separate geographical areas and differ in only minor characteristics, suggesting that they are conspecific, although they may be incipient species (Benson 1961; Hall and Moreau 1970). These swallows have a tendency to wander, and individuals are sometimes recorded outside their normal range.

33 FANTI ROUGH-WINGED SWALLOW Plate 11
Psalidoprocne obscura (Hartlaub)

Hirundo obscura Hartlaub, 1855, J. für Orn., p. 355: Dabocrom, Gold Coast.

FIELD CHARACTERS Fanti Roughwings are entirely dark green, with a strongly forked tail. In the field, they appear to have the darkest plumage and the most deeply forked tail of all the roughwing group. They frequent areas near water and usually occur in small groups. The flight is leisurely.

HABITAT This species is usually seen over or near water in areas of open grass woodland, forest edge, secondary bush, grassland, river floodplains and villages.

DISTRIBUTION AND POPULATION The range is limited to the southern lowland region of West Africa from Senegal and Guinea Bissau east to western Cameroon, west of Mount Cameroon and Kumba, where the northern limit is at about latitude 9°N (Hall and Moreau 1970). The species is locally distributed, but can be numerous where it does occur. Its local distribution depends on the availability of nest sites, which include some artificial ones.

MIGRATION Fanti Roughwings are partly migratory, southern birds moving north in the wet season; and they also make local movements after the breeding season. They are resident all year in some places, such as Enugu in southern Nigeria, but are generally absent from the southern part of the range in the wet season (Elgood *et al.* 1973). In Sierra Leone, they make local migratory movements around Freetown and may move to higher altitudes in the summer. On the Ivory Coast, they also make local movements; they are common from October to May south of 7°30′N, and rarer in the south during the rains, when they invade all the Guinea zone (Thiollay 1985). In Nigeria at Zaria, migrants are present from mid April to mid October, the population being

extended during the breeding season by birds from Sapele to the northern limit of the range at Kari (= a southern concertina migrant) (Elgood *et al.* 1973); it is present as a breeding bird in the Plateau Province of Nigeria from March to October (Bannerman 1953), and around Lagos it is present in large numbers in July and August. In Ghana, it is mainly a dry-season visitor inland from September to March; in the north, it appears in the wet season (Grimes 1988). It is a rare visitor as far as the Gambia between June and November (Gore 1981).

FOOD AND BEHAVIOUR Fanti Roughwings are often seen in pairs or small flocks. When feeding, they sometimes use a tree as a standing point and fly out to hunt from it. They feed low over water, grassland and around trees. The flight is light and graceful (Serle 1949). The diet consists of flying insects, including small beetles (museum specimens). Pairs usually nest in small groups.

BREEDING The limits of the breeding season are not clear, but records of breeding are generally in the rains between May and August (Mackworth-Praed and Grant 1973; Elgood 1982; Grimes 1988). For nesting sites, burrows are dug into vertical banks, including artificial sites such as roadside cuttings and mine shafts. The burrow is horizontal, some 60 cm (2 ft) long, and ends in an enlarged chamber where the nest is placed. The nest is made with plant fibres, twigs, rootlets, palm fibres, and a little moss, but few or no feathers. The eggs are white and measure 18.8 × 12.9 mm (17–19.5 × 12–13.5; weight 1.64). The clutch size is two. There are no details of incubation or fledging periods.

VOICE The call is a soft squeaking but this species is often silent (Marchant 1942).

DESCRIPTION This small swallow is entirely glossy dark green, sometimes with a blue tinge, including the scapulars, median and lesser wing-coverts and tertials. The rump and uppertail-coverts often have more of a dark blue-green sheen. The lores are black and the ear-coverts dark green. The greater wing-coverts are blackish-brown with a slight green gloss. The primaries and secondaries are blackish-brown with a sheen on the outer webs. The tail is black with a dark green gloss on the outer webs and on both webs of the central pair of feathers; it is long and strongly forked on breeding males. The axillaries and underwing-coverts are dark brown without any gloss. The eyes are brown, the bill black and the legs and feet black. The sexes are alike, but females have a shorter tail and lack the serrations that the male has on the outer web of the first primary. Juveniles are brown with a slight green gloss on the upperparts, depending on age; the glossy feathers appear irregularly; the outer tail feathers are also shorter than on adults.

Measurements Length 17 cm (6¾"). Wing 92–101 (mean 96.2); tail of male 86–116 (mean 94.6), of female 73–84 (mean 76); fork of male 50–74 (mean 61.5), of female 20–38 (mean 30.5); bill 6.8–8 (mean 7.2); tarsus 9.2–10 (mean 9.7). Weight 8.8–10.

34 SQUARE-TAILED ROUGH-WINGED SWALLOW   Plate 11
Psalidoprocne nitens (Cassin)

Atticora nitens Cassin, 1857, Proc. Acad. Philad., p. 38: Muni River, Gabon.

Psalidoprocne nitens centralis Neumann, 1904, Kitima Station on the Ituri.

FIELD CHARACTERS The Square-tailed Roughwing is entirely brown with a green gloss, except for a grey-brown chin, throat and cheeks. It can be distinguished from other roughwings (30–33) by its small size and its square rather than deeply forked tail. It frequents forests, where it is usually seen in small groups. Its flight is weak and fluttering. It is a generally silent bird, but individuals in flocks often twitter.

HABITAT Square-tailed Roughwings are restricted to forest habitats, where they are usually seen in clearings, felled or freshly burnt areas, villages and surrounding cultivated ground, rivers, or sometimes over the canopy. They occur in both rainforest and old secondary forest, where they replace the Black Roughwing (32) (Brosset and Erard 1986).

DISTRIBUTION AND POPULATION This species is confined to West Africa. The nominate race occurs from Sierra Leone through southern Nigeria, south through Cameroon and Gabon to the mouth of the Congo River in the extreme west of Zaire. The race *centralis* occurs in the northern and eastern parts of Zaire. The Square-tailed Roughwing has a very localised distribution and is not usually common, although Bannerman (1953) recorded it as abundant in the forests of Cameroon and it can be locally common elsewhere, as in Ghana (Grimes 1988) and Gabon (Brosset and Erard 1986). It is strictly a forest species, not nesting in association with humans, and confined to areas with suitable natural nest sites.

MIGRATION Although Square-tailed Roughwings are not known to migrate, they may make local movements, dispersing after the breeding season. In some areas, such as the Birwa Plateau of Sierra Leone, they are present for only part of the year (Bannerman 1953).

FOOD AND BEHAVIOUR The flight is slow and fluttering and interspersed with periods of perching on small trees. These roughwings are gregarious, usually being seen in small groups, feeding and perching together. They often feed high over clearings or the forest canopy. The diet is not well known, but includes insects such as small beetles and flying ants. The stomachs of six birds contained tiny wood-boring beetles of the family Bostrichidae, with a very few winged ants and a small fly (Chapin 1953). They are known to feed on swarms of flying ants and termites (Brosset and Erard 1986). Pairs usually nest in small groups. Brosset and Erard (1986) described possible mating displays: one bird interrupted its flight by keeping its wings rigid and below the horizontal; a second bird followed, vibrating its wings, which were also held below the horizontal, and spreading its tail. The vibration of the wings produced a clear noise. This second bird described a series of up-and-down flights, alternating this with periods of gliding in which the wings were arched below the horizontal; several times it turned and rejoined the first, holding its head high as if to touch the latter's bill, and calling.

BREEDING The limits of the breeding season are not clear, but seem to be at the end of the dry season and at the beginning of the rains. Breeding has been recorded in January and July–August in the western and central parts of the range and from July to September in Zaire (Dean 1974; Thiollay 1975; Lippens and Wille 1976). In Liberia, birds were in breeding condition in August and September (Colston and Curry-Lindahl 1986). In Gabon, breeding takes place from July to November and in March (Brosset and Erard 1986). For nest sites, these roughwings use holes in vertical sand and clay banks, banks of streams and pitfall traps. The burrow, dug by the birds themselves, is about 0.3 to 2 m (1–6½ ft) long, inclined upwards, and is enlarged towards the end, forming a chamber where the nest is placed. The nest is made of soft vegetation such as *Usnea* and moss (Bannerman 1953; Brosset and Erard 1986). The clutch size is two. Brosset and Erard (1986) found a clutch of four, but this may have been laid by two females. The eggs are white, and are long and pointed. They measure 20 × 13 mm (19–21 × 8–13; weight 1.76). There are no details known of the incubation and fledging periods.

VOICE The call is a soft 'sip', and birds in flocks keep up a low twittering (Fuggles Couchman 1939); a call is given during displays. These roughwings are otherwise apparently quite silent birds.

DESCRIPTION This is the smallest of the African rough-winged swallow group. The upperparts, including the wing-coverts, are dark brown with an oily-green gloss, but the forehead, crown and nape are slightly duller than the rest of the upperparts. The lores are black. The ear-coverts are brown. The chin, throat and cheeks are grey-brown without a gloss. The breast, abdomen, flanks and undertail-coverts have a dark, oily-green gloss, especially on the abdomen and flanks. The underwing-coverts and axillaries are dark grey-brown with a slight oily-green gloss. The primaries and secondaries are blackish-brown, with a green gloss on the outer web; the tertials are as the back. The tail is square and blackish-brown with a purplish-blue gloss, especially on the central pair of feathers. The bill is black, the eyes are brown and the legs and feet are blackish. The sexes are alike, but females lack the male's serration on the outer web of the first primary. The juveniles are a duller dark brown with a faint oily-green gloss.

Measurements Length 11 cm (4¼"). Wing 88–104 (mean 93.7); tail (square) 46–55 (mean 49.3); bill 6.3–8.2 (mean 7.4); tarsus 9–11 (mean 9.8). Weight 8.3–11 (mean 9.8).

RACES *Centralis* is similar to the nominate race, but has a metallic greenish-black throat.

35 WHITE-BACKED SWALLOW   Plate 12
Cheramoeca leucosternus (Gould)
Alternative name: Black-and-white Swallow

Hirundo leucosternus Gould, 1841, Proc. Zool. Soc. Lond., pt. 8 (1840), p. 172: Naomi River, New South Wales. (Often incorrectly spelt *leucosternum*, see Brooke 1974.)

FIELD CHARACTERS This species is distinctive, with its pied coloration, dark rump and deeply forked tail. The crown and mantle are white, the rest of the back is black; below, the throat and upper breast are white, and the lower breast and abdomen black. There is a brown band across the face. These swallows frequent open country near water and are usually seen in flocks, members of which continuously twitter. The flight is rather weak and erratic.

HABITAT White-backed Swallows can be found in any open country with sandy banks along rivers or other watercourses suitable for breeding. They are seen in dry areas but not in forests, except in cleared sites where sandy banks are available for nesting. They have been seen feeding over mudflats.

DISTRIBUTION AND POPULATION White-backed Swallows are endemic to Australia (Blakers *et al.* 1984). They breed in the western and southern regions and in the interior of Australia. They have recently extended their range to the coast of southeastern Queensland (Brisbane River) and New South Wales (south to the Nepean River) (Blakers *et al.* 1984). The range has expanded towards the coast since 1900; previously the only record there was of their having nested in 1896 at Narrabri. The range may also be extending south along the Swan coastal plain and west along the southern coast to Denmark, perhaps further. There have been several recent sightings south of the Swan River. There are no measures of abundance, but this species is generally common, though breeding sites may be localised. Unlike many other swallows, White-backed Swallows do not use artificial structures for nesting and so probably have not benefited from the spread of humans in Australia. Quarrying, mining and similar activities, however, have provided some new nesting sites and may have allowed the population to increase in some areas.

MIGRATION These swallows are generally resident, but some movements do take place (Blakers *et al.* 1984). Thus they are occasional non-breeding visitors to the Kimberley and Rolling Downs regions. In the southern Murray-Darling region they desert colonies after breeding, but their movements in the non-breeding season are not known; numbers in this area vary little over the year, suggesting that there is no migration away from the region as a whole. They are only intermittently present in the edges of the range such as at Mount Isa. One bird recorded moved 121 km (75½ miles) from Moonta to Angle Vale (Blakers *et al.* 1984).

FOOD AND BEHAVIOUR The flight is erratic, fluttering, and includes much swooping with rapid wingbeats. White-backed Swallows generally forage in small flocks or, less usually, alone, and they often fly high above the ground. Sometimes they join flocks of other swallows, especially when not breeding. They take a variety of insects such as beetles in flight (museum specimens). These swallows nest singly or in groups (one group contained 80 pairs:

Blakers *et al.* 1984). They may be territorial to some extent (Lord 1956); one observer noted a dispute, mainly vocal, between the occupants of a nesting area and intruders (Edwards 1948). After the breeding season they usually form small flocks. They roost communally in their own and in other birds' burrows; as many as 27 have been found in one burrow. There have been a few instances of groups being found in a torpid condition during the day in burrows (Serventy 1970; Congreve 1972): Congreve described these torpid birds as cold to the touch, with eyes closed, wings folded, legs and feet tucked in and the plumage dull; this was after 18 days of cold wet weather in June (the austral winter), when insect food would have been scarce.

BREEDING The breeding season lasts from July or August to December and following the rains in arid regions (Macdonald 1973). There is usually one brood raised per season. For nest sites, White-backed Swallows use sandy river banks, embankments, mine workings, pits, quarries, crowns of hills where vertical sandy faces are present, and the burrows of bandicoots and rat kangaroos. They usually excavate their own tunnel, but may also use deserted burrows made by other species. The tunnel is about 6 cm (2½ in) in diameter, and about 60 cm (2 ft) long, although burrows up to 1 m (3⅓ ft) long have been found. An enlarged chamber, in which the nest is placed, is excavated at the end of the burrow. The nest, which is shallow and saucer-shaped, is a collection of dried grass and leaves, sometimes with pieces of seaweed or fine rootlets depending on what is available locally (Campbell 1901; Serventy and Whittell 1962). The clutch size is usually four or five, occasionally six. The eggs are pure white and slightly glossy. They measure 17.3×12.5 mm ($16–18.3 \times 12.2–13.1$; weight 1.42). Up to nine eggs have been recorded in a nest, but this is probably due to two females laying in a single nest (Campbell 1901).

VOICE The contact call is a single 'check' uttered in flight; among flocks, this results in a constant harsh sound. The song is a twittering.

DESCRIPTION This medium-sized swallow has an unusual plumage coloration. Instead of having the upperparts dark and the underparts light-coloured like most hirundines, it is partly white above and blackish below. The forehead, outer parts of the crown and the mantle, the chin, throat and upper breast, and the axillaries and underwing-coverts are pure white. The centre of the crown is dark grey-brown; the crown feathers have dark centres and pale edges giving a slight scaly effect. The face between the bill and the eyes is black, and this continues as a grey-brown band across the face and ear-coverts and onto the hindneck. The rest of the upperparts and the lower breast, abdomen and undertail-coverts are black with a slight blue gloss. The scapulars, wing-coverts, wings and deeply forked tail are brownish-black. The bill is black, the eyes are dark brown and the legs and feet are grey-brown. The sexes are alike. The juvenile is duller and browner, with little gloss, the white areas being more buffy-white and the scaly effect on the crown more extensive so that there appears to be just a line of white above the eyes; the feathers of the wings and upper-tail-coverts have pale edges, and the outer tail feathers are short.

Measurements Length 15 cm (6"). Wing 98–109 (mean 102.1); tail 64–78 (mean 72.2); fork 36–41 (mean 37.8); bill 7.9–9 (mean 8.3); tarsus 10.5–11.8 (mean 11.3). Weight 12–15.8 (mean 14.8).

36 GREY-RUMPED SWALLOW Plate 12
Pseudhirundo griseopyga (Sundevall)

Hirundo griseopyga Sundevall, 1850, Öfv. K. Vet.-Akad. Förh., 7, p. 107: Durban, Natal.

Pseudhirundo griseopyga melbina (Verreaux and Verreaux), 1851, Gabon.

Pseudhirundo griseopyga andrewi (Andrew), 1966, Lake Naivasha, Kenya.

FIELD CHARACTERS Grey-rumped Swallows have a dark brown head, neck, rump and uppertail-coverts, the rest of the upperparts being glossy blue; the underparts are dull white. In the field, the brown head and rump and white underparts of this species are distinctive compared with other swallows. Juvenile House Martins (72) are similar, but have a white rump and shallowly forked tail. This is an open-country species, usually seen in flocks, often in large ones when not breeding. The flight is weak and wavering. It is often silent.

HABITAT These swallows need open areas, especially those near water, for breeding and foraging. They can be found both in mountainous country, mainly up to 2000 m (6600 ft), and in lowland areas where there is grassy or wooded savanna, grassland, vleis, burned ground, woodland clearings, golf courses, polo fields, airfields, flat, marshy ground, ploughed fields, rice-paddies and meadows. The race *melbina* is recorded from wet, humid coastal areas.

DISTRIBUTION AND POPULATION Grey-rumped Swallows are widespread, breeding throughout much of Africa south of the Sahara apart from southwestern Africa (Hall and Moreau 1970). The nominate race ranges widely from southern Ethiopia and the Sudan through Uganda, Kenya and Tanzania, west to Zaire and south through Zambia and eastern Zimbabwe, Malawi and Mozambique to eastern and northern Transvaal, northern Botswana, Caprivi, the lower Zambesi River, northern Natal, Swaziland and Zululand. The race *melbina* occurs patchily in West Africa from Liberia and Guinea Bissau to Gabon and the lower Congo River around Majumba and Landana. The third race *andrewi* has been seen only on migration, in Kenya; it may breed in Ethiopia (Williams 1966).

In many parts of the range these are common or locally abundant swallows, especially in southern localities. In Nigeria, however, they are rare, breeding only sporadically (Elgood *et al.* 1973), and they are uncommon in East Africa (Britton 1980). There are often marked seasonal fluctuations in numbers in many localities. Since Grey-rumped Swallows do not use artificial nesting sites, they have not benefited from the construction of human artefacts; they do, however, favour open areas and have made use of human-made sites such as burnt areas, golf courses, polo fields and airfields (Benson 1980).

MIGRATION In southern Africa, these swallows are resident but are subject to local movements, especially during the rainy season, when they move to lower elevations (Maclean 1985). They have been seen at sea off Angola, possibly migrating

(Took 1967). In Zambia, they move away from flooded areas in January and February and re-appear in the dry season between March and September, numbers fluctuating from year to year (Taylor 1979; Aspinwall 1980). Their movements depend on the rains; in Zimbabwe they are usually present from April to October/November, but will remain in the area later, even all year, if the weather is very dry (Tree 1976; Irwin 1981). In Central and Western Africa, their movements are complex and poorly understood: they are residents in some areas, making local movements, but breed sporadically in others and tend to be nomadic when not breeding (Elgood *et al.* 1973). They are rare vagrants to eastern Cape Province and, in West Africa, to the Gambia and Ivory Coast (Thiollay 1975; Gore 1981; Maclean 1985).

FOOD AND BEHAVIOUR Grey-rumped Swallows are often seen in small flocks or pairs during the breeding season. The flight is weak and erratic; birds often flutter and dart after insects. They feed at an average height of only 8 m (26 ft), predominantly over water but also over open ground and around tree canopies (Waugh 1978). On Mount Nimba in Liberia, they often sweep up one slope and then dive down 30–50 m on the other side to repeat the manoeuvre (Colston and Curry-Lindahl 1986). They sometimes come to the ground to eat large insects caught in flight. The diet is largely unknown, but stomach contents of museum specimens include dipteran flies, beetles and other unidentified insects. This is a fairly gregarious species, breeding in groups on sand banks, although the holes are generally widely spaced. They form large flocks, sometimes of thousands of individuals, before and after the breeding season. They roost communally in reedbeds.

BREEDING The breeding season generally coincides with the dry season (to avoid flooding of burrows), but these birds also breed opportunistically whenever conditions are suitable. In West Africa they usually breed between November and May (e.g. Elgood 1982; Grimes 1988), in Ethiopia there are breeding records from March, April and December (Urban and Brown 1971), and in East Africa they breed in May, July–October and March (Brown and Britton 1980). Maclean (1985) gave dates of May–November for southern Africa and July–November for Zimbabwe, and Earlé (1987b) gave March and May–

July for South Africa. In South Africa 80% of records are in June–July, in Central Africa 86% are from July to August, and in East Africa 64% are from August to September (Earlé 1987b). Most holes are dug in flat sand and penetrate up to 1 m (39 in) into the ground at a fairly steep angle. A nest in the form of a pad of coarse grass, lined with soft fibres, hairs and feathers, is placed at the end of the hole in a chamber some 15 cm (6 in) in diameter (Benson 1951; Serle 1957). These swallows also occupy old rodent burrows in open flat ground, disused kingfisher and bee-eater burrows and old termite mounds.

Estimates of the clutch size vary from two or three in West Africa, two to four in East Africa, three or four in southern Africa and two to five in Zaire. The eggs are white with some gloss, different clutches varying somewhat in size and shape; they measure 16 × 11.9 mm (14.3–17.6 × 11–12.9; weight 1.4). Details of incubation and nestling periods have not been recorded.

VOICE In flight it utters a grating 'chraa', but is often silent. Winterbottom (1939) described its voice as a faint, harsh hiss.

DESCRIPTION These are small swallows with a rather dull plumage. The forehead, crown and nape are brown; the feathers have narrow buffy edges, which gives the slight effect of scales. The areas around the eyes and the ear-coverts are darker than the rest of the head. The lores are black, with a narrow white line above. The mantle, lower back, scapulars and wing-coverts are a glossy deep blue, the feathers of the mantle having white bases which are sometimes visible. The rump is grey-brown. When the feathers are newly moulted, those on the rump have a whitish fringe. The uppertail-coverts are a darker grey-brown. The underparts, including the undertail-coverts, are dull white, with a wash of pale grey-brown towards the sides, especially on the breast. In fresh plumage, the underparts from chin to breast have a pinkish wash. The axillaries are pale smoky-brown; the underwing-coverts are white with a wash of smoky-brown. The wings and tail are brownish-black with a dull blue wash; the tail feathers are edged with pale grey-brown on the outer web, and the outermost two pairs have dull white edges, broadest on the inner web, which abrade with wear. The outermost tail feathers are elongated, forming a deep fork. The eyes are dark brown, the bill black and the legs and feet pale sepia. The sexes are alike. Juveniles are almost identical to adults, having a partly glossy plumage even at the nestling stage; the mantle, scapulars and wings are browner, and the rump is grey-brown with fawn tips; the tips of the feathers of the crown, mantle, greater wing-coverts, inner primaries and secondaries have buffy fringes, the underparts and cheeks are washed with a pinky-buff, and the lores are not so black. The outer tail feathers are also shorter. The moult takes place between October and May, when breeding activity is at a minimum (Earlé 1987b).

Measurements Length 14 cm (5½"). Wing 91–104 (mean 97.2); tail 63–90 (mean 76.8); fork 33–44 (mean 38.3); bill 7.5–9.8 (mean 8.3); tarsus 10.2–11.5 (mean 10.9). Weight 8.3–10.3 (mean 9.5).

RACES The nominate race is the largest. The West African race *melbina* has a very dark brown rump and uppertail-coverts, and a darker brown crown which has a slight blue sheen (wing 91–100); juveniles are paler on the crown and rump. The race *andrewi* is brown above and smoky-grey below, and is the same size as nominate *griseopyga*.

There has been some disagreement over the number of subspecies of *griseopyga*. In 1937, Bannerman described a race *liberiae* from Liberia which is smaller than the nominate and has a clear brown rump and a pale brown, non-glossy head, whiter underwing-coverts and shorter outer tail feathers and wings. Another race from the highlands of northern Cameroon and northeastern Nigeria, *gertrudis*, has also been described; this is smaller than *griseopyga* and has a slightly browner crown and rump. According to White (1961), only the nominate race and *liberiae* are valid. Other authors have recognised all four races. Dowsett (1972), however, suggested that the size and colour differences between *gertrudis* and *griseopyga* were not sufficient to distinguish between these two races; he also concluded that *liberiae* should be merged with *melbina*.

In 1965 Williams collected a swallow from Lake Naivasha which he described as a new species, but which is similar to *griseopyga* although it looks more robust. It is browner above than *melbina* and smoky-grey below. Because of its resemblance to *griseopyga* it is now usually considered to be a race of this species.

37 MASCARENE MARTIN
Phedina borbonica (Gmelin)

Plate 13

Hirundo borbonica Gmelin, 1789, Syst. Nat., 1, pt. 2, p. 1017: Bourbon = Mauritius.

Phedina borbonica madagascariensis Hartlaub, 1860, Madagascar.

FIELD CHARACTERS Mascarene Martins are grey-brown, with streaked upperparts and underparts, although the streaking on the upperparts is not noticeable in the field. They are the only streaked swallow on Madagascar. They resemble Brown-throated Sand Martins (26), but the latter have plain underparts. On mainland Africa they could be confused with Lesser Striped Swallows (57), but they have a more shallowly forked tail without any white patches. They are fairly gregarious and found mainly in open country. The flight is slow and heavy.

HABITAT On Madagascar, this martin is found from sea level to 2200 m (7250 ft), feeding over open ground, desert brush, wooded plains, forest, marshes and ricefields. On the wintering grounds in eastern Africa, it is also seen in open areas such as recently cleared forest (Clancey *et al.* 1969). On Mauritius and Reunion it is locally distri-

buted on the coast, but feeds in areas from sea level up to 1500 m (4930 ft), such as over reservoirs, along cliffs, among *Casuarina* trees, over dense thickets or along the shore.

DISTRIBUTION AND POPULATION This swallow has a restricted breeding range, being endemic to Madagascar and the Mascarene Islands (Cheke 1987a, b). The nominate race occurs on Mauritius and Reunion, and *madagascariensis* occurs on Madagascar. The latter may also breed on Pemba, where it has been recorded between September and March (i.e. its breeding season) (Packrenham 1979). On Mauritius, the breeding sites are along the southern and western coast and inland on cliffs. On Reunion it is locally distributed, mainly at 200–500 m (660–1640 ft), along the east side of the island and around St-Joseph and the Grande Chaloupe.

Mascarene Martins are fairly common

on Madagascar, though locally distributed (Rand 1936; Milon *et al.* 1973). The Mauritius and Reunion race was badly hit by a cyclone in 1861 (Berlioz 1946) and few birds were seen for several years afterwards; by the turn of the century it had recovered, and was reported to be common but local. Staub (1973) found it fairly abundant on Mauritius (with about 300–500 individuals on Reunion). On Mauritius, Cheke (1987a) recorded 70–75 pairs in 1973–74, but there may be more at unrecorded sites. Recent cyclones have apparently had less effect than that in 1861, but the Reunion population was disturbed by a cyclone and heavy rain in 1980 (Cheke 1987b). On Reunion the population in 1974 was about 200 pairs, possibly 200–400 (Barré and Barau 1982; Cheke 1987a); 190 martins were seen perching on wires after a night of heavy rain (Barré and Barau 1982).

MIGRATION The race *borbonica* is resident on Mauritius and Reunion and has not been recorded away from these islands; the breeding sites, however, are deserted from January to mid August, so these martins may make local movements. The Madagascar race is migratory, making local and long-distance movements. On Madagascar it is migratory on the Imerina Plateau, being present only from October to March (Dee 1987b). There are several records of Mascarene Martins wintering in the lowlands of eastern Africa, and they may occur there each year although they are not regularly seen. Clancey *et al.* (1969) found large numbers in late June to mid July in Mozambique in 1968, and hundreds were seen in Malawi at Lake Chilwa in June and July 1944 (Benson 1944). This race is also known from Kenya, Pemba Island, Mauritius, Reunion, the Seychelles, Aldabra and other islands in the western Indian Ocean. Some of these records are probably due to birds being blown off course (Feare 1977); the Amirantes record, for example, followed the passage of cyclone Agatha.

FOOD AND BEHAVIOUR The flight is slow, heavy and fluttering, including a lot of gliding. The martins often feed close to the ground and to bushes or trees, and join flocks of other swallows and swifts. Mascarene Martins are often seen feeding singly or in small groups. They perch on the ground and on wires and bushes. Feeding activity is highest just before dusk. A variety of flying insects is taken, including beetles and Hymenoptera (museum specimens). They breed in groups. Rand (1936) recorded one of about ten pairs. Recently groups on Mauritius have contained three to twelve pairs, and the largest was about 20 pairs. Breeding groups on Reunion also have only a few pairs (Cheke 1987). They roost in flocks of a few birds on buildings, cliffs and bushes, sometimes in company with other birds, for example with Blue-cheeked Bee-eaters *Merops superciliosus*, in the Seychelles (C.J. Feare, pers. comm.).

BREEDING Breeding occurs in the wet season, from August to November in Madagascar and September to early January on Mauritius and Reunion (Milon *et al.* 1973; Cheke 1987a, b). The nests are made usually 3–5 m (10–16 ft) above water, on narrow slate ledges, in rocks, behind tufts of grass or ferns, in roofs, in buildings and subterranean passages, and also in caves on Reunion. The nest is a shallow cup of twigs and vegetable matter such as dry stems, dry grass, *Casuarina* and algae, with a lining of finer vegetation and a few feathers. The female incubates alone, but the male helps to feed the young (Staub 1973). The eggs are white with brown spots and measure 21.6 × 15 mm (19.8–23.4 × 14.5–16; weight 2.5). The clutch size is two on Madagascar and Mauritius, but two or three on Reunion. The chicks are fed by the parents after fledging (Cheke 1987a). There are no details on incubation or fledging periods.

VOICE The song, 'siri-liri siri-liri', is uttered on the wing and when the bird is perched. It comprises three motifs: a warble, a lower-amplitude, more attenuated warble, and one ending with glissando elements (Horne 1987). The 'chip' call is a contact call, but is included in songs as well. There are also pre- and post-copulatory calls and aggressive notes. However, they are fairly quiet swallows (C.J. Feare, pers. comm.).

DESCRIPTION This is a medium-sized swallow. The upperparts are a dark grey-brown with unclear streaks; below it is grey-brown, with white on the throat and abdomen and sooty-black streaks from the chin to the vent. The sides of the breast and flanks are greyish-brown. The lores are blackish and the ear-coverts brown with sepia streaks. The undertail-coverts are grey-brown bordered with white. The underwing coverts and axillaries are dusky grey-brown. The wings and shallowly forked tail are blackish-brown. Fresh tertials have narrow pale edges. The legs, feet and bill are black and the eyes are dark brown. The sexes are alike. Juveniles are similar to the adults but have broad white tips to the tertials. Moult is known to occur in December and January on Mauritius, and in June and July in birds from Madagascar wintering in East Africa (Clancey *et al.* 1969; Cheke 1987a).

Measurements Length about 15 cm (6"). Wing 112–120 (mean 116.6); tail 50–59 (mean 54.6); fork 6–10 (mean 8.2); bill 10.3–12.1 (mean 11.3); tarsus 12.5–14 (mean 13.3). Weight 17.9–23.5–21.1.

RACES The race *madagascariensis* is paler and has a larger bill than *borbonica*. It has white undertail-coverts with dark feather shafts, more pronounced streaks on the breast and abdomen, lighter and greyer upperparts, whiter medio-ventral plane, and less well accentuated shaft streaking, that on the abdomen and undertail-coverts being reduced to very fine black lines.

38 CONGO MARTIN
Phedina brazzae Oustalet

Plate 13

Phedina brazzae Oustalet, 1886, Le Naturaliste, 8, p. 300: Ganciu, i.e. Nganchu, middle Congo River.

FIELD CHARACTERS Congo Martins are brown above, and white with heavy black streaking below. The heavy streaking on the underparts distinguishes this species from most other swallows in its range. It differs from other striped swallows in having a square tail without any white patches. It frequents rivers and is usually seen in small groups. The flight is heavy.

HABITAT Congo Martins are usually seen along rivers, especially where steep banks are available for nesting. One breeding group was seen in a rocky escarpment on the side of a valley (Rand *et al.* 1959).

DISTRIBUTION AND POPULATION There are few records of the Congo Martin, but it probably extends over southern Zaire, southern Congo and the extreme north of Angola (Lippens and Wille 1976). It is known from the type locality near Kwamouth in southern Zaire, Luluabourg and elsewhere in the Kasai, Djambala in the Congo and Lunda in Angola. It is not known to migrate.

FOOD AND BEHAVIOUR The flight is slow and includes periods of gliding. These martins are known to feed over rivers, sometimes in the company of other species of swallow. The diet consists of flying insects, and they have been recorded feeding on swarms of termites (Lynes 1938). Congo Martins nest singly or in small groups in often widely scattered holes in vertical river banks or cliffs. One group contained four pairs (Rand *et al.* 1959).

BREEDING Breeding takes place in July–October, at the end of the dry season and the beginning of the wet season before the river level rises sufficiently to flood the nest sites (Rand *et al.* 1959). The nest, a small pad of dry grass and feathers, is placed at the back of a hole about 50 cm (20 in) long in a bank or other suitable vertical face (Chapin 1953). The clutch size is three. The eggs are pure white and measure 18.5 × 12.5 mm (weight 1.5). The incubation and fledging periods are unknown.

VOICE The calls have not been recorded.

DESCRIPTION Congo Martins are small swallows. The upperparts are ashy-brown or grey-brown, the head being darker than the rest of the plumage. There are indistinct broad shaft streaks on the upperparts from the mantle to the tail-coverts. The ear-coverts and lores are blackish-brown. The underparts are white, with heavy blackish-brown shaft streaks, most dense on the chin and throat, and a brownish wash on the breast. The underwing-coverts and axillaries are dusky brown. The feathers of the undertail-coverts are brown centrally with white edges. The wing-coverts are blackish-brown with some pale margins in fresh plumage. The primaries, secondaries and tail are blackish-brown and the tail is square. The eyes are dark brown and the bill and legs and feet black. The sexes are alike. The juvenile has only diffuse striping on the underparts and has some rufous or buffy edges to the feathers on the upperparts, including the wing-coverts.

Measurements Length about 12 cm (4¾"). Wing 95–103 (mean 100.5); tail (square) 44–49 (mean 46.8); bill 7.9–8.8 (mean 8.5); tarsus 9–10.7 (mean 10). Weight 13.

39 CRAG MARTIN
Hirundo rupestris Scopoli

Hirundo rupestris Scopoli, 1769, Annus 1, Hist-Nat., p. 167: Tirol.

FIELD CHARACTERS The Crag Martin has an ashy-brown plumage, paler below with black underwing- and undertail-coverts. It could be confused with the Sand Martin (27), but is rather larger and stockier, and is a darker brown above and dingier below without a breast-band and with darker underwing- and undertail-coverts. It also has white patches in its tail which Sand Martins lack. The Rock Martin (40) is also similar, but, in areas where the two could be confused, is a smaller, paler and greyer bird. The Crag Martin is a mountain species, usually seen alone or in small groups when breeding, but in large flocks outside the breeding season. The flight is slow. There are several calls, most commonly a 'prrrt'.

HABITAT Crag Martins frequent cliffs in mountainous areas, grassy hills with crags and precipices, and river gorges, usually in dry, warm and sheltered situations. They are not usually associated with human habitation, but are often seen around ancient hill forts in India (Ali and Ripley 1972). They breed mostly up to 2000–2700 m (6600–8900 ft), but will breed at up to 5000 m (16,500 ft) in central Asia.

DISTRIBUTION AND POPULATION Crag Martins are widespread, breeding over much of the mountainous parts of southern Europe, the Mediterranean and Asia. The breeding range extends from the Iberian peninsula and southern and central France, south throughout the Mediterranean to the extreme northwest of Africa and the Persian Gulf and east through the Himalayas to southwestern and northeastern China. The species has recently spread north in Yugoslavia and Romania, but some colonies in France have disappeared and only a few pairs breed in West Germany (Cramp 1988). This species is locally fairly common, but is less numerous than other swallows. It is spreading in some areas, using buildings and motorway bridges to an increasing extent for breeding (Cramp 1988).

MIGRATION Northern populations are migratory; others are resident, though they make local post-breeding movements (Cramp 1988). Even among northern birds, however, some stay in the northern Mediterranean to winter; 2,000–3,000 roost on Gibraltar in winter (Elkins and Etheridge 1974). Others winter in Africa, mainly Morocco, Algeria and Tunisia, but also in Senegal, the Nile Valley, the Red Sea coast and Ethiopia. Russian breeders winter in China south to central Yunnan, the Indian subcontinent and the Middle East. Indian birds are resident, but move to lower ground throughout the peninsula after breeding. The populations in Cyprus and Turkey move to lowland areas in winter.

FORAGING AND FOOD The flight is slow and graceful, with frequent gliding. When breeding, Crag Martins often feed along a cliff face close to their nest, flying back and forth and using any thermals that are present (Farina 1978). At other times they also feed low over alpine meadows or streams. Most prey is taken in flight, but there are a few records of Crag Martins picking insects from rocks, the ground or the surface of water (Cramp 1988). There are few studies of their diet (see Glutz von Blotzheim and Bauer 1985 and Cramp 1988 for a summary). In one study in Spain (Guitián Rivera *et al.* 1980), flies, stoneflies and caddisflies were important prey, and beetles, flies, pond skaters, butterflies and a wasp were recorded in the nest and faeces. In Switzerland, the diet includes brachyceran and nematoceran flies, beetles such as weevils, Lepidoptera, ants and spiders (Glutz von Blotzheim 1962). Small moths are locally important, and stomachs of Asian birds have contained small beetles, bugs, flies and Hymenoptera.

SOCIAL ORGANISATION These martins breed solitarily or in small loose groups of a few pairs, rarely more than ten (Strahm 1953). A few larger groups of 50 or more are known, however (Cramp 1988). The nests are typically well spaced out, usually several metres apart and an average of 30 m (100 ft) in Strahm's (1956, 1963) study. Crag Martins are gregarious outside the breeding season, forming flocks of up to 400 birds and roosting in large numbers on cliff ledges, though migrants usually move in groups of only a few birds (Cramp 1988). They rarely associate with other hirundines.

SOCIOSEXUAL BEHAVIOUR These are aggressive birds, defending a territory around their nest of 200–300 m² (Strahm 1963). They feed partly within and partly outside this territory. Residents dive at intruders with bill open and uttering anger calls. The dive may be followed by a chase or by a fight, with the resident grasping the intruder by the nape and both birds falling locked together (Strahm 1963; Farina 1978). In one apparent threat display, an incubating female gaped and sleeked her plumage when her mate arrived and forcibly tried to relieve her (Farina 1978). Little is known of courtship and mating behaviour (see Glutz von Blotzheim and Bauer 1985 and Cramp 1988 for summaries). At the start of the breeding season chasing can be seen, but this decreases as pairs form and does not seem to be related to mate-guarding as in Sand Martins (Strahm 1954; Cramp 1988). In one display, two birds flew towards each other and touched bills (Strahm 1954). Courtship feeding has been described but does not seem to be typical (Prenn 1937; Hauri 1968). Possible attempted copulations have been recorded in which two birds fly one above the other with tails spread and calling; they touch and hold each other momentarily, then fly together for a few seconds (Strahm 1954).

BREEDING The breeding season is from May to August and two broods are normal (Cramp 1988). Crevices and hollows on cliff faces and sites under overhanging rocks are used for nest sites; buildings and bridges are also used. The nest is a quarter sphere made of mud pellets and well lined with feathers, mixed with dry grass, straw, etc. It is re-used for second broods and in successive years. Both sexes build the nest, usually in a few short bouts each day; taking one to three weeks to complete it (Rivera et al. 1980). The female continues lining the nest during incubation (Strahm 1954).

The clutch size is two to five, with an average of three. The eggs are white, with speckles and blotches of red-brown, grey-brown or purple-brown concentrated at the broad end (the speckling, however, is variable). They measure 20.2 × 14.0 mm (17.2–23.2 × 12.7–15.4; weight 2.08). The female does most or all of the incubation; the male occasionally relieves her for short bouts (Hauri 1968; Farina 1978). The incubation period is 13–17 days, and the nestling period is 24–27 days (Rivera et al.

1980). The nestlings are fed frequently, the parents visiting the nest every two to five minutes (Strahm 1956). The fledglings are fed by the parents for another 14–21 days (Strahm 1956; Hauri 1968; Rivera et al. 1980).

VOICE Crag Martins have a wide range of calls (Stadler 1928; Prenn 1937; Elkins and Etheridge 1978; and see Cramp 1988). The song is a series of soft twittering notes. The most commonly heard call is a contact call 'prrrt', used singly or in series within a flock and between members of a pair. There is a variety of alarm and warning calls: a 'zrrr', uttered when the birds are disturbed; a two-syllable 'gsigsi', given when a predator is seen; a plaintive 'whee', given when the bird is excited; and a descending whistle, 'siu'. During aerial chases, a series of notes such as 'zuirr-schri schri rerere-ririri-twirr' or 'chu-chu-chu-chu-chu' is uttered. A 'rrr' anger call is used when an intruder is attacked. Other calls heard, such as a two-syllable 'pitcha', may be variants of these main calls.

DESCRIPTION The Crag Martin is a medium-sized hirundine with uniform ashy-brown upperparts. In fresh plumage, the feather tips of the mantle, back and rump sometimes have narrow rufous fringes. The sides of the head are brown-grey; the lores are darker and the ear-coverts are sometimes mottled pale grey. The cheeks, chin and upper throat are speckled ashy-brown and grey or buff; the speckling is variable and sometimes merges into a stripe on the cheeks. The lower throat and breast are pale buff, whitish in worn plumage. The pale buff breast grades into the pale brown-grey of the abdomen to the dark brown-grey of the flanks, sides and undertail-coverts; the latter also have white tips. In fresh plumage, the abdomen is more buffy and the undertail-coverts have rufous tips. The underwing-coverts and axillaries are dull black. There are buff fringes to the coverts along the leading edge of the wing. The wings and wing-coverts are dark brown-grey. There is a faint green sheen to the flight feathers, upper primary coverts, bastard wing and lesser upperwing-coverts in fresh plumage; the upperwing-coverts and tertials have white tips when fresh. The tail, which is square, is dark brown, with a white spot on the inner web of each feather except on the central and outermost pairs; however, there is occasionally a spot on the outermost pair as well. The eyes are dark brown, the bill is black with a grey base to the lower mandible, and the legs and feet are brownish-flesh with darker toes. The sexes are alike. Juveniles are similar to adults, but have widespread rufous edges to the feathers and usually less speckling on the cheeks, chin and throat; the rufous colour becomes paler and abrades with wear, rufous edges being retained longest on the tertials and greater coverts; the tail has generally smaller patches than on the adult. The base of the lower mandible is yellowish on juveniles through to about September, in contrast to dark grey-black on adults. Moult usually starts while the birds are breeding, from June onwards, and finishes by December (Cramp 1988).

Measurements Length 15 cm (6"). Wing 126–136 (mean 130.8); tail (square) 52–57 (mean 54.4); bill 10.5–12.2 (mean 11.5); tarsus 10.6–12.5 (mean 11.6). Weight 17–33 (mean 23).

RACES Two races, in central Asia (*centralasica*) and the Atlas Mountains (*theresae*), have been proposed on the basis of slight differences in size and colour, but there is no consistent geographical variation (Vaurie 1951).

40 ROCK MARTIN   Plate 14
Hirundo fuligula Lichtenstein
Alternative name: Pale Crag Martin (northern populations)

Hirundo fuligula Lichtenstein, 1842, Verz. Säugth. Vög. Kaffernland, p. 18: Kaffirland, = Grahamstown, Cape Province.

Hirundo fuligula pusilla (Zedlitz), 1908, Asmara, 3000 m Eritrea.

Hirundo fuligula fusciventris (Vincent), 1933, Namuli Mt, 6200 ft Quelimane Province, Mozambique.

Hirundo fuligula bansoensis (Bannerman), 1923, Bamenda, 4750 ft Cameroon Highlands.

Hirundo fuligula anderssoni (Sharpe and Wyatt), 1887, Damaraland.

Hirundo fuligula pretoriae (Roberts), 1922, Pretoria, Transvaal.

Hirundo fuligula obsoleta (Cabanis), 1850, northeast Africa; restricted to lower Egypt on the right bank of the Nile in the region of Cairo and the neighbouring Moqattam Hills by Vaurie 1951, Am. Mus. Nov., 1529, p. 16.

Hirundo fuligula spatzi (Geyr), 1916, Gara Djenoun (= Garet el Djenoun), Tuareg Mts.

Hirundo fuligula presaharica Vaurie, 1953, Biskra, southern Algeria.

Hirundo fuligula buchanani (Hartert), 1921, Mt Baguezan, Asben, French Sahara.

Hirundo fuligula arabica (Reichenow), 1905, Lahej, Arabia.

Hirundo fuligula perpallida Vaurie, 1951, Hofuf, Hasa district, eastern Saudi Arabia.

Hirundo fuligula peloplasta (Hume), 1872: 'the Gaj. the Nurrinai and other small streams that issue from the bare stony hills that divide Suidh from Kelat . . . the rocky headland of Minora . . . Kurrachee Harbour . . . and along the Mekran Coast' (*pallida* auct. occupied, Brooke 1974).

The northern populations of this species are sometimes considered to be a separate species, *Hirundo obsoleta* (the Pale Crag Martin), but the continuous variation in coloration and size suggests that the races are conspecific (Hall and Moreau 1970; Voous 1977). Thus the *obsoleta* group of pale races from North Africa and Asia intergrades in colour and size with the darker, smaller races from West, Central and East Africa. Birds of the *fuligula* group of races from southern Africa are larger than those of equatorial Africa but intergrade in colour, being generally paler. Rock Martins are the African representatives of the crag martin superspecies, which includes the Crag Martin (39) in Europe and the Dusky Crag Martin (41) in India. Meinertzhagen (1954) treated them as a single species, but the breeding ranges of *rupestris* and the *obsoleta* group overlap, suggesting separate species (Voous 1977).

160

FIELD CHARACTERS Rock Martins are largely earth-brown, with a russet chin and throat. They are distinctive compared with other African *Hirundo* species in having a drab plumage. They resemble Sand Martins (27), but differ in having white patches in the tail feathers. Northern races differ from Crag Martins in being paler and greyer, with a white throat and less contrasting underwing-coverts. Southern races are darker, but still show a paler throat and less dark under-wing. They frequent mountainous areas. They breed in single pairs or small groups, but form larger flocks at other times. The flight is slow.

HABITAT This species replaces the Crag Martin in tropical and arid mountainous areas, but is absent from rainforest zones. The preferred habitat is hilly or terrain with steep cliffs and crags and rocky gorges, but they can be found down to sea level, especially in rocky areas and towns. Unusually for swallows, they are often seen far from water. In North Africa, they also frequent ancient monuments and some desert towns such as Aswan (Cramp 1988).

DISTRIBUTION AND POPULATION Rock Martins breed throughout Africa and the Middle East to western Asia in Afghanistan and Pakistan. Because the variation is clinal the different races tend to intergrade with one another, especially *arabica* and *obsoleta* in Mecca, Jidda and Taif and *pusilla* and *obsoleta* in northern Sudan. Intermediates between *fusciventris* and *fuligula* also occur in southeastern Zimbabwe. The distributions of the races are thus not clearly demarcated, but are indicated as follows:
fuligula: the eastern Cape.
pusilla: Mali to central and western Sudan, Eritrea and most of Ethiopia.
fusciventris: southern Sudan, southern Ethiopia and East Africa south to Zimbabwe and northern Mozambique.
bansoensis: West and Central Africa.
anderssoni: southwestern Cape, south-western Africa to southern Angola.
pretoriae: eastern South Africa from Cape Province to the Transvaal.
obsoleta: Egypt, Sinai, the Dead Sea depression, Arabia (but not in the southwest and northeast) and southwestern Iran.
spatzi: south-central Algeria, southern Libya, Chad and Mali.
presaharica: the Atlas Saharien mountains of Algeria and Morocco south to Timimoun and El Golea and Mauritania.
buchanani: the Air Massif in the south-central Sahara.
arabica: Gebel Elba, the Red Sea Province of the Sudan, southwest Arabia, northern Somalia and Socotra.
perpallida: northeast Arabia and southern Iraq.
peloplasta: central and eastern Iran, Afghanistan and Pakistan.

Within this range, Rock Martins often have a localised distribution because of their preference for rocky areas as nesting sites, but they can be common where they do occur. They also take advantage of artificial structures for breeding, and this may allow populations to expand into flatter country.

MIGRATION Rock Martins are generally resident. Although they do not make long migrations, they do disperse locally after breeding. Thus, the race *arabica* is known as a visitor to Somalia as well as a breeding species (Ash and Miskell 1983); and in Africa Rock Martins move to lower altitudes, and perhaps further north as well, after the breeding season (Irwin 1977). There are local movements in North Africa and Pakistan (Etchécopar and Hüe 1967; Ali and Ripley 1972). Large numbers build up in some areas during the non-breeding season, as in Saudi Arabia and Oman (Gallagher and Woodcock 1980; Jennings 1980).

FOOD AND BEHAVIOUR The flight is slow, with much gliding. The birds are particularly active at dawn and dusk (Mackworth-Praed and Grant 1963). They feed both low over the open ground and along cliff faces, at an average height of 7 m (23 ft) (Waugh 1978). They have also been recorded hawking over rocks on a beach (Skead 1966). When feeding nestlings, they hunt close to the nest (Moreau 1939b). They usually forage alone or in pairs, occasionally in small groups, and they join flocks feeding at grass fires (van Someren 1958). They catch a variety of insects in flight, including Hymenoptera, mosquitoes and other flies, beetles, plant bugs and ants (Bates 1936; Valverde 1957; museum specimens). They have also been seen feeding on the ground on flies (Meinertzhagen 1930). Rock Martins nest in single pairs; occasionally small groups form where plentiful nesting sites are available, particularly south of the Sahara. In South Africa one group held 40 pairs (Cramp 1988). When not breeding, they form usually small flocks, the largest up to 300 (Jennings 1980). Pairs form early on arrival at the breeding grounds. Once a nest site is selected it is aggressively defended from other individuals, including those of other species (Brooke and Vernon 1961). Courtship and copulation behaviour are not known, though in one instance a bird was seen to dive at another repeatedly, eventually mounting and copulating (Bundy and Morgan 1969).

BREEDING The breeding season varies geographically; in many areas it is not well defined. In South Africa Rock Martins breed chiefly from August to February, but in the Kalahari in any month after rain and in Zimbabwe from August to April (Maclean 1985; Earlé 1988a); the peak is August–December in South Africa (Earlé 1988a). In East Africa they breed in all months, with peaks in the rains in March–June, September–November or February–March, depending on the area; the overall peak is April–May and November (Brown and Britton 1981; Earlé 1988a). In Central Africa the peak is August–November and January–April (Earlé 1988a). In Ethiopia they breed in January–March and October–November (Urban and Brown 1971), while in western Africa they breed mainly from May to June and October–December (Mackworth-Praed and Grant 1973; Elgood 1982; Grimes 1988), and in northwestern Africa February–April (Etchécopar and Hüe 1967). In Asia, eggs are laid mainly from April to June (Baker 1934; Ali and Ripley 1972). Pairs often have two broods in a season, and three have been recorded (Sclater and Moreau 1933).

The nest is like that of the European Barn Swallow (42), a deep bowl made of mud pellets built against beams in the porches of buildings, or against a ceiling, an overhang, gable, under eaves, on bridges, dams, rock faces or quarries. The shape varies from a bowl when built on a ledge to a half cup when built against a rock face. Grasses, occasionally feathers, are used for the lining. The nest is built up and re-used for subsequent broods in the season and in subsequent years (Schmidt 1964), as well as for roosting in during the non-breeding season (Taylor 1942). One nest contained 960 pellets (Sclater and Moreau 1933). It is built by both sexes and can take several weeks to complete (Brooke and Vernon 1961).

The clutch size is usually two or three eggs are buffy-white with sepia or brown-grey spots often concentrated at the broad end. The size of the eggs varies from 20.8 × 14.1 mm (17.9–22.9 × 13.2–15.2; weight 2.17) in South Africa to 19.3 × 12.9 mm (18.5–20.0 × 12.0–13.5; weight 1.7) in Asia. Both sexes incubate and feed the nestlings. The incubation period is 16–19 days (Moreau and Moreau 1940; Hull 1944). The feeding rate is about ten visits per nestling per hour. Estimates of the nestling period vary from about 22–24 days to 25–30 days (Moreau and Moreau 1940; Brooke and Vernon 1961; Maclean 1985); the upper estimates may include fledglings that have returned to the nest, as the process of fledging takes several days. The fledglings return repeatedly to the nest (Moreau 1939b); in one case they were fed in the vicinity of the nest by their parents for at least 19 days (Brooke and Vernon 1961).

VOICE The song is a low twitter. There is also a contact call, a high-pitched monosyllabic 'twee'. Other calls have been noted, including a low chirp, a chortle and a rapid 'chir chir chir', but in general this is a quiet species (Frandsen 1982; Cramp 1988).

DESCRIPTION Rock Martins are medium-sized, rather drab brown swallows. The entire upperparts from the forehead to the uppertail-coverts, including the cheeks and ear-coverts, wing-coverts and wings, are earth-brown. The lores are blackish-brown. The chin, throat, and sides of the neck are pinkish-cinnamon, which extends over the upper part of the breast and the underwing-coverts and axillaries, merging into the earth-brown, washed with pale rufous, of the rest of the underparts. The edge of the wing is barred rufous and brown. The undertail-coverts have russet tips. The square tail is dark brown, and each feather, except for the outermost and innermost pairs, has a white patch on the inner web; however, the outermost pairs also occasionally have a small white spot. The eyes are brown, the bill is black and the legs and feet are pinkish-brown. The sexes are alike. Juveniles are similar to adults, but have widespread buffy-white edges on the feathers of the upperparts and buffy margins to the wing-coverts, primaries and secondaries. In northern populations, the moult starts during the breeding season when the birds are incubating or feeding young. In southern, central and eastern populations, moult has been recorded in all months, but few moult in July–September when breeding is often at a peak (Earlé 1988a).

Measurements Length 13 cm (5"). Wing 126–133 (mean 129.9); tail (square) 50–59 (mean 55.9); bill 10.3–11.5 (mean 10.9); tarsus 11.2–11.9 (mean 11.6). Weight (*fusciventris*) 16–30 (mean 22.4).

RACES The races differ mainly in the depth of colour of the plumage and in size. There is a cline in size from north to south, the nominate race being one of the largest; there is also a general cline in colour, from pale grey-brown or whitish-grey birds in the north to dark sooty-brown ones in the south. Northern races also have a whitish chin and throat compared with the rufous-brown of southern races. The plumage coloration thus matches the habitat of the birds, being palest in desert regions.

The race *fuligula* is large and dark (wing 126–133); *pusilla* is slightly paler (wing 110–128); *fusciventris* is small and dark (wing 106–121); *bansoensis* is very dark and small (wing 107–114); *anderssoni* (wing 123–139) is paler than *fuligula*; *pretoriae* is similar to *fuligula*, but slightly larger (wing 127–139); *obsoleta* is grey-brown (paler and greyer than the Crag Martin) (wing 110–125); *spatzi* is dusky brown, with deep buff from the throat to the abdomen (wing 117–121); *presaharica* is paler and sandier than *spatzi* (wing 117–123); *buchanani* is darker and browner than more northern races (wing 110–115); *arabica* is similar to *buchanani*, but slightly larger (wing 110–126); *perpallida* is whitish-grey above, with white chin and upper breast (wing 118–121); *peloplasta* (wing 118–125) is similar to but sandier than *obsoleta*.

41 DUSKY CRAG MARTIN   Plate 14
Hirundo concolor Sykes

Hirundo concolor Sykes, 1832, Proc. Comm. Zool. Soc. Lond., pt. 2 p. 83: the Dukhun.

Hirundo concolor sintaungensis (Stuart Baker), 1933, Sintaung, 6000 ft, Southern Shan States.

Dusky Crag Martins are part of a superspecies with the European Crag Martin (39) and African Rock Martin (40), and they have been considered conspecific (e.g. Meinertzhagen 1954). Both the Dusky Crag Martin and a race of the Rock Martin (*peloplasta*) breed in Pakistan, although at different altitudes, the Rock Martin in the mountains and the Dusky Crag in the plains; thus it is not known if they are sufficiently distinct to avoid hybridising. However, here they are treated as separate species.

FIELD CHARACTERS The Dusky Crag Martin is mostly sooty-brown, rather paler below. It can be distinguished from other sympatric swallows by its dark underparts. It is darker than the migrant European Crag Martin or the Rock Martin. It frequents mountainous areas, and is often seen alone or in small groups. The flight is slow.

HABITAT The typical habitat is hilly and mountainous areas with cliffs, gorges, caves and precipices, but these martins also breed in lowland areas and in towns with old stone buildings and in ancient fortifications. They occur even in large cities such as Bombay (Ali and Ripley 1972).

DISTRIBUTION AND POPULATION The species ranges across northern India to southeast Asia (Ali and Ripley 1972). The nominate race *concolor* occurs in India from along the base of the Himalayas

throughout the peninsula and east to Bihar and western Bengal. The race *sintaungensis* occurs in southwestern China, central and eastern Burma, Tenasserim, the mountains of northern Thailand, northwestern Tonkin, northern Laos and northern Annam; there is also a breeding record from Selangor, Malaysia (Wells 1984). Crag martins are locally distributed, but are common in some areas where nest sites are plentiful. They have probably greatly benefited for many centuries from the presence of humans and their buildings, which afford them excellent nesting sites. They are now frequently associated with human habitation, but still often use natural nest sites.

MIGRATION Dusky Crag Martins are resident, but make some local movements after breeding (Ali and Ripley 1972), Long-distance movements are probably rare, but a crag martin, probably of this species, was recorded in Borneo in 1980 (Vowles and Vowles 1985).

BEHAVIOUR The flight is slow, with frequent periods of gliding. These martins are usually seen feeding alone or in pairs, occasionally in small groups, hawking around crags and buildings. They use ledges and buildings as perches. Their habits appear to be similar to those of the European Crag Martin, although the species has not been well studied. The diet consists of insects caught in flight but is not known in detail (Ali and Ripley 1972). Dusky Crag Martins breed in single pairs, or occasionally in small, scattered groups when plenty of nesting sites are available. Outside the breeding season, they form small flocks.

BREEDING Breeding has been recorded in every month from January to October, but chiefly in February and March and after the start of the rains in July and August (Ali and Ripley 1972). Two broods are often raised. The nest is usually built under the eaves of buildings, including old hill forts, mosques and tombs, under bridges, archways, on the walls of wells, in culverts, or under overhangs and ledges on cliff faces or river banks; caves are also sometimes used. The nest is a half bowl made of mud pellets and lined with dry grass and feathers, built close to an overhang. It is repaired and re-used in subsequent years. The clutch size is usually two to four, exceptionally five. The eggs are white, with reddish-brown speckles and spots, and measure 17.7 × 13 mm (16.1–19.2 × 11.7–14.2; weight 1.57). Both male and female build the nest, incubate the eggs and feed the nestlings. No details are known of the incubation or nestling periods, but they are probably similar to those of the European Crag Martin.

VOICE The calls are like those of the Crag Martin: a soft 'chit-chit' contact call and a twittering song.

DESCRIPTION This small swallow is a darker form of the European Crag Martin and African Rock Martin. The upperparts are a uniform sooty-brown, darkest in fresh plumage. The lores, ear-coverts and sides of the head are dark brown. The underparts are a paler brown, darkening posteriorly. The chin, throat and foreneck are pale, dull rufous with fine black streaks. The axillaries and underwing-coverts are dark brown. The edge of the wing is barred rufous and brown. The tail is short and square, each feather apart from the outermost and innermost pairs having a small white patch on the inner web; however, very occasionally there is a small, faint spot on the outermost pair as well. The eyes are brown, the bill is blackish-brown and the legs and feet are pinkish-brown. The sexes are alike. The juvenile is sooty-brown like the adult, but the upperparts and wings have narrow rufous-grey margins; it also has a paler chin and throat, without the black streaks.

Measurements Length 13 cm (5"). Wing 103–113 (mean 106.9); tail (square) 42–47 (mean 45.2); bill 7.5–9.1 (mean 8.5); tarsus 9.2–10.2 (mean 9.7). Weight 12–14.

RACES Dusky Crag Martins from Burma and Thailand have been described as a separate race *sintaungensis*, which is darker than the nominate race, with more blackish than brown on the back and dark brown underparts. However, it is not clearly distinct from *concolor*, as individuals of the nominate race themselves vary somewhat in the degree of blackness of the plumage, which may also be blacker when fresh (Vaurie 1951).

42 BARN SWALLOW   Plate 15
Hirundo rustica Linnaeus
Alternative names: Swallow, Chimney Swallow, House Swallow

Hirundo rustica Linnaeus, 1758, Syst. Nat., ed. 10, p. 191: Sweden.

Hirundo rustica transitiva (Hartert), 1910, Plains of Esdraclon, Palestine.

Hirundo rustica savignii Stephens, 1817, Egypt.

Hirundo rustica gutturalis Scopoli, 1786, 'in nova Guiana' = Antigua, Panay, Philippine Islands, ex Sonnerat, Voy. à la Nouvelle Guinée, p. 118, pl. 76.

Hirundo rustica tytleri Jerdon, 1864, Dacca.

Hirundo rustica erythrogaster Boddaert, 1783, Cayenne, ex Daubenton, Pl. enlum., pl. 724, fig. 1.

FIELD CHARACTERS The Barn Swallow has steel-blue upperparts, white underparts, rufous-chestnut forehead, chin and throat and a well-defined blue breast-band. This colour pattern, together with the long outer tail feathers, makes this a very distinctive swallow, but in Africa the juvenile, lacking the long tail feathers, is difficult to distinguish from the Red-chested Swallow (43) on the wing, although the latter has a narrower breast-band and more white in the tail. The Barn Swallow frequents open country, nesting on human artefacts. It flies low, zigzagging, with rapid wingbeats.

HABITAT Barn Swallows breed in a wide variety of climates and over a wide altitudinal range, from sea level to 1800 m (5900 ft) in the Alps and to 3000 m (9900 ft) in the Caucasus. The preferred habitat is open country such as farmland where buildings are available for nesting and where water is nearby. In Europe, the House Martin (72) replaces it in towns, but in some areas the Barn Swallow uses urban sites, such as eaves along a street; thus, on Honshu, where the Red-rumped Swallow (60) also occurs, the latter is the rural bird and the Barn Swallow the urban one (Mizuta 1963).

DISTRIBUTION AND POPULATION This is the most widespread swallow species, breeding in North America, Europe and Asia (AOU 1983; Cramp 1988). In Africa south of the Sahara, it is replaced by several similar swallows with which it forms a superspecies. The nominate race breeds throughout Europe and Russia east to the Yenisei valley, south to northern Africa, the Near and Middle East, and the Himalayas as far east as Sikkim. Two races have restricted ranges around the Mediterranean: *transitiva* breeds in southern Turkey, Syria, Lebanon, western Jordan and Israel, and *savignii* breeds in the Egyptian delta south to Luxor. The race *gutturalis* breeds in Asia from the eastern Himalayas east to Japan, Korea and northeastern Burma; and *tytleri* breeds in central Siberia, from the Podkamanaya Tunguska, east to Takutsk and south to Nizhneudinsk and northern Mongolia. The New World race *erythrogaster* breeds throughout much of North America, from Alaska and Canada south through central Mexico to Chiapas; it has also been reported breeding in the wintering range, in Argentina, near Mar Chiquita, at least since 1980 (Martinez 1983).

The Old World subspecies intergrade with one another; populations in the areas of overlap are intermediates and are sometimes referred to as separate subspecies. In the Amur Territory, *tytleri* and *gutturalis* were probably once separated, but both may have colonised this area in the seventeenth century when Russian immigrants arrived and provided nesting sites; the birds in this area are distinct hybrids between the races (Smirensky and Mishchensko 1981).

In the past this species has suffered some declines. In the United States, numbers dropped in the nineteenth century: the blame was put on House Sparrow introductions (Graber *et al.* 1972). It has also declined in central and western Alaska since the mid 1920s and rarely breeds there now (Kessel and Gibson 1978). In most places, however, populations have increased in the past century, probably because of the availability of new nesting sites such as bridges and dams unwittingly provided by humans. In the United States it is increasing in numbers in all regions, especially the central and eastern states, and is extending its range south towards the Gulf of Mexico: numbers have increased in Alabama, Texas, Louisiana and Mississippi in particular (Robbins *et al.* 1986). In Florida it is known mainly as an abundant migrant, but is also beginning to breed on the coast; it first nested there in 1946 (Weston 1965; Robertson and Kushlan 1974). It has also recently colonised northern Alberta, following settlement by humans for agriculture and oil prospecting (Erskine 1979).

In Europe and Asia populations have fluctuated, and have declined recently in some areas, including the Netherlands, West Germany, Denmark, Czechoslovakia, Romania, the Baltic States and Britain. In Israel they disappeared on the coastal plain from the 1950s, perhaps because of use of the pesticide DDT, but are recolonising western Galilee (Paz 1987). (For population sizes, see Glutz von Blotzheim and Bauer 1985 and Cramp 1988.) In Japan, it is also extending its range in Hokkaido (Iijima 1982).

Barn Swallows probably once had a more local and restricted range, occurring mainly around coasts or upland areas where caves and cliffs were available for nesting. They have greatly benefited from the presence of humans and their artefacts.

MIGRATION These swallows make regular

annual migrations between their northern breeding and southern wintering grounds. The main passage south is in September and October, with most birds arriving back in the breeding grounds in April and May. The race *rustica* winters in Africa south of the Sahara, and in Arabia and the Indian subcontinent. The migrants move in a broad front across the Sahara and Middle East. In general, continental western and central European birds winter in Central Africa, while north and east European birds winter in Central and East Africa and eastern South Africa (Zink 1970a). In South and south-western Africa, however, the populations are more mixed, with west, central and east European birds in Namibia and Botswana (Loske 1986). British swallows winter mainly in eastern and southern parts of South Africa, mixed with Russian and central European birds. British and Irish birds have extended their range westwards since the early 1960s, perhaps as a result of climatic changes (Rowan 1968; Mead 1970).

The race *transitiva* is mainly resident, but has been recorded in winter as far south as Egypt, Sudan, Kenya, Uganda and Zambia, and in Sinai in a post-breeding dispersal. In Egypt the race *savignii* is resident, but it disperses from towns and villages to lakes, swamps and cultivated areas after the breeding season. The race *gutturalis* migrates in winter to India, including Sri Lanka, the Laccadive, Maldive, Andaman and Nicobar Islands, southern China, Burma, Thailand, the Malay peninsula, Indochina, the Philippines, through the Sunda Islands, east to the Celebes, the Moluccas, western Papua New Guinea, the Aru Islands and northern Australia, and in small numbers to southeastern Africa. In Australia, *gutturalis* is a regular visitor to the western Kimberley region and Innisfail, but is a scarce migrant to the northern part of Australia and is a vagrant to the south; it was first seen in 1869 in Torres Strait, but since 1960 it has been seen regularly and sometimes even in flocks of up to 300 (Blakers *et al.* 1984). The arrival of the Barn Swallow in Australia may be due to a recent change in wintering range. The race *tytleri* migrates through Japan and China to winter in eastern Bengal, Assam, northern India, east through southern Yunnan, Burma (where it is an erratic visitor), Thailand and the Malay peninsula.

The New World race *erythrogaster* migrates through Mexico, Central America, the West Indies and islands off the Pacific and Atlantic coasts to the main winter range in Panama, Puerto Rico, the Lesser Antilles and throughout South America, although few winter as far south as Tierra del Fuego (AOU 1983; Phillips 1986). It winters locally and irregularly further north in Central America, Mexico, the southwestern United States and southern Florida, and small numbers have been recorded on the Galapagos Islands. The extent of wintering north of Panama is not clear, however, as many birds recorded there may be early or late migrants. Some remain in Argentina and Bolivia during the northern summer.

Such a wide-ranging species inevitably turns up casually or accidentally in many sites, for example in the Hawaiian Islands, northern Alaska and Canada, Banks Island, Bermuda, Greenland, Tristan da Cunha and the Falkland Islands. A few individuals occasionally winter in their breeding grounds, regularly so in North Africa, southern Spain and in the eastern Mediterranean.

FORAGING AND FOOD Barn Swallows fly swiftly, with lots of banking and turning, feeding predominantly low over the ground or water at a mean height of 7–8 m (23–26 ft) (Waugh 1978). They use little gliding flight, especially when catching food for their nestlings. At this stage they usually feed within 200 m of the nest, hunting singly (Bryant and Turner 1982). They feed in pairs during egg-laying, but will feed in loose flocks at other times. The usual method of feeding is to skim low over the ground or water, pursuing insects in flight. They often follow other birds and mammals, including humans, catching the insects disturbed by them. They also skim water to pick up floating insects, and brush past foliage, picking up insects such as caterpillars disturbed from the leaves (Turner 1981). In bad weather, they will also hover and pick insects and spiders from the surface of plants, walls, etc. They occasionally perch on plants, such as trees, or on the ground to pick up invertebrates such as flies and sand-hoppers (e.g. Vietinghoff-Riesch 1955).

In Scotland, the adults when breeding take mainly medium-sized to large flies and beetles, as well as some smaller insects such as midges, parasitic wasps, ants, bees and moths (Waugh 1978; Turner 1980); but in Africa, and probably other wintering sites, Hymenoptera, especially flying ants, are much more important (Waugh 1978). Beetles and termites are also important prey during the non-breeding season, and grasshoppers, plant bugs, Lepidoptera, flies and sandhoppers are also taken. Throughout the breeding range, the nestlings' diet is predominantly flies (62–76%), and most of these are large flies of the family Muscidae, hoverflies, horseflies and robberflies (e.g. Wang 1959; Kožená 1979, 1980; Turner 1980); smaller acalypterate flies and nematoceran flies are also frequently fed. Aphids and other plant bugs form nearly a quarter of the diet and a few beetles, parasitic Hymenoptera, bees, moths, mayflies, dragonflies, grasshoppers, lacewings and caddisflies are fed to the young; the bees are usually stingless drones. Swallows will also collect caterpillars when these are abundant, and spiders are occasionally taken. Grit, particularly calcium-rich grit, is regularly collected. Very rarely, some plant material such as berries is ingested (see Vietinghoff-Riesch 1955; Glutz von Blotzheim and Bauer 1985; Cramp 1988).

SOCIAL ORGANISATION In natural sites, Barn Swallows breed in single pairs or small groups of up to 30 or so pairs (Speich *et al.* 1985). In artificial sites in Europe and Asia there are usually fewer than five nests per group, but groups in North America tend to be larger; large groups of 50 or more nests are occasionally recorded on both sides of the Atlantic. Nests are usually several metres apart (Møller 1983). When not breeding, the swallows form flocks and roosts of up to thousands of birds.

SOCIOSEXUAL BEHAVIOUR The behaviour and breeding biology of Barn Swallows has been extensively studied. (For summaries see Vietinghoff-Riesch 1955; Glutz von Blotzheim and Bauer 1985; Cramp 1988.) Barn Swallows are nearly always monogamous, but there have been records of males pairing with two females and, in colonies, males often copulate with females other than their own mate (Møller 1985). The members of a pair stay together for the second clutch and in successive years. Adults return to their previous nest site in successive years, with only a few per cent changing to other sites (Shields 1987b; Cramp 1988). First-years often return to within 3 km (2 miles) of their natal site, most within 30 km (19 miles) (Davis 1965; Christensen 1981); males are more faithful than females to their natal site (Shields 1987b). Females breed when one year old, but a few males remain unpaired until they are

two (Hemery *et al.* 1979; (Crook and Shields 1987; Møller 1988b). Unmated males will visit the nests of other individuals, and will even kill nestlings, in order to gain mating opportunities (Crook and Shields 1985, 1987; Møller 1988b). Both sexes defend their nest, but breeding males are very aggressive, defending a small area around the nest and guarding their mate from the attention of other males attempting to copulate with her. Mate-guarding is especially pronounced among group pairs and early in the season (Møller 1985). Nest-owner and intruder chase and fight in mid air, sometimes wounding or even killing each other. Nest-owners use a threat display in which they sing, with wings slightly open, feathers sleeked and head thrust forwards.

Adult males arrive first at the breeding grounds and select a nest site, though a few apparently pair before arriving (Hartley 1941). Unattached males perform a nest-showing display (Löhrl 1962): the male circles over the site, singing, then descends towards the nest site, lands and utters enticement calls until the female also lands, then he continues to sing. If the female is interested, the male stops singing and makes pecking movements towards the site. He may show the female several sites before a choice is made. The male solicits mating by singing when the female is perched near the nest. He flies over her, hovering, with tail fanned, then mounts and calls.

BREEDING The main breeding season is April–August (Bent 1942; Cramp 1988). It starts earlier (in March) in the south and later (in May) in the north of the range. These swallows usually have two broods a year, but sometimes attempt three. In the extreme north of the range, where the breeding season is shorter, only one brood is reared. Most nests are built on artificial structures, including bridges, barns, culverts, mine shafts, wells, even vehicles and an underground oil depot. The nest is usually placed inside a building, on a beam close to the ceiling or under eaves, against any suitable projection, even lamp shades, picture frames, etc., usually a few metres above the ground. A few natural sites are known, however: caves, crevices in cliffs, holes in banks, perhaps also in hollow trees (Speich *et al.* 1985). The birds prefer nesting in association with domestic animals, choosing cow and pig sheds and stables most frequently (Møller 1983). Nest-building takes about a week, depending on the weather; repairing an old nest and making a lining takes just a few days. Both male and female build (but the female tends to do more, especially the lining), working mainly in the morning and making some 1,000 trips to collect mud. The nest is a deep bowl of mud pellets (rarely, an old nest of another species is adapted for use). It is usually re-used for second or third broods and in successive years; birds repair it and build it up each year. Nests include vegetable material, usually dry grass but occasionally even seaweed, and algae has been recorded where mud is scarce (Duffin 1973). The nest is lined with feathers.

The usual range of clutch sizes is two to seven, with four or five on average; second clutches are smaller than the first, and clutches decrease in size with increasing latitude (Møller 1984). The eggs are white with reddish or purplish-brown speckles, with some lilac and grey. They average 19.7 × 13.6 mm (16.7–23.0 × 12.3–14.8; weight 1.9) in Europe, but there is some slight geographical variation, with average measurements of 18.8 × 13.5 mm for *erythrogaster* and 18.9 × 13.3 mm for *gutturalis*. The eggs are laid at daily intervals, but the interval may be longer in bad weather. The incubation period is 14–16 days, occasionally 11–19. The fledging period is 18–23 days. In Europe only the female incubates, although males have occasionally been seen on the nest, but in North America males incubate to varying extents, some doing as much as a quarter of the incubation (Ball 1983). Fledglings are lured away from the nest with contact calls. After fledging, broods stay in family groups away from others for about a week while the parents feed them, on perches and in flight. The young show weak recognition of parents, but parents do not recognise their youngsters' calls (Medvin and Beecher 1986). First-brood fledglings occasionally help feed the second brood (Cramp 1988).

Hatching success typically is high at about 90%, and fledging success is about 70–90% of eggs laid. The average annual mortality is about 40–70% for adults and 70–80% for first-years (Cramp 1988). Most live fewer than four years; the record for longevity is 15 years 11 months (Rydzewski 1978).

VOICE Barn Swallows have a large vocal repertoire (Cramp 1988). The song is a melodious twittering mixed with a grating rattle; it is uttered in flight or when perched. There is also a chirping contact call used between members of a pair, between parents and young or in flocks; this is sometimes extended into a low twitter. The female uses a contact call to entice the male to follow her during nest-building and when luring fledglings from the nest. Males utter an enticement call, a wheezing 'wi wi wi', when attracting potential mates. An 'it it it' call is also used during pair-bonding. Whining calls are used during copulation. A stuttering or screeching 'witt titititi' is used as a threat call. There are several alarm calls, ranging in degree of alarm from a warning 'chir chir', through a two-syllable 'tsi wit' to a variety of muffled calls such as 'dewihlik' when in imminent danger.

DESCRIPTION The adult male has striking glossy steel-blue upperparts, including the scapulars, tertials and lesser and median wing-coverts, with black lores and a rufous-chestnut forehead, chin and throat. White bases to the feathers of the hindneck and mantle are sometimes visible. The rest of the underparts are pinky-cream, creamy-white, buffy- or vinaceous-white, separated from the throat by a steel-blue breast-band, and with the deepest colour on the under-tail-coverts. The underparts vary in colour geographically, being generally whiter further north. The underwing-coverts and axillaries are similar to but often darker than the abdomen. The primaries, secondaries and greater wing-coverts are black with a steel-green or blue-green gloss, the gloss being bluer on the coverts. The small coverts along the leading edge of the wing are spotted blue and buff. The tail is black with a blue or blue-green gloss, and has small white patches on the inner webs of all but the central pair of feathers. The outer tail feathers are elongated to form streamers. In worn plumage, the upperparts are duller and the underparts paler. The eyes are dark brown, the bill and the legs and feet black. The female is similar, but has less of a glossy blue on the upperparts and breast-band, whiter underparts, shorter outer tail feathers and a shorter patch on the sixth pair of tail feathers (from the centre). Albinos and partial albinos are known (e.g. Koenig 1962). The juvenile is similar to the adult, but is duller and lacks the elongated tail feathers, and has a paler, more buffy forehead, chin and throat, and, compared with the adult male, often whiter under-parts; the steel-blue gloss is less apparent, and the upperparts and breast-band are browner. Moult usually starts on the winter-ing grounds, but occasionally a few feathers are moulted near the breeding grounds. The southern breeding populations (Africa to China) start moulting on the breeding grounds and finish in the winter quarters; resident populations start moulting earlier, from late April to June (Cramp 1988).

Measurements Length 18 cm (7") Wing of male 120–129 (mean 124.4), of female 118–125 (mean 121.8); tail of male 89–119 (mean 103.4), of female 70–99 (mean 86.9); fork of male 47–78 (mean 61.9), of male 27–57 (mean 44.2); bill 11.2–12.8 (mean 12.3); tarsus 10.2–11.5 (mean 10.8). Weight 14–23.7 (mean 18.9).

RACES The races differ mainly in the tone of the underparts and the extent of the breast-band, although these are also variable within a race. There is also a decline in size from the northwest (*rustica*) and northeast (*tytleri*) to the south and east (*gutturalis*). The race *transitiva* (wing 119–128) has darker rufous-buff underparts, but is similar to some southern European specimens. The race *gutturalis* (wing 110–122) has whitish underparts and an incomplete breast-band. The underparts of *tytleri* (wing 117–127) are cinnamon-rufous to chestnut and the breast-band is incomplete; *savignii* (wing 113–125) also has deep rufous-chestnut underparts, but a complete breast-band. The race *erythrogaster* (wing 114–126) has chestnut or cinnamon-rufous underparts, and the breast-band consists only of patches on the sides of the breast.

HYBRIDISATION Several cases of hybrid-isation with House Martins, Cliff Swallows (67) and Cave Swallows (68) are known (Martin and Selander 1975; Martin 1980; Menzel 1984).

43 RED-CHESTED SWALLOW   Plate 15
Hirundo lucida Hartlaub
Alternative name: Gambia Swallow

Hirundo lucida 'J. Verreaux' Hartlaub, 1858, J. für Orn., p. 42: Casamance River, Senegal.

Hirundo lucida clara Bates, 1932, 70 miles east of Wagadugu, Upper Volta.

Hirundo lucida subalaris Reichenow, 1905, Congo = Stanley Falls *fide* Bannerman, 1939.

Hirundo lucida rothschildi Neumann, 1904, Schubba, Kaffa, Ethiopia.

This swallow is part of the barn swallow superspecies and is sometimes considered con-specific with the Barn Swallow (42) (Hall and Moreau 1970).

FIELD CHARACTERS This species is very similar to the Barn Swallow, with blue upperparts, white underparts, and rufous-chestnut forehead, chin and throat, but it lacks the long tail streamers of the adult of the latter. It is also slightly smaller and has a narrower breast-band, a smaller area of rufous-chestnut on the forehead and more white in the tail, but these differences may be clear only when both birds are seen together. The females and juveniles are par-ticularly difficult to distinguish because of their short tails. It is an open-country swal-low, often seen alone or in small groups. The flight is swift and darting.

HABITAT Red-chested Swallows frequent mainly dry savanna and semi-arid areas in West Africa. In Ethiopia they occur mainly in grassland habitat from 1800 to 2750 m (5900–9060 ft) (Urban and Brown 1971). They are frequently seen in villages.

DISTRIBUTION AND POPULATION Red-chested Swallows have a disjunct distribu-tion in West Africa, the Congo valley and Ethiopia, the latter two populations possibly being relict (Hall and Moreau 1970). The nominate race is resident in West Africa from Senegal east to Ghana, Togo and the extreme west of Nigeria, but does not occur in the wet coastal zone; there is one breed-ing record for Liberia, in April 1880. The race *clara* occurs to the north of *lucida*, on the southern edge of the Sahara in Mali and Upper Volta east as far as western Niger and Nigeria. The race *subalaris* is confined to the lower and upper parts of the valley of the Congo River, while *rothschildi* occurs in central and southwestern Ethiopia. These swallows are common throughout their range, and are abundant in some areas such as the Gambia. Artificial structures such as bridges have provided new nesting sites and have probably allowed populations to increase. They are resident and sedentary all year in the breeding range.

FOOD AND BEHAVIOUR The flight is swift and darting, like that of the Barn Swallow. They feed on insects caught in flight, and have been recorded feeding on swarms of flying termites (Chapin 1953). Pairs nest singly or in small, loose groups, depending on the availability of nest sites. At other times they will form larger flocks.

BREEDING In West Africa, eggs or nestlings have been recorded between February and July (Mackworth-Praed and Grant 1973; Grimes 1988). For the race *clara*, there are also breeding records in June, and August to October. In Ethiopia, *rothschildi* breeds in May and June (Urban and Brown 1971). In Zaire, *subalaris* breeds in the rains in February–May and August–September (Lippens and Wille 1976). Red-chested Swallows have apparently nested in association with humans for a long time; there is one record of a nest in a window seat in an old factory in 1880. Nest sites are typically in buildings, such as the verandahs of bungalows, also under eaves, in huts, on bridges, cliffs, and termite mounds. The nest, like that of Barn Swallows, is made of mud pellets mixed with a few vegetable fibres and is lined with feathers. It is often placed on rafters and beams. The eggs are white, with large brownish-red blotches. They measure 18.9 × 13.2 mm (16.8–20.9 × 12.5–14.2; weight 1.72). The clutch size is three or four throughout the range. Incubation and nestling periods, and details of the breeding biology, are not known, but

are likely to be similar to the Barn Swallow's.

VOICE The calls are similar to those of the Barn Swallow. The song is a weak twittering, which is said to be clearer and louder than that of Barn Swallows.

DESCRIPTION Red-chested Swallows have glossy steel-blue upperparts, including the lesser and median wing-coverts and tertials the gloss is most apparent in fresh plumage. The lores and ear-coverts are black. The forehead, chin, throat and upper breast are a dark rufous-chestnut. The axillaries and underwing-coverts are dull white. The rest of the underparts are white, apart from an incomplete breast-band of steel-blue. The undertail-coverts are a dingier white. The greater wing-coverts, wings and tail are black with a blue gloss. The tail is moderately forked, with large white patches on the innermost webs of all but the central pair of feathers. The eyes are brownish-black, the bill black and the feet and legs brown. The sexes are alike. The juvenile is very like the adult, but has little gloss on the upperparts and breast-band, which are browner, and has paler chestnut on the forehead, chin and throat.

Measurements Length 15 cm (6"). Wing 104–118 (mean 111.8); tail 56–67 (mean 61); fork 18–25 (mean 21.3); bill 9.4.–11.6 (mean 10.9); tarsus 10.1–11 (mean 10.5). Weight 12–14.

RACES The subspecies differ in the depth of colour of the chestnut on the throat, upper breast, chin and forehead. The Saharan race *clara* is the palest and smallest (wing 104–110), and the Congo race *subalaris* is the darkest. The Ethiopian race *rothschildi* is larger, with more violet-blue above and purer white underwing-coverts (wing 109–123).

44 ANGOLAN SWALLOW
Hirundo angolensis Bocage

Plate 15

Hirundo angolensis Bocage, 1868, J. Sci. Math. Phys. Nat. Acad. Sci. Lisboa, 2, no. 5, p. 47: Huilla, Angola.

Hirundo angolensis arcticincta Sharpe, 1891, Mt Elgon, 7000 ft, eastern Africa.

Angolan Swallows are the southern equatorial representative of the barn swallow super-species. Some authors have united them with the northern form, the Red-chested Swallow (43), but their breeding ranges, the limits of which are not well known, at least interdigitate in the lower Congo if not overlap (Moreau and Hall 1970). Hence, for now, it is as well to keep them as separate species.

FIELD CHARACTERS Angolan Swallows have steel-blue upperparts and breast-band and ashy-brown underparts. They are similar to the Barn Swallow (42), but are smaller, have a broken breast-band, rufous-chestnut on the upper breast, and greyish-brown rather than creamy underparts. The outer tail feathers are also relatively shorter, with more extensive white patches. They frequent both open country and forest glades, and are usually solitary. The flight is less active than that of Barn Swallows.

HABITAT Angolan Swallows frequent a variety of habitats, from montane grassland, open and bush grassland and cultivation to the edges of swamps, rivers and forest, and they are often seen around villages and in clearings and open glades.

DISTRIBUTION AND POPULATION The Angolan Swallow occurs across equatorial Africa. The nominate race *angolensis* occurs from Gabon and Zaire east to Ruanda-Urundi and the Kondoa and Kasauli districts of Tanzania, south through Angola to the Kunene and Okavango Rivers and Caprivi, and in northern Zambia and Malawi. The race *arcticincta* occurs in Uganda, western Kenya and northwestern Tanzania (Komo Island). This is an uncommon or rare species throughout most of the range, although it is common in parts of Uganda, Tanzania and Kenya (Britton 1980). In Angola it is rare in the interior. The distribution is possibly a relict one; the species may have been more widespread when the climate was cooler and moister. It has only relatively recently been recorded from Gabon and may have extended its range there (Rand *et al.* 1959). It uses human artefacts to only a small extent for nesting and has not benefited much from the construction of large buildings, bridges and culverts, though the habit may be spreading (Aspinwall 1982).

MIGRATION The movements of this species are not well known. In parts of its range it is resident, but it makes local movements after the breeding season. In East Africa and Zambia it appears to be partly migratory, most records being between August and March, so it may be largely absent in the wetter months (Benson *et al.* 1971). Some local altitudinal movements are likely. It is a vagrant to southern Africa (Maclean 1985).

FOOD AND BEHAVIOUR This is a rather solitary species; it is usually seen alone or in pairs. When flying, it is less active and less manoeuvrable than the Barn Swallow. The diet consists of insects caught in flight, including winged ants (Friedmann and Williams 1969), mayflies and dipteran flies (museum specimens). Pairs often nest singly or in small groups, although a few large groups have been recorded: a group of 150 birds was recorded breeding in a building at Mouila in Gabon (Rand *et al.* 1959).

BREEDING In East Africa it breeds only in the rains; in Uganda this is generally in February–June and October–December, and in Tanzania in November–May (Brown and Britton 1980). In Angola, there are breeding records in September (Dean 1974); in Zambia, in October–December (Benson *et al.* 1971); in Zaire, in August in the south and March–May and December in the east (Lippens and Wille 1976); and, in Gabon, May and September (Rand *et al.* 1959). Two broods may be reared each year. Nests are built under eaves, in verandahs, under overhanging rocks on cliffs, under bridges or in caves. The nest is a half cup made of mud pellets and dry grass, lined with feathers, like that of the Barn Swallow. The nest is sometimes built on a support such as a rafter, but is also often attached to vertical walls under an overhang without any support from below. The clutch size is two to four, usually three, eggs, which are white with red-brown spots and measure 18.8×13.4 mm ($18.3–19.5 \times 13.1–13.5$; weight 1.78). Incubation and fledging periods are not known, but are probably similar to those of the Barn Swallow.

VOICE The song is a weak twittering, often uttered in a display flight in which the wings are downcurved and quivered.

DESCRIPTION These are medium-sized swallows. The entire upperparts, including the scapulars, lesser and median wing-coverts and tertials, are glossy steel-blue with greenish reflections, the gloss being most pronounced in fresh plumage. The lores are velvety black, and the ear-coverts are glossy blue. The forehead, chin, throat and upper parts of the breast are deep rufous-chestnut. There is a narrow, broken, steel-blue breast-band. The rest of the underparts are ashy-brown, palest in the centre of the breast. The undertail-coverts are dark ashy-brown with strongly defined black shaft streaks and buffy tips. The axillaries and underwing-coverts are a darker ashy-grey than the rest of the underparts, with a steel-blue wash on the edge of the wing. The primaries, secondaries and greater wing-coverts are black with a blue sheen. The tail, which is moderately forked, is black with a strong blue gloss; on all but the central pair of feathers the inner web is white, apart from a blue-black tip. The bill is black, the eyes are brown, and the legs and feet are dark brown or purplish-black. The sexes are alike, but females have shorter outer tail feathers. Juveniles are similar to adults, but are duller, with browner, less glossy upperparts and breast-band, and with paler rufous areas and shorter outer tail feathers.

Measurements Length 14–15 cm (5½–6"). Wing 114–129 (mean 199.2); tail of male 59–68 (mean 62.4), of female 55–57 (mean 55.9); fork of male 8–23 (mean 16), of female 8–16 (mean 12); bill 9.6–11.9 (mean 11.2); tarsus 10.2–11.7 (mean 11.1). Weight 16–18.

RACES The race *arcticincta* has a more deeply forked tail, and has more white on the centre of the breast and generally paler underparts than the nominate race. In Angola, the tail fork is 8–15 mm, in East Africa it is 16–23 mm. The underparts of Ugandan specimens, however, are variable, sometimes being dusky, and there is a gradation in size, so the two races may not be distinct (Friedmann and Williams 1969).

45 PACIFIC SWALLOW
Hirundo tahitica Gmelin

Plate 16

Hirundo tahitica Gmelin, 1789, Syst. Nat., 1, pt. 2, p. 1016: Tahiti.

Hirundo tahitica domicola Jerdon, 1844, Nilgiris.

Hirundo tahitica abbotti (Oberholser), 1917, Pulo Manguan, Anamba Islands.

Hirundo tahitica namiyei (Stejneger), 1887, Urassoimagiri, Okinawa, Ryu Kyu Islands.

Hirundo tahitica javanica Sparrman, 1789, Java.

Hirundo tahitica frontalis Quoy and Gaimard, 1830, Dorey (i.e. Manokwari), New Guinea.

Hirundo tahitica ambiens Mayr, 1934, Wide Bay, New Britain.

Hirundo tahitica subfusca Gould, 1856, Moala, Fiji Islands.

The Pacific Swallow has often been split into two species, based on the *javanica* and *tahitica* groups of races, and the Welcome Swallow (46) is also sometimes merged with this species.

FIELD CHARACTERS The Pacific Swallow has steel-blue upperparts, rufous-chestnut chin, throat and forehead and dusky underparts. The western forms are paler below and closely resemble the Barn Swallow (42), but have relatively shorter outer tail feathers and darker underparts, and there is no band below the throat. It occurs in open and forested country and is often seen alone or in small groups, but will roost with flocks of migrant swallows. The flight is rapid.

HABITAT The Pacific Swallow is generally a bird of sea-coasts, breeding on cliffs and in caves, but is also now moving inland, especially to areas of forested hills (Medway and Wells 1976). It frequents open and forested habitats, especially near water, and is common around human habitation. In India it ranges from 700 to 2400 m (2300–7900 ft), feeding on the grassy slopes around tea and coffee plantations (Ali and Ripley 1972). In the Malay peninsula it ranges from the coast to the highlands, occasionally nesting on cliffs, more often on artificial structures over water; it feeds over open country such as grassland, paddyfields and gardens, and along river courses or roads in forested areas.

DISTRIBUTION AND POPULATION The species ranges widely from southern India, through southeast Asia, Indonesia, Wallacea and New Guinea to the islands of the South Pacific. It is replaced by the closely related Welcome Swallow in Australasia. The Indian race *domicola* breeds in the hills of southern India from Nilgiri southwards, and in Sri Lanka. The race *abbotti* occurs in the Philippines, Borneo and parts of Sumatra, and surrounding islands; *namiyei* occurs only on the Ryu Kyu Islands and Taiwan. The race *javanica* occurs from Burma and Thailand south to Wallacea, and *frontalis* occurs in New Guinea; the birds in Wallacea are probably *javanica* (White and Bruce 1986), but have also been described as *frontalis* (e.g. Peters 1960). The race *ambiens* breeds only in New Britain; and *subfusca* occurs in the eastern part of the range, on various groups of Pacific islands. The nominate race *tahitica* occurs only on the Society Islands.

This is a common swallow in its range but is often locally distributed, and is often confined in coastal areas where cliffs are available for nesting. Within the last few decades, however, it has colonised hill stations in Malaysia and is probably extending its range into areas where human artefacts provide new nesting sites.

MIGRATION This swallow is largely sedentary, but some movements have been recorded. For example, transients of *abbotti* have been reported from Lanyu Island and Huoshao Tao (de Schauensee 1984), and in Sri Lanka *domicola* moves down into the foothills of the wet zone after the breeding season (Ali and Ripley 1972). In one study of the movements of Asian birds, Pacific Swallows moved only 10–25 miles (16–40 km) between roost sites over a three-year period (McClure 1974).

FORAGING AND FOOD The flight includes frequent swerves and bankings, with periods of gliding on extended or nearly closed wings. In the hottest part of the day the birds reduce heat stress by exposing their legs in flight, raising their wings and panting (Bryant 1983). They generally feed low down, at about 11 m (36 ft) in forested habitat and 14 m (46 ft) in open habitat, nearly half of the time within 10 m (33 ft) of vegetation, and usually in small flocks of up to five birds (Waugh and Hails 1983). In one study, 60% of their food consisted of Hymenoptera, especially ants and Apocrita, with dipteran flies, mainly of the family Muscidae, making up a third of the diet (Waugh and Hails 1983); other items included beetles and termites. They take, on average, larger prey than Barn Swallows do (Waugh and Hails 1983). The importance of ants in the diet declines in March and April, while the frequency of the larger brachyceran and cyclorraphan flies in the

diet peaks in May, when first broods are being fed (Waugh and Hails 1983).

BEHAVIOUR pairs usually breed singly or in small, scattered groups, but larger groups do occur: at one site under a bridge there were 35 nests spaced 1 m or more apart (Hails 1984); in Tahiti, groups of five to 40 nests are usual (Holyoak 1974). A small area around the nest is defended from conspecifics. When not breeding, they will roost gregariously with other migratory hirundines (Medway and Wells 1976).

BREEDING The breeding season is chiefly March–May in India and Burma, February–May in Sri Lanka, with some nests between December and June, November–December in Tahiti, and February–August in the Malay peninsula. Two broods are sometimes raised in a season. In Hails' (1984) study, 29% of pairs were double-brooded (laying a second clutch after successfully rearing a first, not including replacement layings); no birds attempted a third brood. The re-lay interval after a first brood is 22 days, much longer than the week or so of temperate hirundines. The nest is a half cup of mud pellets, measuring about 12 cm long by 6 cm wide by 8 cm deep (5 × 2½ × 3 in), and lined with fine roots, lichens, dry grass and feathers; feathers are often added once the eggs are laid. Nests are built under eaves on walls or ledges on cliffs, inside buildings on rafters, on verandahs, jetties and bridges, in caves, culverts and tunnels, and on tree stumps. They are built close to an overhang, which protects the nest, and are usually over or close to water. Nests are re-used each year if they survive.

In India the clutch size is two or three, and on Tahiti one or two. In Malaysia the average clutch size is three; in Sri Lanka three, occasionally two or four. Clutches of four are most frequent in April, and clutch size declines during the season (March–July). Hails (1984) recorded two clutches of five, but in both cases one egg was small and did not hatch. The eggs are usually laid at daily intervals, but sometimes a day is missed. The eggs are white, with small speckles of reddish-brown, purple-brown and lavender-grey. Those of the race *domicola* average 17.5 × 12.6 mm (15.7–19.6 × 12–14.2; weight 1.45), of *javanica* 17.8 × 12.9 mm (16–19.8 × 11.9–13.6; weight 1.56), and those of the nominate race measure 19.6 × 13.9 mm (18.5–21 × 13.5–14.2; weight 1.98). Philips (1950) and

Ali and Ripley (1972) stated that in India and Sri Lanka both sexes build the nest, incubate and feed the young. In Hails's (1984) study, only one bird, the female where known, incubated, but both sexes built the nest and fed the young. The male, however, feeds the nestlings less than the female does. The incubation period is 16 (15–17) days. The female incubates for only a third of the daylight hours, less than in temperate-climate swallows. The nestling period is 20 (17–22) days. Feeding rates vary throughout the day, being highest late morning and at dusk. Fledglings return the nest to roost, for several days. Fledging success (as a percentage of eggs laid) was low, only 38%, in Hails' study, with only 54% of eggs hatching. Longevity is poorly known, but one ringed bird was recovered seven years after it was first captured (McClure 1974).

VOICE The calls are 'twsit-twsit-twsit', often run into a twittering, and a 'titswee' with the second syllable higher than the first.

DESCRIPTION This is a small swallow. The nominate race has a dark rufous-chestnut forehead; the rest of the upperparts from the crown to the uppertail-coverts, including the scapulars, are a slightly glossy steel-blue. The lores are black, and the ear-coverts blue. The chin and throat are chestnut, and the breast, abdomen, axillaries and underwing-coverts are brownish-black. The undertail-coverts are grey-brown with a dark subterminal band and pale tips. The wings and tail are dull brownish-black with only a slight gloss on the coverts, most pronounced on the lesser coverts. The tail is slightly forked, and the feathers, apart from the inner two pairs, have a very narrow pale margin to the inner web. The bill is black, the eyes are brown and the legs and feet are black. The sexes are alike. The juvenile is duller, less metallic, with a less sharply defined rufous-chestnut forehead, and paler chin and throat; the tertials and their coverts and the undertail-coverts are edged with pinkish-white at the tips.
Measurements (*javanica*) Length 13 cm (5"). Wing 101–111 (mean 105.1); tail 44–48.9 (mean 59); fork 8–14 (mean 9.2); bill 10.4–12 (mean 11); tarsus 9.6–11.1 (mean 10.4). Weight (*javanica*) 11.1–15.6 (mean 13.1).

RACES The various races differ mainly in the shade of the underparts, the amount of white in the tail and the colour of the upperparts. The race *domicola* is ashy-grey below and glossy green above and has white tail spots; *abbotti* has a greenish gloss, pale grey underparts, the feathers having dark shaft streaks, and white tail spots; *namiyei* has smoky-brown underparts, steel-blue upperparts, and white tail spots. The race *javanica* has purple-blue upperparts, large tail spots, and a larger bill than *domicola* (7.5 versus 6 mm broad); the underparts are pale ashy-brown with dark streaks, whiter on the abdomen. The race *frontalis* has greyer underparts and glossy blue-black upperparts, and large tail spots, but it is not a well-differentiated race. The race *ambiens* is grey below, blue above and has small or no tail spots. The race *subfusca* has less and paler rufous-chestnut on the forehead, a richer rufous-chestnut chin and throat, a dark grey-brown breast and abdomen with a few glossy, blackish-brown feathers in the centre of the breast, and no white in the tail.

There is a distinct cline in coloration among the different races. The eastern group of races are dark-bellied and lack any white in the tail; the western races have a whitish abdomen and much white in the tail (consisting of a row of white spots on the inner webs of the feathers). These groups meet in northern Melanesia (Mayr 1955). Dark birds, indistinguishable from *subfusca*, are found in the Solomon Islands. In New Britain *ambiens* are intermediate between the dark *subfusca* and the light *frontalis* of New Guinea. Individuals from Rook Island (opposite New Britain) are referable to *frontalis*. On Long Island the birds are similar to *frontalis* but are somewhat darker, slightly larger and have less white in the tail, showing an admixture of *ambiens* genes. The races *javanica* and *abbotti* also grade into one another.

46 WELCOME SWALLOW
Hirundo neoxena Gould

Plate 16

Hirundo neoxena Gould, 1843, Proc. Zool. Soc. Lond., pt. 10 (1842), p. 131: 'the whole of the southern coast of Australia and Van Diemen's Land' = Tasmania.
Hirundo neoxena carteri (Mathews), 1912, Broome Hill, Western Australia.

This species forms a superspecies with the Pacific Swallow (45), although it has often just been considered to be a race of that species (Peters 1960).

FIELD CHARACTERS The Welcome Swallow has steel-blue upperparts, rufous-chestnut chin, throat and forehead, and grey-white underparts. It is very similar to the Pacific Swallow, from which it differs principally in having elongated outer tail feathers. Barn Swallows (42) are also similar, but have a clear dark breast-band. It frequents mainly open country, often near water. It is often found alone or in small groups, but will form flocks after the breeding season. The flight is rapid.

HABITAT This swallow is a common bird in a wide variety of habitats except forest and desert, breeding especially around human habitation but also in coastal caves and cliffs. It is often seen near water such as rivers, estuaries, lakes and ponds, especially on farmland, but also feeds in drier areas such as over crops and sand dunes.

DISTRIBUTION AND POPULATION The Welcome Swallow is confined to Australia and, since the late 1950s, New Zealand, although vagrants have been seen outside this range. The nominate race *neoxena* occurs in eastern Queensland, New South Wales, Victoria and adjacent parts of South Australia, Tasmania, and New Zealand, including Great Barrier Island, and the Auckland, Chatham and Kermadec Islands although the extent of breeding on the islands is not clear. The race *carteri* breeds in Western Australia, including Bernier Island. The Welcome Swallow was first recorded in New Zealand in the 1920s and recorded breeding there first in Northland in 1958 (Michie 1959). It has also only recently been recorded as a non-breeding visitor in New Guinea (Beehler *et al.* 1986) and New Caledonia (de Naurois 1979) and on other island groups, including the Auckland Islands (Claridge 1983) and the Kermadec Islands (Craig 1984). Its range outside Australia may thus be increasing, but it has not done so within Australia; there are still no breeding records from the Kimberley, Top End or Cape York regions, although individuals have been recorded in the northern regions (Blakers *et al.* 1984).

This is a common species except in central Australia. There are no measures of abundance, but it may have increased through changing its nest site to artificial structures. In New Zealand it has increased

rapidly in numbers and range: it is now common throughout South Island, and in North Island, in Northland, around the Bay of Plenty and Hawke Bay; it is still spreading, especially in the central North Island and South Island and onto offshore islands (Falla *et al.* 1983). The southern populations may have spread from the north or have been due to successive colonisations (Edgar 1966). Gregory (1978) suggested that individuals crossed the Tasman Sea accidentally on ships; there have been several sightings of this species at sea.

MIGRATION Tasmanian birds migrate north in February–March, returning in August–September (Blakers *et al.* 1984); some, however, apparently remain in Tasmania over winter. Western birds are mainly sedentary, although large flocks sometimes form after the breeding season. Eastern birds are largely migratory; they are breeding visitors in the south and non-breeding visitors in the extreme north, including the Torres Strait. The swallows do not leave the southern parts entirely, but movements and influxes have been recorded. There is an autumn-winter passage in the southern Murray-Darling region, and there is an influx of birds in the north (e.g. at Inverell and Murphy's Creek). They often disappear from breeding localities after the breeding season. New Zealand birds appear not to migrate regularly, but flocks sometimes form in the non-breeding season in areas such as Southland, outside the usual breeding range (Falla *et al.* 1983).

FOOD AND BEHAVIOUR The flight is fast, with frequent banking and turning, usually low over the ground. A wide variety of insects is eaten, including dragonflies, heteropteran bugs, carabid and staphylinid beetles, tipulid, ephydrid and bombyliid flies, caddisflies, moths and wasps (Sharpe and Wyatt 1885–1894; Hughes 1973; Park 1981b). Brock (1978) observed Welcome Swallows walking behind starlings and magpies, flitting up to catch insects disturbed by these other birds; Hobbs (1966) recorded late-autumn breeders feeding at night on moths attracted to lights at a service station, presumably because flying insects were scarce during the day; and Serventy (1958) recorded one entering a hotel saloon bar to catch blowflies at a window. They usually breed singly, but sometimes in loose groups. In one study, the nests were placed 0.1–1 m (4–39 in) apart (Hughes 1973). There are records, for example, of 20–25 nests under one jetty and 500 birds occupying a deserted farmhouse (Blakers et al. 1984). They defend a small area around the nest itself, some individuals being very aggressive, chasing and fighting off intruders. One male was seen to attack nestlings and may have contributed to the death of one (Park 1981b). Outside the breeding season Welcome Swallows form flocks and roosts of usually up to 500 birds; one of about 2,000 has been recorded (Watson 1955).

A pair will return to the same site to breed together in successive years, but the young usually disperse from the natal area (Park 1981a). At the start of the breeding season, the birds engage in chases and aerial displays in which the tail is fanned. Pairs perch together, twittering to each other, and, in one recorded case, raising and fluttering their wings (P. Park, pers. comm.). Park (1981b) observed one possible copulation, when a male mounted a female perched on a girder beside the nest. The male appears to guard the female, accompanying her during nest-building.

BREEDING The breeding season is July–April, with a peak of laying in September–October (Marchant and Fullager 1983). A pair may have two or three broods a year. The nest is a half cup attached to vertical surfaces close to an overhang on a wall or in a cave, or in a hollow of a tree; horizontal or sloping surfaces are also occasionally used. Welcome Swallows have taken advantage of artificial structures and now usually use such sites rather than natural ones (Marchant and Fullager 1983). They will build in verandahs, under eaves, on rafters, bridges, culverts, jetties, mine shafts, water tanks and even 'outback mailboxes'; nests are usually, but not always, on the outside of buildings (Campbell 1901; Serventy and Whittell 1962; Marchant and Fullager 1983). Like the Barn Swallow, the Welcome Swallow takes advantage of any likely place for its nest, and several unusual sites have been recorded, including moving boats, a coach, on top of a bunch of pannikins in a shearing-shed (Campbell 1901) and in a broken Fairy Martin's (70) nest (Ashton 1986). A few natural sites such as caves, cliffs and hollow trees or logs are also used,

for example on the southwestern coastal cliffs of the Nullarbor Plain (Reilly et al. 1975). The nest is made of mud mixed with grass. The mud pellets are collected locally, sometimes together with pieces of dry grass, rootlets and hair. The lining of the nest consists of layers of grass, rootlets, hair, wool and other soft material; even seaweed has been recorded (Campbell 1901). A variable number of feathers are added as a final layer. Some females continue to add feathers even during incubation (Park 1981b). Males are first to bring mud to a site for a nest, but both male and female build the nest (Park 1981b). Nests take six to 24 days to build, most activity occurring in the mornings. Old nests are re-used each year, after being repaired with more mud (Schrader 1976). Pairs that are sedentary will use the nest for roosting in after the breeding season (Storr 1965; Brown et al. ms).

The clutch size is three to five, averaging four, occasionally only two and, rarely, six (Marchant and Fullager 1983): in a study of swallows in Tasmania, 61% of 67 clutches contained four eggs, 19% five eggs, and 16% three eggs, with only two clutches of two, although the latter showed signs of being preyed on (Park 1981b). Clutches tend to be larger inland than on the coast (Marchant and Fullager 1983). The eggs are white, with brown and lavender speckles and blotches which usually form a zone around the broad end (Campbell 1901; Serventy and Whittell 1962). They average 18.4 × 13.6 mm (weight 1.75). There may be some geographical variation in egg size: in western Australia the range is 18.0–19.0 × 13.0–14.0; in New Zealand 16.0–19.2 × 12.0–14.0; and in Tasmania 16.02–19.4 × 13.97–12.12 (Park 1981b). The eggs are laid on successive days early in the morning, though there is sometimes a delay of at least a day between eggs, perhaps associated with poor feeding conditions (Wood 1973; Marchant and Fullager 1983). Usually only the female incubates, although Park (1981b) saw a male sit on the eggs once for a few seconds, and Serventy and Whittell (1962) stated that both birds incubate. Wood (1973) and Schrader (1976) reported that one bird brought food to another, incubating, bird (presumably its mate), but this is probably rare. Incubation lasts 14–18 days (average 15.6 days). The females leave the nest more frequently in cooler weather. The eggs in a clutch hatch synchronously, usually within a day of each other (Marchant and Fullager 1983). The fledging period is 18–23 days (average 20.6 days). Both parents feed the nestlings, nearly always only one chick at a time. The chicks were fed infrequently, at intervals of 30 minutes to an hour, in one study (Crouchley and Crouchley 1979) but at rates of 17–24 feeds per hour at a nest of four chicks in another study (P. Park, pers. comm.). 'Helpers' (individuals other than the parents) were seen feeding nestlings at one nest, where the feeding rate was 56 times in an hour (Salter 1960). Once the nestlings leave the nest, they return there to roost at night for a few days to a few weeks; during the day their parents feed them close by the nest. At one nest, a fledgling from a first brood continued to roost in the nest while the second clutch was laid and incubated; it was sometimes seen on the eggs during the day (Salter 1960).

In Park's study, the mean fledging success was 59% of eggs laid producing fledged young, and in Australia as a whole it averages 53% (Marchant and Fullager 1983). At a site in New Zealand, 52% of eggs and chicks were lost because of infertility, predation, disturbance, nest falls and sparrows taking over the nests (Edgar 1966). Cold weather and heavy rain are also cause of nestling mortality (Schrader 1976; Marchant and Fullager 1983).

VOICE The contact call is a single 'seet' uttered in flight, occasionally from a perch, which is repeated rapidly to form a twittering. The song is a high-pitched mixture of squeaky twittering and trills, often uttered from a perch. The alarm call is a sharp 'twsee', 'sweert', or occasionally a 'tit-swe' with the second syllable stressed.

DESCRIPTION This is a medium-sized swallow with glossy steel-blue-black upperparts from the crown to the uppertail-coverts, including the scapulars. The lores are black, and the ear-coverts are blue. The forehead is bright rufous-chestnut; the chin and throat are similar but the upper breast is slightly paler rufous-chestnut. The lower breast and abdomen are greyish-white. The sides of the body and the underwing-coverts and axillaries are greyish-white with a brown tinge. The undertail-coverts are grey-brown, dark subterminally and with pale tips and edges. The wings are dull blackish-brown, with only a slight gloss on the coverts and tertials, most marked on the lesser coverts. The tail is blackish-brown and deeply forked; all but the central feathers have a subterminal white patch on the inner web. The bill is black, the eyes dark brown, and the legs and feet dark blackish-brown. The sexes are alike, but the male is slightly larger, with a more deeply forked tail. Albino and partial albino birds have been recorded (Klapste and Klapste 1985). Juveniles are duller and browner than adults, though the mantle may show some gloss; the rufous-chestnut areas are much paler and less well demarcated, there is little rufous-chestnut on the forehead, and the upper breast is dull white; the tertials have buffy tips; the outer tail feathers are also shorter. The moult takes place after the breeding season peak, in January–April (Rogers et al. 1986).

Measurements Wing 108–116 (mean 122.9); tail 74–85 (mean 77.7); fork 24–37 (mean 31.6); bill 8.8–10.8 (mean 9.7); tarsus 10.2–11.2 (mean 10.7). Weight 12.5–17.3 (mean 14.7).

RACES There is a cline in size from the large *carteri* (wing 112–118) on the western side of the continent to the small *neoxena* on the eastern side, but the races are not well defined. Queensland birds have less white in the tail than southern and western birds, and have sometimes been described as a separate race, *parsonsi* (Peters 1960).

47 WHITE-THROATED SWALLOW   Plate 16
Hirundo albigularis Strickland

Hirundo albigularis Strickland, 1849, Jardine's Contr. Orn., p. 17–4, pl. 15: Cape Peninsula, South Africa.

FIELD CHARACTERS This swallow has steel-blue upperparts, dull white underparts, a broken blue breast-band and a rufous-chestnut forehead. It differs from the Barn Swallow (42) in having a white throat. It is dusky like the Angolan Swallow (44), but the white throat, well-defined breast-band and whitish underwing-coverts are distinctive. It can be distinguished from the Pearl-breasted Swallow (53) by the well-defined breast-band, rufous-chestnut forehead and white patches in the tail. It can be found in open country, near water, usually alone or in small groups. The flight is swift.

HABITAT White-throated Swallows frequent open country, floodplains, grasslands, especially montane grassland, and highveld, at a range of altitudes, and are usually found near water. They are often seen around human constructions.

DISTRIBUTION AND POPULATION The breeding range extends from Angola and Zambia south throughout much of southern Africa (Maclean 1984). In Malawi, it occurs only on the border with Mozambique (Benson and Benson 1977). The species is usually described as being local but common when breeding. It has benefited from the construction of bridges and dams, which provide many nesting sites, and it has probably extended its range and population size this century.

MIGRATION White-throated Swallows are migratory, wintering in Angola, Zambia and southern Zaire between about April and August. In Zambia, they are resident north of 14°S in small numbers, and breeding has been recorded there, but they are mainly passage migrants and winter visitors from April to October (Irwin and Benson 1967; Aspinwall 1979). There is one record from East Africa, at Malini, and several winter records from Malawi (Benson and Benson 1977; Britton 1980). A few occasionally overwinter in Zimbabwe (Irwin 1981).

FOOD AND BEHAVIOUR The flight is swift, with frequent banking and turning, like that of the Barn Swallow. These swallows are usually seen alone, in pairs, or in small family groups, feeding mainly over water but also over open grassland and roads. They eat aerial insects such as dipteran flies, beetles and wasps (museum specimens), usually while skimming over the ground, but they will also sally out from a perch to catch insects. Rarely, they will feed from the ground (Jensen 1962). They breed in solitary pairs, returning to the same site each year. Males may return to the breeding grounds before females (Jackson 1973a).

BREEDING The breeding season is from August to March, with most records in September–January (Maclean 1985). Pairs often have two or more broods a year.

White-throated Swallows build their nests on bridges, dam walls, culverts, buildings, water tanks and rock faces, but they are not generally associated with human habitation, preferring constructions over or near water. When they use a building, it is usually an outbuilding rather than a house, but they will also use verandahs. The nest is placed below or near an overhang of rock or a projection on a bridge or building. It is often re-used for subsequent broods in the same and in following years, although pairs sometimes aslo switch nests after a successful breeding attempt, perhaps to avoid parasites (Earlé 1988b). The nest is a half bowl made of mud pellets, lined with fine roots, grass, hair and feathers. The clutch size is two to four, usually three, eggs, which are white with red-brown speckles, especially at the larger end where there are also slate-blue markings; they measure 20.9 × 14.6 mm (18.1–23 × 13.5–15; weight 2.35). The incubation period is 15–16 days; the nestling period is 20–21 days, and the fledglings return to the nest for several more days (Maclean 1985). Both parents feed the nestlings. The young can swim short distances if they fall from their nest (McLachlan and Liversedge 1978). The oldest known bird was nine years and eleven months (Earlé 1987d).

VOICE The song is a gentle warble, and there are twittering alarm notes.

DESCRIPTION The White-throated Swallow is a medium-sized hirundine. It is glossy deep steel-blue-black above from the crown to the uppertail-coverts, including the scapulars. The forehead is rufous-chestnut. The lores, the areas around the eyes and the ear-coverts are dull blue-black. The chin and throat are pure white. The breast-band is 10–12 mm deep and is steel-blue-black; it is broadest at the shoulder, tapering slightly towards the centre, and is often broken or interrupted by an extension of white from the throat. The rest of the underparts are dull white washed with brown-grey. The axillaries and underwing-coverts are vinaceous-white. The wings are black with a slight steel-blue wash, most pronounced on the lesser and median coverts and tertials. The tail is glossy steel-blue-black, with a large, white subapical patch on the inner web of all but the central pair of feathers; the outermost feathers are elongated and narrowed to form a deep fork. The eyes are brown, the bill is black and the legs and feet are black. The sexes are alike, but females have shorter outer tail feathers. Juveniles are duller, with little gloss; they lack the bright rufous forehead, their breast-band is browner, and their outer tail feathers are also shorter.

Measurements Length 14–17 cm (5½–6¾"). Wing 118–136 (mean 128.5); tail of male 70–84 (mean 76), of female 65–75 (mean 70.5); fork of male 26–37 (mean 32.5), of female 25–32 (mean 28.5); bill 11–13 (mean 12.2); tarsus 10–15 (mean 12). Weight 16–28 (mean 21.3).

RACES The birds breeding in the northern part of the range in Angola, Zambia and Malawi have shorter wings and tail and are sometimes referred to as a separate race, *ambigua.* They are not, however, completely distinct from the other populations. Rather, there is a cline in size, from birds with wings of 126–136 mm in South Africa to those with wings of 118–124 mm in Angola.

48 ETHIOPIAN SWALLOW   Plate 16
Hirundo aethiopica Blanford

Hirundo aethiopica Blanford, 1869, Ann. Mag. Nat. Hist. (4) iv., p. 329: Barakit, Tigre, Abyssinia.

Hirundo aethiopica fulvipectus Amadon, 1954, Farniso, near Kano, Nigeria.

Hirundo aethiopica amadoni White, 1956, Geloher.

FIELD CHARACTERS The upperparts of this species are steel-blue, the underparts are white, and there is an incomplete breast-band. The forehead is rufous-chestnut. It is very similar in pattern and size to the Red-chested Swallow (43), but has a broader rufous-chestnut forehead and a much paler throat and breast; the patches of white in the tail feathers are also smaller. The pale throat and dark breast patches are the best identification features. It frequents open country and woodland, and is rather solitary. The flight is swift.

HABITAT Ethiopian Swallows breed in savannas, areas of mixed bush and grass, montane grassland, open woodland and semi-arid areas across a wide altitudinal range, from sea level up to about 3000 m (9900 ft). Although this species prefers open habitats, it will penetrate forests where there are large clearings, as in southwestern Nigeria. It also frequents towns and villages. In East Africa it is often seen on the coast.

DISTRIBUTION AND POPULATION The Ethiopian Swallow is widespread in Central Africa (Hall and Moreau 1970). The race *fulvipectus* is found across the savanna belt of West Africa from the Ivory Coast, Nigeria and the Cameroons east to the White Nile in Sudan. The nominate race *aethiopica* occurs in Ethiopia, northern Kenya, northern Uganda and northeastern Tanzania; and *amadoni* in Somalia south along

the east coast to eastern Kenya. This is a common, widespread swallow, especially near and in towns, although it is found only locally on the Ivory Coast (Thiollay 1985). It breeds almost exclusively in association with humans. Its use of artificial structures, particularly large European-style buildings, may have been the cause of its recent expansion south into East Africa (Grant and Lewis 1984). It was scarce in the interior of Kenya and unknown in Uganda in the early part of this century, but there are now numerous records as far as eastern Tanzania (Britton 1980). It has also expanded its range westwards in West Africa since the 1960s (Grimes 1988).

MIGRATION This species is generally resident, but it makes some post-breeding movements. It is resident in West Africa, but in some areas numbers increase during the breeding season (Grimes 1988). It is reported to be a summer visitor to Kordofan and Darfur, while being resident further east in Khartoum (Bannerman 1939). It is also resident in Ethiopia (Urban and Brown 1971), but is mostly a breeding-season visitor to Eritrea (Smith 1957). In north-western Somalia it is a partial migrant, with few present in December–March and numbers increasing from April (Clarke 1985). In Chad it is absent in the dry season from December to March (Salvan 1969). In East Africa it is also mainly a resident (Britton 1980).

BEHAVIOUR The flight is rapid, entailing lots of circling, swerving and dipping. The diet consists of a variety of insects caught on the wing. These swallows are known to drink on the wing, and often perch on twigs, wires and rafters. They can be seen in pairs, family units and flocks of up to 80 or 100. Bannerman (1939) described the courtship as follows. The pair sit side by side, the male singing and the female twittering; every few minutes they dash out of and around the nest site, returning to the same perch. Then first the male, then the female, makes a series of short flights, hovering opposite the site where the nest is to be built. The male then squawks, flies up to the female and hovers above her. Singing starts well before nest-building. Ethiopian Swallows breed in single pairs or in loose groups, depending on the availability of nest sites. Buildings are often used for roosting, and juveniles have been seen roosting in nests in November in Nigeria (Bannerman 1939). Pairs may stay near their nest site all year around (Grant and Lewis 1984).

BREEDING The breeding season in West Africa is between March and August, and in Ethiopia between April and December; in East Africa it is in the rains in March–June and December (Brown and Britton 1980). There are usually two broods in a season. Nest sites are almost exclusively inside buildings such as mud huts, sheds, stables and houses or under eaves or verandahs. Nests are also built under bridges. Both rural and suburban sites are used. Natural nest sites include hollows in baobab trees, and in sea caves and coral overhangs along the Kenya coast, but in the interior only artificial sites are used. The nest is open and semi-circular, made of mud pellets mixed with grass and lined with dry grass, rootlets, horsehair and feathers; coconut fibre, palm-leaf fibre and possibly seaweed have also been recorded (Grant and Lewis 1984). The nest is built against a vertical or slightly sloping surface such as a roof beam or wall close to the ceiling, and may be re-used in subsequent years; it is rarely supported from below. Most building takes place in the morning, and the nest takes some two weeks to complete. Old nests of other swallows and swifts are sometimes used as a foundation for a new nest.

The clutch size is usually three or four, sometimes five, but is smaller (two to four, usually three) in East Africa than elsewhere in the range. Clutches of six and seven have been recorded (Serle 1950a) though these may have been laid by more than one female. The eggs are white, speckled and blotched with red-brown and rufous, with grey or lavender secondary markings, concentrated in a band at the blunt end. Their average size is 18.7 × 13.2 mm (16.9–20.1 × 11.9–14.0; weight 1.7). They are laid at daily intervals. Both sexes build the nest and feed the nestlings. The female does most of the two weeks' incubation. The nestlings fledge at 21–25 days and continue to roost in the nest for a week or more (Grant and Lewis 1984). The oldest known bird was seven years (Rydzewski 1978).

VOICE The song is a low, weak twittering; it has been described as sweet, melodious and varied, stronger than a Barn Swallow's (42). It is usually uttered from a perch, sometimes in flight. Other calls are a repeated 'cheep', a 'chi', and an alarm call 'preut'.

DESCRIPTION Ethiopian Swallows are small hirundines. The entire upperparts from the crown to the uppertail-coverts, including the scapulars, are a glossy steel-blue, but sometimes appear to have a steel-green sheen. The forehead and forecrown are deep rufous-chestnut. The lores are sooty-black; the ear-coverts are blackish with a blue gloss. The chin, throat and upper breast are a buffy-white; the rest of the underparts are white. There is an incomplete breast-band: narrow crescents of steel-blue extend along the sides of the breast but do not meet. The undertail-coverts, underwing-coverts and axillaries are white; the undertail-coverts also have dark shaft streaks. The wings are black with a slight steel-blue gloss, most pronounced on the lesser and median coverts and tertials. The tail is glossy steel-blue; the tail feathers, apart from the central pair, have small white patches on the inner webs. The tail is strongly forked, the outer feathers being elongated with blackish points. The eyes are brownish-black and the bill, legs and feet are black. The sexes are alike. The juvenile is duller, with a brown crown, blackish-brown upperparts with steel-blue and purple fringes, and brown breast patches; it lacks the rufous-chestnut forehead; the outer tail feathers are also shorter.
Measurements Length 13 cm (5"). Wing 103–111 (mean 106.6); tail 56–77 (mean 63.4); fork 23–33 (mean 27.5); bill 9.6–11.1 (mean 10.5); tarsus 9.9–11.8 (mean 10.9). Weight 10.5–15 (mean 13).

RACES There are three races: *fulvipectus,*
amadoni and *aethiopica.* Compared with
the nominate race, *fulvipectus* has a more
buffy chin, throat and breast, while the

remainder of the underparts are washed
buff. The race *amadoni* has a whiter throat
and breast and a slight buff tinge to the chin.

49 WIRE-TAILED SWALLOW   Plate 17
Hirundo smithii Leach

Hirundo smithii Leach, 1818, Append. Tuckey's Vog. Congo, p. 407: Chisalla Island, Lower
Congo River.

Hirundo smithii filifera Stephens, 1825, Kanpur, Uttar Pradesh, India.

FIELD CHARACTERS Wired-tailed Swallows
have blue upperparts, apart from a rufous
forehead and crown. The underparts are
creamy-white. The fine streamers and
chestnut head are distinctive in the field, but
the former can be difficult to see in flight.
This species frequents open country, near
water. It is usually solitary or in small groups.
The flight is swift.

HABITAT Open country such as grasslands,
lightly wooded grassland, open woodland,
forest edge, village clearings and the tops of
rocky hills, in the vicinity of pools, rivers and
other bodies of water, are typical habitat for
this species. It is more often found near
water than many other species of swallow.
It is normally a bird of low to mid altitudes;
in Africa it is most common below 2000 m
(6600 ft), and in Asia it is usually found up to
1500 m (4930 ft), but has been recorded
breeding at 2700 m (8900 ft) (Ali and Ripley
1972). In Africa it nests up to about 3000 m
(9900 ft) (Urban and Brown 1971).

DISTRIBUTION AND POPULATION This is a
widespread species throughout much of
Africa south of the Sahara, and southern
Asia as far as southeast Asia, and it is extending its range in some areas. The African
race, *smithii,* is widely distributed outside of
the central rainforest zone and the dry
southwest, occurring from the Sudan and
Ethiopia, through Uganda, Kenya and
Tanzania, to Zimbabwe, Mozambique,
northeastern Transvaal and eastern Natal in
the east, and from Senegal and the Gambia
east to Zaire and south to Angola, Caprivi
and northern Botswana in the west. It is
more locally distributed at the edges of its
range in the Ivory Coast, the Gambia and
South Africa (Clancey 1964; Gore 1981;
Thiollay 1985). The Asian form, *filifera,*
occurs in southern Buchara, Afghanistan,
Baluchistan, most of India east to Assam and

Bangladesh, south to North Kerala and the
Nilgiris, and in the plains of Burma, northern
Thailand, Laos, and southern Annam. This
species may also be present in parts of
China, in southwest Tibet, and in western
and southern Yunnan, as it occurs in
northwest India and has been recorded in
the northwestern Himalayas and near the
border of Yunnan east of Myitkyina (Delaney *et al.* 1982; de Schauensee 1984).

In parts of Africa it is locally abundant
and is the main swallow species along rivers
and in cultivated areas, especially below
1000 m (3300 ft) (Urban and Brown 1971;
Clancey 1973). It is probably extending its
range to the west and southwest in southern
Africa, benefiting from the presence of
artificial nest sites. In Zimbabwe it has.
become more widely distributed during the
20th century on the Mashonaland Plateau
and Chipinga Uplands, extending its range
from the lower valleys (Irwin 1981). In the
Gambia there were no records of it until
1962, but it is now regularly reported, particularly breeding on artificial structures
(Gore 1981); in such sites, however, the
nests are sometimes usurped by House
Sparrows. In Asia, the species is also locally
common.

MIGRATION In the equatorial parts of its
range, the Wire-tailed Swallow is resident,
but it is a summer breeding visitor to the
more seasonal environments within its
range. The African race is largely resident
but is subject to some seasonal movements,
for example in Natal (Clancey 1964; Aspinwall 1980). In Gabon it is an irregular
migrant, being present from October to
January (Brosset and Erard 1986). The Asian
race is a summer visitor to Pakistan and
northern India, where the winters are cold.
Elsewhere it is resident, although it does
undertake local post-breeding movements

and it has been recorded as a vagrant in Sri Lanka (Ali and Ripley 1972).

FORAGING AND FOOD The flight is swift, with characteristic swoops, glides, turns and banking movements. These swallows usually fly low over the ground, at an average height of 4–5 m (13–16 ft), feeding predominantly over water, but also over open, though generally sheltered, areas (Waugh 1978). The Wire-tailed Swallow feeds in pairs or loose flocks. Its food is mainly midges, gnats, other dipteran flies, ants and termites (Ali and Ripley 1972). Food brought to nestlings in three African nests consisted mainly of small Hymenoptera, such as flying ants, and small beetles; winged termites, small bugs, small Lepidoptera and muscid flies were also taken (Moreau 1939a). Insects such as locust hoppers are occasionally taken from the ground (e.g. Fuggles Couchman 1939). These swallows will also follow tractors and large animals to catch insects disturbed by them (Benson and Benson 1977).

BEHAVIOUR In general this species nests solitarily; nests are sometimes built near each other and several pairs may nest in the same building, but they are not clustered together into colonies. Pairs are territorial and aggressively chase intruders from the nest area (Nyandoro 1987). Resident pairs stay near the breeding site and roost in their nest when not breeding (Hanmer 1976).

BREEDING The breeding season generally coincides with the start of the rains. In East Africa, however, these swallows breed in all months of the year, but 64% of records are between February and July, with peaks in April–May and October (Packenham 1979; Brown and Britton 1980; Earlé 1988a). In Ethiopia the main breeding season is March–September (Urban and Brown 1971). In West Africa, there are breeding peaks in January–March and July–August in the Gambia, and March–May, August and December–January in Ghana; and there are also two peaks in Central Africa, in February–April and August–October (Gore 1981; Irwin 1981; Earlé 1988a; Grimes 1988). In South Africa breeding occurs in all months, but mainly August–October and February–April, with 40% of records in September–October and 50% in April–May (Maclean 1985; Earlé 1988a). In India the breeding season is generally between March and September (Ali and Ripley

1972), but varies locally. Where nests are built along river banks, breeding takes place before the height of the wet season, when water levels are still low (Betts 1952). Pairs often have two broods in a season, and three or, rarely, four have been recorded (Ali and Ripley 1972; Beesley 1972; Hanmer 1976).

Nowadays the nest site is usually on or in an artificial structure such as a building, verandah, culvert or bridge, but cliffs, rocks or trees overhanging water, and caves are also used. Nest sites are often along the banks of rivers or streams, or in mid stream, for example on boathouses, piers or fallen trees in the water; one record from the Gold Coast (on the Black Volta at Kintampo) is of a nest in the stern of a pontoon which regularly crossed a river (Bannerman 1939). The nest is a shallow half bowl of pellets of mud or mud mixed with straw, lined with dry grass and feathers, attached to a vertical surface such as a wall or on a rafter of a roof, but usually at least 2 m (6½ ft) above the ground. Both male and female build the nest, taking about a week. Nest sites and old nests are often re-used for later broods and in subsequent years, and occasionally nests are based on old nests of other swallows (Nyandoro 1987).

The clutch size is usually three, sometimes two or four, in Africa, and three to five in India. The eggs are white or pinkish-white, slightly glossed, with red-brown specks, spots and blotches. In Africa, they measure 17.7 × 13.1 mm (15.8–19.6 × 12.2–14.2; weight 1.6), and in Asia 18.4 × 13.1 mm (16.1–20.3 × 11.6–14; weight 1.65). The incubation period is usually 14 or 15 days, sometimes up to 18 days (Moreau and Moreau 1940; Brooke 1958). Only the female incubates the eggs and broods the chicks, but the male helps to feed them as soon as they hatch. At first the female brings little food to the nest, but increases the number of feeding visits until she is usually making more than the male (Moreau 1939b). There is no marked diurnal variation in feeding rate, but the parents feed less in the early morning and during rain, unless winged termites, which fly during rain, are available nearby. The nestlings fledge after 18–21 days, but return to the nest for several days afterwards (Moreau 1939a; Brooke 1958).

VOICE The male has a typical swallow's twittering song, a double 'chirrik-weet, chirrik-weet', repeated every couple of seconds from a perch near the nest (Ali and Ripley 1972). There is also a 'chit-chit' contact call, uttered when flying; and, when the swallows are alarmed, a 'chichip chichip' call is used. In the African race, at least, the adult uses a 'chit-chit' call when landing on the nest to feed the young, and a soft 'chee' as a contact call (Shaw 1979).

DESCRIPTION This is a small swallow with a rufous-chestnut forehead and crown. The colour of the forehead and crown varies between individuals, however, and it pales with wear. The lores are black and the ear-coverts are glossy blue. The upperparts, including the nape of the neck, rump and uppertail-coverts, are glossy blue. The wing-coverts and tertials are glossy blue with a purple sheen. The rest of the wings are black with a strong blue gloss. The underparts are creamy-white, apart from a patch of glossy blue on either side of the breast and on the sides of the flanks. The undertail-coverts and axillaries are white, and the underwing-coverts are white edged with brown along the wing margin. The tail is glossy blue, with large white patches on the inner web of all but the central pair of feathers. The outermost tail feathers are greatly elongated into very fine filaments on the male; they are also elongated, but less so, on the female. The eyes are dark brown, and the bill, feet and legs black. The sexes are alike, except in the length of the tail streamers. Juveniles have a paler, browner head, with less glossy upperparts and breast patches; the greyish-brown bases to the feathers of the upperparts are more prominent; they also have shorter outer tail feathers. Moult starts towards the end of the breeding season (Hanmer 1976); in Africa the moult takes place generally from November to early February, when breeding activity is low (Earlé 1988).

Measurements Length 14 cm (5½"). Wing 105–118 (mean 110); tail of male 62–118 (mean 92), of female 47–68 (mean 52.8); fork of male 36–67 (mean 50.8), of female 13–19 (mean 16.1); bill 9–11 (mean 9.9); tarsus 9.7–10.7 (mean 10.1). Weight 11–17 (mean 13.9).

RACES The Asian race *filifera* differs from the nominate race only in being larger, with longer tail streamers (wing 108–124; tail of male 101–202, of female 53–87). The colour of the forehead and crown is also more variable.

50 WHITE-THROATED BLUE SWALLOW   Plate 17
Hirundo nigrita Gray
Alternative name: Little Blue Swallow

Hirundo nigrita G.R. Gray, 1845, Gen. Birds 1, pl. 20: Niger River

FIELD CHARACTERS The brilliant wholly blue plumage, with contrasting white throat spot and white in the tail, makes this swallow easily distinguished from other species at close hand, but at a distance it may appear wholly black. The white marks are usually visible, however, when the bird spreads its tail in flight. It is a solitary, riverine species. The flight is fast and low.

HABITAT It is found only near water: along forested rivers and streams, mangroves and lagoons, probably more often along small streams than large rivers.

DISTRIBUTION AND POPULATION This species occurs over a wide area in the rainforest zone of West and Central Africa, from Sierra Leone east to Zaire and south to northern Angola and possibly northwestern Zambia (Mwinilunga District) (Hall and Moreau 1970). Within this area these swallows are locally distributed, but often common, in suitable habitat. They can be very common along certain rivers in Sierra Leone and the major rivers of the Ivory Coast (Thiollay 1985). There are few records of this species using artificial structures such as buildings and bridges for nest sites, but the habit may be spreading, perhaps allowing an expansion of the population.

MIGRATION White-throated Blue Swallows are sedentary residents, and there appear to be no regular long-distance migratory movements, although there may be some post-breeding dispersal.

FOOD AND BEHAVIOUR The flight is fast, with many banking and twisting movements, like that of the Barn Swallow (42).

The birds are often seen hawking for insects along rivers, within a few feet of the water, following the course of a current rather than over the vegetation along the banks of the river. They perch on tree trunks, branches or rocks in the river, and also on open ground, telegraph wires and houses. They are usually seen in isolated pairs, or small groups. Each pair appears to range over a limited section of the river around its nest site. They feed on a variety of aerial insects, including swarming termites and ants, beetles, vespiform Hymenoptera, small dragonflies and dipteran flies, especially tabanids (Germain *et al.* 1973; Brosset and Erard 1986). These swallows nest solitarily, each pair being very territorial and aggressive to intruders. At one site, six pairs were spread out over a 3-km (1.9-mile) stretch of river (Germain *et al.* 1973). In the wet season, when the water level is high, small flocks are occasionally seen.

BREEDING Breeding is usually in the dry season, timed to coincide with periods when the rivers are running low, to avoid the nests being flooded (Germain *et al.* 1973; Brosset and Erard 1986). There are two main breeding periods, December–March and June–August, but times vary locally. Some pairs have two broods. The nest is a shallow half bowl, made of pellets of mud mixed with some dry grass and lined with feathers, pieces of bark and dry grass. It is similar to that of the Barn Swallow. Nest sites are closely associated with water: the nests are built in hollow tree trunks projecting over water, or on the underside of a snag, dead tree or branch overhanging a river, usually 1–2 m (3–6½ ft) above it and isolated from the banks and from other vegetation. One nest was built only some 40 cm (15 in) from a wasp's nest (Young 1946). There are also records of nests built on rocks projecting from a river, under bridges, on piers, and even on buildings under roofs or verandahs and in railway culverts (Holman 1947; Serle 1949, 1950b; Dean 1974; Brosset and Erard 1986). Old nests are often re-used; new ones can take three weeks to complete (Brosset and Erard 1986).

The eggs are white, with numerous reddish-brown or brown blotches and spots and underlying ashy-purple spots. They measure 18.7 × 13.3 mm (17–19.5 × 13–13.8; weight 1.73). The clutch size is two to four, but usually three. Incubation takes at least 15 days. Only the female incubates, while the male perches nearby and defends the site from intruders. The fledging period is 17–18 days (Brosset and Erard 1986). Families seem to stay together for a while after the young have fledged.

VOICE The song is a weak twittering, often uttered in flight (Serle 1949).

DESCRIPTION The White-throated Blue Swallow is a small hirundine on which the upperparts, from the forehead and crown to the uppertail-coverts, including the wing-coverts, are a bright glossy steel-blue with purple reflections, especially on the head (the purple sheen is more noticeable in the field than on museum specimens). The lores are black and the ear-coverts are glossy blue. There is a patch of white hidden on each side of the lower back. Most of the underparts, including the undertail-coverts, are glossy steel-blue. The chin and sides of the throat have a purplish-blue sheen, but the middle of the throat is white. The under-wing-coverts are blackish with a blue sheen, and the axillaries are black. The primaries and outer secondaries are black with a purple sheen, the inner secondaries and tertials are glossy blue. The tail is short and broad, slightly forked, with only the outer-most feathers being slightly elongated. The central tail feathers are pure blue; the remainder are glossy blue on the outer web and on the tip and margin of the inner web, but the middle of each inner web is white, producing a striking white and blue pattern. The eyes are dark brown, and the bill and legs and feet are black. The sexes are alike. There is no geographical variation. Juveniles are similar to adults, but are much duller, with brownish underparts and little gloss; the spots on the throat and in the tail are also smaller than on the adult.

Measurements Length 12 cm (4¾"). Wing 102–111 (mean 106.1); tail 36–50 (mean 42.8); fork 3–7 (mean 5.8); bill 10.1–11.8 (mean 11.1); tarsus 9.5–11 (mean 10.5). Weight 16–19.

Hirundo leucosoma Swainson, 1837, Bds of West Africa, ii, p. 74: Senegal.

FIELD CHARACTERS Pied-winged Swallows have bright blue upperparts and white underparts, with large white areas in the wings. This is an easily identified swallow, the wing patches being very conspicuous in flight. It is the only swallow in West Africa with a wing patch. It frequents open country and forest clearings, and is usually solitary or in pairs. The flight is rapid.

HABITAT The typical habitat is savanna and farmland, especially near the borders of forests and sometimes in forest clearings. It is frequently seen in and around native villages and even around larger towns.

DISTRIBUTION AND POPULATION The range is restricted to West Africa, from Senegal and Gambia to Nigeria. It has also been recorded once in the Cameroons. Pied-winged Swallows are generally scarce and locally distributed throughout the range, although locally they may not be uncommon (Grimes 1988). They are not limited to natural sites, but nest extensively on buildings.

MIGRATION The movements of this species are very poorly known. It appears to be resident in many places, but in some it is a partial migrant. Thus, on the Accra Plain, it is mainly a wet-season visitor, while it occurs in some coastal districts of Ghana only in the dry season (Grimes 1988).

BEHAVIOUR The flight is rapid, involving much banking and turning. These swallows are usually seen alone or in pairs, or occasionally in small groups, feeding low over open areas of grassland, including lawns. They sometimes join larger flocks of other species of swallows and often perch on telegraph wires and trees. The diet consists of a variety of insects caught in flight, but is not known in detail. This species nests almost exclusively in single pairs.

BREEDING The breeding season is generally May–June; in the Gambia it is April–June (Gore 1981). The nest is a small, shallow cup made of pellets of mud and lined with fibres such as dry grass. It is built mainly in buildings, on projections from walls such as pegs, at the junction of wall and ceiling, on overhanging rafters, or on similar supports, usually close to the ceiling or roof. The nest may be re-used in successive years. A nest has also been recorded 4.6 m (15 ft) down a well and another 6 m (20 ft) up a water tower (Traylor and Parelius 1967). The usual clutch is four, sometimes three; the eggs are pure white and measure 19.7 × 13.1 mm (19–20.3 × 12.5–13.5; weight 1.77). Both male and female build the nest. The incubation and nestling periods are not known.

VOICE Pied-winged Swallows are rather silent birds, but they have a low 'chut' contact call, often uttered when the bird is perched.

DESCRIPTION The Pied-winged Swallow is a small hirundine. The upperparts, from the forehead and crown to the uppertail-coverts, including the lesser wing-coverts, are a glossy steel-blue, with white bases to the feathers of the mantle. The lores and ear-coverts are duller. The breast-band consists only of small glossy blue patches on either side of the breast. The underparts from the chin to the undertail-coverts, including the underwing-coverts and axillaries, are white. The outer greater wing-coverts, primaries and outer secondaries are black, with blue-purple reflections. The outer scapulars, inner secondaries and tertials are white with dark tips and shafts; these, plus the inner greater wing-coverts, form a white patch when the wing is spread. The tail is also steel-blue, but has green reflections; the central pair of feathers is plain, the next pair has a small white patch on the inner web, and the remainder have large white patches, increasing in size towards the outermost feathers, which are elongated and tapered. The tail is only slightly forked. The eyes are brown and the bill, legs and feet are black. The sexes are alike. Juveniles are similar to adults, but are duller, and the head is brown rather than glossy blue; the outer tail feathers are also shorter and less tapered.

Measurements Length 12 cm (4¾"). Wing 96–101 (mean 99.1); tail 44–53 (mean 48.5); fork 10–16 (mean 13.6); bill 7.8–10 (mean 9.8); tarsus 9.4–10.6 (mean 10.1).

52 WHITE-TAILED SWALLOW
Hirundo megaensis Benson

Hirundo megaensis Benson, 1942, Bull. Brit. Orn. Club, 63, p. 10: ten miles west of Mega, 4000 ft, Ethiopia.

FIELD CHARACTERS White-tailed Swallows are blue above and white below, with an almost wholly white tail. The triangle of white in the tail is very conspicuous and is a good guide to identification. This species frequents open grassland with thorn bushes.

HABITAT The habitat is mainly open, arid, short-grass areas with scattered thorn bushes (Benson 1946). Altitudes have been given as 1220–1370 m (3970–4500 ft), uncommon up to 2400 m (7900 ft), by Urban and Brown (1971); and 1220–1520 m (1370–4990 ft) by Benson (1942). Its two main sites, Yavello and Mega, however, are both at above 2000 m (6600 ft), and the intervening country is at or above 1500 m (4930 ft).

DISTRIBUTION AND POPULATION The White-tailed Swallow is endemic to southern Ethiopia between Yavello and Mega, extending about 50 km (31 miles) north of Yavello, 15 km (9 miles) north-northeast of Yavello, and about 50 km east and southeast of Mega towards the Ethiopian-Kenyan border. There were sight records from the Addis Ababa area between 1800 and 2750 m (5900–9030 ft) just before 1970 (Urban and Brown 1971), but none was seen there between 1969 and 1977 (Collar and Stuart 1985). It is restricted to an area of about 10,000 km², but is common within that range (Benson 1946; Ash 1983). In a 60-km (37-mile) stretch of road, 15–20 birds were seen per day (C. Erard, cited in Collar and Stuart 1985). Why its range is so restricted is unknown. Altitude is probably one factor. South of Mega, the altitude drops sharply owing to an escarpment; and the two main sites Yavello and Mega are surrounded by the 1500-m contour, with several areas of land above 1500 m to the east of Mega. The site 50 km east of Mega is on one of these high points (and is probably the same site as that said to be 50 km southeast of Mega). Thus, the species may be restricted by an altitudinal boundary. So far as is known, it does not migrate.

It is not protected, but is listed as rare in the *Threatened Birds of Africa* (Collar and Stuart 1985). Range-management schemes have been implemented elsewhere in the region, and similar schemes, or any other development of its habitat, might endanger this species. It is so poorly known that a study of its biology is necessary before recommendations can be made to ensure that this species does not decline.

BEHAVIOUR This species has been seen feeding in the lee of flowering trees, and it is often associated with termitaria.

BREEDING It probably nests in holes in termitaria, which are common in the area. There are no records of it nesting in buildings. The breeding season is probably January–February, as a young specimen was taken in March (Benson 1942). No other details of its breeding biology are known.

VOICE The calls have not been recorded.

DESCRIPTION The White-tailed Swallow is a small hirundine without any rufous colouring. The forehead, crown, hindneck, mantle, scapulars, lesser wing-coverts, rump and uppertail-coverts are glossy steel-blue. The lores and ear-coverts are blackish-blue. The underparts are whitish, including the underwing-coverts, axillaries and undertail-coverts. The wings are black with a blue sheen, most pronounced on the coverts. The tail is largely white, the feathers having white inner webs and dusky tips. The outer tail feathers, which are slightly elongated, have a white band on the inner web and blue-black outer webs; the penultimate pair has less blue-black, which extends onto the inner web; the next pair is greyish towards the tip of the outer web; the rest of the tail feathers are white with black shaft streaks. The female is similar to the male, but has shorter outer tail feathers, is less strongly blue and has less white in the tail; the tips of her tail feathers are dark, and the innermost pair whitish at the margins. The juvenile is duller than the adult, with some brownish tips to the feathers; the tail is a dull steel-blue with white on the outer webs and white spots on the inner webs; the outer feathers are edged with black, and the outermost are slightly elongated and more rounded at the tip than on the adult female. **Measurements** Length 13 cm (5″). Wing 99–104 (mean 102); tail of male 59–61 (mean 60), of female 48–55 (mean 52); fork of male 21–25 (mean 23.3), of female 8–16 (mean 12); bill 8.9–9.8 (mean 9.2); tarsus 9.5–10.8 (mean 10.3).

53 PEARL-BREASTED SWALLOW
Hirundo dimidiata Sundevall

Plate 18

Hirundo dimidiata Sundevall, 1850, Öfv. K. Vet.-Akad. Förh., 7, p. 107: Upper Caffraria. Type from Leroma, Transvaal.

Hirundo dimidiata marwitzi Reichenow, 1903, Malangali, Usafua, north of Lake Nyasa.

FIELD CHARACTERS Pearl-breasted Swallows have contrasting wholly blue upperparts and white underparts. They can be distinguished from similar species of *Hirundo* by the absence of white in the tail and wing. They frequent scrub and woodland, and are usually seen alone or in small groups. The flight is swift.

HABITAT The preferred habitat is semi-arid scrub, edges and clearings of miombo woodland and farmland. The species is frequently seen near human habitation, especially in drier areas. In the Cape, it has been seen feeding over newly cut hayfields and in dry thorn-euphorbia woodland (Clancey 1964). It has also been recorded over swampy ground and along the edges of pans (Benson *et al.* 1971).

DISTRIBUTION AND POPULATION Pearl-breasted Swallows are found in southern Africa from Angola, southern Zaire and Tanzania southwards (Maclean 1985). The race *marwitzi* is known from Angola, Zaire, Zambia, Zimbabwe, southwestern Tanzania and Malawi. The nominate race *dimidiata* breeds to the south of *marwitzi*, in Damaraland, the Transvaal, Orange Free State, Swaziland and Cape Province. It is absent from large parts of southern Africa, however, including much of Natal, eastern Orange Free State, Lesotho, northern Botswana, southern and eastern Mozambique and eastern Tanzania. This is a sparsely distributed, scarce and rarely seen species, though it can be fairly common in areas. Although it nests in artificial sites, it seems to prefer isolated places, where it nests solitarily, rather than in towns and villages, and so as yet the population has not taken advantage of many artificial nesting sites. There are also suggestions of recent declines in some areas (e.g. Irwin 1981).

MIGRATION In the northern part of the range, including Zimbabwe, Namibia and the Transvaal lowveld, it is resident all year (Maclean 1985). In the southwestern Cape, however, it is a summer breeding visitor, from late August or September until early March in the western part of its range; it breeds a month later in the east. Birds from the Cape are non-breeding, winter visitors to the highveld of the Transvaal; they are absent from the Cape from April to August (Benson 1949). Some may also winter in Zimbabwe, where there is an influx of birds in the dry season (Irwin 1981). Numbers in Zambia are also highest in the dry season. The migrations are, however, poorly known.

FOOD AND BEHAVIOUR Pearl-breasted Swallows are rather solitary, usually seen in pairs or family parties, though large flocks of up to 100 or so are occasionally seen (Benson *et al.* 1971). They often perch on dead twigs on treetops. Their flight is swift and similar to that of the Barn Swallow (42). Although they feed on flying insects, details of their diet are not known. They frequently perch on the ground or on small stones, especially around farmyards, where they feed on insects such as flies associated with livestock (R.A. Earlé, pers. comm.); they also feed on insects flushed by moving animals (Dean and MacDonald 1981). Little is known of their breeding behaviour, but Schmidt (1959) recorded males fluttering in front of perched females before they attempted to copulate and uttering a 'kss-kss' sound. These swallows usually nest as solitary pairs, particularly in the southern part of the range; there have, however, been reports of their nesting in small groups, and Lippens and Wille (1976) state that they do so in Zaire, which may reflect a racial difference in behaviour.

BREEDING The breeding season is from August to December in the Cape, to March in the eastern Cape and to April in Zimbabwe, with 77% of records for South

Africa in September–November (Earlé 1988a); in Zambia it is August–September; and in Central Africa it is from August to February, with a peak in September in the wet season (Earlé 1988a). There are usually two broods. Nest sites are in houses, especially huts with thatched roofs, verandahs, barns, old poultry houses, culverts, wells, mine shafts, pits, on cliffs and in antbear burrows, but this swallow prefers isolated and disused buildings to occupied ones. It has been recorded using nests of the Greater Striped Swallow (56) (Winterbottom 1962). One nest was built in the broken-off end of a hollow bough some 9 m (30 ft) above the ground (Priest 1935). Nest sites can be used for a long time: one site on a farm was used for about 30 years (Schmidt 1959). The nest is a half bowl made of mud pellets strengthened with dry grass or horsehair, and lined with fine roots, grasses, and horsehair; feathers seem to be rarely used. The nest is usually built against a wall or beam close to a ceiling or overhang, and is often re-used for subsequent broods. The nest measures about 130 mm (5.1 in) in diameter and is about 45 mm (1.8 in) deep externally. When it is built close to a ceiling, the sides of the nest are often extended upwards to meet it. Both male and female build the nest, but the male seems to do more than the female; they work in the mornings and can take three to four weeks to complete it (Schmidt 1959).

The clutch size is two or three, rarely four, eggs, which are pure white and measure 17.3 × 12.6 mm (14.8–19.5 × 11.3–14.0). They are laid at daily intervals. The incubation period is 16 or 17 days, and the nestling period is 20–23 days. Only the female incubates, but both parents feed the nestlings. Fledglings return to the nest for a few nights to roost; during the day they sit on wires and trees. Their parents feed them, perched or in flight, for up to 29 days after fledging; the fledglings stay around the nest site until the second clutch is laid (Schmidt 1959).

VOICE The song is a chittering 'chip-cheree-

chp-chip' (Maclean 1985). There is a guttural 'kss-kss' heard during courtship, and a succession of 'twit' calls uttered by both sexes in flight (Schmidt 1959). The parents call when they visit the nest to feed the nestlings.

DESCRIPTION This is a small blue and white swallow. The upperparts from the forehead to the uppertail-coverts, including the scapulars and lesser wing-coverts, are glossy blue-black with a slight purplish wash. The lores and ear-coverts are duller. The entire underparts are dull grey-white. The breast and sides of the body have a buffy-grey wash, and many of the feathers have a narrow, dusky medial streak. The axillaries and underwing-coverts are a darker greyish-white. The undertail-coverts have dark shafts and tips. The wings are black with a glossy blue wash, most pronounced on the coverts. The tail is metallic blue-black, usually without any white although, very occasionally, there is some diffuse white on the outer feathers. The outermost feathers are elongated and taper to a point, forming a moderate fork. The eyes are brown, and the bill, legs and feet are black. The female resembles the male, but has shorter outer tail feathers. The juvenile is duller than the adult, being mainly dusky black with a little blue-green gloss, especially on the head and mantle, and has shorter outer tail feathers. The primary moult is from November to July, after the peak in breeding (Earlé 1988a).

Measurements Length 13 cm (5″). Wing 100–110 (mean 102.8); tail of male 57–70 (mean 63.5), of female 54–61 (mean 57); fork of male 22–26 (mean 24), of female 15–19 (mean 16.4); bill 8.5–9.9 (mean 9.4); tarsus 9.3–10.9 (mean 10.2). Weight 10–12.

RACES The race *marwitzi* is darker, more greyish below, and is somewhat smaller (wing 91–108) than the nominate race. The differences, however, are slight, and the species could be regarded as monotypic. The races are particularly difficult to distinguish when in worn plumage.

54 BLUE SWALLOW
Hirundo atrocaerulea Sundevall

Plate 19

Hirundo atrocaerulea Sundevall, 1850, Öfv. K. Vet.-Akad. Förh., 7, p. 107: Umvoti, Natal.

Hirundo atrocaerulea lynesi Grant and Mackworth-Praed, 1942, Njombe, Tanzania.

The Blue Swallow is most closely related to the Black-and-rufous Swallow (55). They are similar in size and shape of bill, wings and tail. Their underparts differ in colour, but on both species these feathers are blackish and white at the base. Neither uses pellets of mud to make its nest. This is, however, a distinctive swallow, as it lacks both red in the plumage and white in the tail and it is strongly sexually dimorphic. Roberts (1922) erected a new genus (*Natalornis*) for it, but it is now usually kept in the genus *Hirundo*.

FIELD CHARACTERS In the field, this swallow is very distinctive, with its wholly blue plumage and, on the male, elegant tail streamers. It frequents open grassland and is usually solitary or in small groups. It flies fast, keeping low over the ground.

HABITAT Both races prefer to nest and feed in open grassland with streams that form potholes, rather than in forested areas (Snell 1969). The nest area needs to be relatively free of vegetation so that the birds have a clear flight path to the nest itself. They are typically birds of mountainous areas, occurring mostly between 1500 and 2200 m (4930–7260 ft) in Zimbabwe, but at lower levels further south; those at low latitudes breed at higher altitudes than those further from the Equator.

DISTRIBUTION AND POPULATION This swallow breeds in restricted parts of southern and eastern Africa (Earlé 1987c). It is known from parts of Natal, Zululand, Swaziland, eastern Transvaal, eastern Zimbabwe and adjacent Mozambique, Malawi, northeastern Zambia, southeastern Zaire and southwestern Tanzania. Its southernmost limit is now a ridge of high ground between the upper Umvoti River and the Karkloof River. The nominate race breeds from southern Zimbabwe to eastern Natal, and *lynesi* from Tanzania to Malawi. It is locally distributed, in South Africa occurring mainly in the Natal Midlands, and it breeds at low densities.

Although probably never common (Priest 1935 described the species as rare in 'Rhodesia' and nowhere common south of the Zambezi), it has declined to very low numbers in South Africa and Zululand, although numbers wintering in Uganda have been maintained (Collar and Stuart 1985). The status of the population in South Africa is 'endangered', and in Zimbabwe it is 'vulnerable' (Brooke 1984). Densities are low, with no more than five or six pairs per km². Snell (1969) estimated that there were only three or four pairs per km² in one area of Zimbabwe, and this decreased in later years; indeed, Blue Swallows have not bred at Snell's study site since December 1983

(M.L. Snell, pers. comm.). This decline is believed to be due to extensive planting of pine and Australian wattle, and other forms of development which destroy both the nest sites and feeding areas. In addition, control of fires leads to nest sites becoming cluttered with vegetation and thus unsuitable; overgrazing and excessive burning cause erosion of the nest sites. This species is no longer found at its type locality in Natal, which was at the southernmost part of its range; it has declined generally in Natal and has disappeared from the lower-lying parts of its former range, this again attributed to the commercial planting of pine, eucalyptus, wattle and, to a lesser extent, sugar cane which has taken place over the last 20 or so years. Out of at least 29 former breeding sites in the Transvaal, Swaziland and Natal, only eight are still used, supporting only 63 pairs, most of which are threatened with destruction (Allan 1988). In Malawi, however, where afforestation is controlled, there is a large population on the Nyika Plateau; the species is also common on the Viphya Plateau, but scarce on the Misukas and extinct on the Zomba Plateau following heavy plantation. There is still suitable habitat for it in Tanzania, but the population there is probably also endangered (Brooke 1984). In the Transvaal, some 470 ha (1160 acres) on the Berlin State Forest have recently been set aside for a population of about ten pairs, and the threat of afforestation removed from other sites (Anon. 1987; Allan 1988). It is legally protected by local conservation ordinances, and in Natal is a specially protected bird.

In the past, populations of this species have probably been limited by the availability of natural nest sites, since it needs areas that are not subject to erosion and are relatively free of vegetation. It is, however, starting to nest on artificial structures (although infrequently at present) and may spread as a result, though it consequently has to compete with other species such as the Greater Striped Swallow (56), White-throated Swallow (47) and White-rumped Swift *Apus caffer* for nest sites.

MIGRATION From the breeding grounds in southern Africa, the Blue Swallow regularly migrates north to Uganda, western Kenya and northeastern Zaire (Earlé 1987c). The eastern population also migrates to the north of its range after the breeding season. In South Africa and Zimbabwe it arrives on the breeding grounds in September and leaves in March or early April. In Zambia it arrives in October and leaves in April.

FOOD AND BEHAVIOUR The Blue Swallow is usually seen alone or in groups of a few individuals, feeding over open grassland, vleis and forest edges. Like other swallows, it hunts aerial insects, flying quickly and actively, usually skimming low over the ground and often keeping to a small area. Only occasionally does it fly high. Priest (1935) described it as engaging in brief periods of flying, interspersed with long periods of perching on low bushes and shrubs, less commonly on wires. Snell (pers. comm.), however, notes that breeding pairs are on the wing almost continuously by day, occasionally perching near the nest. Drinking and bathing are performed on the wing. The diet includes dipteran flies (museum specimens). Like other swallows, the birds return each year to the same breeding site. Breeding birds often keep to a favoured perch near the nest throughout the breeding season. The male and female of a pair keep together and do not flock with other swallows. They are very solitary, and are apparently one of the most territorial of swallows, readily and aggressively driving off intruders near the nest. Nest sites are about 400 m (440 yards) apart on average (Allan 1986), and Snell (1969) reported them nesting no closer than 8 km (½ mile) from each other. During courtship, males pursue females in flight while singing and fluttering the wings.

BREEDING The Blue Swallow is double-brooded, breeding from September to February, with over three-quarters of records from November to January (Earlé 1987c). Snell (1979) recorded three broods being raised in each of two years at an artificial site. The nests are built underground in potholes, antbear burrows and banks; they are attached to the wall or roof under an overhang, up to 5 m (16 ft) below ground level. There are several records of nests being built on artificial structures such as mine shafts, road culverts and the eaves of houses, but this seems to be a relatively recent phenomenon. One unusual site was on a vertical surface underneath a corrugated garage roof, the nest itself being built in the normal way: this nest was later taken over by Greater Striped Swallows, and the following year the Blue Swallows at this site took over the nest of a pair of White-throated Swallows (Snell 1969); at the same site in subsequent years, Blue Swallows built nests on a rafter in the porch of a house and in a thatched roof. Blue Swallows nested successfully at this site for about 20 years (Snell 1979). The nest itself, which is often repaired and re-used, is a half bowl made of mud and grass, unsupported below. Unlike other *Hirundo* species, Blue Swallows mix the mud and grass as they collect it instead of using mud pellets; both male and female build the nest. The lining is made of grass, rootlets and feathers.

The clutch is usually of three but sometimes two eggs, which are white and spotted and streaked; these emaculations have been variously described as purple-brown, rufous, yellowish-brown, brown and grey. The eggs average 18.3 × 13.2 mm (17.7–19.5 × 12.5–13.8; weight 1.67). The incubation period is 14–16 days, and the nestling period 20–24 days. Only the female incubates, but the male helps to feed the nestlings, which have a conspicuous yellow gape which becomes white by the time they leave the nest. Predators appear to be few, but nests are subject to the vagaries of weather and erosion, and well-used sites are abandoned when erosion, particularly after heavy rain, causes the nests to collapse (Snell 1979). One brood died as a result of a late ground frost, and a pair deserted a clutch of eggs when a cyclone brought down pieces of shrubs and ferns that obscured the entrance of the hole (Snell 1979).

VOICE The song is a plaintive, monotonous series of six to eight notes. The male sings during courtship, and also on many other occasions when the pair is feeding and while the female is incubating. The alarm call, also used when attacking intruders in the territory, is a high-pitched 'peep peep'. Snell (1969) also described a quiet, unmusical 'chip chip', heard in flight, which seems to be a contact call between the male and female.

DESCRIPTION The whole of the upperparts and underparts of this large and spectacular swallow are a brilliant, iridescent steel-blue.

The flanks and the side of the rump show some white feathers, but these are often visible only when the bird is preening. The wings are metallic blue-black, the primaries having a slightly greener gloss. The tail is black, with a blue-green wash and whitish feather shafts. The outer tail feathers are narrow and greatly elongated on the male, forming impressively long, thin streamers; these are shorter on the female, but the sexes are otherwise alike (though on a few females the breast is duller, perhaps a result of abrasion at the nest: Earlé 1987c). The bill, legs and feet are black, and the eyes are brown. The juveniles are sooty-black, with some blue gloss above, and with a brownish throat; they have short outer tail feathers like the female.

Measurements Length 20 cm (8"). Wing of male 104–120 (mean 113), of female 101–111 (mean 107); tail of male 93–132 (mean 135), of female 60–81 (mean 71); fork of male 58–108 (mean 92), of female 25–32 (mean 30); bill 9.1–10.9 (mean 10); tarsus 9.1–12.5 (mean 10.2).

RACES The population in eastern Africa is sometimes considered to be a separate race, *lynesi*. It is similar to *atrocaerulea*, but its plumage is washed with violet.

55 BLACK-AND-RUFOUS SWALLOW   Plate 19
Hirundo nigrorufa Bocage

Hirundo nigrorufa Bocage, 1877, J. Sci. Math. Phys. Nat. Acad. Sci. Lisboa, 6, no. 22, p. 158: Caconda, Angola.

FIELD CHARACTERS In the field, this is a very dark swallow, appearing almost black above with distinctive rufous underparts and a characteristic dark tail with little white in it. It frequents open country, usually alone or in small groups. It flies swiftly, close to the ground.

HABITAT These swallows frequent open savanna and grassland such as dambos (grassland along drainage courses), marshy valleys and watershed plains, particularly areas that are seasonally flooded, and often near streams or other waterbodies. In Mwinilunga District, they favour narrow valleys where there is a strip of grassland along a stream, bordering miombo woodland (Bowen 1983). Pairs have also been seen in the grassy margins of a swamp, at a fish pond and feeding over a burnt, cleared area of miombo woodland (Bowen 1983).

DISTRIBUTION AND POPULATION This species has a restricted range in Angola, southernmost Zaire and Zambia (Bowen 1983). In Angola it occurs in the Central Plateau east to southern Lunda and northern Moxico. In Zambia it occurs in the Northern and Luapula Provinces, the northern part of the North-Western Province and in the northern Mwinilunga District eastwards to Solwezi. It is uncommon throughout its range, although it is quite common and widespread in the northern Mwinilunga District of Zambia

where nest sites are still plentiful (Bowen 1983). It is limited by the availability of natural nest sites as it does not use artificial ones.

MIGRATION The extent of any migratory movements is unclear. It does not make long-distance migrations but, at least in the Mwinilunga District, it disperses after breeding. It is absent from its breeding grounds there between late November and early March, during the peak of the rains (Bowen 1983). It is not known where the birds move to. Elsewhere records are scarce, and it is not clear whether dispersal occurs.

FOOD AND BEHAVIOUR The flight is quick, with short wingbeats, the bird frequently turning around the same point (Lippens and Wille 1976). They usually feed low over the ground, skimming the vegetation; occasionally they feed higher, especially during the breeding season (Bowen 1983). Although groups of four or five are occasionally seen and larger groups form before and after breeding, this species is usually seen alone or in pairs. It perches frequently, often low down on bushes, stems, termite mounds or fences (Bowen 1983). The diet includes flies and other small insects (museum specimens). Bowen (1983) observed individuals chasing one another; several were singing on the wing and displaying by turning their wings up and down in flight. This display flight is similar to that of Blue Swallows (54). Black-and-rufous Swallows nest as solitary pairs; Bowen (1983) recorded nests 100 m

(110 yds) apart, even where nest sites were plentiful.

BREEDING In Zambia breeding starts in July, after the rains, eggs being laid from July to October (Bowen and Colebrook-Robjent 1984). In Zaire, a clutch was found in July, in the dry season (Lippens and Wille 1976). Most broods have fledged by mid October. It is not known whether these swallows have two broods; late clutches in September and October may be second clutches or replacements. The nest is attached to bare earth banks of rivers or streams under overhangs (Bowen 1983; Bowen and Colebrook-Robjent 1984). One at Kasama was attached to the side of a pit. It is usually built away from obstructing vegetation and about half way up the bank, 20 cm (8 in) or more from the water. It is a half bowl made of mud (not as pellets) and rootlets, with a lining of grass and sometimes a few feathers, but never very many. One nest measured 80 mm wide and 55 mm from front to back (3.2 × 2.1 in); inside it was 60 mm (2.4 in) in diameter and 45 mm (1.8 in) deep (Bowen 1983). There are no records of buildings or other artificial sites being used. The usual clutch size is three, sometimes two. The eggs are blunt to long-oval, and are glossy, cream to white, and well marked with specks or spots of warm, dark or chocolate-brown over ashy-grey or lilac-grey; the markings tend to be concentrated around the blunt end and vary between clutches. The eggs are very similar to those of the Blue Swallow (Bowen and Colebrook-Robjent 1984); they measure 18.7 × 13.3 mm (16.5–19.5 × 12.3–13.8;

weight 1.73). The incubation and nestling periods are not known.

VOICE Black-and-rufous Swallows are rather silent. They have a warbling song uttered on the wing, and a short, strident, repeated alarm note (Bowen 1983).

DESCRIPTION The Black-and-rufous Swallow is a medium-sized hirundine. The upperparts from the forehead and crown to the uppertail-coverts, including the wing-coverts, are glossy violet-blue, this colour extending down the sides and onto the undertail-coverts. The lores and ear-coverts are duller. The primaries and secondaries are a duskier blue. The underparts from the chin to the abdomen, including the under-wing-coverts and axillaries, are deep rufous. The tail feathers are dusky blue, with narrow white edges to the inner webs rather than the patches characteristic of other *Hirundo* species; the outer feathers are slightly elongated. The eyes are chestnut-brown and the bill, legs and feet are black. Females are similar to males, but are slightly paler below and tend to have shorter wings. Juveniles are duller and browner above, with only a slight, greener, sheen, and their underparts are pale rufous; the lores, ear-coverts and undertail-coverts are sepia, the latter having rusty tips, and the outer tail feathers are shorter than on the adult.

Measurements Length 16 cm (6¼"). Wing of male 108–116 (mean 112), of female 106–110 (mean 108); tail 50–70 (mean 60.4); fork 10–20 (mean 16); bill 9–9.7 (mean 9.4); tarsus 9.9–10.8 (mean 10.3). Weight 13.

56 GREATER STRIPED SWALLOW   Plate 19
Hirundo cucullata Boddaert

Hirundo cucullata Boddaert, 1783, Tab. Pl. enlum., p. 45: Cape of Good Hope, ex Daubenton, Pl. enlum., pl. 723, fig. 2.

FIELD CHARACTERS The Greater Striped Swallow has a blue mantle, rufous-chestnut crown and rump, and streaked underparts. The latter feature distinguishes this species from most other South African swallows apart from the Lesser Striped Swallow (57), which it closely resembles (the two species form a superspecies) and whose range it overlaps. Where they do overlap, it differs from the Lesser Striped in being larger, and having a paler rump, buffier underparts with

less bold streaking, and paler ear-coverts. It frequents more open country than the Lesser Striped Swallow. It is usually seen alone or in small groups. Flight is slow, with few wingbeats.

HABITAT These swallows frequent mainly mountainous open country such as high-veld, and montane grassland, but avoid woodland and forest. They often associate closely with humans, and frequently breed in suburban as well as rural areas.

DISTRIBUTION AND POPULATION Greater Striped Swallows are confined to southern Africa (Maclean 1985). They breed in Cape Province, and South-West Africa east to Natal, western Zululand, western Swaziland, Orange Free State, Basutoland, the highveld of the Transvaal, and Matabeleland in Zimbabwe. This is a very common species in its breeding range, partly at least because of its willingness to use abundant artificial nesting sites around human habitation, which has probably led to an increase in numbers. It sometimes suffers competition from White-rumped Swifts *Apus caffer* for nest sites; the swifts are known to eject young swallows and take over the nest (Schmidt 1962). In some places it probably also competes for nest sites with Lesser Striped and Rufous-chested Swallows (58).

MIGRATION In winter these swallows migrate north to Angola, southwestern Tanzania and southern Zaire (Maclean 1985). Those recorded in Zambia in winter appear to be largely if not wholly passage migrants, being present mainly from April to May and September to November (Aspinwall 1972). They also occur as a rare migrant in Malawi. They are present in their breeding range from August to April or, rarely, June. Very occasionally individuals overwinter in South Africa. The only long-distance recovery is of an individual ringed near Cape Town and recovered in Kazanza, Zaire, 3156 km (1960 miles) to the north (R.E. Earlé, pers. comm.).

FOOD AND BEHAVIOUR The flight is leisurely, with frequent gliding. They appear to be less agile and manoeuvrable than the Lesser Striped Swallow, and have a relatively less deeply forked tail (Waugh 1978). They feed close to their nest site, low over the ground, usually alone or in pairs. Family groups are seen towards the end of the breeding season. In the non-breeding season, small flocks form, often with other swallows and swifts. They are fearless of humans and appear quite tame. The diet consists of aerial insects such as flying ants (museum specimens), but they have been known to eat mulberries *Acacia cyclops* (Broekhuysen 1960); they are often attracted to grassland fires. Pairs nest singly, although several pairs may nest on the same building. First-years return to the vicinity of the nest where they hatched, and there is one record of a female apparently mating with her father at her natal nest (Schmidt

1962). Males and females return to the same nest each year, but females sometimes move nests if they lose their mates. The male displays when singing, perched or in flight, by throwing the head back and puffing out the throat feathers. Unpaired males advertise to females by flying with shallow wingbeats and singing; once the male has a female's attention, he leads her to the nest (R.A. Earlé, pers. comm.).

BREEDING The breeding season is long, extending between August and March in Zimbabwe, September–March in the Cape and October–April in Transvaal, Natal and Orange Free State (Clancey 1964; Maclean 1985). Two, sometimes three, broods are usual in all parts of the range. Nest sites are largely on a wide variety of artificial structures, including verandahs, lofts, barns, culverts, bridges and drainpipes; the birds prefer to nest high up (for example, choosing the highest culverts available). They will adapt the nests of other swallows (Snell 1969) and use nestboxes and holes in walls after constructing a mud tunnel over the entrance (e.g. Pringle 1948). Natural sites are in caves or on rock faces, or on the underside of fallen trees. The nest is a large bowl of mud pellets, with a long tubular entrance and a lining of soft fibres and feathers, even pieces of cloth, and may be re-used in subsequent years; scarcely any vegetable matter is used to strengthen the mud. The shape of the nest is adaptable, depending on where it is built: one nest constructed around an electric-light fitting had two tunnels (Shillingford 1965). Both parents build the nest and can take at least two or three weeks to complete it; they continue to bring in feathers during and after laying the eggs (Schmidt 1962).

The clutch size is two to four, occasionally five, but usually three; it tends to decrease during the season (Schmidt 1962). The eggs are glossy white, occasionally with a few brownish spots, and measure 21.4 × 14.8 mm (19–24.5 × 13.5–16.5; weight 2.45); they are usually laid at daily intervals, but sometimes a day is missed. The incubation period is 17–20 days (average 18 days); late broods tend to have longer incubation periods than early ones. Only the female incubates, but both male and female feed the nestlings. The nestling period is 23–30 days. Fledglings return to the nest to roost for at least another nine days (Schmidt 1962). The oldest known bird was six years and eight months old (Earlé 1987d).

VOICE The contact note is a twittering 'chis-sick', frequently heard from flocks. The song is short: an initial chuckling phrase of two or three notes is followed by a gargled trill, 'trip trip trirrr'(Maclean 1985).

DESCRIPTION Greater Striped Swallows are large members of the *Hirundo* genus. The forehead and crown are dark rufous-chestnut, with a lighter rufous-chestnut on the sides of the neck and nape. The feathers on the crown have conspicuous blue-black bases. The mantle and scapulars are glossy deep blue. The rump is light rufous-chestnut. The upper series of uppertail-coverts are rufous-chestnut, while the lower series are glossy blue-black. The lores are dusky, and the cheeks and ear-coverts are buffy with dark brown streaks. The underparts are a light buff to creamy, darker on the sides, and with narrow sepia streaks. The undertail-coverts are a light cream, with shaft streaks and occasional dark subterminal spots. The axillaries and underwing-coverts are buffy-white with dark shafts to the feathers. The wings are blackish-brown. The wing-coverts, especially the lesser coverts, have a slight blue gloss, but the shafts of the feathers are duller and greener. The edge of the wing is mottled with black and white. The tail is blackish-brown with a blue-violet gloss: each feather, apart from the inner-most two pairs, has a large white patch on the inner web, although the extent of white on the feathers is variable; the outer feathers are extended and attenuated to form streamers. The bill is black, the eyes and legs and feet are dark brown. The sexes are similar, but females have shorter outer tail feathers. Juveniles are duller, have thicker streaks on the underparts and shorter outer tail feathers; the crown has more black mixed with the rufous-chestnut on the crown, and the tertials and wing-coverts have tawny tips.

Measurements Length 18–20 cm (7–8"). Wing 117–131 (mean 125); tail of male 99–108 (mean 102), of female 90–99 (mean 94.4); fork of male 44–55 (mean 51), of female 38–47 (mean 43); bill 9.5–11.1 (mean 10.2); tarsus 13.9–15.5 (mean 14.6). Weight 19–35–27.

57 LESSER STRIPED SWALLOW   Plate 19
Hirundo abyssinica Guérin-Méneville

Hirundo abyssinica Guérin-Meneville, 1843, Rev. Zool., p. 322: Ethiopia.

Hirundo abyssinica puella Temminck and Schlegel, 1847, Guinea Coast.

Hirundo abyssinica maxima Bannerman, 1923, Kuribo, 5500 ft, Nigerian highlands.

Hirundo abyssinica bannermani Grant and Mackworth-Praed, 1942, Aribo Valley.

Hirundo abyssinica unitatis Sclater and Mackworth-Praed, 1918, Pinetown, Natal.

Hirundo abyssinica ampliformis Clancey, 1969, Linyanti, Caprivi Strip.

FIELD CHARACTERS This swallow should be readily identifiable from its heavily striped underparts and rufous-chestnut crown and rump. The only species it resembles is the Greater Striped Swallow (56), which, where they occur together, is larger, has a light-coloured rump and finer streaks on the underside. It frequents more wooded country and its flight is often swifter than that of the Greater Striped Swallow.

HABITAT It generally prefers wooded country, but also occurs in open grassy areas at a range of altitudes, though usually at lower ones. It is most common up to about 2000 m (6600 ft); at higher levels in montane grassland it is replaced by the Greater Striped Swallow. It frequents open woodland, savanna, forest edge, forest clearings, cultivation and grassland, and is often seen around villages and towns. In West Africa it is typical of the semi-arid and grass-woodland belts in both farmland and bush, particularly near rocky streams or towns and villages. In mountainous areas it frequents valleys and grassland, and is rarely seen over forests. In Zambia it is usually seen in lightly wooded country or along rivers in more heavily forested areas. In Mozambique it is most common in acacia-thorn country (da Rosa Pinto and Lamm 1958).

DISTRIBUTION AND POPULATION They range over much of Africa south of the Sahara (Clancey 1969a). Lesser Striped

Swallows in Sudan, Eritrea, Ethiopia and Somalia are referable to the nominate race. Those in southern Sudan, Uganda, Kenya, Tanzania, Pemba, Zanzibar and the Mafia Islands, Ruanda-Urundi, and Zaire, western Angola, north to Gabon, south through Malawi, Zambia and Zimbabwe to the eastern Transvaal, Mozambique, Natal and eastern Cape Province are of the race *unitatis*. Over a large area of southern Sudan and Kenya, however, individuals of this species are intermediate between these two races. The race *puella* is locally distributed, from Sierra Leone to Nigeria as far south as Ondo and Benin and to Bornu and Zaria in the north, in Upper Volta and the Gold Coast; it has been recorded once in the Gambia and as far east as Cameroon and Gabon. The race *maxima* occurs in Cameroon and adjacent parts of Nigeria; *bannermani* is found in western Darfur on the Jebel Marra and in the western Basin; and *ampliformis* occurs in Zimbabwe on the Zambesi above the Victoria Falls, western Zambia, the Caprivi Strip and adjacent northern Botswana and eastern Angola.

Lesser Striped Swallows are very common and widespread throughout their range, although in some peripheral areas they are only locally common. They are one of the most abundant African swallows, especially in Zaire and eastern Africa. Populations in some areas are probably increasing (Benson 1980), particularly where they are using artificial structures for nest sites. Artificial sites may also have allowed them to expand into more open country, where they thus come into competition with the Greater Striped Swallow.

MIGRATION This species is a migrant in the northern and southern parts of its range. Its movements, however, are poorly known. In West Africa, it is a wet-season (breeding) visitor in the north, moving south in the dry season; elsewhere, however, it is a partial migrant, with some individuals staying in the non-breeding season (Elgood *et al.* 1973; Grimes 1988). In South Africa it is a summer breeding migrant, from July to March or April (Maclean 1985). The wintering grounds of this southern race *unitatis* are unclear; they are probably in the southern equatorial belt. In Zimbabwe it is partially resident, but local movements may occur and birds from further south may move into Zambia and Zimbabwe in the dry season, when the breeding population has left

(Aspinwall 1981; Irwin 1981). Populations in Botswana and southern Mozambique and Zimbabwe are also migratory, moving north after breeding. Elsewhere, Lesser Striped Swallows appear to be largely resident, although they may make local post-breeding movements, partly to lower altitudes. In East Africa they are more common in dry areas in the rains, and they are a breeding visitor to the Mafia Islands (Britton 1980).

FOOD AND BEHAVIOUR The flight is erratic and wavering, including lots of fluttering and gliding, but it can be swift and direct and these swallows are more manoeuvrable and agile than the Greater Striped Swallow (Waugh 1978). They feed both at mid levels and low over the ground, often over open water, at an average height of 6 m (19 ft) (Waugh 1978). They sometimes feed around cattle and other large animals, catching the insects disturbed by them. They are often seen in pairs or small flocks, and they often perch on wires and treetops. Their diet is not known in detail, but includes dipteran flies, flying ants and other small insects (Friedmann and Williams 1969; museum specimens). There is also a record of flocks hovering and taking caterpillars off standing crops (Priest 1935), and they have been seen catching flying termites. Unusually for hirundines, they have also been recorded feeding on fruit: Maclean (1988) recorded individuals eating the fruit of the pigeonwood tree *Trema orientalis*. These swallows nest both as isolated pairs and in small groups of usually fewer than ten, but even in groups the nests are usually spaced out; in one group of 48, the nests were 25 cm (10 in) or more apart (Dean 1974).

BREEDING Breeding takes place chiefly in the rains, but often extends through much of the year. North of the Equator, from West Africa to Ethiopia, it lasts mainly from February or March to July or August, but from April to November in Gabon (Serlé 1950a, b; Urban and Brown 1971; Brosset and Erard 1986; Grimes 1988). In East Africa the peak is in the long rains from March to June, with another small peak in the short rains of November and December (Brown and Britton 1980). The population in southern Africa breeds later in the year than the eastern one: in South Africa breeding peaks in October–December, and in Zimbabwe, Zambia, Malawi and Angola it peaks in

September–November (Earlé 1988c). Two broods are usual in the southern part of the range and probably also in West Africa.

Nest sites include natural ones, such as the underside of boulders in rivers, under overhanging rocks on cliff faces, gullies and caves, in clefts in crags, under large branches of trees such as baobabs and acacias and in partly hollowed ant-mounds; but many nests are now built on artificial structures such as bridges, culverts, usually with a diameter of at least 65 cm (26 in), mine shafts, wells, barns, outhouses and houses, both used and disused, on verandahs, beams inside houses, close to the ceiling and under eaves. In highland areas, the eaves of mountain huts and rest houses are often used. The nests are usually at least a couple of metres above ground level. Nest-boxes are also used, a mud tunnel usually being added to the entrance hole. There are a few records of this species using an old nest of other swallows such as the Wire-tailed Swallow (49) or Rock Martin (40) as a base, enclosing it and adding a tunnel (Benson and Benson 1977). The race unitatis often nests on rocks or concrete structures, but ampliformis still usually nests under branches (Irwin 1981). The retort-shaped nest is made of mud pellets and lined first with dry grass, then with feathers; the nest chamber is about 15 cm long and 10 cm deep (6 × 4 in). The mud is picked up with a sideways jerk of the closed bill. One nest was estimated to have contained 1,589 pellets (Sclater and Moreau 1933). The nest can take up to six or seven weeks to build; both male and female construct it, starting with a flat cup, building up the sides and adding the tunnel last (Sclater and Moreau 1933). Two to four eggs, usually three, make up the clutch. The eggs are white, occasionally with a few red-brown speckles; even within a clutch one or more eggs may be marked while the rest of the clutch is pure white (James 1926). They measure 19.7 × 13.9 mm (17.3–21.8 × 12.5–15.4). Incubation lasts about 14–16 days, and the nestling period is 17–19 days (Moreau and Moreau 1940). The male perches by the nest while the female incubates. Both parents feed the young. The young return to the nest for several more days to roost. The oldest known bird was five years and eleven months (Earlé 1987d).

VOICE These are very vocal swallows. The song is more vigorous and warbler-like than that of the Barn Swallow (42). It consists of nine or ten squeaky notes, 'chip-chip-chwip, kreek, kree-kree, kreep, chwip, kreeee' (Maclean 1985). They have a loud, wheezy call note, 'tee-tee-tee'.

DESCRIPTION Lesser Striped Swallows are medium-sized hirundines. The forehead, crown, sides of the head and the neck are rufous-chestnut. The lores are greyish and the ear-coverts are rufous-chestnut. The mantle and scapulars are blue-black, and the rump is rufous-chestnut like the head. The shorter uppertail-coverts are rufous-chestnut, but the longer ones are blue-black. The underparts are white with broad shaft streaks of sepia, most dense on the chin and throat. The underwing-coverts and axillaries are pale tawny. There is a buffy wash on the breast and sides in fresh plumage. The undertail-coverts are white, rarely with tawny streaks. The upperwing-coverts, wings and tail are black with a slight blue gloss, strongest on the coverts. All but the central two pairs of tail feathers have white patches on the inner webs, although the extent of the patches is variable. The outer tail feathers are elongated, forming a deep fork. The bill is black and the eyes, legs and feet are brown. The female is like the male, but has shorter outer tail feathers. The juvenile is duller than the adult, with some black on the head, tawny tips to the wing-coverts, tertials and secondaries, and a tawny wash on the chest and flanks; the outer tail feathers are also shorter. The moult starts after the breeding season and appears not to overlap the latter, at least for the southern African population, migrant birds moulting on the wintering grounds (Earlé 1988c).

Measurements Length 15–19 cm (6–7½"). Wing 102–117 (mean 106); tail of male 93–116 (mean 100), of female 72–87 (mean 79.9); fork of male 47–52 (mean 50.4), of female 29–47 (mean 35.7); bill 8–9.9 (mean 9); tarsus 11–12.8 (mean 11.9). Weight 15–21 (mean 17).

RACES The races differ mainly in the extent of striping on the underparts, the shade of the rufous-chestnut areas, the amount of white in the tail and the presence or absence of streaks on the undertail-coverts, all the races but abyssinica having streaks. The race unitatis (wing 101–117) is more heavily striped below than abyssinica. The race maxima is large (wing 107–117) and has even heavier, broader and blacker stripes; the rufous areas are a more

saturated chestnut and it has small white tail patches. The race *bannermani* has fine, narrow streaks, and paler rufous areas, but it is not clearly separable from *abyssinica*. The race *ampliformis* has heavy, deep black stripes; it is more tawny than *maxima* and has more white in the tail. The race *puella* is small (wing 95–106), with fine streaks.

58 RUFOUS-CHESTED SWALLOW   Plate 20
Hirundo semirufa Sundevall
Alternative name: Red-breasted Swallow

Hirundo semirufa Sundevall, 1850, Öfv. K. Vet.-Akad. Förh., 7, p. 107: Magliesberg, Transvaal.

Hirundo semirufa gordoni Jardine, 1851, Gold Coast.

FIELD CHARACTERS This species is similar to the Mosque Swallow (59), having a blue crown and mantle and rufous underparts and rump, but it is slightly smaller, with longer streamers; the dark crown extends below the eye rather than being level with the eye, and there is no white on the underparts. The juvenile is similar to the Redrumped Swallow (60), but on the latter the sides of the head are red rather than blue. It frequents more open country than the Mosque Swallow. It is usually seen alone or in pairs. The flight is slow, with few wingbeats.

HABITAT The typical habitat is open, lowland country, usually up to 1700 m (5600 ft). In West Africa, it frequents the semi-arid and grass-woodland belts, large clearings in forests, farmland, open plantations, bush and villages and towns. In eastern areas, the main habitats are bushed grassland and cultivation. In south Africa, it is found in dry, open country such as grassland, vleis, open bushveld and thornveld. In Zimbabwe, it generally avoids the river valleys, being found from 900 to 1500 m (2950–4930 ft) (Irwin 1981). It avoids heavily wooded areas, where it is replaced ecologically by the similar Mosque Swallow (Benson *et al.* 1971). It often uses artificial open areas, such as airfields, sportsfields and gardens.

DISTRIBUTION AND POPULATION Rufous-chested Swallows are found over much of Africa south of the Sahara. The nominate race ranges over southern Africa from the eastern Cape north to the Orange Free State, Zululand, Transvaal, Natal, eastern Botswana, Zimbabwe, Malawi, northern Namibia and Angola; it has also probably bred in Mozambique (Clancey 1969b). The race *gordoni* ranges across West and Central Africa from Senegal east to the Sudan and south to northern Angola in the west, through Zaire and Uganda to northwestern Tanzania and southwestern Kenya west of the Rift Valley. Birds in the southern part of this range are intermediate between the two races (in colour, and with a wing of 111–130) and have sometimes been considered to be a separate race, *neumanni*. This is a common and widely distributed swallow throughout most of its range, though only locally common in East Africa. The development of railways and roads, with their bridges and culverts, has provided many new breeding sites and contributed to an extension in the range and an increase in numbers (Cooper 1963; Irwin 1981).

MIGRATION These are migratory swallows in much of the range north and south of the Equator. In southern Africa it is a summer breeding visitor from July to March, wintering in tropical Africa (Aspinwall 1980). Its movements and wintering sites are not well known, however. A few may overwinter in southern Africa (Irwin 1981). In West Africa it is apparently resident in some areas, such as southeastern Nigeria (Elgood *et al.* 1973), but is a wet-season breeding visitor to northern areas, as in Sierra Leone, Ghana and Cameroon (Louette 1981; Grimes 1988). In Gabon it is sedentary (Brosset and Erard 1986).

FOOD AND BEHAVIOUR The flight is often slow and buoyant, with few wingbeats, and includes much gliding. Usually, these swallows feed at fairly low heights, about 6 m (19 ft) above the ground (Priest 1935), swooping or occasionally hovering over vegetation. They rarely land on the ground, but perch on wires and twigs; they have, however, been recorded basking on roads and dust-bathing (Bannerman 1939), and also foraging on the ground. They are usually seen alone or in pairs, even when not breeding. The diet consists of aerial insects, including flies and small beetles (Sharpe and Wyatt 1885–1894). This is a generally solitary species, and breeds in single pairs, rarely in groups. The males are sometimes bigamous (Earlé 1987f).

BREEDING In West Africa, the main breeding season coincides with the rains in April to July or August, but the species may also breed in other months (Serle 1950a, b). In East Africa, breeding takes place in the rains from May to June (Brown and Britton 1980). In Zimbabwe, the breeding season is from August to April, but mainly September–March (Irwin 1981); in South Africa, from September to March (Maclean 1985); and, in Zaire, October–December and April–July (Lippens and Wille 1976). There are often two broods. The nests are built on a variety of natural and artificial sites, including rock faces, hollows in trees, fallen logs, rafters in houses, roofs of sheds, tops of windows, drainpipes, ant-bear holes, hollow termite mounds and ant hills, holes in high banks, hollows in banks dug out by large mammals, and under culverts and bridges; they are usually placed quite low (e.g. Roberts 1939; Plowes 1944; Earlé 1987f). In some areas, artificial sites are now more important than natural ones (Brosset and Erard 1986). The nest is a large bowl measuring about 18 cm (7½ in) across , with an extended entrance some 20 cm (8 in) long, made of small mud pellets, with thick walls and lined with fine grasses, seed inflorescences, hair and feathers (Vincent 1949; Mack 1972); it is built against the ceiling or roof of a cavity. Both male and female collect mud for and build the nest; one pair took five weeks to build a nest (Young 1946) and another three weeks (Mack 1972). The nest sites are re-used each year.

The clutch size is two to five, usually three. The eggs are white with some gloss, occasionally lightly streaked and speckled with reddish-brown, and average 23.2 × 15.5 mm (20.0–25.1 × 13.7–16.3; weight 2.9). Incubation and nestling periods have not been recorded. The oldest known bird was five years nine months (Earlé 1987d).

VOICE The song is a low, sweet gurgling, softer and less vigorous than that of the Barn Swallow (42). The call note is a plaintive 'seeur seeur' or 'chik-chitrrperree'; there is also a high-pitched alarm call, 'weet weet' (Young 1946).

DESCRIPTION This is one of the largest African swallows. The adult male is a glossy blue-black on the forehead, crown, mantle, scapulars and lesser wing-coverts, with a bright rufous rump and shorter uppertail-coverts; the longer uppertail-coverts are blue-black. The lores, the area around the eyes and the ear-coverts are a duller blue-black. The malar stripes, side of neck and underparts, including the undertail-coverts, are bright rufous, being darkest on the abdomen and sides. The axillaries and underwing-coverts are buffy. The wings are blackish-brown with a dark blue sheen, most pronounced on the coverts and tertials; the edge of the wing is rusty-white and black. The tail is blue-black, with a white patch on the inner web of all but the innermost feathers; the outer feathers are elongated and attenuated to form long, narrow streamers. The bill, legs and feet are black, and the eyes are dark brown. The sexes are similar, but the female has slightly shorter streamers. Juveniles are duller, brownish above and paler below, and have short outer tail feathers; the tertials have buff tips.

Measurements Length 24 cm (9½"). Wing 125–139 (mean 132); tail of male 121–167 (mean 136.6), of female 108–128 (mean 116.4); fork of male 70–96 (mean 83.4), of female 57–66 (mean 61.6); bill 10.4–12 (mean 11.1); tarsus 13–16 (mean 14.7). Weight 28–34 (mean 30).

RACES The race gordoni is a less rich rufous below and is smaller (wing 110–123) than the nominate race. There is some variation in the nominate race, from small northern to large southern individuals (tail of male 135–167 in the south, 122–135 in the north). Eastern birds are a more vinaceous-rufous below and may be a separate race (Clancey 1982).

Hirundo senegalensis Linnaeus, 1766, Syst. Nat., ed. 12, 1, p. 345: Senegal.

Hirundo senegalensis saturatior Bannerman, 1923, Accra, Gold Coast.

Hirundo senegalensis monteiri Hartlaub, 1862, Angola.

FIELD CHARACTERS The Mosque Swallow has a blue crown and mantle, and rufous nape of the neck, rump and underside. It is similar to the Red-rumped Swallow (60), but is larger and has whiter underwing-coverts and rufous undertail-coverts. It also resembles the Rufous-chested Swallow (58), but the rufous of the underparts extends further onto the nape, the lores are white rather than black, the sides of the face, throat and upper breast are much paler, and the nominate race lacks the white in the tail of the latter species. It frequents more wooded country than the Rufous-chested Swallow. Its flight is slow and fluttery, and it is usually seen alone or in small groups.

HABITAT Mosque Swallows are more typical of woodland than the similar Rufous-chested Swallow, but they frequent many habitats with trees available, excluding rainforest and deserts; they are not usually seen above about 2800 m (9200 ft). They are also not so closely associated with human habitation as are many other swallows. In West Africa, the species is widespread in the savanna belt and in open parts of the forest area, in forest clearings, along rivers and around villages; in the rainy season it occurs in the dry semi-arid belt as far as the edge of the Sahara. In Ethiopia, it is frequent up to 2750 m (9030 ft), but rare below 1200 m (3900 ft) (Urban and Brown 1971). In East Africa, it occurs mainly in wooded grassland, forest edge and clearings, light woodland and cultivation (Britton 1980). In southern Africa, it occurs mainly in woodland and dry acacia forest, though usually near water, especially along river valleys, around cultivation and near human habitation. In Zambia, it occurs in enclosed, heavily wooded areas, but also in montane grassland (Benson et al. 1971).

DISTRIBUTION AND POPULATION This species occurs over much of Africa south of the Sahara. The nominate race occurs from Senegal east to the Sudan, south to about latitude 8°N. The race *saturatior* occurs in the coastal districts of West Africa east across Central Africa to Ethiopia, Uganda and Kenya (but not in the south). The race *monteiri* occurs in southern Africa from Angola, Zaire, Zambia and southern East Africa (Tanzania and coastal Kenya) south to Caprivi, Ovamboland, eastern and northern Zimbabwe, the Transvaal lowveld, Malawi and Mozambique as far as the Limpopo River. Individuals around Mombasa, Tsavo and Nairobi intergrade between *saturatior* and *monteiri*, having varying amounts of white in the tail; *senegalensis* and *saturatior* also intergrade, in southern Sudan.

Mosque Swallows are generally scarce in much of their range, although Bannerman (1939) noted that they were quite common and widespread in West Africa. There may have been some decline in this population, as Elgood *et al.* (1971) recorded it as uncommon and very localised in Nigeria. However, it is common elsewhere in West Africa (Gore 1981; Grimes 1988) and widespread in East Africa (Britton 1980). In Zambia it is common and generally widespread, especially in areas where the Rufous-chested Swallow is absent (e.g. Barotse Province), but scarcer in the south (Benson *et al.* 1971). It is an uncommon swallow in the southernmost parts of its range. It generally avoids occupied human dwellings for nesting, and so has not benefited much from artificial nest sites.

MIGRATION The movements of this species are not well understood, but they do not migrate long distances and seem to be fairly sedentary. After breeding, the birds often disperse locally or make short-distance migrations, but some remain in the breeding areas. North of the Equator it is often a wet-season visitor to drier areas. In the Gambia some Mosque Swallows move south to wetter areas for the non-breeding season (Gore 1981), and in Ghana the species is resident in the north but a wet-season visitor in some places (Grimes 1988). In northeastern Gabon it is a visitor from November to April (Brosset and Erard 1986), and in Chad numbers increase in the wet season (Salvan 1969(. Local movements to occur in eastern and southern Africa (Aspinwall 1980; Irwin

1981). Occasionally dispersal is further afield: the race *monteiri* has been recorded as a vagrant in Zululand and Somalia (Ash and Miskell 1983; Maclean 1985).

BEHAVIOUR The flight is slow and heavy, consisting of periods of gliding interspersed with fluttering; this characteristic makes them look like a small kestrel or merlin. They are usually seen flying in pairs or in small groups, and are often seen perched on trees or telegraph wires. They typically feed high up, over the treetops or water, at an average height of 25 m (80 ft) (Waugh 1978). They feed on flying insects. Pairs usually nest solitarily or in small, loose groups, with the nests well separated.

BREEDING The breeding season is chiefly before and during the rains, in May–October, in West Africa. In Ethiopia, breeding occurs in April, July and November (Urban and Brown 1971). In East Africa, it is mainly in the long rains in March–June and December (Brown and Britton 1980). In southern Africa, breeding is mainly between August and April (Maclean 1985). Two broods are usual. A frequent nest site is a hole in a tree, especially baobabs, but these swallows also nest inside or on buildings, on cliffs, in caves, on termite mounds, on walls or on the underside of a bridge; when they nest in buildings, these are usually outbuildings or deserted, undisturbed places. The nest is a large closed construction of mud and dry grass, with a long tubular entrance, and lined with grass and feathers, plastered against an overhanging rock, ceiling or eave. If birds use a hole in a tree or roof, they may not make the full retort-shaped nest but use mud to fill up the hole to a suitable size (Winterbottom 1942). In houses they often make a small version of the nest, consisting of little more than a rim of mud on a suitable surface which they line with feathers. The nest is repaired and re-used each year (Pitman 1931). Nests of other swallows are sometimes taken over, being built up and with a tunnel added. The birds collect mud with a sideways jerk of the bill. They can take several weeks to build a nest (Sclater and Moreau 1933; Verhayen 1954).

The clutch size is two to four, usually three or four in southern Africa. The eggs are pure white and those of the nominate race measure 21.7 × 14.7 mm (21–22.1 × 14–15; weight 2.45); the eggs of *saturatior* are larger at 24.7 × 17.5 mm (24–25.3 × 17–18). The incubation and nestling periods

have not been recorded. The fledglings return to the nest for a while to roost; where the species is sedentary, they may do so for several weeks (Beesley 1972).

VOICE Mosque Swallows have several calls: a reedy trill; a guttural croak preceded by a 'naga'; and a metallic 'harrrp harrrp' (Maclean 1985). Individuals in flocks utter a nasal 'nya' contact call.

DESCRIPTION The Mosque Swallow is a large hirundine. Most of the upperparts, including forehead, crown, lesser wing-coverts and longer tail-coverts, are glossy purplish-blue, sometimes steel-blue. The lores are whitish with some blue-black mottling. A rufous collar extends around the base of the neck and sides of the head. The rump and shorter uppertail-coverts are rufous, but some tail-covert feathers are blue with rufous tips. The chin, throat and cheeks are cream, this colour merging into the pale rufous of the breast and the deep rufous of the abdomen, flanks and under-tail-coverts; there is sometimes a black spot at the tips of the feathers of the undertail-coverts. The underwing-coverts and axillaries are creamy-white. The wings are blackish-brown with a purple-blue gloss, strongest on the coverts and tertials. The tail is also blackish-brown with a purple-blue sheen, lacking white patches; the outer feathers are elongated into long streamers. The eyes are dark brown, and the bill and legs and feet black. The sexes are alike; both have long tail streamers, though on females they tend to be shorter. Juveniles are duller: the crown, mantle and wings are dark brown with glossy blue tips to the feathers, the collar is indistinct and the sides of the neck are white, tinged with buff, and the rump is also very pale; the throat is white, the breast is pale rufous and white, with dull blackish feathers on each side, and the rest of the underparts are pale rufous; the tail lacks the streamers of the adult, and the wing-coverts, innermost secondaries and uppertail-coverts have some rufous tips.

Measurements Length 24 cm (9½"). Wing 137–156 (mean 144.7); tail of male 94–122 (mean 107), of female 80–115 (mean 102.9); fork of male 38–68 (mean 56.3), of female 36–64 (mean 53.6); bill 12.5–14.9 (mean 13.7); tarsus 17–19.1 (mean 18.4). Weight 29–50 (mean 42.5).

RACES The race *saturatior* (wing 137–154) is darker than *senegalensis*, the neck, breast, belly, sides of the body, rump and undertail-coverts being a deep chestnut. The race *monteiri* (wing 137–152) is almost as dark as *saturatior*, but has a pale throat and a large white patch on the inner webs of all but the innermost tail feathers; the amount of white in the tail is variable.

60 RED-RUMPED SWALLOW
Hirundo daurica Laxmann

Plate 20

Hirundo 'daurica Laxmann, 1769, K. Vet.-Akad. Handl., vol. xxx, p. 209. pl.7: the Sunghua Chiang, Heilungkiang, China, near its confluence with the Amur River.

Hirundo daurica japonica Temminck and Schlegel, 1847, Japan.

Hirundo daurica nipalensis Hodgson, 1837, central region of Nepal.

Hirundo daurica erythropygia Sykes, 1832, Poona, India.

Hirundo daurica hyperythra Blyth, 1849, Sri Lanka.

Hirundo daurica rufula Temminck, 1835, Egypt, Sicily, Japan (Japan erroneous).

Hirundo daurica domicella Hartlaub and Finsch, 1870, Casamance.

Hirundo daurica disjuncta Bates, 1930, Birwa Peak, 4700 ft, Kono District, Sierra Leone.

Hirundo daurica kumboensis Bannerman, 1923, Kumbo, 5500 ft, northern Nigeria.

Hirundo daurica emini Reichenow, 1892, Bussisi and Bukoba, Tanzania.

Hirundo daurica melanocrissa (Rüppell), 1845, Province of Barakit and Gondar, Ethiopia.

FIELD CHARACTERS This species has a blue crown and mantle, chestnut collar and rump, and buffy underparts with narrow shaft streaks. It can be distinguished from similar swallows by its chestnut collar and rump and by the absence of a breast-band or rufous throat. It differs from other red-rumped African swallows in not having any white patches in the tail. It frequents open hilly country and is often seen alone or in small groups. Its flight is slow and graceful.

HABITAT The natural habitat of Red-rumped Swallows is open, hilly country and river gorges and valleys where cliffs, caves or old fortifications are available for nesting, but they also increasingly often frequent cultivated areas, human habitation and clearings around roads and railways where artificial nest sites are available. In West Africa they occur in the southern semi-arid belt and the northern grass-woodland belt. They breed at a range of altitudes, up to 3300 m (10,830 ft) in the Himalayas. This species is restricted more to warm climates than the Barn Swallow (42).

DISTRIBUTION AND POPULATION The species has an extensive range over southern Europe, Asia and Africa (Glutz von Blotzheim and Bauer 1985; Cramp 1988). The nominate race *daurica* breeds in south-ern Siberia from the Irtysh east to the Amur and the mouth of the Ussuri and south to northern Mongolia and Transbaikalia; the limits between *daurica* and *japonica*, however, are unclear (*japonica* breeds in Korea, Japan and eastern China). The race *nipalensis* breeds from the central Himalayas to Yunnan; those birds from Szechwan north to Kansu and in western Inner Mongolia are sometimes considered to be a separate subspecies, *gephyra*. The race *erythropygia* breeds in India along the base of the Himalayas from the Punjab to western Bengal and south to the Nilgiris; *hyperythra* is resident in Sri Lanka up to about 1200 m (3900 ft). The race *rufula* breeds from the Iberian peninsula and Morocco eastwards to Kazakhstan, Kashmir and Himachal Pradesh; it has also bred in Somalia (Meinertzhagen 1954; Ash and Miskell 1983). In Africa, *domicella* occurs from Senegal and Gambia west to the Sudan and the extreme northwest of Uganda, *kumboensis* is restricted to the highlands of Kumbo and Obu in the Cameroons, while *disjuncta* occurs only on the Birwa Plateau in the Tingi Mountains, Sierra Leone; *disjuncta* is separated from *kumboensis* by *domicella*. The race *emini* occurs in eastern Africa from southern Sudan through the highlands of eastern

Zaire, Uganda, Kenya and Tanzania to Malawi, and *melanocrissa* occurs throughout much of Ethiopia.

Throughout its range this species is common, if sometimes locally distributed. In Europe its range has been extending in recent years, mainly since the mid 1950s when it started to breed further north in Portugal and Spain (Glutz von Blotzheim and Bauer 1985; Cramp 1988). It first bred in southern France in the early 1960s, and since the mid 1970s a few pairs have bred regularly there. There has been an extension into Italy and Corsica; and one northwards into the Balkan States, with breeding recorded in Romania since the mid 1970s. In addition, there are increasing numbers of vagrants turning up in western, central and northern Europe. The expansion may be due to changes in climate, or to an increased use of artificial sites such as bridges and abandoned country buildings for nesting, or a combination of factors (Simeonow 1968; von Wicht 1978; de Lope Rebollo 1981, pers. comm.).

MIGRATION The northern populations of the Red-rumped Swallow are migratory and are only summer visitors to their breeding grounds, leaving mainly in September and October and returning in March and April. Their winter ranges, however, are unclear, in part because the various races overlap during winter and are difficult to distinguish in the field. The winter range of *daurica* is unclear, but it is known from northeast India, the Himalayas and Indochina; it is also a vagrant to north Heilungkiang and south to northeast Kirin. The race *japonica* winters in the southern part of the breeding range and to India, northern Thailand and possibly northern Indochina; *nipalensis* winters throughout India and northern Burma, and descends to lower altitudes than when breeding. The winter range of *rufula* is not known, but it is a regular migrant in the eastern Mediterranean and North Africa (there may be two migration routes, West Africa for western birds and the Nile for eastern ones: Etchécopar and Hüe 1967); there is a pronounced spring and autumn passage across the Straits of Gibraltar. It is a common migrant to the western highlands and northeast of Ethiopia (Urban and Brown 1971) and has been recorded from Chad, Mali and Senegal. The Indian and Sri Lankan races are not migratory, but make local post-breeding move-

ments (Henry 1971; Ali and Ripley 1972).

The migratory status of the African races is not clear. In many parts of the range the species appears to be resident all year, but in parts it is a visitor. Thus, in Nigeria it is a late-dry-season or early-wet-season visitor to southwestern areas and at Zaria numbers fall in the non-breeding season (Elgood *et al.* 1973). Similar seasonal variations are known in East Africa (Britton 1980). Vagrants are occasionally recorded in southern Africa (Maclean 1985).

Vagrants are often reported, for example in western, northern and central Europe, including the British Isles, mainly when returning migrants overshoot their breeding range, but there are a few autumn records as well.

FORAGING AND FOOD The nominate race is poorly known, and most of the available information concerns the European form, *rufula* (see Glutz von Blotzheim and Bauer 1985 and Cramp 1988 for detailed summaries). The flight is graceful, more buoyant and slower than that of the Barn Swallow. These swallows usually feed alone or in small loose groups. When breeding they feed close to the nest site, low over vegetation, but will also feed up to 100 m or more. Most food is obtained in flight, but very occasionally they feed from the ground. Meinertzhagen (1954) recorded them coming down to camel dung to take flies, and they have been seen taking termites from the ground and insects from plants (Cramp 1988). They frequently feed at grass fires and around human structures that attract insects, such as markets, bazaars and shipping docks in India and occasionally around human settlements in Spain (Ali and Ripley 1972; de Lope Rebollo, pers. comm.). The adults' diet includes grasshoppers, beetles, plant bugs, flies, bees and mosquitoes (Show Tsen-Hwang 1930; Cheng Tso-hsin 1964; Cramp 1988). In a study in France (Prodon 1982), nestlings aged 25 days were fed mainly winged ants, with a few other Hymenoptera, flies, beetles and a cockroach; prey included non-flying insects. Cicadas, spiders and termites are also taken.

SOCIAL ORGANISATION These swallows usually breed solitarily or in loose groups of three to five pairs, although there are a few records of larger groups of up to 50 nests and one of 100 nests (Glutz von Blotzheim and Bauer 1985). In Iberia, however, they are always solitary (de Lope Rebollo, pers. comm.). There are records of nests built close together (Cramp 1988), but these birds are usually aggressive to other swallows in the vicinity of the nest (Prodon 1982). The size of the defended area may depend on the dispersion of the nests (Cramp 1988). When not breeding, they form small flocks, and migrate singly or in groups of a few individuals.

SOCIOSEXUAL BEHAVIOUR Adults return to the previous year's site to breed, old birds before first-years (Cramp 1988). Once a male has selected a nest site, he defends it against intruders (de Lope Rebollo 1980). Courtship consists of a flight in which the male circles the female, giving contact calls. During the display the male may vibrate his wings and dive steeply, ending with wings outspread, or throw his head back and raise his tail. The female usually perches near the nest, while the male flutters towards her and sings, sometimes spreading his tail. Prior to copulation, the female perches with wings drooped and tail raised: the male sidles towards her, singing; the female vibrates her wings, and the male briefly mounts her and copulates. Preening, sometimes mutual, may follow.

BREEDING The breeding season varies regionally. In the Soviet Union, it is chiefly June–July; in the Himalayas, India and Sri Lanka, April–August; in Europe, April–September (Dementev and Gladkov 1968; Ali and Ripley 1972; Cramp 1988). In West Africa the breeding season is chiefly October–May, but varies locally (e.g. Grimes 1988). In Ethiopia breeding takes place in most months, but especially January and April–August (Urban and Brown 1971). In East Africa breeding takes place in the rains, especially the long rains in April–May; in Malawi, October–February; in Zaire, August and January–March (Lippens and Wille 1976; Britton 1980). There are often two or three broods in a season, pairs re-using a nest for the second and third ones. Most pairs have a second brood, but less than a quarter attempt a third (de Lope Rebollo 1980).

A variety of natural and artificial nest sites is used, including crevices in walls and rock faces, under overhangs, on cave roofs, under eaves of houses or mosques, under bridges and culverts and in verandahs, roofs and bunkers. This species is much less reliant on artificial structures than is the Barn Swallow, but will use inhabited as well as empty buildings. In some areas such as Bulgaria and the Iberian peninsula, where it has recently extended its range, more than a third of nests are on bridges. The nest is retort-shaped, made of mud pellets sometimes mixed with dung, and with only a few or no pieces of dry grass; it has a tunnel entrance, and is lined with a mixture of feathers, rootlets, leaves, hair, pine needles or dry grass. Nests on bridges are longer and have thicker walls than cliff nests. The nest is built against a ceiling or overhang, often facing east to south if built on a cliff. It is usually placed within 4.5 m (15 ft) of the ground, rarely up to 20 m (65 ft), and in Spain some nests are only 0.5 m (20 in) above the ground (de Lope Rebollo, pers. comm.). A nest can take a couple of weeks to complete, and is re-used for subsequent broods that year and in future years. Both male and female build the nest, the male accompanying his mate on trips to collect mud, from patches within usually 150 m (165 yds) of the nest site; the tunnel is the last part to be built and is sometimes left until the clutch has been laid.

In Asia the clutch size is usually three or four, rarely five, but is usually five or six in the Soviet Union and is only two, rarely three, in Sri Lanka. In Europe clutches are of three to five, rarely six or seven eggs, but four or five are usual (de Lope Rebollo 1980). In Africa the clutch size is smaller, with two or three eggs being usual. Clutch size decreases during the season (de Lope Rebollo 1980). The eggs are laid at daily intervals, but the laying interval is occasionally longer. The eggs are white or, rarely, white with a few orange-brown specks. Egg size does not vary much geographically: the eggs of *daurica* average 21 × 14.3 mm (18–22.5 × 13.1–15.2; weight 2.25); and those of *rufula* measure 20.3 × 14.2 mm (18.2–22.5 × 13.1–15.5) (de Lope Rebollo 1980). Both male and female incubate the eggs and feed the chicks, but females do the greater part of the incubation and of the feeding of older nestlings. The incubation period is 14 or 15 days (sometimes 11–16 days), and the nestling period is 22–27 days. The nestlings come to the tunnel entrance to be fed when about 16 or 17 days old. The fledglings are fed by the parents for another five or six days, return to the nest for two to three weeks, and continue to remain in groups before migration. (See de Lope Rebollo 1980; Prodon 1982; Cramp 1988).

Hatching success and fledging success (of eggs laid) are high, some 80% and 74%, respectively, in de Lope Rebollo's study. One seven-year-old bird has been recorded (Rydzewski 1978).

VOICE The male has a twittering song that sometimes ends in a trill; it is shorter and quieter than that of the Barn Swallow. The commonest call is a short contact call, 'djuit', softer than the song; it is used between pairs, between parents and young, and in aggressive chases of intruders, and is uttered once or twice and often repeated. A longer version of the contact call is used by the male in alternation with singing. There is also a territorial call by the male which sounds like a cat's mewing; a short, whistling alarm call; and a short, hard 'krr' used by a male attacking an intruding swallow near the nest (Prodon 1982).

DESCRIPTION Red-rumped Swallows are medium-sized hirundines. The forehead, crown, mantle and scapulars are a deep metallic blue. There is an incomplete chestnut collar, extending from the sides of the head; the central hindneck is deep blue. The lores, cheeks and ear-coverts are chestnut, slightly mottled with grey-brown. The sides of the feather bases of the mantle and inner scapulars are pale cream or off-white, more visible in worn plumage. The lower back, rump and shorter uppertail-coverts are chestnut but the rump and tail-coverts pale with wear. The longer uppertail coverts are black with a blue gloss. The sides are pale cinnamon-buff. The underparts are buffy or ochreish with a somewhat lighter throat, paling with wear. A few feathers on the sides of the breast have black centres. The rump is faintly streaked and the underparts bear long, blackish-brown streaks. The underwing-coverts and axillaries are buff or pinky-buff. The undertail-coverts are black with buffy bases. The wings are brownish-black, only slightly metallic, the deepest gloss being on the lesser coverts. The tail is brownish-black with a slight blue-green gloss, and is deeply forked. The eyes are dark brown and the bill, legs and feet are blackish-brown. The sexes are alike, but females have shorter wings and outer tail feathers. Juveniles are duller, browner versions of the adults, with less pronounced streaking, a paler collar, rump and underparts, and shorter outer tail feathers; the tertials, wing-coverts and longer uppertail-coverts have buff-tips and the inner primaries and secondaries have pale edges along the tips. Fresh feathers on the crown, mantle and scapulars also have buffy tips. Northern populations start moulting late, probably just before migration or on the wintering grounds; non-migratory races start the moult earlier (Cramp 1988).

Measurements Length 16–17 cm (6¼–6¾ in). Nominate *daurica*: wing 121–138; tail 93–119; weight 33. Race *rufula*: wing of male 120–128 (mean 124.5), of female 118–127 (mean 121.4); tail of male 94–107 (mean 101.9), of female 89–99 (mean 95.6); fork of male 53–64 (mean 59.3), of female 46–56 (mean 52); bill 9.3–12.5 (mean 11.1); tarsus 13.2–14.7 (mean 14); weight 15.2–29 (mean 19.1).

RACES The numerous races differ mainly in the degree of streaking, the development of the collar and the colour of the underparts and rump. There is some clinal variation and intergrading of forms. The race *japonica* has bolder streaks than the nominate race, and is slightly smaller (wing 114–125). The best-known race, *rufula*, has faint, narrow streaks and a broad complete collar. The Indian races are slightly smaller still (wing 102–123): *nipalensis* has narrower streaks than *japonica*, variable streaking on a dark rump and the neck-collar is sometimes complete; *erythropygia* has similar streaks to *nipalensis* below, but those on the rump are faint or absent; *hyperythra* is rufous-chestnut below with narrow streaks, has no neck-collar, and has faint streaks on the rump. The African races have little or no streaking, but vary in the colour of the underparts: *domicella* (wing 110–116) is creamy-white below; *disjuncta* (wing 106–115) is pale rufous below; *kumboensis* (wing 110–120) is also pale rufous below, but is larger than *disjuncta*; *emini* is large (wing 116–129), with chestnut underparts and rump and faint streaking; and *melanocrissa* (wing 119–129) has less chestnut on the face and little or no streaking below.

61 STRIATED SWALLOW

Plate 20

Hirundo striolata Temminck and Schlegel
Alternative name: Mosque Swallow

Hirundo striolata Temminck and Schlegel, 1847, in Siebold's Fauna Japonica, Aves, p. 33: Java.

Hirundo striolata mayri Hall, 1953, Singhaling Hkamti, Upper Chindwin.

Hirundo striolata stanfordi Mayr, 1941, Tamu, 1000 ft, Myitkyina District, upper Burma.

Hirundo striolata vernayi Kinnear, 1924, Longlung, Siam.

Hirundo striolata badia (Cassin), 1853, Malacca.

This swallow is sometimes considered to be a subspecies of the Red-rumped Swallow (60). The two species are very similar, particularly nominate Striated and the race *japonica* of Red-rumped, but they do not intergrade; rather, sharp breaks in characters occur. Thus, in the Brahmaputra area, Red-rumped Swallows to the north are small and narrowly streaked, whereas the Striated Swallows to the south are large and heavily streaked (Vaurie 1951). The two species appear not to breed together, and as their status is still very unclear I have kept them separate.

FIELD CHARACTERS The Striated Swallow has a blue crown and mantle, streaked underparts and a chestnut rump and indistinct collar. It is very like the Red-rumped Swallow, differing in being a little larger, more heavily streaked and having a less distinct or absent neck-collar. It frequents open hilly areas, and is often seen alone or in small groups. Flight is slow and graceful.

HABITAT Striated Swallows frequent open, often hilly areas with river gorges and rocky outcrops, but they are also seen in forest clearings, scrub, villages and cultivation.

DISTRIBUTION AND POPULATION This swallow replaces the Red-rumped Swallow in southern and southeastern Asia (Vaurie 1951; Deignan 1963; Etchécopar and Hüe 1983). Nominate *striolata* occurs in Taiwan, the Philippines, Borneo, Sumatra, Java and the Lesser Sunda Islands: Lombok, Flores, Alor, Wetar, Sumba, Timor. The race *mayri* occurs in northeastern India (south of the Brahmaputra), and the hills of Bangladesh, and in northwestern Burma. The race *stanfordi* breeds in northeastern Burma, northern Thailand and south Yunnan, and probably also in northern Laos. The race *vernayi* is known only from the Thailand-Tenasserim border and western Thailand. The race *badia* occurs in the Malay peninsula, from Thailand south to Selangor State. Throughout its range the Striated Swallow is a common breeding bird, frequently using artificial structures for nest sites.

MIGRATION Striated Swallows are resident in some areas, but are migratory in others

(Vaurie 1951). The island forms and the Malay race *badia* are resident, although vagrants have turned up outside the breeding areas: thus, *striolata* is known from southwestern Sarawak and from New Guinea (Smythies 1968; White and Bruce 1986). On the continent these swallows are partial residents, and local movements occur between breeding and wintering areas. The race *mayri* occurs in winter in the southern Shan States, northern Thailand and northern Indochina. In winter the race *stanfordi* has been recorded from Laos, Tonkin and Annam (Burma, Thailand).

FOOD AND BEHAVIOUR The flight is slow and buoyant compared with that of the Barn Swallow (42). These swallows frequently feed with other swallow species, but do not use communal town roosts (Medway and Wells 1976). They feed low over the ground and frequently hawk around cliffs (Allen 1948). The diet consists of flying insects, including cicadas, mosquitoes and other flies. Striated Swallows usually breed alone or in small groups with scattered nests.

BREEDING The breeding season is mainly April–July throughout the range (e.g. Smythies 1953; Ali and Ripley 1972; Medway and Well 1976). The nests are built in houses under the ceiling, under the eaves of verandahs and temples, on bridges and in culverts, and on the roofs of limestone caves. The nest is retort-shaped, made of mud pellets and lined with dry grass, fibres and a few feathers; the tunnel is long, about a third of the length of the nest (Allen 1948).

The nest, which can take several weeks to build, is typically attached to a horizontal surface, within a crevice or on an irregularity. The usual clutch is three to four eggs, usually four, rarely five, but the clutch size of *badia* is usually two. The eggs are pure white, but rarely have faint reddish specks at the larger end. They measure 20.5 × 14.6 mm (17.5–24.5 × 13.1–15.8; weight 2.3). The eggs of Burmese, Javan and Assam birds are larger than Chinese ones: 19.3 × 13.9 mm (17.5–20.4 × 13.1–14.4) in China; 21.4 – 14.7 mm (20.2–23.2 × 14.3–15.8) in India; and 23.1 × 15.6 mm (22–24.5 × 14.8–16.6) in Java.

VOICE The contact call is 'pin' or a long drawn-out 'quitsch'; the song is a soft twittering; and the alarm call is a repeated 'chi-chi-chi' (Allen 1948).

DESCRIPTION This is a large swallow. It has steel-blue or blue-green upperparts with greyish bases to the feathers, the bases being most visible in worn plumage. The rump is chestnut with narrow black shaft streaks. The shorter uppertail-coverts are also chestnut, and the longer ones are black with a blue gloss. There is a poorly defined chestnut collar, extending along the head, above the eye, but this is often absent. The lores, cheeks and ear-coverts are white with sepia streaks. The underparts are white with strong, coarse, blackish-brown striations, which are densest on the chin and throat.

Some feathers on the sides of the breast have black centres, forming a black patch. The undertail-coverts are blackish-brown with a greenish gloss. The axillaries and underwing-coverts are white with a buffy wash. The upperwing-coverts and wings are blackish-brown with a slight blue gloss, deepest on the lesser wing-coverts. The tail is blackish-brown with a slight blue gloss, and is deeply forked. The eyes are brown, the bill is brownish-black and the legs and feet are dark brown. The sexes are alike. The juvenile is browner and duller, with a paler rump, sides of head and collar; the outer tail feathers are shorter, and there are buff tips to the wing-coverts and tertials.

Measurements Length 19 cm (7½"). Wing 119–132 (mean 124.6); tail 92–108 (mean 98.6); fork 43–58 (mean 51); bill 9. 9–12.1 (mean 11); tarsus 14.2–16 (mean 15.1). Weight 22.

RACES The races differ mainly in the degree of streaking on the underparts and rump. The races *mayri* and *stanfordi* have broad streaks but *stanfordi* has a more well-defined black patch near the thighs; *vernayi* is more rufous below and has only faint streaking on the rump; *badia* is deep rufous below, with faint streaking on the underparts and none on the rump. (Wing of *mayri* 119–130; of *stanfordi* 129–135; of *badia* 132–141; of *vernayi* 129.) Other races have been suggested, but are not clearly distinguishable from these (Vaurie 1951).

62 PREUSS'S CLIFF SWALLOW
Hirundo preussi (Reichenow)

Plate 21

Lecythoplastes preussi Reichenow, 1898, Orn. Monatsber. vi, p. 115: Edea, Cameroon.

FIELD CHARACTERS This swallow has blue upperparts, a buffy rump and underparts and a rufous patch behind the eye. In the field, the pale rump and underparts are distinctive. The head and tail markings, however, are often not clearly visible. It frequents open country near cliffs, and is highly gregarious throughout the year. Its flight is slow and fluttery.

HABITAT Preuss's Cliff Swallow is found in the savanna zone of western Africa. It frequents a variety of habitats, but is usually near cliffs and rivers where rock faces are available for nesting. It is now less tied to these habitats, however, as road and rail-

way culverts and bridges and human habitation provide some sites for breeding.

DISTRIBUTION AND POPULATION This cliff swallow is confined to part of western and Central Africa, occurring irregularly from Guinea-Bissau, Sierra Leone and Mali east to Cameroon. Some of the known breeding areas are several hundred kilometres apart. There is also a record from northeastern Zaire (Chapin 1953). It is a rare and scattered species, although it can be locally abundant. It does, however, appear to be increasing in numbers. Its known range has recently been extended through western Nigeria (Ashford 1968; Broadbent

1969) to Sierra Leone (Tye 1985), although it may have been present but overlooked before. New breeding colonies develop especially on bridges, and the presence of these artificial nesting sites may have allowed the populations to expand.

MIGRATION Preuss's Cliff Swallows make some migratory movements, but these are not well known. In Nigeria they make irregular movements, appearing and disappearing, shifting nesting areas between years and disappearing in August and September (Elgood 1982). They also appear to be partial migrants in Mali (Lamarche 1981).

FOOD AND BEHAVIOUR The flight is slow and includes frequent periods of gliding. The birds feed in often large flocks. The diet is not known in detail, but consists of a variety of insects caught in flight, including flying ants (Germain *et al.* 1973). Like other cliff swallows, this species nests in large colonies, sometimes containing hundreds of pairs, with the nests touching each other: one colony contained 1,000 nests and another 2,000, both on bridges (Germain *et al.* 1973). Within a 'colony' the nests may be arranged in smaller clusters: at one site, for example, 150 nests were separated into seven groups, with 70 nests in the largest cluster (Ashford 1968).

BREEDING Breeding takes place largely at the end of the dry season in West Africa, mainly February–June, but November–July in Mali (Mackworth-Praed and Grant 1973; Lamarche 1981). In Nigeria, Ashford (1968) noted building taking place at the end of January, and eggs were present in March. The natural nest sites of this species are cliff faces or rocks, often overhanging streams and rivers, with the nest built several metres above the water (Jourdain 1935), but artificial structures, especially bridges, are increasingly being used. There are records of colonies in mine shafts, tunnels in dams, large pipes, on beams under the roofs of huts and under the eaves of buildings (Bannerman and Bates 1926; Jourdain 1935; Serle 1965). The nest is bottle-shaped, built with mud pellets, and sparsely lined with fine grass, hairy seeds and a few feathers (Ashford 1968). It has a wide spout which projects vertically down. The clutch size is usually two, sometimes three, eggs (Jourdain 1935). The eggs are glossy, with a cream or pinkish-white ground colour, and with pale grey-violet and rufous freckles which are sometimes concentrated at the larger end (Jourdain 1935); some eggs also have a few black speckles. Egg size and colour are similar between clutches; the amount and intensity of speckling, however, is variable. The eggs average 18.8 × 12.9 mm (17–21.8 × 11.9–13.5; weight 1.63). Both male and female build the nest, and building is synchronous within the colony (Serle 1965). Incubation and nestling periods are not known.

VOICE The song is an energetic and noisy twittering (Bannerman 1939). Ashford (1968) recorded two calls: a 'prrp prrrp', and a single 'pseep' used as an alarm call.

DESCRIPTION Preuss's Cliff Swallow is a small hirundine. The forehead and crown, nape of the neck, mantle and back and scapulars are deep glossy blue. The white edges of the mantle feathers are sometimes visible. There is a patch or streak of rufous-chestnut behind the eye. The feathers at the base of the bill and the lores are buffy. The rump is creamy or sandy-buff. The upper-tail-coverts are browner with pale rufous edges. The cheeks, chin, throat, breast and abdomen are plain, pale buffy-rufous. The undertail-coverts are pale rufous, with blackish terminal portions edged with rufous. The underwing-coverts and axillaries are pale rufous. The wings are black with a faint blue sheen. The tail is dark brown and slightly forked; each feather, apart from the innermost pair, has a white patch on the inner web. This patch is smallest and faintest on, and sometimes absent from, the outer pair. The eyes and legs and feet are dark brown, and the bill is black. The sexes are alike. Juveniles are similar to adults, but are duller and browner with little gloss; they have a dirty white rump and underparts, and the throat and breast are marked with grey-brown; the inner secondaries have buffy tips; the rufous streak behind the eye is very pale.

Measurements Length 12 cm (4¾"). Wing 92–100 (mean 95.8); tail 50–57 (mean 53.2); fork 8–17 (mean 11.3); bill 7.6–9.2 (mean 8.3); tarsus 10.1–11.2 (mean 10.7).

63 ANGOLAN CLIFF SWALLOW
Hirundo rufigula Bocage

Plate 21

Hirundo rufigula Barboza du Bocage, 1878, J. Sci. Math. Phys. Nat. Acad. Sci. Lisboa, 6, no. 24, p. 256: Caconda, Benguela.

This species is very close to Preuss's Cliff Swallow (62), differing in small details of plumage. Hall and Moreau (1970) and Dowsett and Dowsett-LeMaire (1980) considered the two to be conspecific though perhaps incipient species; they are, however, more likely to be separate species (R.A. Earlé, pers. comm.).

FIELD CHARACTERS This cliff swallow has a blue head and mantle, pale rufous underparts and a rufous rump and throat. The rufous throat is the most distinctive feature. The species differs from the similar Preuss's Cliff Swallow in the colour of the throat and rump, and in lacking any rufous behind the eyes. It frequents open country near cliffs and is highly gregarious. The flight is fluttery.

HABITAT Angolan Cliff Swallows frequent many open habitats, often near water, and particularly near cliffs and rocky gorges where nesting sites are available.

DISTRIBUTION AND POPULATION The breeding range is restricted to Angola, southwestern Zaire and western Zambia with a recent extension into southern Gabon (Mackworth-Praed and Grant 1973; Lippens and Wille 1976; Christy 1984). The species is increasing in numbers and forming new breeding colonies, especially on bridges (Taylor 1979).

MIGRATION This cliff swallow is clearly migratory, although its wintering areas are not known. Thus it is absent from Zambia and Zaire between November and May (Benson 1982).

FOOD AND BEHAVIOUR The flight is slow and the birds often glide. They usually feed in flocks. The diet consists of flying insects, including dipteran flies (in museum specimens), but is not known in detail. The species breeds in colonies of sometimes hundreds of birds, with the nests built against each other.

BREEDING The breeding season is mainly June and July in Zaire, September and October in Zambia and May–June in northern Angola; in southern Angola, however, breeding has been recorded from July to September (Cannell 1968; Dean 1974; Benson 1982). Natural nest sites are usually on cliffs in rocky gorges or in caves, but nowadays this species often nests under bridges and on dams and buildings. The nest is bottle-shaped, built with mud pellets, and with a 5 cm (2 in) wide entrance tunnel. It is lined with fine grass, but not usually feathers (Hall 1960). The clutch size is two or three. The eggs are pinkish-white or white, with rufous and chestnut-brown and violet speckles which sometimes form a cap at the larger end; they measure 18–20 × 12.5–14 mm. Both sexes incubate and feed the young.

VOICE The song is a rapid twittering. Christy (1984) noted a harsh 'tre-tre-tre' uttered by birds in flocks.

DESCRIPTION Angolan Cliff Swallows are small hirundines. The upperparts from the forehead to the mantle, back and scapulars are glossy blue-black. The feathers of the hindneck, sides of the neck and the mantle have dull white edges, producing a streaked appearance. The ear-coverts are rufous with blue-black streaks, and the feathers at the base of the bill and the lores are pale rufous. The cheeks are rufous with dark streaks. The rump is rufous and the uppertail-coverts are rufous-brown. The underparts are a paler rufous, with a few dark streaks on the breast and a darker chestnut on the chin and throat. The underwing-coverts and axillaries are pale rufous. The undertail-coverts are deep chestnut, and the longer ones have black subterminal patches. The wings and tail are blackish with a faint blue-black gloss, deepest on the lesser wing-coverts and tertials; the tail is only slightly forked, and has small, oblong white patches on the inner webs of the feathers apart from the innermost pair. The eyes are chestnut-brown, the bill is black and the feet and legs are blackish. The sexes are alike. The juvenile is duller and browner, with paler rufous areas.
Measurements Length 12 cm (4¾"). Wing 95–100 (mean 97); tail 42–54 (mean 50.4); fork 9–11 (mean 9.7); bill 7.1–9 (mean 8.1); tarsus 10–11 (mean 10.7).

64 ANDEAN CLIFF SWALLOW

Hirundo andecola d'Orbigny and Lafresnaye

Hirundo andecola d'Orbigny and Lafresnaye, 1837, Syn. Av. in Mag. Zool., cl. 2, p. 69: La Paz, Bolivia.

Hirundo andecola oroyae (Chapman), 1924, Oroya, 12,500 ft, Junin, Peru.

Although usually placed with the cliff swallows, this species differs in some respects, such as the lack of pale edges to the iridescent feathers of the mantle and in having the rump concolorous with the back and no red in the adult plumage (although the juvenile has a rufous rump). However, it is too poorly known for its relationships to be clear (Earlé 1987e).

FIELD CHARACTERS The upperparts are blue, apart from a brownish rump, and the underparts are grey-brown. The blue head and mantle distinguish it from the Brown-bellied Swallow (15) and the greyish underparts from the Blue-and-white Swallow (18). It breeds in the high puna outside the altitudinal range of most swallows, frequenting rock faces and towns. It is gregarious and regularly glides when flying.

HABITAT Andean Cliff Swallows are high-altitude specialists. They breed in the puna zone, above about 3400 m (11,160 ft), in open mountainous country with puna or montane scrub vegetation where cliffs are available for nest sites, including desert puna and tola heaths and mountain villages and towns (Fjeldså and Krabbe 1989). They are often seen over water. They are less commonly seen in the arid temperate zone on the western slopes of the Andes at 2500–3400 m (8200–11,160 ft), and only occasionally below 2500 m. They range outside the habitat used by other resident swallows, but they occasionally occur in the same places as Blue-and-white Swallows along the edges of the highlands.

DISTRIBUTION AND POPULATION This swallow has a very limited range, in the central Andes of Peru, Chile and Bolivia (Fjeldså and Krabbe 1989). The nominate race *andecola* occurs in the puna zone of southern Peru in the departments of Arequipa, Cuzco and Puno, northern Chile in the mountains of the provinces of Tarapacá and Arica, and northern and western Bolivia in the departments of La Paz, Cochabamba, Oruro, Potosi and Tarija; it probably also occurs in adjacent parts of northwestern Argentina. The race *oroyae* has a more restricted range, occurring only in the puna zone of central Peru. The status of the population is unknown, but Johnson (1967) described it as not abundant in Chile.

It seems, however, to be common if not abundant locally in Peru (Morrison 1939). Fjeldså (1987) found it to be common, even numerous in places, and recorded several thousand at Laguna Tacahua.

MIGRATION The movements of this swallow are very poorly known. It probably makes only local post-breeding movements at most. Morrison (1939) noted that birds were breeding in the Department of Huancavelica in Peru in September and October, but were absent in December.

BEHAVIOUR This species is extremely poorly known. Its flight is rather slow and includes periods of gliding; it often flies with stiff wings. It frequently feeds over water in small groups, catching insects on the wing, but the diet is not known in detail. Pairs nest in colonies, the size of the group probably depending on the availability of crevices. One group was of three or four nests in a roof (N.K. Krabbe, pers. comm.).

BREEDING The breeding season is not well known. In Peru, birds were in breeding condition in September and October (Morrison 1939); but birds with enlarged gonads, as well as eggs and fledglings, have been recorded in December–March in Bolivia (Niethammer 1956; Fjeldså 1987; N.K. Krabbe, pers. comm.). It has been found nesting on cliffs and in roofs. The nest is placed within a crevice or a hole in a vertical wall of a bluff or escarpment; the bird will sometimes make or enlarge a crevice by digging with its bill and scraping with its feet (Johnson 1967). Holes in roofs are also used (N.K. Krabbe, pers. comm.). The eggs are white with brown spots. No details of incubation or nestling periods are known.

VOICE The song is a characteristic harsh, short, dry 'trrrrt'. The bird may start singing an hour or so before dawn, while sweeping to and fro in flight (N.K. Krabbe, pers.

comm.). The contact call is a soft 'trui' (Fjeldså and Krabbe 1989).

DESCRIPTION The Andean Cliff Swallow is a medium-sized hirundine. The upperparts, including the scapulars, are a glossy blue-black or greenish-black, apart from the rump and uppertail-coverts which are brownish; on older individuals, however, the rump and uppertail-coverts become more like the back. The lores are black and the ear-coverts are grey. On the underparts, the sides of the head, chin, throat and breast are grey-brown, fading into a pale greyish-white abdomen and undertail-coverts. The undertail-coverts are long, full and broad; the longer ones are dark grey with pale edges. The sides, axillaries and underwing-coverts are grey-brown. The wings and tail are brownish-black with a blue gloss; the tail is almost square. The eyes are brown, the bill is black, and the legs and feet are horn-coloured. The sexes are alike. The juvenile is duller and browner, with white-tipped tertials and buffy tips to the greater wing-coverts; the rump is rufous-brown, the lower abdomen and undertail-coverts are washed pale rufous, and the uppertail-coverts are tinged tawny.

Measurements Length 14 cm (5½"). Wing 113–122 (mean 115.7); tail (square) 54–58 (mean 56); bill 8.8–9.9 (mean 9.4); tarsus 11.2–11.9 (mean 11.3). Weight 14–19 (mean 17).

RACES There are two races: *oroyae* has a longer wing (122–128) than *andecola* and has whitish rather than brownish primary shafts, bluer upperparts, and a longer and broader bill (10–11). The validity of the race *oroyae* has been questioned (Hellmayr 1935), but Zimmer (1955) found that specimens from central Peru were larger than and different in colour from *andecola*.

65 TREE MARTIN   Plate 23
Hirundo nigricans Vieillot

Hirundo nigricans Vieillot, 1817, Nouv. Dict. Hist. Nat., 14, p. 523: New Holland (error = Hobart, Tasmania, see Mathews, 1913, Austral. Av. Rec., 2, p. 65).

Hirundo nigricans timoriensis (Sharpe), 1885, Timor.

Hirundo nigricans neglecta (Mathews), 1912, northwest Australia, type from Fitzroy River.

FIELD CHARACTERS Tree Martins have a blue crown and mantle, whitish underparts and rump and a rufous forehead. They can be distinguished from other Australian swallows by their shallowly forked tail, whitish rump and small amount of rufous on the face. The Fairy Martin (70) is most similar, but has a rufous head and nape. They frequent woodland and are usually seen in small groups in the breeding season, but often in large flocks at other times. The flight is swift and they fly high.

HABITAT Tree Martins are typical of open woodlands, especially those with large wide-spreading trees which afford plenty of nest holes. They are often also seen in suburban or urban situations, breeding even in large cities, especially Adelaide and Perth (Blakers *et al.* 1984).

DISTRIBUTION AND POPULATION Tree Martins are widespread throughout Australia and apparently also breed in Wallacea (Blakers *et al.* 1984). The race *timoriensis* occurs on Timor in the Lesser Sunda Islands, and possibly also on Flores, but its status as a breeding bird is not clear (White and Bruce 1986). The race *neglecta* occurs in West and North Australia. The nominate race *nigricans* breeds in Queensland (except the most northern part), New South Wales, Victoria, eastern South Australia and Tasmania; it has bred at least once in New Zealand, at Oamaru in 1893 (one pair) (Oliver 1930).

This is a common species in Australia. Most breeding, however, occurs in the south, with only two breeding records north of 20°S, in the Atlases in the Atherton region (Blakers *et al.* 1984). Its relatively new and possibly increasing habit of nesting on artificial structures may lead to an expansion of the population in Australia. The presence of a race on Timor, however, suggests that the species may once have been more widespread in Wallacea. Though population sizes have not been estimated, at Boola Boola a density has been recorded of 0.5 birds per ha (1.2 per acre) in gullies in eucalypt forest (Blakers *et al.* 1984).

MIGRATION Those Tree Martins in the south are summer breeding visitors, those in the north non-breeding visitors; their status is less clear in the west, where there are long passage movements (Macdonald 1973). In the southwest and in Perth they are seen all year, but there is a long passage movement, with birds travelling north in the autumn and winter and south in the spring and summer. They are present all year near Innisfail, but are migratory from December to September above 1000 m (3300 ft) on the tableland. There is an influx into the Atherton region in winter, but they do breed there. They are present all year at Coonabarabran. In Tasmania, Tree Martins leave in February–March and return in August, often via Flinders Island. In Darwin they are present all year in small numbers, but are more common from May to August (Blakers et al. 1984).

Both vagrants and small flocks, probably from Tasmania, sometimes occur in New Zealand (Falla et al. 1983). These are mainly in the south, in Nelson Province and near Farewell Spit, but have turned up throughout the islands. They have also wintered at Blenheim and Featherston in New Zealand. In winter, Tree Martins occur widely in the Torres Strait, New Guinea and surrounding islands, especially the Aru Islands, Kei Islands, the Bismarck Archipelago and the Solomon Islands (Draffan et al. 1983; Beehler et al. 1986). They are also an irregular seasonal visitor to the island of Flores (White and Bruce 1986).

FOOD AND BEHAVIOUR The flight is swift, with frequent twists and turns. Tree Martins usually fly higher than Welcome Swallows (46), often more than 6 m (19 ft) above the ground, and sometimes considerably higher. Feeding sites are typically over and around the canopies of trees; over waterbodies such as creeks, pools, lakes, rivers and estuaries; and over farmland, especially pasture, and low scrub. They have also been recorded over the sea. A variety of aerial insects is taken, including flies, wasps, elaterid and other beetles, and bugs; spiders are also eaten (Green 1966, museum specimens). Tree Martins nest solitarily or gregariously, depending on what nest sites are available. When groups do occur, however, they are small, often just two to ten pairs in the same vicinity, and nests are not usually adjoining; one of the largest known colonies is of at least 50 pairs nesting

in crevices in the ceiling of a cave in the Otway Range in Victoria (Pescott 1978). The birds usually flock outside the breeding season, and sometimes they roost in large flocks, of even hundreds or thousands, especially in reedbeds or gum trees (Blakers et al. 1984); they often form flocks on the ground before roosting, and have been recorded gathering on patches of charcoal (Mollison and Green 1962). Their breeding behaviour is poorly known; they have been observed apparently mating in flight (Hastwell 1985).

BREEDING The breeding season is July or August to January (Macdonald 1973). In the southwest they breed mainly from August to November (Serventy and Whittell 1962). In arid areas, the season is less regular and the birds breed opportunistically following the rains. There are often two broods a year. Tree Martins most often use natural nest sites, mainly holes in dead trees or stumps, or crevices in cliffs or caves, but they sometimes use crevices in bridges, piers and buildings, although to a lesser extent than the Welcome Swallow and Fairy Martin do. The use of artificial structures seems to be more common in western Australia (at least there are few records from eastern localities: Bell 1979): nests have been recorded in such places as the beams of piers, ventilators and in verandahs in crevices under the roof or in a wall. Tree Martins also occasionally use the nests of Welcome Swallows, refurbishing the lining with leaves, building up to the roof with mud, and even driving off the original owners (Sharland 1943; Mellor 1967); they also readily use nestboxes. The nest is made of dry grass and leaves, especially green eucalypt leaves, or pine needles, and sometimes feathers as well (Campbell 1901). Such a scanty nest is unusual for a cliff swallow, but Tree Martins betray their origins by using mud on occasions; when they nest in holes they often reduce the size of the opening, if necessary, with a mixture of mud and plant fibres such as grass stems, building up a wall of several centimetres. In addition, they sometimes make a full mud nest, a half bowl like that of the Welcome Swallow's, especially under the eaves and verandahs of buildings (Sedgwick 1949; Serventy and Whittell 1962; Bell 1979). They use the same nest sites every year (Lord 1956).

There are usually four eggs, sometimes three or five, white, with light brown and mauve spots, concentrated at the larger end (Campbell 1901; Serventy and Whittell 1962). They measure 17.9 × 13.3 mm (16.3–21 × 12–14.5; weight 1.6). Incubation and nestling periods are not known.

VOICE The contact call is a 'tsweet', uttered in flight or when perched, and flocks twitter constantly on the wing. The song is a high-pitched twitter.

DESCRIPTION Tree Martins are small hirundines. A pale red band extends across the forehead towards the top of the eyes. The lores are black and the ear-coverts are smoky-brown. The upper forehead, crown, nape, mantle, back and scapulars are glossy blue-black, with grey-white feather bases which are often visible. The rump is dull white with a buffy wash, and with brownish-black shaft streaks on most feathers. The uppertail-coverts are dusky with paler margins. The cheeks, chin and throat are dull white with a buff tinge and with faint brownish-black streaks. The rest of the underparts are dull white, greyer on the breast, with a pale rufous tinge, especially on the flanks. There is a marked chestnut-brown tinge to the undertail-coverts. The

upperwing-coverts, wings and tail are dull blackish-brown, and the tail is slightly forked. The secondaries have narrow pale margins and the tertials have broader ones. The bill is black, the eyes are dark brown, and the legs and feet are blackish-brown. The sexes are alike. The juvenile is duller, with a browner back and paler forehead and underparts, the feathers of the back being dark with pale fringes; glossy feathers appear irregularly; the scapulars, tertials, secondaries and lesser and median coverts have brown fringes, paler on older juveniles, the throat is white with brown streaks, and the flanks are white. The primary moult occurs after breeding, from January to March (Rogers *et al.* 1986).

Measurements Length 13 cm (5"). Wing 103–115 (mean 107); tail 46–60 (mean 52.1); fork 6–9 (mean 7.4); bill 8.5–9.9 (mean 9); tarsus 10.5–11.5 (mean 10.9). Weight 13.8–19.3 (mean 15.9).

RACES Within Australia, eastern birds of the nominate race *nigricans* are somewhat larger than western *neglecta* (wing 100–106). The race *timoriensis* is small (wing 90–94), with dark shaft streaks on the throat and foreneck.

66 SOUTH AFRICAN CLIFF SWALLOW   Plate 21
Hirundo spilodera Sundevall

Hirundo spilodera Sundevall, 1850, Öfv. K. Vet.-Akad. Förh., vol. vii, p. 108: Caffraria. Type from Mooi River, Potchefstroom, Transvaal.

FIELD CHARACTERS South African Cliff Swallows are distinctive swallows, with a blue mantle, brown crown, rufous rump and pale rufous or whitish underparts. They are the only swallow in their breeding area with both metallic plumage and a square tail. They frequent open country, and are highly gregarious throughout the year. The flight is fluttery.

HABITAT The South African Cliff Swallow is an open-country species, preferring flat grassland, savanna and semi-arid areas, but is limited to areas with suitable nest sites.

DISTRIBUTION AND POPULATION The breeding range is restricted largely to South Africa from the eastern Cape to Natal, Orange Free State and the highveld of Transvaal, with a few breeding localities in South West Africa (Earlé 1987a). This species has also bred in Zimbabwe to just

north of Bulawayo, but has probably not done so recently (Irwin 1981). The range was extended in the Karoo and into Namibia and Zimbabwe after the very wet years of 1961–62 (Earlé 1987a). Locally these swallows are generally common except in the west of the range, although there are few records from this area. They were probably once more restricted by the need to be near cliffs or other natural breeding sites. Nowadays a wide variety of artificial nest sites is available, and the population has greatly benefited from this; indeed, no natural breeding sites are known at present (R.A. Earlé, pers. comm.). The range has expanded in the eastern Cape with the construction of large buildings, bridges and other artificial sites; in Orange Free State and the Karoo area, the lack of suitable breeding sites probably restricts its distribution (Earlé 1987a).

MIGRATION This species makes regular migrations between its breeding and non-breeding grounds, which are widely separated (Earlé 1987a). It arrives at the breeding sites in August and leaves in April, returning to the wintering grounds in the basin of the lower Congo River in Zaire from May to July. It probably migrates through Botswana, Angola and western Zambia (Dowsett 1979; Earlé 1987a). Probable stragglers have also been recorded in Malawi and on the Namibian coast (Medland 1985). There are a few records of this species in its breeding range in June and July, but the latter may have been early arrivals (Broekhuysen 1974; Earlé 1987a).

FORAGING AND FOOD The flight is fluttery, with short periods of gliding when the birds are feeding, but more direct when collecting mud. Feeding sites are usually open ground near the colonies. Most individuals feed alone, but they sometimes feed in small groups; social foraging is more frequent after the first young have fledged. The mean foraging height is 2 m (6½ ft), but nearly half the foraging is done less than 1 m above the ground (Earlé 1985d). They sometimes feed with other animals, including sheep, cattle, guineafowl, Cattle Egrets and Ostriches, catching the insects disturbed by the larger animals; they will also follow tractor-drawn ploughs and settle on the ground to pick up insects (Skead 1979; Earlé 1985d; Herholdt 1986). Ground foraging also occurs when termites are swarming after a period of rain or overcast weather. Cliff swallows are attracted to fires, and they also flush moths from bushes by hovering above the vegetation. They seem to feed from the ground and from vegetation more frequently than most swallows, perhaps because the high densities of birds around colonies may deplete the aerial food sources (R.A. Earlé, pers. comm.).

Earlé (1985d) has made a detailed study of the diet from the stomachs of 163 birds. Many types of insect were taken, but the main ones were beetles, flies, ants, parasitic wasps and bugs: of the beetles, scarabeid dung beetles and curculionid weevils were most often taken; fruit flies and those of the muscid family were the main flies. Flightless carabid beetles, moth and beetle larvae, termite workers and spiders were all taken in small numbers, presumably from the ground or vegetation. Few very small insects such as Thysanoptera and aphids were taken, although they were abundant in the environment. Small stones were found in 11% of stomachs, even in nestlings. Captive chicks produced pellets of indigestible sand, grass and some insect chitin.

SOCIAL ORGANISATION Cliff swallows are highly social, defending the colony as a group and collecting mud pellets socially. They always nest in colonies, which can number 15–20 to hundreds or thousands of nests. They remain gregarious outside the breeding season.

SOCIOSEXUAL BEHAVIOUR When they first arrive at the breeding site, the swallows, if not taking over an old nest, squat at a site on the wall (Earlé 1985c); these birds are apparently all males. The squatter starts on its own to build a ledge for the base of the nest, but usually soon forms a pair bond with another bird and the two continue to build together; most individuals approaching the squatter are chased off, but the prospective mate is allowed to alight. Unmated individuals on half-completed nests, however, lure prospective mates down by crouching on the nest and singing at birds flying past. Once a prospective mate alights on the nest, the singing bird turns its tail towards the newcomer and quivers its wings; if the newcomer does not enter the nest, it is chased off. Individuals that are accepted are repeatedly allowed to alight at the nest until the pair bond has formed. Copulations occur in the nest, or at least on the nest site.

Nests need to be defended from other swallows. Strangers sometimes follow nest-owners into nests (this may be related to intraspecific parasitism and extra-pair copulations); in addition, nest-builders steal mud and lining materials from each other (Earlé 1985c). The nest site is defended by both partners. Birds flying close by are threatened, and any alighting near the nest are attacked and chased. The threat posture involves several phases (Earlé 1985c). First, the crown feathers are raised when an intruder is sighted. Then the defender opens its bill and utters a threat call. If the intruder alights, the defender quivers its wings and either pecks at it or chases it off; the intruder usually escapes before being attacked. Most attacks are the result of birds returning to the nest to find an intruder there. The owner attacks the nape or head of the intruder with its bill and clings to its back;

then the combatants fall to the ground. The attacker, always a male, usually attempts to mate with the intruder, although there is no evidence of sperm being transferred. The intruder gives an alarm call, attracting other birds and stimulating mating among them. Other birds are also attracted to the fight and join in. Victims seem to be from other colonies, perhaps seeking mates. If an intruder tries to enter an occupied nest, it is pecked at and sometimes gripped so that it hangs from the nest. Fights sometimes take place inside nests, but usually last only a few seconds before the intruder is chased off; one such fight, however, lasted 30 minutes. Neighbours are not aggressive towards each other, but collectively chase off an intruder. These swallows are not usually aggressive towards other species.

BREEDING The breeding season is chiefly September–March, with laying peaking after rainfall. Some pairs (14% in one colony studied: Earlé 1986a) have two or three broods, and a few have four. The usual nest sites are on the eaves of buildings, in barns, bridges, culverts, quarries, water tanks and cliffs; when nesting on public buildings and churches, the birds can be a nuisance because of their droppings. The nest is a closed half sphere made of mud pellets, and lined with plant down, fibres such as sheep's wool and a few feathers; the entrance is towards the top, facing outwards. Nests are usually adjoining; where they are very close, the entrances face away from each other. The shape depends on the location; at one colony nests were built partly in crevices, and mud was used only to make the entrance smaller and to form a tunnel (Earlé 1985b). The first nests are built high on a vertical face close to an overhang or horizontal roof; later nests are built below and to either side. In Earlé's study in the Orange Free State, the nests were generally above the reach of a human, not always over water but never on a building lived in by humans, or in a barn. Mud is gathered up to about 300 m (330 yds) from the colony, from puddles or the edges of streams; the type of mud used is variable, sometimes containing sand or clay. The progress of building depends on the weather and is delayed in dry weather. Building occupies only 3.7 h a day on average (Earlé 1986c). The birds will hover over seed heads to collect seed plumes of Compositae; they also collect feathers in

flight and pull sheep's wool from fences. Feathers are brought throughout incubation and even in the nestling period. Nests are re-used from year to year after being repaired, and the lining is added to each year (Earlé 1985b).

Two nests took five and seven days, respectively, to build. They contain some 1,300–1,800 pellets, which can be added to the nest very rapidly when the bird is building. At a new site, a ridge of pellets is first formed along the vertical surface of the wall by all the males; this forms the base for all the new nests. The bird clings to the site and deposits about 50–100 pellets to give him a foothold from which he can guard his site. A nest base is then constructed on an area of about 10 cm (4 in) on the ridge, to which mud pellets are added ventrally and laterally to form a cup. The lateral walls are extended upwards until they reach the roof, and the opening is filled in to form a narrow retort; then the lateral walls are joined to form the roof, and the entrance tunnel is constructed. At this final stage, the lining is collected. All building is done from inside the nest.

The clutch size is one to four eggs, but usually two or three. Most four-egg clutches probably include eggs of a second female parasitising the first (Earlé 1986a). Clutch size decreases during the season. The eggs are white with fine spots and blotches of red-brown or inky-purple, which are more numerous towards the larger end. The eggs average 20.2 × 14.4 mm (17.8–22.9 × 12.7–15.2; weight 2.2), and are laid at intervals of 24 hours. The incubation period is 14 days, and the nestling period is 24 or 25 days. Both sexes incubate and feed the young, taking about equal turns. Feeding rates are highest around noon, before the hottest part of the day. The young return to the nest for a few days after fledging.

Predators are few, as the nests are high up or over water. A monitor lizard and red ants have been recorded attacking chicks in the nest; red ants are the main threat, causing one colony at Bloemfontein in 1983/84 to be abandoned (Earlé 1985a). Humans also destroy nests and take the chicks. House Sparrows *Passer domesticus* and Cape Sparrows *P. melanurus* remove eggs and take over the nests; House Sparrows also chase off swallows from neighbouring nests, and can disrupt small colonies but probably have little effect on large ones. House Sparrows are relative newcomers to

South Africa, but other sparrows have been recorded occupying swallow nests as early as 1879 (Winterbottom 1962). Chicks sometimes fall from nests, probably as a result of harassment by ticks *Ornithodoros peringueyi* (Earlé 1985a). In one study the fledging success from eggs laid was 72%, but was low in one year because of high mortality caused by the mite *Ornithonyssus bursa* (Burgerjon 1964); in Earlé's (1986a) study, breeding success was variable between sites and years but averaged 57%.

VOICE These swallows are quite vocal for a colonial species. They have seven types of call, although no song equivalent to that of the Barn Swallow (42) (Earlé 1986b). These are: a chatter call, which is a series of warbles and may be a low-intensity territorial song; a threat call, similar to the chatter call but used when defending the nest and usually accompanied by the threat display; a short nest-relief call, given when either partner relieves its mate at the nest; low- and high-intensity alarm calls; a harsh distress call; and a contact call of two or three notes, which may be individually recognisable. Nestlings have individually recognisable contact calls.

DESCRIPTION South African Cliff Swallows are medium-sized hirundines which are very variable in colour. The top of the head is dark brown (blue-black in fresh plumage). The nape of the neck, mantle and back are metallic blue-black, but the feathers have vinaceous-white edges so the upperparts appear mottled. The scapulars are a duller blue-black. The uppertail-coverts and rump are rufous, pale rufous or buffy (in worn plumage), the longer coverts with blue-black tips and rufous margins. The forehead and the lores are buffy-orange to pale rufous, although the facial markings are variable and the forehead is sometimes blue-black. The ear-coverts are dull blue-black. The chin is pale rufous; and the throat and upper breast are pale rufous or whitish, with a variable amount of black and rufous speckling. The rest of the underparts are pale rufous or whitish with a variable amount of rufous streaking, apart from the undertail-coverts which are cinnamon with dusky subterminal spots. The wings and tail are brownish-black with a faint metallic greenish sheen, especially on the coverts; the tail is square, and lacks any white patches. In fresh plumage, the tertials have buffy edges. The bill, legs and feet are black; the eyes are dark brown. The sexes are alike. Juveniles are duller, with a paler rump, breast and undertail-coverts, and the tertials have white fringes. The primary moult takes place between March and the end of August, mainly on the wintering grounds, but about 2% of adults start before migrating (Earlé 1987a).

Measurements Length 14 cm (5½"). Wing 105–119 (mean 111); tail (square) 45–57 (mean 51); bill 7–9.2 (mean 8.4); tarsus 11.7–17.8 (mean 13.9). Weight 16–26 (mean 20.6).

RED SEA SWALLOW
Hirundo perdita Fry and Smith

Hirundo perdita Fry and Smith, 1985, Ibis, 127, 1–6: Sanganeb Light House, Red Sea.

In May 1984, on Sanganeb Light House in the Red Sea, a single specimen of a previously unknown type of cliff swallow was found (Fry and Smith 1985). It closely resembled the South African Cliff Swallow (66) but had a steely-blue crown, blackish forehead and lores, grey rump, white chin, and bluish-black throat and upper breast. Photographs indicate that fresh rump feathers may have extensive brownish fringes (S C Madge and N J Redman, pers. comm.). Fry and Smith named it as a new species *Hirundo perdita*, the Red Sea Swallow, and suggested that it might breed in the Red Sea hills of Sudan or Ethiopia. The specimen they found had probably wandered away from its usual range — its scientific name indeed means 'the lost swallow'. No more was heard about this swallow until late in 1988 when 'unidentified' cliff swallows were seen by a cliff face at Lake Langano (about 20 birds) and in the Awash National Park (about three to eight birds) in Ethiopia (G Edwards, pers. comm.; SC Madge and N Redman, pers. comm.). The newly discovered swallows had blue-black upperparts with a rump varying from off-white to pale pink or rufous. The birds seen by Madge and Redman (in Awash National Park) were described as having brownish throats and brownish-white underparts; those seen by Edwards (at both sites) had

Red Sea Swallow

off-white underparts with buffy sides of the breast. Neither exactly resembles the Red Sea Swallow description but cliff swallows are variable and the specimen found by Fry and Smith may not be typical of its species. Whether the newly discovered swallows are the same species as the Red Sea Swallow or an entirely new form is too early to judge. At the time of going to press no photographs or skins were available.

67 CLIFF SWALLOW   Plate 22
Hirundo pyrrhonota Vieillot

Hirundo pyrrhonota Vieillot, 1817, Nouv. Dict. Hist. Nat., 14, p. 519: Paraguay.

Hirundo pyrrhonota tachina (Oberholser), 1903, Langtry, Texas.

Hirundo pyrrhonota hypopolia (Oberholser), 1920, Fort Norman, Mackenzie.

Hirundo pyrrhonota melanogaster Swainson, 1827, table land of Mexico = Real del Monte, Hidalgo.

FIELD CHARACTERS Cliff Swallows have a blue mantle with white streaks, a cinnamon-rufous rump, rufous throat and whitish underparts. The cinnamon or rusty-coloured rump, whitish forehead, square tail and dark throat patch readily distinguish this species from most of the other swallows in North America. The closely related Cave Swallow (68) differs mainly in having a darker forehead and lighter throat patch. The Cliff Swallow frequents open country and towns and is highly gregarious throughout the year. When feeding, it tends to soar more than other swallows.

HABITAT Although originally a cliff dweller in the mountainous areas of the west, most now associate with humans, frequenting a variety of open habitats such as farms and also nesting in towns.

DISTRIBUTION AND POPULATION Cliff Swallows breed throughout much of North America and Mexico (Behle 1976; AOU 1983). The nominate race breeds on the eastern side of North America west to Manitoba and the Rocky Mountains, and from southwestern British Columbia south to northwestern Baja California. In the Great Basin, its range is split in two by the race *hypopolia*, which breeds from Alaska and western Canada south to parts of California, Nevada, Utah, Montana and Wyoming. Individuals from southwestern Utah, the lower Colorado valley, and parts of Baja California, Arizona (except the southeast),

New Mexico (except the southwest) and southern Texas, along the Rio Grande valley, are referable to *tachina*. Those breeding from southeastern Arizona and southwestern New Mexico, through eastern Sonora, western Chihuahua and southern Coahuila, on the Mexican plateau south to Oaxaca, and the Pacific plains to Nayarit are of the race *melanogaster*.

Cliff Swallows have always been most numerous in the mountainous western side of North America where cliffs provide nest sites (AO Gross in Bent 1942; Erskine 1979). Nowadays they use human artefacts for nest sites, and numbers have been increasing in eastern areas: in New York State they first bred in 1817, and by the beginning of this century were widespread (Bull 1974). In Canada perhaps less than a quarter of nest sites are natural ones, and those nearly all in the west (Erskine 1979). In the nineteenth and early twentieth centuries, when the availability of unpainted barns declined, numbers of Cliff Swallows in the eastern United States also declined; painted barns may not provide good sites for attaching nests, although Cliff Swallows do use them (for example in British Columbia: RW Butler, pers. comm.). Competition for nest sites from introduced House Sparrows probably also contributed to the decline: at one area in North Dakota, the population increased at an annual rate of 87% when the local House Sparrows were removed (Krapu 1986). Since the start of construction of dams and highway bridges, however, there have been plenty of new sites and consequently numbers have increased greatly, the species re-occupying areas where it had been extirpated and extending its range into the southeastern states of the USA, although it is still scarce there (Robbins *et al.* 1986).

MIGRATION In winter, Cliff Swallows migrate to Brazil, Paraguay, northern and central Argentina and, rarely, Chile, although small numbers winter as far north as Panama; there are casual records as far south as Tierra del Fuego and out to sea near the Galapagos Islands (AOU 1983; Phillips 1986). They migrate via Central America, Colombia and Venezuela; they are rarely seen in the Caribbean. The race *pyrrhonota* winters from southern Brazil to Paraguay and northeastern Argentina; *melanogaster* winters in southern Brazil and northwestern Argentina. The winter ranges of *tachina* and *hypopolia* are not known.

FORAGING AND FOOD Cliff Swallows generally feed in close-knit flocks, individuals tending to leave the breeding colony together for the feeding grounds. Most foraging is done within 0.4 km (¼ mile) of the colony, but the birds will feed up to 6.1 km (4 miles) away (Emlen 1952, 1954). Sometimes they feed low over the ground, but in warm weather they feed at higher altitudes, perhaps moving with insects in thermals (RW Butler, pers. comm.). The colony serves as an 'information centre' in which unsuccessful foragers are able to follow more successful birds to a source of food; flock feeding also allows individuals to be more successful on average at capturing prey (Brown 1985a, 1986, 1988b). A specialist feeder, the Cliff Swallow takes mainly small, swarming insects. Beal (1918) recorded the diet of adults as consisting of 27% beetles, especially small dung beetles and weevils, 27% hemipteran bugs and 14% dipteran flies; in California, nestlings were fed mainly Hymenoptera and Diptera (Beal 1907). In Nebraska, however (Brown 1985a), over half the insects brought to nestlings were plant bugs (Homoptera), mainly cicadellids and aphids, while dipteran flies, especially muscids, empidids and chironomids, accounted for about a fifth of the diet, and Hymenoptera, mainly ants, for about a tenth; a few mayflies, dragonflies, grasshoppers, hemipteran bugs, lacewings, beetles, moths and spiders were also taken. Cliff Swallows have been known to feed on the ground on accumulations of insects (e.g. Hobson and Sealy 1987).

SOCIAL ORGANISATION Colonies can be enormous, containing 2,000 or 3,000 nests, although they average a few hundred (Brown 1985a). Cliff Swallows are also gregarious outside the breeding season.

SOCIOSEXUAL BEHAVIOUR Many adults return to the same colony to breed each year (Mayhew 1958; Sikes and Arnold 1984). In Mayhew's study, first-year birds tended to disperse away from where they hatched, but Sikes and Arnold did not find such a trend. At the colony there are frequent disputes, with birds attempting to steal grass or mud, females laying eggs in the nests of others (sometimes even carrying their eggs to another nest), and males copulating with females who are not their mates (Brown 1985a; Brown and Brown 1988). Mud-gathering is a social activity. At mud-gathering sites males attempt to mate forcibly with females coming to collect mud (Butler 1982b) Nests are fiercely defended against intruders, at first by threatening and jabbing, but if the intruder persists fights ensue which sometimes lead to the death of a bird. However, males do not guard their mates, presumably so that the nest can be defended at all times by one or other of a pair (Butler 1982b; Brown 1985a).

Males sometimes sing while in flight, with throat feathers extended and wings stiff and fluttering; this often leads to chases among males. At the start of the season, males claim a breeding site and defend it, crouching with neck drawn in, bill raised and wings quivering, and singing. Other individuals hover nearby or perch erect near the 'squatter', turning their head out and partially opening their wings, and sometimes singing; the squatter usually snaps at or chases these birds. Over a number of days, one of these secondary individuals persists and is accepted as a mate. Copulations between the members of a pair (rather than extra-pair copulations) occur in the nest: the male moves into the nest cup and crouches; after several minutes the female will follow him, crouch and allow him to mount, which he does with quivering wings. They may copulate several times a day (Emlen 1954).

BREEDING The breeding season is from April to August in the southern part of the range, but starts in May, in the northerly sites (AO Gross in Bent 1942). Breeding within a colony is highly synchronised (Brown 1985a). The majority of pairs raise a single brood per season, but a few have a second. The natural cliff sites are still used a little, but most colonies are now on bridges, in culverts and on buildings; the swallows prefer sites with an overhang and which are at least a couple of metres above ground (less if they are over water). Occasionally they will nest on other sites such as burrows in sand banks or on trees, or inside buildings. The nests, built of mud pellets with a little dry grass and sparsely lined with grass and feathers, are often packed close together; they are domed, with a narrow entrance tunnel which usually points downward and away from neighbouring nests (Emlen 1954). The nests vary in size and shape; if built close to an overhang the roof may not be completed, and the length of the entrance tunnel is variable. The nest is started by the male, who first makes a narrow crescent of mud; this is extended to form a ledge from which the pair continues to build. The lateral and ventral walls are then built until a cup is formed; the lateral walls are usually extended into a roof, then the walls and floor are extended forward and the nest opening narrowed. Egg-laying usually starts at this stage: thus, in one study, the first egg was laid in a colony when a third of the nests had floor and walls but no tunnel and the remainder could not hold eggs (RW Butler, pers. comm.). Some nests are left with a wide entrance, others have a short, unroofed entrance tunnel; most have an enclosed tunnel some 15–20 cm (6–8 in) long (Emlen 1954). Mud is gathered from near the colony, and the nest is worked on a few hours a day for a week or more. Old nests from a previous year are often re-used, but colonies tend to switch nesting sites between seasons, probably to avoid parasites present in old nests (Sikes and Arnold 1984; Loye ms). Both sexes build, incubate, and feed the chicks.

The female lays two to five eggs, but usually three or four. The eggs are white with, usually, brown dots or blotches, and measure 20.4 × 14 mm (18–22.9 × 12.7–15.2; weight 2.1). Early clutches are larger than later ones (Samuel 1971b). The eggs are laid at daily intervals. The incubation period is about 12–14 days, though periods of 15 or 16 days have been recorded, and the nestling period is about 24 days. Once the young have fledged, they and their parents leave the colony for a crèche, which can be several kilometres away; the juveniles perch together on a wire or in a tree, where they continue to be fed by their parents, who recognise their own offspring's calls (Stoddard and Beecher 1983; Beecher et al. 1986).

Some studies have reported relatively low hatching successes of 65–75% (e.g. Samuel 1971b; Grant and Quay 1977), but losses at this stage are usually low. Nestlings sometimes die of starvation owing to bad weather during which the insect prey are scarce (e.g. Stewart 1972). In large colonies, the swallow bug Oeciacus vicarius can greatly retard the growth of nestlings and reduce their chances of survival (Brown and Brown 1986). Breeding success is generally high, about 70% of eggs laid producing fledglings in Grant and Quay's (1977) study, but in Samuel's (1971b) study it was less than 60%. Annual mortality is about 45–50%, higher for juveniles (65–84%) than for adults; most individuals live for only a few breeding seasons, but there are records of nine-year-olds (Mayhew 1958; Samuel 1971b; Sikes and Arnold 1984).

VOICE Cliff Swallows have relatively few vocalisations (Samuel 1971a; Brown 1985b). The 'twitter-squeak' song is a rapid, often creaky, twittering, usually by the male when perched, but occasionally in flight. The alarm note is a plaintive single call (the 'purr' call). Cliff Swallows also use 'chur' calls, for example when flocking or between the members of a pair. There is also a 'squeak' used to use to indicate that they have found a source of food (Brown 1985a; Stoddard 1988).

DESCRIPTION Cliff Swallows are small hirundines. The forehead varies from a dull white to a pale wood-brown, and fades with wear. The crown is glossy blue-black and the hindneck is grey-brown. The mantle, back and scapulars are glossy blue-black, with pale grey or whitish streaks on the former. The rump is light cinnamon-rufous. The uppertail-coverts are grey-brown with pale margins. The lores are blackish. The ear-coverts, sides of the head, chin and throat are chestnut. There is a patch of glossy black on the throat, extending over the upper part of the breast. The upper breast, sides and flanks are pale grey-brown, with a pale chestnut tinge to the upper breast. The rest of the underparts are whitish. The longer undertail-coverts are dusky or dark grey-brown with white margins. The underwing-coverts and axillaries are pale grey-brown. The upperwing-coverts, wings and tail are blackish-brown; the wing-coverts, secondaries and tertials have very pale margins, sometimes almost white at the tips. The bill is black, the eyes are brown, and the legs and feet are dusky

or horn-coloured. The sexes are alike. The juvenile is duller, being dull black on the head, mantle and scapulars, with very little gloss, and having a dull chestnut forehead, a mixture of grey-brown, dusky and dull chestnut on the sides of the head, chin and throat and a pinkish or vinaceous-buff wash on the underparts; the feathers of the upperparts have paler terminal margins, and the tertials have pale vinaceous-cinnamon terminal margins. The coloration on the head is variable, and partial albinism is not uncommon. The moult may start on the breeding grounds or on migration, but occurs mainly on the wintering grounds.

Measurements Length 13 cm (5"). Wing 105–113 (mean 109); tail (square) 45–51 (mean 48); bill 8.9–10.6 (mean 9.7); tarsus 11.3–13.2 (mean 12.5). Weight 17.5–26.7 (mean 21.6).

RACES The race *hypopolia* is larger (wing 110–115) than nominate *pyrrhonota*, with a larger, whiter frontal band, a whiter breast, greyer flanks and pectoral region, and paler rump and more rufescent underparts. The race *tachina* is smaller (wing 99–108) than *pyrrhonota* and has a cinnamon or fawn forehead; *melanogaster* is the same size as *tachina*, with a deep cinnamon/rufous or chestnut forehead and a deep cinnamon rump. However, there is a great deal of intergradation between the races, which form a cline in size and plumage characteristics from north to south. Some individuals from Oregon, with pale underparts and a buff forehead, have been described as a separate race, *aprophata*, but, because there is a great deal of individual variation in the species, it is unlikely that these are distinct from *hypopolia* (Behle 1976). Similarly, small, pale individuals from Arizona are probably *melanogaster*, rather than a separate race *minima*.

68 CAVE SWALLOW
Hirundo fulva Vieillot

Plate 22

Hirundo fulva Vieillot, 1807, Ois. Amer. Sept., 1, p. 62, pl. 32: Santo Domingo.

Hirundo fulva pelodoma (Nelson), 1902, Saltillo, Coahuila, Mexico (*pallida* auct. occupied, Brooke 1974).

Hirundo fulva citata (Van Tyne), 1938, Chichén Itzá, Yucatan.

Hirundo fulva chapmani (Chapman), 1924, Alamor, Province of Loja, Ecuador (*aequatorialis* auct. occupied, Brooke 1974).

Hirundo fulva rufocollaris Peale, 1848, near Callao, Peru.

FIELD CHARACTERS Cave and Cliff Swallows (67) are very similar. The former can be distinguished by the dark chestnut forehead and cinnamon-buff throat, sides of neck and collar. It breeds in open, craggy country or along coastal cliffs and is highly gregarious throughout the year. The flight is slow with much gliding.

HABITAT Cave Swallows frequent a variety of open-country areas, often near water and suitable nesting sites such as caves. They are typical of rocky ravines, coastal cliffs and headlands in the Greater Antilles especially, as well as cultivated areas, and can be found nesting in many villages in Mexico. The Peruvian race *rufocollaris* frequents cultivated areas and human habitation in the river districts between the coast and the mouths of the Andean valleys.

DISTRIBUTION AND POPULATION The breeding range is disjunct, with populations being restricted to southern North America and Mexico, the Greater Antilles, and Ecuador and Peru (AOU 1983). The nominate race *fulva* breeds in the Greater Antilles: Puerto Rico, Cuba, Isle of Pines, Hispaniola (including Gonave, Tortue, Ile à Vache); and Jamaica. The race *pelodoma* breeds in southeastern New Mexico, south-central Texas, southern Arizona and northeastern Mexico; *citata* occurs in the Yucatan peninsula; *chapmani* in southwestern Ecuador, and perhaps in northwestern Peru; and *rufocollaris* in western Peru.

In parts of the range, including Texas and the Greater Antilles, Cave Swallows are locally common. Although nesting on houses is probably a well-established habit in Peru and Mexico, the use of artificial sites in the United States is recent, although Cave Swallows as yet use them less than Barn Swallows (42) do. The known range has been expanding over the last century, in part because of the new nesting sites. These swallows were not known to breed in the United States until 1914, and the first report for New Mexico was in 1952, although two had been collected in 1930 and misidentified as Cliff Swallows; recently they have also bred at the University of Arizona campus in Tucson (Huels 1984, 1985). The first known sites were all in caves or sink holes. Competition from Cliff and Barn Swallows may have restricted their nesting sites (Selander and Baker 1957), although all three species use the same buildings in Mexico (Amadon and Eckelberry 1955;

Baker 1962). More recently, however, they have spread to concrete highway culverts and buildings and breed in association with both other species, but particularly Barn Swallows. As a result of this change in habits, Cave and Barn Swallows now sometimes hybridise (Martin 1980).

MIGRATION The nominate race is resident on most of its breeding islands, but on Cuba it is present only locally during winter, and is a summer resident on the Isle of Pines. The winter range of *pelodoma* is unknown; it has been recorded on migration in Chiapas and Tamaulipas, there are a couple of sight records from Panama (Wetmore *et al.* 1984) and there is also a questionable sight record from Costa Rica. The race *citata* is resident. Cave Swallows are occasionally recorded in southern Florida, including the Dry Tortugas, and accidentally north to Nova Scotia, and in the Virgin Islands. There is also a record from Trinidad, and a questionable record of *fulva* from Panama. The South American races are probably resident.

FOOD AND BEHAVIOUR The flight is similar to that of the Cliff Swallow, with frequent periods of gliding. It feeds in small flocks and is known to feed in mixed flocks with Cliff and Barn Swallows (Baker 1962), but generally higher than Barn Swallows. In South America, it will also join flocks of other species such as the Blue-and-white Swallow (18) (Mischler 1986). Stomachs of Puerto Rican specimens contained over 50% beetles, especially of the genus *Platypus* and of the families Chrysomelidae and Nitidulidae, about 16% flies and nearly 10% ants; a few parasitic wasps, true bugs and plant bugs and a moth were also present (Wetmore 1916). Another stomach contained mainly nymphs of aquatic bugs (*Zaitha anura*) and some tenebrionids (Beatty and Danforth 1931). Flies, small beetles and bugs have been recorded in the diet of Cuban and Hispaniolan birds (Danforth 1929, 1935b). Cave Swallows breed colonially, usually in groups of a few tens of nests, but sometimes a few hundred pairs nest together. Some 1,500 nests were found in one cave in Texas (Selander and Baker 1957).

BREEDING The breeding season in the Antilles is April–July, in Peru, June and in Texas April–August. There are two broods, and three have been recorded in culverts. Cave Swallows do not restrict their nesting to caves, but nowadays also use artificial structures, including culverts, bridges, walls, cathedrals, ruined forts and other buildings, where they nest under the eaves or on beams under gables and verandahs; colonies sometimes form in village plazas, especially on the cathedral. The nest is usually at least a couple of metres above the ground, but if over water it may be less than 1 m above the high-water line; in caves, the nests are built in the twilight zone. In Peru, *rufocollaris* nests both on cliffs and on houses. The nests are not so close together as in Cliff Swallow colonies; many are built in isolated crevices rather than on flat walls. Nesting is less synchronous than in the Cliff Swallow. The nest is usually a crescent-shaped open half bowl made of mud pellets, rarely closed with an entrance spout like the Cliff Swallow's; mud substitutes such as guano are used when available. The shape of the nest differs slightly between races: *pelodoma* nests are open, but those of *fulva* are sometimes enclosed with an entrance tunnel, and those of *rufocollaris* are enclosed like those of the Cliff Swallow but with long necks. The nest is lined with a pad of vegetable fibres such as cactus hair, down from seed pods, dry grass, bark and feathers. Old nests are repaired and re-used both within and between seasons. There is a record of an old Cliff Swallow nest being used (Huels 1984).

The usual clutch size is three to five, though only two or three are usual on Hispaniola (Balat and Gonzales 1982); *pelodoma* lays three to five, occasionally one, two or six eggs. Clutch size decreases during the season (Martin 1981). The eggs are white with reddish-brown and lilac speckles and spots, and resemble those of the Cliff Swallow. They average 19.4 × 13.9 mm (17.7–23 × 13.4–15.2; weight 1.96). Both male and female incubate (Wetmore 1916). The incubation period is 15 or 16 days, and the nestling period 22–26 days. The fledglings stay near the colony and return to the nest for several days. Fledging success (from eggs laid) in Martin *et al.*'s (1977) study was 55%, and 54–72% in Martin's (1981) study, higher in culverts than in coves.

VOICE The calls are a 'chu-chu', a 'weet' or 'cheweet' (uttered in flocks), and a short 'choo' which may be an alarm call. There is also a song consisting of squeaks followed by a warble and ending in a series of double-toned notes (Selander and Baker 1957).

DESCRIPTION The Cave Swallow is a small hirundine. It has a deep chestnut forehead. The crown is glossy blue-black or greenish-black. The hindneck is grey-brown. The mantle, back and scapulars are glossy blue-black, with white streaks along the former. The rump is chestnut or cinnamon-rufous. The uppertail-coverts are hair-brown, sometimes with paler margins. The lores are blackish. The ear-coverts, sides of the head, chin and throat vary from white with a cinnamon-rufous tinge to pale cinnamon-rufous; the upper breast, sides and flanks are similar, but have a grey-brown tinge. The undertail-coverts are hair-brown with broad white margins, sometimes with a pale cinnamon-rufous tinge. The lower breast and abdomen are whitish. The axillaries and underwing-coverts are pale hair-brown. The wings and tail are blackish-brown, the secondaries sometimes having paler margins; the tail is almost square. The bill is black, the eyes are brown and the legs and feet are a horn colour. The sexes are alike. The juvenile is much duller than the adult, with a dull black mantle and scapulars, a narrow dull chestnut forehead, cinnamon margins to the tertials and uppertail-coverts, dusky ear-coverts, and white chin and throat, sometimes with dusky flecks. The white facial markings, however, vary geographically (Martin *et al.* 1986). In Texas, the moult is more or less completed by the time the birds migrate (Selander and Baker 1957).

Measurements Length 12 cm (4¼"). Wing 97–108 (mean 102.1); tail (square) 42–48 (mean 44.5); bill 7.8–9.9 (mean 8.9); tarsus 11.3–14.7 (mean 12.5). Weight 14.4–17.5 (mean 15.1).

RACES The race *pelodoma* is larger (wing 104–113) than *fulva*, with a pale cinnamon-rufous rump, paler undertail-coverts, and pale grey-brown sides and flanks. The race *citata* is a small (wing 94–103), dark race, with darker sides of the head, chin, throat, sides and undertail-coverts than *fulva* and a paler forehead and rump. The birds on Cuba have sometimes been considered a separate race, *cavicola*, but there are no consistent differences between these island birds. A minority of *fulva* and *pelodoma* have black throat markings like those of the Cliff Swallow. The South American *rufocollaris* has sometimes been considered a separate species: it has a chestnut neck-collar and rump, the throat and sides of the head are white with a buff tinge, the upper breast and sides are dull chestnut, and the rest of the underparts are buffy-white; the undertail-coverts are chestnut-brown with buffy-white fringes. The race *chapmani* is small (wing 93–95), with the buff and chestnut areas of the lower parts and sides of head deeper and more extensive than on *rufocollaris*.

HYBRIDISATION Cave Swallows are known to hybridise with Barn Swallows (Martin and Selander 1975), and one was recorded paired with a Cliff Swallow (Huels 1985).

69 INDIAN CLIFF SWALLOW   Plate 23
Hirundo fluvicola Blyth

Hirundo fluvicola Blyth, 1855, J. Asiat. Soc. Bengal, 24, p. 471: Somar and Kane Rivers, Bundelkund.

FIELD CHARACTERS Indian Cliff Swallows have blue upperparts, a chestnut forehead and crown, pale brown rump and buffy, streaked underparts. The combination of dark crown, pale rump and streaked underparts with a square tail is distinctive. They occur in mountainous areas and around human habitation, and are highly gregarious throughout the year. The flight is slow and fluttery.

HABITAT The typical natural habitat is open mountainous areas with cliffs for nesting, but they equally frequent human habitation and cultivated areas, especially near water, which also provide nest sites. They will even breed in busy towns (Ali and Ripley 1972).

DISTRIBUTION AND POPULATION Indian Cliff Swallows breed from northeastern Afghanistan (Kabul), northern Pakistan and most of India from Kashmir, east along the lower Himalayas to Gonda and Mirzipur Districts in Uttar Pradesh and south to Coimbatore at about 11°N (Ali and Ripley 1972). There are some breeding records from eastern Nepal (Inskipp and Inskipp 1986). This is a common swallow in India, particularly in the Gangetic Plain. Its widespread use of artificial nesting sites has allowed it to spread into new habitats such as towns.

MIGRATION In the south this species is resident, but makes some post-breeding movements (Ali and Ripley 1972). Birds from the higher altitudes in the northern parts of the range move down to the plains in the non-breeding season. There is some post-breeding dispersal, and individuals do turn up outside the breeding range; there is one record from Sri Lanka. In Afghanistan, northern Pakistan and northwestern India, where the winters are cold, it is migratory, visiting the area to breed between the end of February and September. There are several records from Nepal, mainly in January, April and August (Inskipp and Inskipp 1986).

BEHAVIOUR The flight is weak and fluttering, with fewer swoops than in the Barn Swallow (42). The birds usually feed in flocks, often with other swallows, and often over water. The diet consists of a variety of insects caught in flight (Ali and Ripley 1972). Like other cliff swallows, they nest colonially in groups of from a few tens of nests to a few hundreds; one of the largest known colonies contained 600 nests (Baker 1934).

BREEDING There are records of breeding throughout the year, but in the southern part of the range there appear to be two peaks, in December–April and in July–October; in the northern part of the range, breeding occurs chiefly in March–June (Ali and Ripley 1972). There are often two, perhaps three, broods. Indian Cliff Swallows use both natural nest sites such as cliffs, and artificial ones such as buildings, gateways, mosques, bridges and culverts; they will use both deserted and inhabited buildings, but prefer sites over water. The nest is retort-shaped and made of mud pellets: the bowl of the nest is about 10 cm (4 in) in diameter, and the entrance, which projects outwards, is about 5–15 cm (2–6 in) long; the lining is of fibres such as dry grass, horsehair and feathers. The nests are built adjoining one another. The colony site is re-used every year, some nests being repaired, others replaced. The birds collect mud in flocks, working especially in the early morning and late afternoon; some extra-pair copulation appears to take place in these flocks, as happens in the American Cliff Swallow (67) (Ali and Ripley 1972). Both sexes build the nest. There are usually three, sometimes four, eggs in a clutch. These are white, sometimes with spots of pale sepia or yellowish-brown, especially at the larger end. They average 18.5 × 13.1 mm (16.0–20.8 × 11.8–14.0; weight 1.65). Both male and female incubate the eggs and feed the nestlings. The incubation and nestling periods are not known.

VOICE There are two calls: a sharp 'trr trr' uttered in flight; and a twittering chirp which may be a territorial song, as it is given on the nest and is accompanied by a shivering wing display (Ali and Ripley 1972).

DESCRIPTION Indian Cliff Swallows are small hirundines. The mantle, back and scapulars are glossy steel-blue, the feathers of the mantle having visible white edges and blue tips. The lores are white with blackish-brown streaking, and the ear-coverts are dark brown with streaks of rufous-brown. The forehead, crown and nape are dull chestnut with faintly indicated shaft streaks, and the rump is pale brown with dark shafts and buffy tips to the feathers. The uppertail-coverts are smoky-brown. The underparts are buffy-white with blackish-brown streaks, particularly on the sides of the head, chin, throat and breast. The under-wing-coverts and axillaries are grey-brown with narrow shaft streaks, and the undertail-coverts are white with dusky shaft streaks. The upperwing-coverts, wings and tail are blackish-brown, with pale white or buffy-white margins to the secondaries and tertials; the tail is almost square. The eyes are brown, the bill is black, and the legs and feet are blackish-brown or black. The sexes are alike. The juvenile is duller, with a brownish head, buffy-rufous margins to the feathers of the mantle, scapulars and wing-coverts, and buffy or whitish margins to the feathers of the rump; the throat is more faintly streaked than on the adult, the centres of the crown feathers are dusky, the upper parts of the breast and flanks are light brown, and the tertials have buffy-white tips. There is a single post-breeding moult, which is irregular as there is no fixed breeding season (Vaurie 1951).

Measurements Length 11 cm (4¼"). Wing 89–97 (mean 91.6); tail (square) 40–47 (mean 44); bill 7.2–8.9 (mean 8.3); tarsus 9–10.8 (mean 10.2). Weight 8–12 (mean 9.7).

70 FAIRY MARTIN
Hirundo ariel (Gould)

Plate 23

Collocalia ariel Gould, 1843, Proc. Zool. Soc. Lond., pt. 10 (1842), p. 132: New South Wales.

The Fairy Martin appears to be most closely allied with the Indian Cliff Swallow (69) and has been considered conspecific with it (Vaurie 1951; Hall and Moreau 1970). The plumage, size and shape are similar. Both have a rufous crown and streaked throat, and the same glossy upperparts with a dull rump; the Indian species differs in having a brown rather than a white rump (although the feathers are tipped with white or buff) and more intense streaking. The juveniles are almost identical, with faint streaking, whitish rump, blackish centres to the crown feathers and white-tipped tertials.

FIELD CHARACTERS Fairy Martins have a blue back, pale rump, rufous forehead and crown and buffy-white underparts. The streaking on the underparts is not easily seen in the field. They closely resemble Tree Martins (65), but the latter have a blackish crown. They frequent open country, often near water, and are highly gregarious throughout the year. The flight is weak.

HABITAT Fairy Martins frequent any open country, particularly open woodland, but are often seen near water. They avoid heavily forested areas.

DISTRIBUTION AND POPULATION Fairy Martins are endemic to Australia. They breed mainly in eastern Australia from Port Denison (near Bowen) south to Victoria, South Australia; but also in western Australia, although not in the southwest forested area or (except sporadically) south of Gingin or west of the Great Southern Railway (Blakers *et al.* 1984). In southwestern Australia they are largely replaced by the Tree Martin (Sedgwick 1958). They formerly bred in Tasmania, where nests were recorded in the last century and an unoccupied one was found in 1968 (Vincent

1972), but they no longer do so. The range may be expanding across the Tasman Sea to New Zealand: in the last ten years there have been several sightings of Fairy Martins and possible records of breeding (e.g. Bell 1984; Nevill 1984; Riddell and Taylor 1984). There are no measures of abundance, but the species is widespread and generally common; it is often seen in large flocks or colonies. It suffers competition from House Sparrows, pardalotes and Zebra Finches, and predation by kingfishers which break open the nest (Blakers et al. 1984).

MIGRATION The Fairy Martin shows some post-breeding movements, but not all individuals leave the breeding areas (Blakers et al. 1984). It migrates north to south in eastern Australia. It is common in summer at Murphy's Creek, leaving in April, though a few also overwinter there (Lord 1956). In the southern Murray-Darling region, it arrives in August and leaves in January–March. Numbers increase in winter in Cape York and Atherton regions and around Darwin, decreasing in the southeast although a few are present all year. There seems not to be a regular migration in the southwest region. The longest recorded movement is of 129 km (80 miles) from Waikerie to Salters Springs. It is occasionally recorded in New Guinea and Torres Strait, and there are non-breeding records from the Cape York region and the Top End north of 14°N. It occurs as a vagrant in Tasmania in spring and summer.

FOOD AND BEHAVIOUR The flight is slow and fluttery. It usually feeds in flocks, often high up. The diet consists of a variety of insects taken in flight, but is not known in detail. Fairy Martins have also been recorded perching on a newly cut lawn, eating injured moths (Baldwin 1965). Nesting is colonial: the number of nests is variable and often only a few tens of nests form a colony, but one of the largest known contained 700 (Blakers et al. 1984).

BREEDING The breeding season is from August to January; two or three broods may be reared in a season (Campbell 1901; MacDonald 1973). The natural nest sites are under overhangs on cliffs and rocks, in cave entrances, river banks and in hollows in tree trunks. Nowadays, however, Fairy Martins frequently use artificial structures such as bridges, culverts, pipes, mine shafts, wharves and the eaves or verandahs of buildings, providing they have a clearance of at least 0.4 m (16 in) for the nest (Reilly and Garrett 1973). The nests are clustered together. Adults return to breed in later years at most but not all sites (Lane 1965). The nest is retort-shaped and made of mud pellets: one nest was made of more than 1,000 pellets (Sedgwick 1958). The bowl is more or less round and is about 15 cm (6 in) in diameter, and the tunnel entrance is 5–30 cm (2–12 in) long and curves down at the outer end; the bottom of the bowl is lined with grass and feathers (Serventy and Whittell 1962). The nest can take a week to build. The clutch size is four, sometimes five. The eggs are white, often with reddish-brown specks, and measure 17.5 × 12.5 mm (15.7–19.6 × 11.7–13; weight 1.42).

VOICE The contact call is a short 'chrrr' or 'prrrt-prrrt'. The song is a high-pitched twittering. The calls are more high-pitched than those of the Tree Martin.

DESCRIPTION Fairy Martins are small hirundines. The head from the forehead to the nape is dark rufous-brown with faint black shaft streaks. The face is dark grey-brown. The lores are blackish, and the ear-coverts are dark brown. The mantle, back and scapulars are glossy blue-black, the former lightly streaked with white. The rump is dull white or buffy-white. The uppertail-coverts are dusky grey-brown with buffy-white margins. The underparts are mainly dull white. The chin, throat and upper breast are greyish and finely streaked with black. The flanks, sides, axillaries and underwing-coverts are white, tinged with brown. The undertail-coverts are white with a grey tinge. The upperwing-coverts, wings and slightly forked tail are dull brownish-black. The tertials and secondaries have narrow, pale buffy or white margins. The eyes are dark brown, the bill is black and the legs and feet are blackish-brown. The sexes are alike. Juveniles are duller than adults: the wing-coverts have buffy tips, and the tertials are broadly tipped with buffy-white; the crown is grey with brownish tips, the rump is white with a slight rufous tinge, and the uppertail-coverts are grey with a pale fringe. The underparts are white with a slight rufous tinge, brownish on the upper breast and flanks, and with faint streaks on the throat.

Measurements Length 11 cm (4¼″). Wing 89–95 (mean 91.9); tail 43–52 (mean 47.6); fork 4–9 (mean 6.5); bill 7.1–8.8 (mean 7.8); tarsus 9.8–10.8 (mean 10.2). Weight 9.1–14 (mean 11.2).

71 FOREST CLIFF SWALLOW

Plate 21

Hirundo fuliginosa (Chapin)
Alternative name: Dusky Cliff Swallow

Lecythoplastes fuliginosa Chapin, 1925, Ibis, p. 149: Lolodorf, southern Cameroon.

The affinities of this poorly known species are not clear. It differs in several respects from the other cliff swallows (Earlé 1987e). It lacks any iridescent feathers on the mantle or any red in the plumage apart from a rufous tinge to the throat, and the rump is concolorous with the back; the bill also differs in shape. Its eggs are usually white, not spotted, and it appears not to breed colonially. In addition, though the nest is like that of cliff swallows, the spout of the nest is longer (RA Earlé, pers. comm.). Some of these differences, such as the dark coloration and solitary breeding, may just be local adaptations to the forest environment. Earlé (1987e), however, suggested that it is not a cliff swallow, although it probably does belong to the genus *Hirundo*. It has also been suggested that this species is related to the *Phedina* group (African martins), but it differs in habits and in the proportion and shape of the wings and tail, and this seems less likely than a relationship with the cliff swallows.

FIELD CHARACTERS The Forest Cliff Swallow is blackish-brown with a green sheen. It is almost identical to the Square-tailed Rough-winged Swallow (34), but lacks the serrations on the wings and has a stouter bill, a brighter throat and a slightly more forked tail. In the field the two are very difficult to tell apart. It occurs in forests and is usually seen alone or in small groups.

HABITAT These are typically forest swallows; they have been seen in clearings and around villages (Bannerman 1951). They appear unafraid of humans, and are known to enter inhabited buildings through doors and windows in order to build nests.

DISTRIBUTION AND POPULATION The Forest Cliff Swallow has a very restricted range, in the lowland forests of Cameroon, equatorial Guinea and Gabon (Hall and Moreau 1970). It appears to be rare, but its status is unclear as it has probably often been misidentified as a rough-winged swallow. Although it was described as a new species only in 1925, Bates (1909) for example recorded a small dark swallow, said to build mud nests, that may have been this species.

MIGRATION The movements of this swallow are not well known, and it is probably largely sedentary. However, it may make local movements and birds on passage have been recorded very irregularly in northeastern Gabon in January, March and July (Brosset and Erard 1986).

BEHAVIOUR Forest Cliff Swallows hawk for insects in open areas of the forest and in grassy clearings, and have been seen in company with other swallows such as the Square-tailed Roughwing (Bannerman 1951). The diet is not known in detail, but consists of insects caught in flight. This species appears to nest solitarily, but few nest records are available. Serle (1954) recorded a pair courting in March: the pair billed for several seconds while singing. He also noted a pair roosting on the wall of a verandah. Individuals also roost in nests; on at least two occasions four were recorded roosting in a single nest during the nest-building stage (Chapin 1948).

BREEDING Breeding has been recorded in January, April–June and in November (Earlé 1987e). Eggs are known from April to June and young in January and November. Known nest sites are under boulders and overhanging rocks, in caves, buildings or verandahs, where the nest is plastered to the roof or ceiling (Chapin 1948; Bannerman 1951; Serle 1954; RA Earlé, pers. comm.); hollows in trees are probably also used. The nest is retort-shaped, with a long entrance spout; it is made of mud pellets and lined with vegetable fibres. Serle (1954) noted one nest, on the roof of a cave, which had two short entrance funnels diametrically opposite each other. Both sexes build; one nest took two weeks to construct (Chapin 1948). The clutch size is two or three eggs, which are white and measure 18.3×12.9 mm ($17.0–19.0 \times 12.5–13.1$); Serle (1954) stated that the eggs sometimes have a few orange-brown speckles. The incubation and nestling periods have not been recorded.

Good (cited in Chapin 1948) described the birds as uttering a lisping call.

DESCRIPTION The Forest Cliff Swallow is a small drab hirundine. The crown is black with a dull metallic sheen, paling to black-brown on the lores, ear-coverts, the sides of the head and the neck. The rest of the upperparts, including the wings and tail, are blackish-brown with a faint oily-green sheen; the sheen is strongest on the mantle. The chin and throat have a rusty tinge, the feathers being dark at the base with rufous tips. The rest of the underparts are dark brown, a little paler than the back, but the underwing-coverts and axillaries are darker blackish-brown. The tail is very slightly forked and lacks any white patches. The eyes are brown, the legs and feet are pinkish-brown with yellowish soles, and the bill is blackish-brown above and paler brown below. The sexes are similar, but the female has little or no rufous on the throat. Juveniles are similar to adults, with scarcely any rufous on the throat.

Measurements Length 11\cm (4¼"). Wing 85–96 (mean 88.6); tail 42–49 (mean 44.8); fork 4–6 (mean 5.6); bill 7.4–9 (mean 8.3); tarsus 9.6–11 (mean 10.5).

72 HOUSE MARTIN
Delichon urbica (Linnaeus)

Plate 24

Hirundo urbica Linnaeus, 1758, Syst. Nat., ed. 10, p. 192: Sweden.

Delichon urbica lagopoda (Pallas), 1811, Dauria.

FIELD CHARACTERS The combination of blue upperparts, white underparts and a white rump distinguishes this species from other swallows in the breeding range. In Africa, juveniles may be confused with Grey-rumped Swallows (36), but have a paler rump and less deeply forked tail. The House Martin frequents open country, including mountainous areas, and also urban areas. It is highly gregarious throughout the year. When feeding, it flies slowly, often very high up.

HABITAT House Martins frequent open areas such as cultivated land, but penetrate more into rocky mountainous regions up to 2000–3000 m (6600–9900 ft) and are more of an urban dweller, breeding in villages, towns and cities. Colonies are usually near waterbodies or vegetation cover, especially deciduous trees, which provide a good source of insect food (Bouldin 1968; Turner 1982a). In Britain, densities are highest in mixed farmland and lowest in moorland areas. Some natural colonies occur, mainly on cliffs in coastal areas, but most are on human artefacts (Cramp 1988).

DISTRIBUTION AND POPULATION House Martins breed throughout Eurasia to the Arctic Circle, and south to North Africa, Asia Minor, Mongolia and Manchuria (Glutz von Blotzheim and Bauer 1985; Cramp 1988). The nominate race *urbica* breeds in Europe and western Asia from about 71°N in Scandinavia to about 62°N in Siberia, east to the Yenisei, central Mongolia, the Tien Shan and the western Himalayas, and south to the Iberian peninsula, the Mediterranean (including northwestern Africa), Asia Minor, northwestern India, and since the 1970s in Israel; breeding in Iceland, the Faroes and Malta is sporadic. There are also several records of its breeding in the wintering grounds in South Africa and Namibia. The race *lagopoda* breeds in eastern Asia from the upper Yenisei, northeast through the middle Lena and Yana valleys to the Kolyma delta, south to northern Mongolia, central Manchuria, the middle Amur and northern China.

House Martins are common in much of their range, taking advantage of artificial structures for nesting. Locally, population sizes tend to fluctuate, and declines in large colonies have often been noted; recent declines have been particularly marked in the Netherlands (Cramp 1988). Bad weather, and the consequent scarcity of food, during the breeding season and on migration have had major effects on populations (Glutz von Blotzheim and Bauer 1985). Air pollution also has an adverse effect; in Britain a reduction in pollution since the Clean Air Act of 1956 has allowed House Martins to spread into the heart of cities such as London (Cramp and Gooders 1967). The development of new housing estates and other buildings has also provided new nest sites and allowed populations to expand. On a more local scale, House Martins can suffer from competition with House Sparrows, which damage or take over nests and attack adults, eggs and young; Lind (1962) blamed House Sparrows for declines in colonies in Finland. Some mortality in farmyard colonies has been associated with the use of fungicides or pesticides (e.g. Oliver 1975). House Martins usually suffer little interference from humans, but the accumulation of faeces under colonies can be a nuisance and nests are sometimes removed because of this. There have been many estimates of population sizes and densities in Europe (see Glutz von Blotzheim and Bauer 1985; Cramp 1988); in Britain and Ireland, the population size is 300,000–600,000 pairs, with densities of two to five pairs per km^2 in rural areas (Sharrock 1976).

MIGRATION The winter range covers Africa south of the Sahara, India and southeast Asia (see Glutz von Blotzheim and Bauer 1985 and Cramp 1988 for summaries). The nominate race winters predominantly throughout Africa south of the Sahara, but there are also winter records from India, mainly on the western side (Ali and Ripley 1972). The eastern race winters in southern China, Burma, Thailand and Indochina, and has been recorded in Sakhalin in Japan. A few House Martins winter in North Africa, and there are occasional winter records in Europe, including Britain. The autumn migration takes place on a broad front south through Europe and Asia to the winter quarters; the peak of migration is from the end of August to the beginning of October in western and central Europe, later in southern parts of the range. The main return to the breeding grounds is in April and May. In its winter quarters this species is usually seen in small flocks; it is a less conspicuous winter visitor than the Barn Swallow, partly because it is more nomadic and flies at greater heights (it is seen commonly only in highland areas of eastern Africa: Britton 1980). Vagrant House Martins are known over a wide area, including the Azores, Bermuda, Ascension Island, Cape Verde Islands, South Georgia, Nepal, Maldives, Iceland, Greenland, and western Alaska.

FORAGING AND FOOD The flight is slow, consisting mainly of gliding rather than flapping. House Martins usually fly high, at an average of 21 m (70 ft) above the ground when breeding, lower in wet weather (Bryant 1973), catching aerial insects on the wing. Exceptionally, they will perch on trees or walls to pick up insects, and have been recorded taking caterpillars hanging by threads from trees (Cramp 1988). They will follow ploughs and large animals to feed on the insects disturbed, but rarely visit grass fires. They feed in small groups up to about 2 km (1¼ miles) from the nest when breeding, though on average feed about 450 m (500 yds) away (Bryant and Turner 1982); the hunting grounds are often over open ground or water, the latter especially in bad weather. On the wintering grounds they feed even higher, at over 50 m (165 ft) on average (Waugh 1978).

There have been several studies of the diet of nestling House Martins (e.g. von Gunten 1961; Bryant 1973; Kožená 1975; and see Menzel 1984; Glutz von Blotzheim and Bauer 1985; Cramp 1988). House Martins take smaller prey than do Barn Swallows, the main items being aphids, midges and other small flies: in one study in Switzerland, for example, 33% of the nestlings' diet consisted of aphids and 45% consisted of small flies, mainly Brachycera and Nematocera (von Gunten 1961), and in the USSR (near Moscow) aphids and flies also predominate (Arkhipenko et al. 1968). Small numbers of other insects, such as beetles, parasitic wasps, stoneflies, mayflies, moths, lacewings, caddisflies, as well as some spiders, are also taken. The types of insect eaten vary during the breeding season: for example, in England, aphids make up half the diet in May and small flies make up three-quarters late in the season (Bryant 1975). In a study in Poland (Kozena 1975), aphids and other plant bugs made up 58% of the diet and flies 31% in July, while in August 48% consisted of flies and 25% plant bugs. The adults bring back several dozen insects at a time for the nestlings. The adults' diet is less well known, but includes aphids, beetles, small flies and other small insects. On the wintering grounds they also take flying ants (Chapin 1953).

SOCIAL ORGANISATION This species is colonial, often breeding in groups of tens or sometimes hundreds of nests, although the average group size is four or five and occasionally pairs nest singly (Lind 1960; Cramp 1988). There are records of colonies of thousands of nests. Town colonies are usually smaller than ones in farms and villages or on cliffs. When not breeding, they will form flocks of several hundred birds.

SOCIOSEXUAL BEHAVIOUR Males tend to arrive at the colony first. Typically the male occupies an old nest or selects a nest site and guards it; he holds his wings open and drooped and ruffles his flank feathers (Lind 1960). If an intruder approaches, the resident bird utters a threat note and ruffles his head feathers. There are frequent disputes over building materials. Intruders are pecked at, and a chase or fight may ensue. Pairs usually form before nest-building starts, and may form on migration (von Gunten 1963). The male leads a potential mate to the nest site while uttering contact calls, then alights and utters enticement calls (Lind 1960); the female may hover at the site or at a different one. If the latter, the male tries to coax her back; this coaxing can continue for several hours, and the male and female are often aggressive to one another in the early stages of pair-formation. Copulation usually takes place in the nest. The male often sings in flight, then lands and solicits the female by crouching and approaching her; in this display his head is lowered, the throat and rump feathers are ruffled, the wings are held open and drooping and sometimes vibrated, and the tail is fanned. If the female is ready to mate, she calls and allows the male to hold her nape or crown and to mount (Lind 1960).

The older birds are the first to arrive at the colony, usually occupying old nests, and they also lay early (Rheinwald et al. 1976). First-years usually build new nests, have smaller clutches and less often have a second brood (Bryant 1979; Hund and Prinzinger 1985). Few females return to their natal place to breed; most settle several kilometres away. Young males disperse less far, however, and many breed where they were hatched (Hund and Prinzinger 1979b). Adults generally use the same breeding site each year, though rarely with the same mate, and females are more likely than males to move elsewhere (von Gunten 1963). Within a season they will change their nest site or mate if a brood is unsuccessful, though again males are more faithful to their site than are females (Hund and Prinzinger 1979b).

BREEDING The breeding season is generally between May and August, earlier in the south of the range than in the north (Glutz von Blotzheim and Bauer 1985; Cramp 1988). Martins in North Africa start laying at the end of March or in April, those in Lapland in the middle of June. There are sometimes still nestlings present in September or mid October in northwestern and central Europe. Two broods are often reared, but only one in the extreme northern and southern parts of the range, and very occasionally three are attempted (Lind 1960). Natural nest sites are cliff faces, rock clefts, and occasionally caves and trees. These were still used widely at the beginning of the 20th century, but nowadays most nests are on the outer walls of buildings or occasionally on bridges, and relatively few cases of cliff breeding are known; the insides of buildings are seldom used. Nests are also occasionally built on other artificial structures, including street lamps and ships. The nest is made of mud pellets and lined with vegetable fibres and feathers; other materials, such as dung or even cement or seaweed, are occasionally included. The shape is variable depending on where the nest is attached, but is often a half to a quarter sphere, with only a narrow entrance near the top and facing away from neighbouring nests; it is usually attached to a vertical face immediately below an overhang, often in the angle between a roof and a wall or above a window, and often contiguous with other nests. Nests are re-used in the same and subsequent years. Both sexes build the nest, collecting mud from up to a few hundred metres from the nest site: they start by building a base, then build up the walls, working from within the structure, and usually take one to two weeks to complete the nest (see Lind 1960 for further details).

The clutch size is usually four or five eggs, but varies between two and six, and it decreases during the season (Bryant 1975; Kondelka 1978; Hund and Prinzinger 1979a; Møller 1984); second clutches are usually of three or four eggs. There is little geographical variation in clutch size, but the size of the second clutch increases with longitude (Møller 1984). The eggs are pure white and average 19.0×13.3 mm (15.9–22.0 $\times$ 11.2–14.7; weight 1.7); they are usually laid at daily intervals, but in bad weather laying can be suspended for a day or more (Hund 1976). The sexes share all parental duties but the female does most of the incubation and brooding. Incubation lasts 14–16 days, but hatching may be delayed by bad weather when the adults leave the eggs unattended for long periods. The eggs often hatch asynchronously

(Bryant 1978a). The nestling period is variable, depending partly on brood size, and may be lengthened by bad weather, but it is usually 22–32 days (Bryant 1978b, 1975; Hund and Prinzinger 1979a). The nestlings come to the nest entrance to beg when about nine days old. When the nestlings are ready to fledge, the parents will hover at the nest entrance and utter contact calls to lure them out (Lind 1960). Once fledged, the young return to the nest for several days to roost and to be fed, and can remain in the colony for several more weeks. They sometimes disperse from where they hatched, before migrating south. Juveniles from the first brood occasionally help to feed their parents' second brood (Menzel 1984).

The hatching rate is high, at about 90%. Fledging success (of eggs laid) depends strongly on local weather conditions, but is generally 60–80% (Balat 1974; Kondelka 1978; Bryant 1988). Bad weather can lead to nestlings dying of starvation, although they may survive for a few days without food as they have large fat reserves and can also become torpid (Prinzinger and Siedle 1986, 1988). Predation and the effects of parasites are generally minor causes of nestling mortality. Adult mortality, which is about 40–60% (Cramp 1988), occurs mainly when the birds are not breeding; females who rear two broods a year survive less well to breed the following year than single-brooded females (Bryant 1979). Most birds breed for only one year, but a few breed for five or six years (Bryant 1988). They rarely live longer than this, but individuals of ten and 14 years have been recorded (Rydzewski 1978).

VOICE The song is a twittering, rather softer and less melodious than that of the Barn Swallow, uttered in flight or at the nest (Lind 1960). There is also a shrill contact call of one or a few syllables, used between members of a pair and by parents to fledging young; it is usually lower-pitched in males than females. A longer version of this call is given on nest relief during incubation. Males give an enticement call, a rapid 'za za za', when attracting a mate. Conspecific intruders at the nest elicit a threat call. There is also a series of warning and alarm calls of increasing pitch (see Cramp 1988).

DESCRIPTION House Martins are medium-sized hirundines. The upperparts, including the forehead, crown, nape, mantle, back and scapulars, are deep glossy blue; white feather bases are sometimes visible on the hindcrown, hindneck, mantle and inner scapulars. The lores and ear-coverts are blackish. The rump and shorter uppertail-coverts are white with indistinct shaft stripes, but the longer tail-coverts are black with a faint blue gloss. The flanks are slightly grey. The underparts are pure white from the cheeks and chin to the undertail-coverts, though the latter have black shaft stripes and are occasionally spotted or dusky. The axillaries and underwing-coverts are a pale smoky colour. The coverts along the leading edge of the wing are black with white tips. The upperwing-coverts, primaries and secondaries are blackish-brown, with a slight blue gloss on the coverts; there are faint white edges to the tips of the secondaries and the tip of the longest fresh tertial has a white fringe. The tail is blackish with a faint gloss, and is moderately forked. In worn plumage, the feather bases are more visible (grey on the crown, rump and chest, white on the neck and mantle), and new grey-brown feathers appear on the rump, chin, throat and chest. The eyes are dark brown, the bill black, and the legs and feet pink with white feathering as far as the toes. The sexes are similar, but the female has greyer underparts, often with grey spots on the undertail-coverts and sometimes on the rump as well. In winter, in both sexes, the cheeks, chin, throat, flanks, rump and shorter tail-coverts are pale grey-brown, but this varies individually. Juveniles are similar but duller, with gloss usually only on the mantle: the chin, throat, breast, flanks and undertail-coverts are pale brownish-buff, and the rest of the underparts are white; the rump and shorter uppertail-coverts are white and the longer uppertail-coverts are brown with white fringes along the tips; the inner primaries and secondaries have narrow white tips, and the tertials have broad ones; the tail is less deeply forked than the adult's. The moult often starts near the breeding grounds with a few body feathers or primaries, but is mostly suspended until the birds reach the tropics. Grey feathers obtained during winter are replaced in spring by white ones.

Measurements Length 13 cm (5"). Wing 105–116 (mean 110.5); tail 56–65 (mean 60.8); fork of male 17–23 (mean 20.2), of female 16–21 (mean 18.6); bill 8.7–10.8 (mean 9.9); tarsus 10.6–12.3 (mean 11.5). Weight 13–23 (mean 18.3).

RACES Individuals in countries around the Mediterranean and in western Asia are smaller and have been described as a separate subspecies, *meridionalis*, but the difference between northern and southern populations is clinal (Vaurie 1951; Loske 1986b). The race *lagopoda* has more extensive white on the lower back, including all the uppertail-coverts, and the depth of the tail fork is intermediate between that of the nominate race and that of the Asian House Martin (73).

HYBRIDISATION Hybrids between House Martins and European Barn Swallows have often been recorded, and individuals are occasionally albinistic (Menzel 1984).

73 ASIAN HOUSE MARTIN
Delichon dasypus (Bonaparte)

Plate 24

Chelidon dasypus 'Temm.' Bonaparte, 1856, Consp. Av., 1, p. 343: Borneo.

Delichon dasypus cashmiriensis (Gould), 1858, Cashmir.

Delichon dasypus nigrimentalis (Hartert), 1910, Kuatun, Fokien.

The Asian and European House Martins (72) are sometimes treated as races of one species because of the similarity in plumage and morphology. The breeding ranges are largely separate, but both breed in the west Himalayas, Khamar-Daban and eastern Sayan, apparently without hybridising (Glutz von Blotzheim and Bauer 1985), suggesting that they are true species. There are also differences in the shape of the nests, in breeding biology and in diet (Durnev *et al.* 1983), although such differences may be racial rather than specific ones.

FIELD CHARACTERS Asian House Martins are very similar to the European species, but the upperparts are darker and less glossy, the streaking on the rump is more distinct, the underparts are washed with a darker grey, the underwing-coverts are darker, and the tail is less deeply forked. The race *lagopoda* of the European House Martin bridges the two species in having a tail fork intermediate between those of nominate House Martin and Asian House Martin. The Asian species frequents mountainous areas and sea-coasts. It is highly gregarious throughout the year. The flight is slow and fluttery.

HABITAT The preferred habitat consists of gorges, valleys and hilly or mountainous areas, or sea-coasts where cliffs and caves are available as nest sites. It also breeds around mountain villages.

DISTRIBUTION AND POPULATION Asian House Martins replace the European species in central and eastern Asia. The nominate race *dasypus* breeds in the southeastern Soviet Union, the Kurile Islands and Japan; it has bred on the eastern coast of Korea, but is now a rare summer visitor there (Gore and Won 1971). The race *cashmiriensis* breeds in the Himalayas from southeastern Afghanistan through central and south Kashmir and Kuman to Sikkim, north to southern Gilgit and Ladak; and in central China, west of 105°E (except in south Shansi) west to Kansu, southeast Tsinghai, Szechwan and south Tibet, and possibly in north Hopeh. The race *nigrimentalis* breeds in southeastern China in the provinces of Fokien and Kwangsi, and in Taiwan. This species is generally locally abundant, but as yet is more restricted to areas with natural cliff nest sites than is the European House Martin. Its range in southern Siberia has expanded recently into the Khamar-Daban region, where it is sympatric with the House Martin (Stepanyan and Vasil'chenko 1980; Durnev *et al.* 1983; Vasil'chenko 1987).

MIGRATION The nominate race *dasypus* migrates through eastern China to winter in small numbers in the Malay peninsula south to Singapore, the Philippines, Borneo, Sumatra and Java, though it is a rare migrant to Indonesia (Medway and Wells 1976; White and Bruce 1986); one has been seen as far as Palau. In Japan, a few remain around the hot springs in mild winters (Austin and Kuroda 1953). It is not usually seen in large flocks in winter and does not join mixed hirundine roosts. The winter range and migratory routes of *nigrimentalis* are unknown, but it is an uncommon visitor to Hong Kong. The race *cashmiriensis* is not a long-distance migrant, but in India and southeast Asia it moves down to lower levels after breeding to avoid the most severe weather (Ali and Ripley 1972); it is also occasionally recorded at this time in the plains of northeastern India, and vagrants turn up further east as far afield as Burma and northern Thailand (Smythies 1953; Deignan 1963).

FOOD AND BEHAVIOUR The behaviour of this martin is not well known, but is probably similar to that of the European House Martin. The flight consists of frequent glides, swoops and banking movements. Like the European species, it feeds high above the ground; loose flocks are often seen with other aerial feeders high above gorges, valleys, terraced fields and forest fires, and also over canals and waterways (Ali and Ripley 1972). The diet consists mainly of small flies (especially nematoceran and brachyceran flies), plant bugs (such as aphids), beetles, and winged ants and other Hymenoptera, including wasps, bees and sawflies (Ali and Ripley 1972; Durnev et al. 1983); butterflies and moths, caddisflies, lacewings, stoneflies and hemipteran bugs are also taken. A few springtails and lepidopteran larvae have been recorded in the diet, suggesting that these martins occasionally pick up food from the ground, perhaps during bad weather (Durnev et al. 1983). Asian House Martins nest in small colonies of a few tens of pairs, occasionally singly; unlike those of the House Martin, the nests often tend to be scattered along a cliff rather than abutting one another (Ali and Ripley 1972). However, closely grouped nests are also built at suitable sites such as deep clefts in rocks (Durnev et al. 1983).

BREEDING The breeding season is May–July in India, April–July in China and March-October in northern parts of the range (Austin and Kuroda 1953; Dementev and Gladkov 1968; Ali and Ripley 1972; Etchécopar and Hüe 1983). Two broods are usual, but the race *cashmiriensis* may have only one a year (Ali and Ripley 1972). Nest sites are usually cliffs or caves, but bridges, houses and, particularly, large buildings such as temples, hotels and power plants are also occasionally used (Baker 1934; Jahn 1942; Bates and Lowther 1952). Asian House Martins, however, are not as closely associated with artificial nest sites as are European House Martins. The nest is a deep bowl made of mud pellets, often mixed with grass, rootlets and moss, and lined mainly with feathers, but also occasionally with pieces of grass, pine needles, leaves, moss, lichen and straw. The shape of the nest, particularly its depth and the diameter of the entrance hole, varies somewhat according to the substrate but, unlike that of the European House Martin, it is often open at the top; open nests resemble structurally those of Barn Swallows (42) but are long and conical at the bottom (Durnev et al. 1983). In Durnev et al.'s study, nearly half the nests were open. The nest is usually built close to an overhanging rock or eave, or in a window corner, with a gap or entrance hole below the roof just large enough for the bird to enter by.

The clutch size is usually three or four throughout the range, but varies from two to six. The eggs are pure white, and average 20.2 × 14.1 mm (19.3–21.1 × 13.7–14.8; weight 2.1). There is some geographical variation: eggs of the race *cashmiriensis* average 17.9 × 12.7 mm, and those of *nigrimentalis* 18.4 × 13.1 mm. Both male and female build the nest, incubate the eggs and feed the nestlings. Incubation and fledging periods are not known, but are probably similar to those of the European House Martin. Fledglings return to the nest for a few nights to roost (Ali and Ripley 1972)

VOICE The calls are similar to those of the European House Martin, including a soft twittering song and a shrill flight call (Jahn 1942).

DESCRIPTION Asian House Martins are small hirundines. The forehead, crown, nape, mantle, back and scapulars are glossy blue-black, though less glossy than the European House Martin. The lores and ear-coverts are blackish, the black of the lores extending along the base of the lower mandible to the chin. The rump and shorter uppertail-coverts are white; the longer uppertail-coverts are black with a faint blue gloss. The underparts are white from the cheeks and chin to the vent; the white portions of the plumage have a smoky-grey wash, and the feathers have slightly indicated dark shaft streaks. The axillaries and underwing-coverts are dark grey-brown. The undertail-coverts vary from grey with white edges of the longest to darker grey with dusky centres of the shorter. The wings and tail are blackish-brown with a slight blue sheen, and the tail is very slightly forked. The bill is black, the legs and feet are pink and are covered with white feathers reaching to the toes, and the eyes are dark brown. The sexes are alike. The juvenile has a white rump, sometimes with a pale vinaceous wash, dark brown upperparts, including the wings and tail, with a slight gloss on the mantle and scapulars; the underparts are grey-white, sometimes with a pale vinaceous wash; the outer tail feathers are less deeply forked than on the adult.

Measurements Length 12 cm (4¾"). Wing 105–112 (mean 108.1); tail 42–53 (mean 47.7); fork 3–9 (mean 5.1); bill 7.8–9.9 (mean 8.7); tarsus 10.2–11.8 (mean 11.0). Weight 18.

RACES The race *cashmiriensis* has brighter blue upperparts and whiter rump and underparts than nominate *dasypus*, and is intermediate in coloration between it and the European House Martin. It is intermediate in size between *dasypus* and the third, smallest race *nigrimentalis* (*cashmiriensis* wing 98–109; *nigrimentalis* wing 97–105); *cashmiriensis* also often lacks the narrow extension of the lores to the chin.

74 NEPAL HOUSE MARTIN   Plate 24
Delichon nipalensis Horsfield and Moore

Delichon nipalensis Horsfield and Moore, 1854 (Nov.), Cat. Birds Mus. Hon. E. I. Co., 1 (1856), p. 384: Nepal.

Delichon nipalensis cuttingi Mayr, 1941, Gangfang, 5500 ft, near the Burma-Yunnan border.

FIELD CHARACTERS Nepal House Martins are similar to the European and Asian forms (72, 73), but differ in having a black or blackish throat, more extensive blue-black on the head, black undertail-coverts and dark terminal bands on the uppertail-coverts, and a distinctly square tail. Hence, the white 'rump' is narrow, and the black tail base looks square. The broken white collar is very narrow and is not easily seen in the field. They frequent mountainous areas and are highly gregarious. The flight is fast compared with that of the House Martin.

HABITAT The Nepal House Martin breeds at between 1000 and 4000 m (3300–13,200 ft), but mostly between 1000 and 3000 m (3300–9900 ft), in river valleys and wooded mountain ridges with cliffs. It moves down to about 350 m (1150 ft) in the non-breeding season (Ali and Ripley 1972).

DISTRIBUTION AND POPULATION This martin has a restricted range, overlapping that of the Asian House Martin, but is not found only in Nepal (Vaurie 1951; Ali and Ripley 1972; Inskipp and Inskipp 1986). The nominate race *nipalensis* is resident in the Himalayas from Garhwal through Nepal to Arunachal Pradesh, northeastern India and Bangladesh to the Arakan Mountains in western Burma. The race *cuttingi* is found only in northern Burma and the Burma-Yunnan border, and in northern Tonkin. In Nepal this species is fairly common (Inskipp and Inskipp 1986), but it is locally distributed, depending on the availability of natural cliff nest sites.

MIGRATION This species is resident, and individuals can be seen around the nesting colonies throughout the year, using their nests for roosting (Stresemann and Stresemann 1969). It is, however, subject to some local movement, mainly between altitudes, sometimes moving to lower altitudes when not breeding and sometimes making sporadic appearances and disappearances (Ali and Ripley 1972). A small flock of 30 birds has also been seen in the non-breeding season in north-central Thailand, where it may be a winter visitor (Tye and Tye 1986).

FOOD AND BEHAVIOUR The flight is fast, with many glides, swoops and tight turns. These martins feed in scattered flocks often high in the air, climbing and diving, hawking along ridges or cliffs or skimming the tree-tops and bushes. They feed on small aerial insects. The diet is not well known, but it includes dipteran flies (Ali and Ripley 1972). They sometimes join flocks of other aerial feeders such as the Himalayan Swiftlet *Collocalia grevirostris* (Stanford and Mayr 1941). They are gregarious, nesting colonially (often 25–50 together), although not usually with the nests touching each other (Ali and Ripley 1972). Several different clusters of nests may be present on a cliff: Baker (1934) recorded an instance of about 3,000 nests on a cliff, in three main and several small colonies; there were about 700 nests in each of the main colonies.

BREEDING The breeding season is March–July in Nepal, April–July in India, and from April–May in Burma, the peak periods varying with locality and altitude (Ali and Ripley 1972; Smythies 1953). Two broods a year are normal, laid in March/April and June (Ali and Ripley 1972). Nest sites are nearly always on vertical cliffs under an overhang (Ali and Ripley 1972); nests on artificial structures are rare, although Baker (1934) recorded a case of three nests in one house attached to a wooden beam. The nest is a deep bowl of mud pellets, deeply lined with fine grass and feathers, with a gap or a small entrance hole near the top. The clutch size is three or four, rarely five. The white, unmarked, eggs are smaller than those of the European House Martin, measuring 18.6 × 12.8 mm (17.2–20.0 × 11.3–13.4; weight 1.6). Both sexes build the nest, incubate the eggs and feed the young. The incubation and fledging periods are unknown, but are probably similar to those of the European and Asian House Martins.

VOICE These are usually silent birds. They sometimes utter a short, high-pitched 'chi-i' in flight (Lister 1954).

DESCRIPTION The Nepal House Martin is a small hirundine. The forehead, crown, nape, mantle, back and scapulars are glossy blue-black. The lores and ear-coverts are black. The blue-black on the sides of the head extends to below the eyes — further down than in the other house martins. The rump is pure white, and the uppertail-coverts are white with black bands. There is a broken white collar on the back of the neck. The chin and throat are black; the undertail-coverts are glossy black; the underwing-coverts are dark grey-brown; and the rest of the underparts are pure white. The wings and tail are brownish-black with a faint blue sheen, and the tail is square. The legs and feet are a pale brownish-flesh colour and are covered with white feathers; the eyes are brown and the bill is black. The sexes are similar, but females tend to have less and greyer black on the throat, and greyer underparts. Juveniles are less glossy, with less black on the throat, and the white underparts are washed with buff. The primary moult is unusually protracted, starting in August/September and continuing through the next breeding season; it is interrupted only during the coldest months (mid November to mid March: Stresemann and Stresemann 1969).

Measurements Length 13 cm (5"). Wing 90–98 (mean 95.7); tail (square) 36–41 (mean 38.5); bill 7.1–8.9 (mean 7.9); tarsus 10.2–12 (mean 11.2). Weight 14–16.

RACES The race *cuttingi* is larger (wing 99–106) and has more black on the throat than the nominate race. The difference in throat colour, however, is clinal, from the western Himalayas, where the birds have a faint black throat or the black is confined to the chin, to Burma, where the black covers the whole throat (Vaurie 1951).

BIBLIOGRAPHY

Abdulali, H (1975) On the validity of *Riparia riparia indica* Ticehurst and extension of range of *Riparia riparia ijimae* (Lonnberg). *J. Bombay Nat. Hist. Soc.* 72: 853–4.

Adams, W, and Templeton, R (1979) Ornithology. In: *Cambridge Expedition to Tierra del Fuego 1977*. Unpublished Report. pp. 32–53. Cambridge University.

Alerstam, T, and Enckell, P H (1979) Unpredictable habitats and evolution of bird migration. *Oikos* 33: 228–32.

Ali, S, and Ripley, S D (1972) *Handbook of the Birds of India and Pakistan. Vol. 5.* Oxford University Press, Oxford.

Allan, D (1986) The Blue Swallow, next bird for extinction. *Quagga* 15: 27–9.

—— (1988) The Blue Swallow in with a chance. *Quagga* 22: 5–7.

Allen, E F (1948) Nidification and other field notes on some Malayan birds. *Malay Nat. J.* 3: 82–6.

Allen, R W, and Nice, M M (1952) A study of the breeding biology of the Purple Martin. *Am. Midl. Nat.* 47: 606–65.

Amadon, D, and Eckelberry, D R (1955) Observations on Mexican birds. *Condor* 57: 65–80.

Anon. (1987) Future of the Blue Swallow now assured. *Bokmakierie* 39: 122.

AOU (1983) *The Checklist of North American Birds. 6th edn.* American Ornithologists' Union, Baltimore.

Aravena, K O (1928) Notas sobre la alimentación de las aves. *Hornero* 4: 38–49, 153–66.

Arbib, R (1979) The blue list for 1980. *Am. Birds* 33: 830–5.

Arkhipenko, E V, Panov, E N, and Rasnicyn, A P (1968) Comparative analysis of the trophic relations of co-existing *Delichon urbica urbica* and *Hirundo rustica rustica*. *Probl. evoljucii TI Novosibirsk, 'Nauka'* 208–11.

Asbirk, S (1976) Studies on the breeding biology of the Sand Martin in artificial nest sites. *Vidensk. Medd. dansk naturh. Foren.* 139: 147–77.

Ash, J S (1969) Spring weights of trans-Saharan migrants in Morocco. *Ibis* 111: 1–10.

—— (1983) Over fifty additions to birds to the Somalia list including two hybrids, together with notes from Ethiopia and Kenya. *Scopus* 7: 54–79.

——, **and Miskell, J E** (1983). Birds of Somalia, their habitat, status and distribution. *Scopus Special Suppl.* 1 EANHS, Nairobi.

Ashford, R W (1968) Preuss's Cliff Swallow, *L. preussi*, breeding in western Nigeria. *Bull. Niger. Orn. Soc.* 5: 42–4.

Ashton, C B (1986) Welcome Swallow breeding in a Fairy Martin nest. *Aust. Bird Watcher* 11: 210–11.

Aspinwall, D R (1972) Greater Striped Swallow records from southern Zambia. *Bull. Zambian Orn. Soc.* 4: 21.

—— (1979) Movement analysis charts. *Zambian Orn. Soc. Newsletter* 72–4, 168–9.

—— (1980) Movement analysis charts. *Zambian Orn. Soc. Newsletter* 59–60, 130–2, 147–8, 166–7.

—— (1981) Movement analysis charts. *Zambian Orn. Soc. Newsletter* 149–50.

—— (1982) Movement analysis charts. *Zambian Orn. Soc. Newsletter* 102–3, 118–20, 149–50.

—— (1983) Movement analysis charts. *Zambian Orn. Soc. Newsletter* 5–6.

Austin, O L, Jr, and Kuroda, N (1953) Birds of Japan: their status and distribution. *Bull. Comp. Mus. Zool. Harv.* 109: 280–637.

Baepler, D H (1962) The avifauna of the Soloma region in Huehuetenango, Guatemala. *Condor* 64: 140–53.

Baker, J K (1962) Associations of Cave Swallows with Cliff and Barn Swallows. *Condor* 64: 326.

Baker, S (1934) *Nidification of the Birds of the Indian Empire. Vol. 3.* Taylor & Francis, London.

Balat, F (1974) Gelegrösse, Höhe der Brutverluste und Bruterfolg bei der Mehlschwalbe. *Zool. Listy* 23: 343–56.

——, **and Gonzalez, H** (1982) Concrete data on the breeding of Cuban birds. *Acta. Sc. Nat. Brno* 16: 1–46.

Baldwin, M (1965) Birds eating charcoal. *Emu* 64: 208.

Ball, G F (1983) Functional incubation in male Barn Swallows. *Auk* 100: 997–8.

Bangs, O, and Penard T E (1918) Notes on a collection of Surinam birds. *Bull. Mus. Comp. Zool. Harv.* 62: 83.

Bannerman, D A (1939) *The Birds of Tropical West Africa. Vol. 2.* Oliver & Boyd, Edinburgh.

—— (1951) *The Birds of Tropical West Africa. Vol. 8.* The Crown Agents for the Colonies, London.

—— (1953) *Birds of West and Equatorial Africa. Vol. 2.* Oliver & Boyd, Edinburgh.

——, **and Bates, G L** (1926) On some birds of Adamawa and New Cameroon. *Ibis* XII(2): 783–802.

Barré, N, and Barau, C A (1982) *Oiseaux de la Réunion.* Imprimerie Arts Graphiques Modernes, St-Dénis, Reunion.

Basilio, A (1963) *Aves de la Isla de Fernando Poo.* Editorial Coculsa, Madrid.

Bates, G L (1909) Field notes on the birds of Southern Kamerun, West Africa. *Ibis* IX: 28–9.

—— (1930) *Handbook of the Birds of West Africa.* John Bale, Sons and Danielson, London.

—— (1936) Birds in Jidda and central Arabia collected in 1934 and early in 1935, chiefly by Mr Philby. *Ibis* 13, 531–56, 674–712.

Bates, R S P, and Lowther, E H N (1952) *Breeding Birds of Kashmir.* Oxford University Press, Oxford.

Beal, F E L (1907) Birds of California in relation to the fruit industry, pt. 1. *US Dept. Agric. Biol. Surv. Bull.* 30.

—— (1918) Food habits of the swallows, a family of valuable native birds. *Bull. U.S. Dept. Agric.* 619.

Beatty, H A, and Danforth, S T (1931) Puerto Rican Ornithological Records. *J. Dept. Agric. Puerto Rico* 15: 33–106.

Beebe, W (1924) *Galapagos: World's End.* Putnam & Witherby, London.

Beecher, I M, and Beecher, M D (1983) Sibling recognition in Bank Swallows (*Riparia riparia*). *Z. Tierpsychol.* 62: 145–50.

Beecher, M D, and Beecher, I M (1979) Sociobiology of Bank Swallows: reproductive strategy of the male. *Science* 205: 1282–5.

——, **Beecher, I M, and Lumpkin, S** (1981a) Parent-offspring recognition in Bank Swallows: I. Natural history. *Anim. Behav.* 29: 86–94.

——, **Beecher, I M, and Nichols, S H** (1981b) Parent-offspring recognition in Bank Swallows: II. Development and acoustic basis. *Anim. Behav.* 29: 95–101.

——, **Medvin, M B, Stoddard, P K, and Loesche, P** (1986) Acoustic adaptations for parent-offspring recognition in swallows. *Exp. Biol.* 45: 179–83.

Beecher, W J (1953) A phylogeny of the oscines. *Auk* 70: 270–333.

Beehler, B M, Pratt, T K, and Zimmerman, D A (1986) *Birds of New Guinea.* Princeton University Press, Princeton.

Beesley, J S S (1972) Birds of the Arusha National Park, Tanzania. *J. E. Afr. Nat. Hist. Soc. and Natn. Mus.* 132: 1–32.

Behle, W H (1976) Systematic review, intergradation and clinal variation in Cliff Swallows. *Auk* 93: 66–77.

—— (1985) *Utah Birds: Geographic Distribution and Systematics.* Utah Museum of Natural History, Salt Lake City.

Belcher, C F (1941) Birds of a Kenya Highland District. *Ostrich* 11: 75–96.

Bell, B D (1979) Tree Martins nesting in buildings. *Aust. Bird Watcher* 8: 102.

—— (1984) The Fairy Martin, *Petrochelidon ariel*, in New Zealand. *Notornis* 31: 172–3.

Belton, W (1985) Birds of Rio Grande do Sul, Brazil. Part 2. Formicariidae through Corvidae. *Bull. Am. Mus. Nat. Hist.* 180: 1–241.

Benson, C W (1942) A new species and ten new races from southern Abyssinia. *Bull. Brit. Orn. Club* 63: 8–19.

—— (1944) The Madagascar Martin from Nyasaland. *Bull. Brit. Orn. Club* 65: 4–5.

—— (1946) On the birds of southern Abyssinia. *Ibis* 88: 287–306.

—— (1949) Systematics and migration of the Pearl-breasted Swallow. *Ostrich* 20: 137–43.

—— (1951) Breeding and other notes from Nyasaland and the Lundaza district of northern Rhodesia. *Bull. Mus. Comp. Zool. Harv.* 106: 69–114.

—— (1953) *A Checklist of the Birds of Nyasaland.* Nyasaland Society, Blantyre.

—— (1961) The African rough-winged swallows. *Bull. Brit. Orn. Club* 81: 27–33.

—— (1980) Man-induced changes in Malawi birds. *Proc. IV Pan Afr. Orn. Congr.* 373–81.

—— (1982) Migrants in the Afrotropical region south of the equator. *Ostrich* 53: 31–49.

——, **and Benson, F M** (1977) *The Birds of Malawi.* Mountford Press, Limbe, Malawi.

——, **Brooke, R K, Dowsett, R J, and Irwin, M P S** (1971) *The Birds of Zambia.* Collins, London.

——, **Colebrook-Robjent, J F R, and Williams, A** (1976) Contribution à l'ornithologie de Madagascar. *L'Oiseau* 46: 368–86.

——, and Pitman, C R S (1957) Some breeding records from Northern Rhodesia. *Ibis* 30: 7–11, 21–7, 37–43.

Bent, A C (1942) Life histories of North American flycatchers, larks, swallows and their allies. *Bull. U.S. Natn. Mus.* 179: 1–555.

Berlioz, J (1946) *Oiseaux de la Réunion*. Librairie LaRose, Paris.

Betts, F N (1952) The breeding seasons of birds in the hills of southern India. *Ibis* 94: 621–8.

Bitterbaum, E J (1986) The comparative behavior of three species of swallows (Genus *Progne*). Ph.D. thesis, University of Florida.

Blake, C H (1948) The flight of swallows. *Auk* 65: 54–62.

—— (1953) Notes on the Rough-winged Swallow. *Bird-banding* 24: 107–8.

Blakers, M, Davies, S J J F, and Reilly, P N (1984) *The Atlas of Australian Birds*. Melbourne University Press, Carlton.

Bond, J (1928) The distribution and habits of the birds of the republic of Haiti. *Proc. Acad. Nat. Sci. Phil.* 80: 483–521.

—— (1936) *Checklist of the Birds of the West Indies*. Philadelphia National Academy of Sciences.

—— (1943) Nidification of the passerine birds of Hispaniola. *Wilson Bull.* 55: 115–25.

—— (1971) Supplement to the Checklist of the Birds of the West Indies. *Phil. Natn. Acad. Sci.* 16: 6–7.

—— (1985) *Birds of the West Indies – Greater Antilles, Lesser Antilles and Bahama Islands*. 5th edn. Collins, London.

Bouldin, L E (1968) The population of the House Martin in East Lancashire. *Bird Study* 15: 135–46.

Bowen, P St J B (1983) Some observations on the Black-and-rufous Swallow, *Hirundo nigrorufa*, in Zambia. *Bull. Zambian Orn. Soc.* 13: 15–23.

——, and Colebrook-Robjent, J F R (1984) The nests and eggs of the black-and-rufous Swallow, *Hirundo nigrorufa*. *Bull. Brit. Orn. Club* 104: 146–7.

Britton, P L (1980) *Birds of East Africa, their Habitat, Status and Distribution*. EANHS, Nairobi.

Broadbent, J (1969) A note on the Preuss's Cliff Swallow, *Lecythoplastes preussi*, at Oyo new Reservoir. *Bull. Nigerian Orn. Soc.* 6: 34.

Brock, B J (1978) Unusual feeding behaviour of swallows. *South Aust. Orn.* 27: 288.

Brodkorb, P (1942) Notes on some races of the Rough-winged Swallow. *Condor* 44: 214–7.

Broekhuysen, G J (1960) Larger Stripe-breasted Swallow *Cecropis cucullata* feeding on vegetable matter. *Ostrich* 31: 26.

—— (1974) Third report on migration in Southern Africa. *Ostrich* 45: 235–50.

——, and Stanford, W P (1954) Display in the South African Sand Martin. *Ostrich* 25: 99–100.

Brooke, R K (1958) Incubation and nestling periods revealed by Rhodesian nest record cards. *Ostrich* 29: 133–6.

—— (1972) Generic limits in Old World Apodidae and Hirundinidae. *Bull. Brit. Orn. Club* 92: 53–7.

—— (1974) Nomenclatural notes on and the type localities of some taxa in the Apodidae and Hirundinidae (Aves). *Durban Mus. Nov.* 10: 127–37.

—— (1975) *Cotyle paludibula* Rüppell, 1835. *Bull. Brit. Orn. Club* 95: 90–1.

—— (1984) South African Red Data Book – Birds. *S. Afr. Nat. Sci. Prog. Rpt.* 97: 1–213.

——, and Vernon, J C (1961) Aspects of the breeding biology of the Rock Martin. *Ostrich* 32: 51–2.

Brosset, A, and Erard, C (1977) New faunistic records from Gabon. *Bull. Brit. Orn. Club* 97: 125–32.

——, —— (1986) *Les Oiseaux des Régions Forestieres du Nord-est du Gabon. I*. Société Nationale de Protection de la Nature, Paris.

Brown, C R (1978a) Clutch size and reproductive success of adult and subadult Purple Martins. *Southwest. Nat.* 23: 597–604.

—— (1978b) Double-broodedness in Purple Martins in Texas. *Wilson Bull.* 90: 239–47.

—— (1978c) Post-fledging behavior of Purple Martins. *Wilson Bull.* 90: 376–85.

—— (1978d) Sexual chase in Purple Martins. *Auk* 95: 588–90.

—— (1979a) Territoriality in the Purple Martin. *Wilson Bull.* 91: 583–91.

—— (1979b) Chick recognition in Purple Martins. *Southwest. Nat.* 24: 683–5.

—— (1980) Sleeping behavior of Purple Martins. *Condor* 82: 170–5.

—— (1981a) Impact of Starlings on Purple Martin populations in unmanaged colonies. *Am. Birds* 35: 266–8.

—— (1981b) Purple Martin feeding on cicadas. *Southwest Nat.* 25: 553.

—— (1983) Vocalizations and behavior of Violet-green Swallows in the Chiricahua mountains, Arizona. *Wilson Bull.* 95: 142–5.

—— (1984a) Light-breasted Purple Martins dominate dark-breasted birds in a roost: implications for female mimicry. *Auk* 101: 162–4.

—— (1984b) Vocalizations of the Purple Martin. *Condor* 86: 433–42.

—— (1985a) The costs and benefits of coloniality in the Cliff Swallow. Ph.D. thesis, Princeton University.

—— (1985b) Vocalizations of Barn and Cliff Swallows. *Southwest. Nat.* 30: 325–34.

—— (1986) Cliff Swallow colonies as information centers. *Science* 234: 83–5.

—— (1988a) Social foraging in Cliff Swallows: local enhancement, risk sensitivity, competition and the avoidance of predators. *Anim. Behav.* 36: 780–92.

—— (1988b) Laying eggs in a neighbor's nest: benefit and cost of colonial nesting in swallows. *Science* 236: 518–9.

——, **and Brown, M B** (1986) Ectoparasitism as a cost of coloniality in Cliff Swallows (*Hirundo pyrrhonota*). *Ecology* 67: 1206–18.

——, —— (1987) Group-living in swallows as an advantage in avoiding predators. *Behav. Ecol. Sociobiol.* 21: 97–107.

——, —— (1988) A new form of reproductive parasitism in Cliff Swallows, *Nature, Lond.* 331: 66–8.

Brown, L H, and Britton, P L (1980) *The Breeding Seasons of East African Birds.* EANHS, Nairobi.

Brown, R J, Brown M N, and Pessotto, B (ms) Sedentary Welcome Swallows *Hirundo neoxena* in the southwest of Western Australia.

Brudenell-Bruce, P G C (1975) *The Birds of New Providence and the Bahama Islands.* Collins, London.

Bruderer, B (1979) Zum Jahreszyklus schweizerischer Schwalben *Hirundo rustica* und *Delichon urbica*, unter besonderer Berücksichtigung des Katastrophenjahres 1974. *Orn. Beob.* 76: 293–304.

Bryant, D M (1972) The breeding biology of the House Martin *Delichon urbica* in relation to aerial insect abundance. Ph.D. thesis, London University.

—— (1973) Selection of food by the House Martin. *J. Anim. Ecol.* 42: 539–64.

—— (1975) Breeding biology of House Martins *Delichon urbica* in relation to aerial insect abundance. *Ibis* 117: 180–216.

—— (1978a) Establishment of weight hierarchies in the broods of House Martins *Delichon urbica*. *Ibis* 120: 16–26.

—— (1978b) Environmental influences on growth and survival of nestling House Martins *Delichon urbica*. *Ibis* 120: 271–83.

—— (1979) Reproduction costs in the House Martin. *J. Anim. Ecol.* 48: 655–75.

—— (1983) Heat stress in tropical birds: behavioural thermoregulation during flight. *Ibis* 125: 313–23.

—— (1988) Lifetime reproductive success of House Martins. In: *Reproductive Success: Studies of Individual Variation in Contrasting Breeding Systems.* Ed. by T. H. Clutton-Brock. Pp. 173–88. University of Chicago Press, Chicago.

——, **and Hails, C J** (1983) Energetics and growth patterns of three tropical bird species. *Auk* 100: 425–39.

——, **and Turner, A K** (1982) Central place foraging by swallows (Hirundinidae): the question of load size. *Anim. Behav.* 30: 845–56.

——, **and Westerterp, K R** (1983a) Short-term variability in energy turnover by breeding House Martins *Delichon urbica*: a study using doubly-labelled water (D_2O^{18}). *J. Anim. Ecol.* 52: 525–43.

——, **and Westerterp, K R** (1983b) Time and energy limits to brood size in House Martins (*Delichon urbica*). *J. Anim. Ecol.* 52: 905–25.

Bryant, H (1859) A list of birds seen at the Bahamas, from Jan. 20th to May 14th, 1859, with descriptions of new or little known species. *Proc. Boston Soc. Nat. Hist.* 7: 102–34.

Buden, D W (1987) *Birds of the Southern Bahamas.* British Ornithologists' Union, London.

Bull, J (1974) *Birds of New York.* Doubleday, New York.

Bundy, G, and Morgan J H (1969) Notes on Tripolitanian birds. *Bull. Brit. Orn. Club* 89: 139–44, 151–9.

Burgerjon, J J (1964) Some census notes on a colony of South African Cliff Swallows, *Petrochelidon spilodera* (Sundevall). *Ostrich* 35: 77–85.

Butler, R W (1982a) Possible use of legs as dissipators of heat in flying Cliff Swallows. *Wilson Bull.* 94: 87–9.

—— (1982b) Wing-fluttering by mud-gathering Cliff Swallows: avoidance of 'rape' attempts? *Auk* 99: 758–61.

—— (1988) Population dynamics and migration routes of Tree Swallows, *Tachycineta bicolor*, in North America. *J. Field Orn.* 59: 395–402.

——, **and Campbell, C A** (1987) Nest appropriation and interspecific feeding between Tree Swallows, *Tachcineta bicolor*, and Barn Swallows, *Hirundo rustica*. *Can. Field Nat.* 101: 433–4.

Büttiker, W (1976) Parasiten und Nidicolen der Uferschwalbe. *Mitt. Schweiz. Entomol. Ges.* 42: 205–20.

Campbell, A J (1901) *Nests and Eggs of Australian Birds*. Private, Sheffield.

Cannell, I C (1968) Notes from Angola. *Ostrich* 39: 264–5.

Chapin, J P (1925) A new swallow from Cameroon. *Ibis* XII(1): 149–51.

—— (1948) Field notes on *Petrochelidon fuliginosa*. *Ibis* 90: 474–6.

—— (1953) The Birds of the Belgian Congo. Part 3. *Bull. Am. Mus. Nat. Hist.* 75A: 1–821.

—— (1954) The African River Martin and its migration. *Ann. Mus. Congo Tervuren Zool.* 1: 9–15.

Chapman, F M (1917a) *Birdlife in Colombia*. American Museum of Natural History, New York.

—— (1917b) *Birdlife in Ecuador*. American Museum of Natural History, New York.

—— (1929) Relationships of the races of *Phaeoprogne tapera* and their probable significance. *Auk* 46: 348–57.

Chapman, L B (1935) Studies of a Tree Swallow colony. *Bird-banding* 6: 45–57.

—— (1955) Studies of a Tree Swallow colony. *Bird-banding* 26: 45–70.

Cheke, A S (1987a) The ecology of the smaller land-birds of Mauritius. In: *Studies of Mascarene Island Birds*. Ed. by A W Diamond. Pp. 151–207. University of Cambridge Press, Cambridge.

—— (1987b) The ecology of the surviving native land-birds of Réunion. In: *Studies of Mascarene Island Birds*. Ed by A W Diamond. Pp. 301–58. University of Cambridge Press, Cambridge.

Cheng, Tso-hsin (1964) *China's Economic Fauna: Birds*. US Department of Commerce, Washington, DC.

Cherrie, G K (1916) A contribution to the ornithology of the Orinoco region. *Misc. Brooklyn Inst. Arts and Sci. Sci. Bull.* 2: 1–374.

Christensen, P V (1981) Recoveries of Danish Swallows, *Hirundo rustica*. *Dansk. Orn. Foren. Tidsskr.* 75: 47–50.

Christy, B H (1940) Mortality among Tree Swallows. *Auk* 57: 404–5.

Christy, P (1984) The Red-throated Cliff Swallow (*Petrochelidon rufigula*) in Gabon. *Oiseau* 54: 362–3.

Clancey, P A (1964) *The Birds of Natal and Zululand*. Oliver & Boyd, Edinburgh.

—— (1969a) Miscellaneous taxonomic notes on African birds XXVII. *Durban Mus. Nov.* 8: 243–74.

—— (1969b) A catalogue of birds of the South African sub-region. Suppl. No. 1 *Durban Mus. Nov.* 8: 276–324.

—— (1972) A catalogue of birds of the South African sub-region. Suppl. No. 2. *Durban Mus. Nov.* 9: 163–200.

—— (1982) Namibian ornithological miscellanea. *Durban Mus. Nov.* 13: 55–63.

——, **and Irwin, M P S** (1966) The South African races of the Banded Sand Martin. *Durban Mus. Nov.* 8: 23–33.

——, **Lawson, W J, and Irwin, M P S** (1969) The Mascarene Martin *Phedina borbonica* (Gmelin) in Mozambique: a new species to the South African list. *Ostrich* 40: 5–8.

Claridge, J C R (1983) Welcome Swallows at the Auckland Islands. *Notornis* 30: 282.

Clarke, G (1985) Bird observations from north-west Somalia. *Scopus* 9: 24–42.

Cohen, R R (1981) Dispersal in adult female Tree Swallows (*Iridoprocne bicolor*) in Colorado. *J. Colo-Wyo Acad. Sci.* 13: 62.

—— (1984a) Criteria for distinguishing breeding male Tree Swallows from brightly colored females prior to capture. *N. Am. Bird-Bander* 9: 2–3.

—— (1984b) Behavioral determinants of nest-site tenacity and mate fidelity patterns in Tree Swallows (*Tachycineta bicolor*). *J. Colo-Wyo. Acad. Sci.* 16: 16.

—— (1987) Violet-green Swallows (*Tachycineta thalassina*) have at least ten distinct vocalizations. *J. Colo.-Wyo. Acad. Sci.* 19: 18.

—— (ms) Vocalizations section. In: *Tree Swallow Biography* (By R.J. Robertson, B. Stutchbury, and R.R. Cohen).

Collar, N J, and Stuart, S N (1985) *Threatened Birds of Africa and Related Islands. ICBP/ IUCN Red Data Book. Part 1. 3rd edn.* ICBP/ IUCN, Cambridge.

——, **and Andrew, P** (1988) *Birds to Watch: The ICBP World Checklist of Threatened Birds*. ICBP, Cambridge.

Colston, P R, and Curry-Lindahl, K (1986) *The Birds of Mount Nimba, Liberia*. British Museum (Natural History), London.

Combellack, C R B (1954) A nesting of Violet-green Swallows. *Auk* 71: 435–42.

Congreve, P (1972) Torpidity in the White-backed Swallow. *Emu* 72: 32–3.

Cooper, K H (1963) On the range of the Red-breasted Swallow, *Cecropis semirufa*, in Natal. *Ostrich* 34: 171.

Cory C B (1890) *The Birds of the Bahama Islands.* Estes & Lauriat, Boston.

Cowley, E (1979) Sand Martin population trends in Britain, 1965–1978. *Bird Study* 26: 113–6.

—— (1983) Multi-brooding and mate infidelity in the Sand Martin. *Bird Study* 30: 1–7.

Craig, J L (1984) Swallows at sea and established on the Kermadec Islands. *Notornis* 31: 201–2.

Cramp, S (1970) Studies of less familiar birds 159: Crag Martin. *Brit. Birds* 63: 239–43.

—— (ed.) (1988). *The Birds of the Western Palearctic. Vol. V.* Oxford University Press, Oxford.

——, **and Gooders, J** (1967) The return of the House Martin. *Lond. Bird Rep.* 31: 91–8.

Crook, J R, and Shields, W M (1985) Sexually selected infanticide by adult male Barn Swallows. *Anim. Behav.* 33: 754–61.

——, —— (1987) Non-parental nest attendance in the Barn Swallow (*Hirundo rustica*): helping or harassment? *Anim. Behav.* 35: 991–1001.

Crouchley, G, and Crouchley, D (1979) Multiple clutches by Welcome Swallows in the Wairarapa. *Notornis* 26: 309–10.

Daguerre, J B (1922) Lista de aves coleccionadas y observadas en Rosas, F.C.S. *Hornero* 2: 259–71.

Danforth, S T (1929) Notes on the birds of Hispaniola. *Auk* 46: 358–75.

—— (1934) The birds of Antigua. *Auk* 51: 350–64.

—— (1935a) *The Birds of St Lucia.* University of Puerto Rico.

—— (1935b) Investigations concerning Cuban birds, with special reference to the economic status and considerations of those which might be desirable for introduction into Puerto Rico. *J. Agric. Univ. Puerto Rico* 19: 421–38.

—— (1936) The birds of St Kitts and Nevis. *Trop. Agric.* 13: 213–7.

—— (1939) The birds of Guadeloupe and adjacent islands. *J. Agric. Univ. Puerto Rico* 23: 9–46.

da Rosa Pinto, A A, and Lamm, D W (1958) Contribution to the study of the ornithology of Sul do Save, Mozambique. *Me. do Mus. Dr Alvaro de Castro* 4: 107–67.

Davis, J, and Miller, A H (1962) Further information on the Caribbean Martin in Mexico. *Condor* 64: 237–9.

Davis, P (1965) Recoveries of Swallows ringed in Britain and Ireland. *Bird Study* 12: 151–69.

Dean, W R J (1974) Breeding and distributional notes on some Angolan birds. *Durban Mus. Nov.* 10: 109–25.

——, **and MacDonald, I A W** (1981) A review of African birds feeding in association with mammals. *Ostrich* 52: 135–55.

Dearborn, N, and Cory, C B (1907) Catalogue of a collection of birds from Guatemala. *Field Mus. Nat. Hist. Chicago* 1: 69–138.

Dee, T J (1986) *The Endemic Birds of Madagascar.* ICBP, Cambridge.

Deignon, H G (1963) *Checklist of the birds of Thailand.* Smithsonian Institution, Washington, D.C.

Delaney, S, Denby, C, and Norton, J (1982) Ornithology: Ladakh Expedition 1980 Report. Pp. 5–153. University of Southampton.

de Lope Rebollo, F. (1980) Biologie de la reproduction de l'Hirondelle rousseline en Espagne. *Alauda* 48: 99–112.

—— (1981) La invasion de *Hirundo daurica rufula* Temm. en la Peninsula Iberica. *Doñana, Acta Vert.* 8: 313–18.

Dementev, G P, and Gladkov, N A (1968) *Birds of the Soviet Union. Vol. 6.* Israel Programme for Scientific Translation, Jerusalem.

de Naurois, R. (1979) Welcome Swallows in New Caledonia. *Bonn. Zool. Beitr.* 31: 160–1.

de Schauensee, R M (1984) *The Birds of China.* Oxford University Press, Oxford.

——, **and Phelps, W H** (1978) *A Guide to the Birds of Venezuela. Princeton University Press,* Princeton, New Jersey.

De Steven, D (1978) The influence of age on the breeding biology of the Tree Swallow. *Ibis* 120: 516–22.

De Weese, L R, Cohen, R R, and Stafford, C J (1985) Organochlorine residues and eggshell measurements for Tree Swallows *Tachycineta bicolor* in Colorado. *Bull. Env. Contam. Toxicol.* 35: 767–75.

——, **McEwen, L C, Hensler, G L, and Petersen, B E** (1986) Organochlorine contaminants in the passeriformes and other avian prey of the Peregrine Falcon in the western United States. *Env. Toxicol. & Chem.* 5: 675–93.

Diamond, A W (1987) *Studies of Mascarene Island Birds.* Cambridge University Press, Cambridge.

Dickey, D R, and van Rossem, A J (1938) *The Birds of El Salvador.* Field Museum of Natural History, Chicago.

Dickinson, E C (1986) Does the White-eyed River Martin breed in China? *Forktail* 2: 95–6.

Dinelli, L (1924) Notas biologicas sobre aves del noroeste de la Argentina. *Hornero* 3: 253–8.

Donnelly, B G (1974) Vertical zonation of feeding swallows and swifts at Kariba, Rhodesia. *Ostrich* 45: 256–8.

Dowsett, R J (1972) Geographical variation in *Pseudhirundo griseopyga*. *Bull. Brit. Orn. Club* 92: 97–100.

—— (1979) Recent additions to the Zambian list. *Bull. Brit. Orn. Club* 99: 94–8.

——, **and Dowsett-Lemaire, F** (1980) The systematic status of some Zambian birds. *Gerfaut* 70: 151–200.

Draffan, R D W, Garnett, S T, and Malone, G (1983) Birds of the Torres Straits. *Emu* 83: 207–34.

DuBowy, P J, and Moore, S N (1985) Weather-related mortality in swallows in the Sacramento Valley of California. *Western Birds* 16: 49–50.

Duffin, K (1973) Barn Swallows use freshwater and marine algae in nest construction. *Wilson Bull.* 85: 237–8.

Durnev, Yu A, Sirokhin, I N, and Sonin, V D (1983) Materials to the ecology of *Delichon dasypus* (Passeriformes, Hirundinidae) on Khamar-Daban (South Baikal Territory). *Zool. Zh.* 62: 1541–6.

Dyrcz, A (1984) Breeding biology of the Mangrove Swallow, *Tachycineta albilinea*, and the Grey-breasted Martin, *Progne chalybea*, at Barro Colorado Island, Panama. *Ibis* 126: 59–66.

Earlé, R A (1985a) Predators, parasites and symbionts of the South African Cliff Swallow *Hirundo spilodera* (Aves: Hirundinidae). *Navors. nas. Mus., Bloemfontein* 5: 1–18.

—— (1985b) The nest of the South African Cliff Swallow *Hirundo spilodera* (Aves: Hirundinidae). *Navors. nas. Mus., Bloemfontein* 5: 21–36.

—— (1985c) A description of the social, aggressive and maintenance behaviour of the South African Cliff Swallow *Hirundo spilodera* (Aves: Hirundinidae). *Navors. nas. Mus., Bloemfontein* 5: 37–50.

—— (1985d) Foraging behaviour and diet of the South African Cliff Swallow *Hirundo spilodera* (Aves: Hirundinidae). *Navors. nas. Mus., Bloemfontein* 5: 53–66.

—— (1986a) The breeding biology of the South African Cliff Swallow. *Ostrich* 57: 138–56.

—— (1986b) Vocalizations of the South African Cliff Swallow, *Hirundo spilodera*. *S. Afr. J. Zool.* 21: 229–32.

—— (1986c) Time budget of South African Cliff Swallows during breeding. *S. Afr. J. Zool.* 21: 57–9.

—— (1987a) Distribution, migration and timing of moult in the South African Cliff Swallow. *Ostrich* 58: 118–21.

—— (1987b) Moult and breeding seasons of the Grey-rumped Swallow. *Ostrich* 58:181–2.

—— (1987c) Measurements, moult and timing of breeding in the Blue Swallow. *Ostrich* 58: 182–5.

—— (1987d) Ringing and recovery details of four southern African swallow species. *Safring News* 16: 67–72.

—— (1987e) Notes on *Hirundo fuliginosa* and its status as a 'cliff swallow'. *Bull. Brit. Orn. Club* 107: 59–63.

—— (1987f) A case of bigamy in the Redbreasted Swallow *Hirundo semirufa*. *S. Afr. J. Zool.* 22: 325–6.

—— (1988a) The timing of breeding and moult in three African swallows (Aves, Hirundinidae). *Revue. Zool. Afr.* 102: 61–70.

—— (1988b) Nest rotation by Whitethroated Swallows *Hirundo albigularis* during the breeding season. *Hirundo* 1: 11–12.

—— (1988c) The timing of breeding and moult of the Lesser Striped Swallow *Hirundo abyssinica*. *Ibis* 130: 378–83.

Edgar, A T (1966) Welcome Swallows in New Zealand 1958–1965. *Notornis* 13: 27–60.

Edson, J M (1943) A study of the Violet-green Swallow. *Auk* 60: 396–403.

Edwards, E O (1948) Have the White-backed Swallows their 'territories'? *Emu* 47: 314.

Eisenmann, E (1959) South American migrant swallows of the genus *Progne* in Panama and northern South America with comments on their identification and molt. *Auk* 76: 528–32.

——, **and Haverschmidt, F** (1970) Northward migration to Surinam of South American martins (*Progne*). *Condor* 72: 368–9.

Eisentraut, M (1956) Notizen über einige Vögel des Kamerungebirges. *J. für Orn.* 97: 291–300.

—— (1963) *Die Wirbeltiere des Kamerungebirges*. Paul Parey, Hamburg.

Elgood, J H (1965) The birds of the Obudu Plateau, eastern region of Nigeria. *Nigerian Field* 30: 60–9.

—— (1976) Montane birds of Nigeria. *Bull. Niger. Orn. Soc.* 12: 31–4.

—— (1982) *Birds of Nigeria*. British Ornithologists' Union, London.

——, Fry, C H, and Dowsett, R J (1973) African migrants in Nigeria. *Ibis* 115: 1–45, 375–411.

Elkins, N, and Etheridge, B (1974) The Crag Martin in winter quarters at Gibraltar. *Brit. Birds* 67: 376–87.

Elliott, J J (1939) Wintering Tree Swallows at Jones Beach, fall and winter 1938 and 1939. *Bird Lore* 41: 11–16.

Emlen, J T, Jr (1952) Social behavior in nesting Cliff Swallows. *Condor* 54: 177–99.

—— (1954) Territory, nest building and pair formation in Cliff Swallows. *Auk* 77: 16–35.

—— (1977) Land bird communities of Grand Bahama Island: the structure and dynamics of an avifauna. *Orn. Monogr. No. 24.* American Ornithologists' Union, Washington, D.C.

Erard, C (1981) Sur les migrations de *Pseudochelidon eurystomina* Hartlaub au Gabon. *L'Oiseau* 51: 244–6.

Erskine, A J (1979) Man's influence on potential nesting sites and populations of swallows in Canada. *Can. Field Nat.* 93: 371–7.

—— (1984) Swallows foraging on the ground. *Wilson Bull.* 96: 136–7.

Etchécopar, R D, and Hüe, F (1967) *The Birds of North Africa.* Oliver & Boyd, Edinburgh.

——, —— (1983) *Les Oiseaux de Chine: Passereaux.* Société Nouvelles des Editions Boubée, Paris.

Falla, R A, Sibson, R B, and Turbott, E G (1983) *The New Guide to the Birds of New Zealand and Outlying Islands.* Collins, Auckland.

Farina, A (1978) Breeding biology of the Crag Martin. *Avocetta* 2: 35–46.

Feare, C J (1977) *Phedina borbonica madagascariensis* in the Amirantes. *Bull. Brit. Orn. Club* 97: 87–9.

ffrench, R (1980) *A Guide to the Birds of Trinidad and Tobago.* Aza Wright Nature Center.

Finlay, J C (1971) Breeding biology of Purple Martins at the northern limit of their range. *Wilson Bull.* 83: 255–69.

Fjeldså, J (1987) *Birds of Relict Forests in the High Andes of Peru and Bolivia.* Zoological Museum, University of Copenhagen.

——, and Krabbe, N K (1986) Some range extensions and other unusual records of Andean birds. *Bull. Brit. Orn. Club* 106: 115–26.

——, —— (1989) *Birds of the High Andes.* Brill, Leiden.

Forster, T (1817) Observations of the Natural History of Swallows; with a Collateral Statement of Facts Relative to their Migration and to their Brumal Torpidity. 6th edn. T & G Underwood, London. (Reprinted 1972, Paul P B Minet, Chicheley, Bucks.)

Fraga, R A (1979) Helpers at the nest in passerines from Buenos Aires Province, Argentina. *Auk* 96: 606–8.

Frandsen, J (1982) *Birds of the Southwestern Cape.* Cape Town.

Freeman, W G (1922) Notes on the food and habits of some Trinidad birds. *Bull. Dept. Agric. Trin. & Tobago* 20: 1–189.

Freer, V M (1977) Factors affecting site tenacity in New York Bank Swallows. *Bird-Banding* 50: 349–57.

Friedmann, H (1948) Birds collected by the National Geographic Society Expeditions to northern Brazil and southern Venezuela. *Proc. US Natn. Mus.* 97: 373–569.

——, and Williams, J G (1969) The birds of the Sango Bay forests, Buddu County, Manaka District, Uganda. *Contr. Sci. LA Mus. Nat. Hist.* 162.

Fry, C H, and Smith, D A (1985) A new swallow from the Red Sea. *Ibis* 127: 1–6.

Fuggles-Couchman, N R (1939) Notes on some birds of the eastern Province of Tanganyika Territory. *Ibis* 3: 76–106.

Gallagher, M, and Woodcock, W (1980) *The Birds of Oman.* Quartet Books, London.

Gaunt, A S (1965) Fossorial adaptations in the Bank Swallow. *Univ. Kans. Sci. Bull.* 46: 99–146.

—— (1969) Myology of the leg in swallows. *Auk* 86: 41–53.

Gauthreaux, S A Jr (1982) The ecology and evolution of avian mating systems. In: *Avian Biology* Ed by D S Farner, J R King and K C Parkes. Pp. 93–168. Academic Press, New York.

Germain, M, Dragesco, J, Roux, F, and Garcin, H (1973) Contribution à l'ornithologie du Sud-Cameroun II. Passeriformes. *L'Oiseau* 43: 212–59.

Gifford, E W (1919) Field notes on the land birds of the Galapagos Islands and of Cocos Island. *Proc. Calif. Acad. Sci.* 2: 189–258.

Glutz von Blotzheim, U N (1962) *Die Brutvögel der Schweiz.* Aarau.

——, and Bauer, K M (1985) *Handbuch der Vögel Mitteleuropas. 10. Passeriformes. Alaudidae–Hirundinidae.* Akademische Verlagsgesellschaft Wiesbaden.

Gochfeld, M, Keith, S, and Donahue, P (1980) Records of rare or previously unrecorded birds from Colombia. *Bull. Brit. Orn. Club* 100: 196–201.

Godfrey, W E (1986) *The Birds of Canada.* Chicago University Press, Chicago.

Gore, M E J (1981) *Birds of the Gambia.* British Ornithologists' Union, London.

——, and Won, P-O (1971) *The Birds of Korea.* R. As. Soc. Korea, Seoul.

Graber, R R, Graber, J W, and Kirk, E L (1972) Illinois birds: Hirundinidae. *Biol. Notes* 80: 1–56. Illinois Natural History Society.

Grant, C H B, and Mackworth-Praed, C W (1942) On the occurrence of *Riparia cincta cincta* (Boddaert) in Eastern Africa during the non-breeding season. *Bull. Brit. Orn. Club* 62: 67–9.

Grant, G S, and Quay, T L (1977) Breeding biology of Cliff Swallows in Virginia. *Wilson Bull.* 89: 286–90.

Grant, L, and Lewis, A D (1984) Breeding of the Ethiopian Swallow *Hirundo aethiopica* in interior Kenya. *Scopus* 8: 67–72.

Green, R H (1966) Gut contents of some Tasmanian birds. *Emu* 66: 105–12.

Gregory, M R (1978) Accidental dispersal of the Welcome Swallow through 'hitch-hiking' on ships. *Notornis* 25: 91–4.

Grimes, L G (1988) *Birds of Ghana.* British Ornithologists' Union, London.

Griscom (1929) Notes on the Rough-winged Swallow (*Stelgidopteryx serripennis* Aud.) and its allies. *Proc. New Engl. Zool. Club* 11: 67–72.

Guerra, E R (1969) Golondrinas que invernan. *Hornero* 11: 59–60.

Guitián Rivera, J, Sánchez Canals, J L, de Castro Lorenzo, A, and Bas López, S (1980) Sobre *Hirundo rupestris* (Scop) en Galicia. *Ardeola* 25: 181–91.

Gullion, G W (1947) Use of artificial nesting sites by Violet-green and Tree Swallows. *Auk* 64: 411–5.

Hails, C J (1979) A comparison of flight energetics in hirundines and other birds. *Comp. Biochem. Physiol.* 63A: 581–5.

—— (1982) A comparison of tropical and temperate aerial insect abundance. *Biotropica* 14: 310–13.

—— (1984) The breeding biology of the Pacific Swallow, *Hirundo tahitica*, in Malaysia. *Ibis* 126: 198–219.

Hall, B P (1960) The ecology and taxonomy of some Angolan birds. *Bull. Brit. Mus. Nat. Hist.* 6: 369–453.

——, and Moreau, R E (1970) *Atlas of Speciation of African Passerine Birds.* British Museum (Natural History), London.

Hallinan, T (1924) Notes on some Panama Canal Zone birds with special reference to their food. *Auk* 41: 304–26.

Hanmer, D B (1976) Birds of the lower Zambezi. *Southern Birds* 2: 1–66.

—— (1980) A coastal form of the African Saw-wing (*Pristoptera p. holomelaena*) in S. Malawi. *Nyala* 6: 134–5.

Harris, M P (1973) The Galapagos avifauna. *Condor* 75: 265–70.

Harris, R N (1979) Aggression in Tree Swallows. *Can. J. Zool.* 57: 2072–8.

Hartlaub, G (1861) Ueber einige neue Vögel Westafrica's. *J. für Orn.* 9: 3–11.

Hartley, G I (1917) Nesting habits of the Grey-breasted Martin. In: *Tropical Wildlife in British Guiana.* Ed. by W Beebe, G I Hartley and P G Howles. Pp. 328–41. New York Zoological Society, New York.

Hartley, P H T (1941) The sexual display of Swallows. *Brit. Birds* 34: 256–8.

Hastwell, K (1985) Tree Martins mating in flight. *Aust. Bird Watcher* 11: 64.

Hauri, R (1968) Die Felsenschwalbe im bernischen Mittelland. *Orn. Beob.* 65: 192–4.

Haverschmidt, F (1968) *Birds of Surinam.* Oliver & Boyd, Edinburgh.

—— (1982) The status of the Rough-winged Swallow, *Stelgidopteryx ruficollis*, in Suriname. *Bull. Brit. Orn. Club* 102: 75–7.

Hayward, C L, Cottam, C, Woodbury, A M, and Frost, H H (1976) *Birds of Utah.* Brigham Young University Press, Provo, Utah.

Hebblethwaite, M L, and Shields, W M (in press) Social influences on Barn Swallow foraging in the Adirondacks: a test of competing hypotheses. *Anim. Behav.*

Hellmayr, C E (1935) Catalogue of the Birds of the Americas. Part 8. *Field Mus. Nat. Hist. Zool.* Ser. 13: 1–541.

Hellyar, R H (1927) Notes on the nesting of the Sand Martin. *Brit. Birds* 21: 166–71.

Hemery, G, Nicolau-Guillaumet, P, and Thibault, J C (1979) Etude de la dynamique des populations françaises d'Hirondelles de cheminée de 1956 à 1973. *L'Oiseau* 49: 213–30.

Henny, C J (1972) An analysis of the population dynamics of selected avian species. *Fish Widl. Serv. Wild. Res. Rep.* 1: 1–99.

Henry, G M (1971) *A Guide to the Birds of Ceylon.* Oxford University Press, Oxford.

Herholdt, J J (1986) South African Cliff Swallows feeding in association with other birds. *Bokmakierie* 38: 122.

Hespenheide, H A (1975) Selective predation by two swifts and a swallow in Central America. *Ibis* 117: 82–99.

Hilty, S L, and Brown, W L (1986) *A Guide to the Birds of Colombia.* Princeton University Press, Princeton, New Jersey.

Hobbs, J N (1966) Nocturnal feeding by Welcome Swallow. *Emu* 66: 116.

Hobson, K A, and Sealy, S G (1987) Foraging, scavenging, and behavior of swallows on the ground. *Wilson Bull.* 99: 116–21.

Holman, F C (1947) Birds of the Gold Coast. *Ibis* 89: 623–50.

Holroyd, G L (1975) Nest site availability as a factor limiting population size of swallows. *Can. Field Nat.* 89: 60–4.

Holt, E G (1926) On a Guatemalan specimen of *Progne sinaloae* Nelson. *Auk* 43: 550–1.

Holyoak, D T (1974) Les Oiseaux des Iles de la Société. *L'Oiseau* 44: 153–81.

Hoogland, J L, and Sherman, P (1976) Advantages and disadvantages of Bank Swallow coloniality. *Ecol. Monogr.* 46: 33–58.

Horne, J F M (1987) Vocalisations of the endemic land-birds of the Mascarene Islands. In: *Studies of Mascarene Island Birds* Ed. by A W Diamond. Pp. 101–50. University of Cambridge Press, Cambridge.

Houston, M I, and Houston, C S (1987) Tree Swallow banding near Saskatoon, Saskatchewan. *N. Am. Bird-Bander* 2: 103–8.

Howell, T R (1972) Birds of the lowland pine savanna of northeastern Nicaragua. *Condor* 74: 316–40.

Hudson, W H (1920) *Birds of La Plata. Vol. 1.* J M Dent, London.

Huels, T R (1984) First record of Cave Swallows breeding in Arizona. *Am. Birds* 38: 281–3.

——— (1985) Cave Swallow paired with Cliff Swallows. *Condor* 87: 441–3.

Hughes, O R (1973) Observations on nesting sites of the Welcome Swallow. *Mauri Ora* 1: 61–4.

Hull, R L (1944) Nesting of the Red-throated Rock Martin *Ptyonoprogne rufigula. J. East. Afr. Nat. Hist. Soc.* 18: 94–5.

Humphrey, P S, Bridge, D, Reynolds, P W, and Peterson, R T (1970) *Birds of Isla Grande (Tierra del Fuego).* Smithsonian Institution, Washington, D C.

Hund, K (1976) Beobachtungen, insbesondere zur Brutbiologie, an oberschwäbischen Populationen der Mehlschwalbe. *Orn. Mitt.* 28: 169–78.

———, **and Prinzinger, R** (1979a) Untersuchungen zur Biologie der Mehlschwalbe in Oberschwaben. *Okologie der Vögel* 1: 133–58.

———, ——— (1979b) Untersuchungen zur Ortstreue, Paartreue und Überlebensrate nestjunger Vögel bei der Mehlschwalbe in Oberschwaben. *Vogelwarte* 30: 107–17.

———, ——— (1985) Die Bedeutung des Lebensalters für brutbiologische Parameter der Mehlschwalbe. *J. für Orn.* 126: 15–28.

Hussell, D J T (1982) Longevity and fecundity records in the Tree Swallow. *N. Am. Bird-Bander* 7: 154.

——— (1983a) Tree Swallow pairs raise two broods in a season. *Wilson Bull.* 95: 470–1.

——— (1983b) Age and plumage color in female Tree Swallows. *J. Field Orn.* 54: 312–18.

Iijima, Y (1982) Breeding of *Hirundo rustica* at Taiki in the southern part of Tokachi District, Hokkaido. *Tori* 31: 17–22.

Inskipp, C, and Inskipp, T (1986) *A Guide to the Birds of Nepal.* Croom Helm, London.

Irwin, M P S (1977) Variation, geographical arcs and gene flow within the populations of the Rock Martin *Hirundo (Ptyonoprogne) fuligula* in eastern, southern and southwestern Africa. *Honeyguide* 91: 11–9.

——— (1981) *The Birds of Zimbabwe.* Quest, Salisbury.

———, **and Benson, C W** (1967) Notes on the birds of Zambia. *Arnoldia* 3: 1–30.

Jackson, H D (1973a) Faunal notes from the Chimanimani Mountains based on a collection of birds and mammals from the Miucrera River, Mozambique. *Durban Mus. Nov.* 10: 23–42.

——— (1973b) Records of some birds and mammals in the Central Chimanimani Mountains of Mozambique and Rhodesia. *Durban Mus. Nov.* 9: 291–305.

Jahn, H (1942) Zur Oekologie und Biologie der Vögel Japans. *J. für Orn.* 90: 7–301.

James, H W (1926) Marked eggs of the Lesser Stripe-breasted Swallow (*Hirundo puella unitatis* Sclater & Praed). *Ool. Rec.* 6: 47.

Jennings, M C (1980) *Birds of the Arabian Gulf.* George Allen & Unwin, London.

Jensen, R (1962) Birds at modern sewage disposal works. *Ostrich* 33: 26.

Johnson, A W (1967) *The Birds of Chile and Adjacent Regions of Argentina, Bolivia and Peru. Vol. II.* Platt Establecimientos Graficos SA, Buenos Aires.

Johnston, D W, Blake, C H, and Buden, D W (1971) Avifauna of the Cayman Islands. *Q. J. Fla Acad. Sci.* 34: 142–56.

Johnston, R F (1965) Breeding birds of Kansas. *Univ. Kans. Publ.* 12: 575–655.

—— (1966) The adaptive bases of geographical variation in color of the Purple Martin. *Condor* 68: 219–28.

—— (1967) Seasonal variation in the food of the Purple Martin *Progne subis* in Kansas. *Ibis* 109: 8–13.

——, **and Hardy, J W** (1962) Behavior of the Purple Martin. *Wilson Bull.* 74: 243–62.

Jones, G (1986a) The distribution and abundance of Sand Martins breeding in Central Scotland. *Scot. Birds* 14: 33–8.

—— (1986b) Sexual chases in Sand Martins *(Riparia riparia)*: cues for males to increase their reproductive success. *Behav. Ecol. Sociobiol.* 19: 179–85.

—— (1987a) Selection against large size in the Sand Martin, *Riparia riparia*, during a dramatic population crash. *Ibis* 129: 274–80.

—— (1987b) Parental foraging ecology and feeding behaviour during nestling rearing in the Swallow. *Ardea* 75: 169–74.

—— (1988) Concurrent demands of parent and offspring Swallows *Hirundo rustica* in a variable feeding environment. *Ornis Scand.* 19: 145–52.

Jourdain, F C R (1935) Notes on a collection of eggs and breeding habits of birds near Lokoja, Nigeria. *Ibis* XIII(5): 623–63.

Kasparek, M (1981) *Die Mauser der Singvögel Europas – ein Feldführer.* Dachverband Deutscher Avifaunisten, Langede.

Kespaik, J, and Lyuleeva, D S (1968) Controlled hypothermy in birds of the family Hirundinidae. *Soob. Pribalt. Komiss. po Izuch. Migratsii Ptits.* 5: 122–45.

Kessell, B, and Gibson, D D (1978) Status and distribution of Alaska birds. *Cooper Orn. Soc. Stud. Avian Biol.* 1: 1–100.

Kilgore, D L, and Knudson, K L (1978) Analysis of materials in Cliff and Barn swallow nests: relationship between mud selection and nest structure. *Wilson Bull.* 89: 562–71.

King, B, and Kanwanich, S (1978) First wild sighting of the White-eyed River Martin. *Biol. Conserv.* 13: 183–6.

King, W B (1981) *Endangered Birds of the World. The ICBP Bird Red Data Book.* Smithsonian Institution, Washington, D.C.

Kitti, T (1968) A new Martin of the genus *Pseudochelidon* from Thailand. *Thai Nat. Sci. Papers Fauna* Ser. 1: 1–10.

—— (1969) Report on an expedition in Northern Thailand to look for breeding sites of *Pseudochelidon sirintarae* (21 May to 27 June 1969). Applied Scientific Research Corporation, Thailand, Bangkok (Research Report).

Klapste, J, and Klapste, P (1985) Dusting, sunning, albinism in Welcome Swallows, *Hirundo neoxena. Aust. Bird Watcher* 11: 98–9.

Koenig, O (1962) Weisse Rauchschwalben. *Die Pyramide*, 2.

Koepcke, M (1983) *The Birds of the Department of Lima, Peru.* Harrowwood Books, Pennsylvania.

Kondělka, D (1978) The breeding biology of the House Martin. *Folia Zool.* 27: 37–45.

Kožená, I (1975) The food of young House Martins (*Delichon urbica*) in the Krkonose Mountains. *Zool. Listy*, 24: 149–62.

—— (1979) A study of the qualitative composition of the diet of young Swallows (*Hirundo rustica*) in an agricultural farm. *Folia Zool.* 28: 337–46.

—— (1980) Dominance of items and diversity of the diet of young Swallows (*Hirundo rustica*). *Folia Zool.* 29: 143–56.

—— (1983) Comparison of the diets of young Swallows (*Hirundo rustica*) and House Martins (*Delichon urbica*). *Folia Zool.* 32: 41–50.

Krapu, G L (1986) Patterns and causes of change in a Cliff Swallow colony during a 17-year period. *Prairie Nat.* 18: 109–14.

Kuerzi, R G (1941) Life history studies of the Tree Swallow. *Proc. Linn. Soc. N.Y.* 52–3: 1–52.

Kuhnen, K (1985) On pair formation in the Sand Martin *Riparia riparia. J. für Orn.* 126: 1–13.

Lamarche, B (1981) Liste commentée des oiseaux du Mali. Part II. *Malimbus* 3: 73–102.

Land, H C (1970) *The Birds of Guatemala.* Livingston, Wynnewood.

Lane, J A (1978) *A Birders' Guide to the Rio Grande Valley of Texas.* C & P Press, Denver, Colorado.

Lane, S G (1965) Seasonal banding of Fairy Martins. *Aust. Bird-Bander* 3: 67–70.

Leffelaar, D, and Robertson, R J (1985) Nest usurpation and female competition for breeding opportunities by Tree Swallows. *Wilson Bull.* 97: 221–4.

——, —— (1986) Equality of feeding roles and the maintenance of monogamy in Tree Swallows. *Behav. Ecol. Sociobiol.* 18: 199–206.

Lehmann, E (1960) Contribuciones estudio fauna Colombia. *Nov. Colomb.* 1: 270–1.

Lentino, M (1988) *Notiochelidon flavipes*: a swallow new to Venezuela. *Bull. Brit. Orn. Club* 108: 70–1.

Lind, E A (1960) Zur Ethologie und Ökologie der Mehlschwalbe. *Ann. Zool. Soc. Vanamo* 21: 1–123.

—— (1962) Verhalten der Mehlschwalbe, *Delichon urbica urbica* (L.) zu ihren Feinden. *Ann. Zool. Soc. Vanamo* 23: 1–38.

Linsdale, J M (1936) *The Birds of Nevada.* Cooper Ornithological Society, Berkeley, California.

Lippens, L, and Wille, H (1976) *Les Oiseaux du Zaïre.* Lannoo Helt.

Lister, M D (1954) A contribution to the ornithology of the Darjeeling area. *J. Bombay Nat. Hist. Soc.* 52: 20–68.

Livingstone, D A (1975) Late quaternary climatic change in Africa. *Ann. Rev. Ecol. Syst.* 6: 249–80.

Lörhl, H (1962) Paarbildung und Polygamie der Rauchschwalbe. *Vogelwelt* 83: 116–22.

Lombardo, M P (1986a) Attendants at Tree Swallow nests I. Are attendants helpers at the nest? *Condor* 88: 297–303.

—— (1986b) Extrapair copulations in the Tree Swallow. *Wilson Bull.* 98: 150–2.

—— (1987) Attendants at Tree Swallow nests II. The exploratory-dispersal hypothesis. *Condor* 89: 138–49.

—— (1988) Evidence of intraspecific brood parasitism in the Tree Swallow. *Wilson Bull.* 100: 126–7.

Lord, E A R (1956) The birds of the Murphy's Creek district, southern Queensland. *Emu* 56: 100–28.

Loske, K-H (1983a) Zur Kolonietreue mehr- und einjähriger Uferschwalben (*Riparia riparia*) in Mittelwestfalen – ein Zwischenbericht. *Beih. Veröff. Naturschutz. Landschaftpflege. Bad-Württ.* 37: 79–87.

—— (1983b) Zur Verbreitung der Uferschwalbe in Westfalen im Jahre 1981 – ein vorläufiger überblick. *Beih. Veröff. Naturschutz. Landschaftpflege. Bad-Württ.* 37: 43–52.

—— (1986a) The origins of European Swallows wintering in Namibia and Botswana. *Ring. Migr.* 7: 119–21.

—— (1986b) Masse und Gewichte in einer mittelwestfälischen Populationen der Meschwalbe (*Delichon urbica*). *Vogelwarte* 33: 332–5.

Louette, M (1981) *The Birds of Cameroon. An Annotated Check-list.* AWLSK, Paleis der Akademien, Brussels.

Low, S (1934) Nest distribution and survival ratio of Tree Swallows. *Bird-banding* 5: 24–30.

Lowe, P R (1938) Some anatomical notes on the genus *Pseudochelidon* Hartlaub with reference to its taxonomic position. *Ibis* 14: 429–37.

Loye, C E (ms) Ectoparasites mediate colony use in a swallow.

——, **and Hopla, C E** (1983) Ectoparasites and micro-organisams associated with the Cliff Swallow in west-central Oklahoma ll. Life-history patterns *Bull. Soc. Vector Ecol.* 8: 71–84.

Lunk, W A (1962) The Rough-Winged Swallow: a study based on its breeding biology in Michigan. *Publ. Nuttall Orn. Club* 4: 1–155.

Lynes, H (1938) Contribution to the ornithology of the southern Congo Basin. *Rev. Zool. Bot. Afr.* 31: 1–129.

Lyuleeva, D S (1973) Features of swallow biology during migration. In: *Bird Migration: Ecological and Physiological Factors*. Ed. by B E Bykhovskii. Pp. 219–72. John Wiley, Chichester.

Macdonald, J D (1973) *Birds of Australia.* Witherby, London.

Mack, C (1972) Nesting notes on Swallows. *Bokmakierie* 24: 55.

Mackworth-Praed, C W, and Grant, C H B (1960) *African Handbook of Birds. Series 1. Vol. 2. Birds of Eastern and Northeastern Africa.* Longmans, London.

—— (1963) *African Handbook of Birds. Series 2. Vol. 2. Birds of the Southern Third of Africa.* Longmans, London.

—— (1973) *African Handbook of Birds. Series 3. Vol. 2. Birds of West Central and Eastern Africa.* Longmans, London.

McLachlan, G R, and Liversidge, R (1978) *Roberts Birds of South Africa, 4th edn.* Trustees of the John Voelcker Bird Book Fund, Cape Town.

Maclean, G L (1985) *Roberts Birds of Southern Africa. 5th edn.* Trustees of the John Voelcker Bird Book Fund, Cape Town.

McLean, S (1968) Lesser Striped Swallows feeding on fruit. *Bokmakierie* 40: 21.

McClure, H E (1974) *Migration and Survival of the Birds of Asia.* US Army Medical Component, SEATO Medical Project, Bangkok.

March, W T (1863) Notes on the birds of Jamaica. *Proc. Acad. Nat. Sci. Phil.* 15: 283–305.

Marchant, S (1942) Some birds of the Owerri Province, S. Nigeria. *Ibis* 6: 137–96.

—— (1958) The birds of the Santa Elena Peninsula, south-west Ecuador. *Ibis* 100: 349–87.

—— (1984) CBC index report 1982–83. *BTO News* 134, September.

——, and Fullager, P J (1983) Nest records of the Welcome Swallow. *Emu* 83: 66–74.

Marelli, C A (1919) Sobre el contenido del estómago de algunas aves. *Hornero* 1: 221–8.

Marsh, R L (1979) Development of endothermy in nestling Bank Swallows (*Riparia riparia*). *Physiol. Zool.* 52: 340–53.

——, R L (1980) Development of temperature regulation in nestling Tree Swallows. *Condor* 82: 461–3.

Marshall, J T, Jr (1943) Additional information concerning the birds of El Salvador. *Condor* 45: 21–33.

Martin, J, and Broekhuysen, G J (1961) Some records of birds using the nests of others. *Ostrich* 32: 104–6.

Martin, R F (1980) Analysis of hybridization between the hirundinid genera *Hirundo* and *Petrochelidon* in Texas. *Auk* 97: 148–59.

—— (1981) Reproductive correlates of environmental variation and niche expansion in the Cave Swallow in Texas. *Wilson Bull.* 93: 506–18.

——, Martin, M W, and Lanier-Martin, N G (1986) Geographic variation in white facial markings of juvenile Cave Swallows. *Southwest. Nat.* 31: 402–3.

——, Miller, G O, Lewis, M R, Martin, S R, and Davis, W R, III (1977) Reproduction of the Cave Swallow: a Texas cave population. *Southwest. Nat.* 22: 177–86.

——, and Selander, R K (1975) Morphological and biochemical evidence of hybridization between Cave and Barn Swallows. *Condor* 77: 362–4.

Martinez, M M (1983) Nidificación de *Hirundo rustica erythrogaster* (Boddaert) en la Argentina (Aves, Hirundinidae). *Neotropica* 29: 83–6.

Mayhew, W W (1958) The biology of the Cliff Swallow in California. *Condor* 60: 7–37.

Maynard, C J (1896) *The Birds of Eastern North America*. Rev. edn. Newtonville, Massachusetts.

Mayr, E (1955) Notes on the birds of northern Melanesia 3. Passeres. *Am. Mus. Nov.* 1707: 1–46.

——, and Bond, J (1943) Notes on the generic classification of the swallows. *Ibis* 85: 334–41.

——, and Greenway, J C (1956) Sequence of passerine families (Aves). *Breviora* 58: 1–11.

——, and Short, L L (1970) Species taxa of North American birds. *Publ. Nuttall Orn. Club* 9: 1–127.

Mead, C (1970) Winter quarters of British Swallows. *Bird Study* 17: 229–40.

—— (1975) Juvenile hirundines starting primary moult in Europe. *Ring. Migr.* 1: 57.

—— (1979a) Colony fidelity and interchange in the Sand Martin. *Bird Study* 26: 99–106.

—— (1979b) Mortality and causes of death in British Sand Martins. *Bird Study* 26: 107–12.

—— (1980) Sand Martins moulting primaries in Britain. *Bird Study* 27: 51–3.

—— (1984) Sand Martin slump. *BTO News* 133, July.

——, and Harrison J D (1979a) Sand Martin movements within Britain and Ireland. *Bird Study* 26: 73–86.

——, and Harrison J D (1979b) Overseas movements of British and Irish Sand Martins. *Bird Study* 26: 87–98.

Medland, R D (1985) South African Cliff Swallow *Hirundo spilodera* in Malawi. *Nyala* 11: 26–7.

Medvin, M B, and Beecher, M D (1986) Parent-offspring recognition in the Barn Swallow *Hirundo rustica*. *Anim. Behav.* 34: 1627–39.

Medway, Lord, and Wells, D (1976) *Birds of the Malay Peninsula. Vol. V.* Witherby, London.

Mees, G F (1985) Nomenclature and systematics of birds from Suriname. *Proc. Koninkl. Nederl. Ak. Werensch. Ser. C.* 88: 86–8.

Meinertzhagen, R (1930) *Nicholls' the Birds of Egypt*. Oliver & Boyd, Edinburgh.

—— (1954) *Birds of Arabia*. Oliver & Boyd, Edinburgh.

Mellor, J W (1967) Notes on swallows and martins. *S. Aust. Orn.* 10: 204–8.

Menzel, H (1984) *Die Mehlschwalbe. Neue Brehm-Bücherei No. 548*. Ziemsen, Wittenberg Lutherstadt.

Michie, R H (1959) Welcome Swallows nesting in Northland – a new bird for New Zealand. *Notornis* 8: 61–2.

Miller, A H (1941) A review of centers of differentiation for birds in the western Great Basin region. *Condor* 43: 257–67.

Milon, P, Petter, H, and Randrianasolo, G (1973) *Faune de Madagascar 35: Oiseaux.* Tanarive & Paris: ORSTOM/CNRS.

Mischler, T C (1986) Die Avifauna des Rio Lurin bei Cieneguilla, Departamento Lima, Peru. *Bonn. Zool. Beitr.* 37: 257–79.

Mitchell, M H (1957) *Birds of Southeastern Brazil.* University of Toronto Press.

Mizuta, K (1963) Local distribution of two Swallows of genus *Hirundo* and breeding success of *H. rustica. Res. Popul. Ecol.* 5: 130–8.

Møller, A P (1974) Population density and nestling production in a population of Swallows, *Hirundo rustica* 1971–73. *Dansk orn. Foren. Tidsskr.* 68: 81–6.

—— (1983) Breeding habitat selection in the Swallow *Hirundo rustica. Bird Study* 30: 134–42.

—— (1984) Geographical trends in breeding parameters of Swallows, *Hirundo rustica* and House Martins *Delichon urbica. Orn. Scand.* 15: 43–54.

—— (1985) Mixed reproductive strategy and mate-guarding in a semi-colonial passerine, the Swallow *Hirundo rustica. Behav. Ecol. Sociobiol.* 17: 401–8.

—— (1987a) Intraspecific nest parasitism and anti-parasite behaviour in Swallows, *Hirundo rustica. Anim. Behav.* 35: 247–54.

—— (1987b) Advantages and disadvantages of coloniality in the Swallow, *Hirundo rustica. Anim. Behav.* 35: 819–32.

—— (1988a) Female choice selects for male sexual tail ornaments in the monogamous Swallow. *Nature, Lond.* 332: 640–2.

—— (1988b) Infanticidal and anti-infanticidal strategies in the Swallow *Hirundo rustica. Behav. Ecol. Sociobiol.* 22: 365–71.

—— (in press) Male tail length and female mate choice in the monogamous Swallow, *Hirundo rustica. Anim. Behav.*

Mollison, B C, and Green, R H (1962) Mist-netting Tree Martins on charcoal patches. *Emu* 61: 277–80.

Monroe, B L (1968) A distributional survey of the birds of Honduras. *Am. Orn. Monogr.* 7.

Moojen, J, Candido de Carvalho, J, and de Souza Lopes, H (1941) Observacoes sobre o contenido gástrico das aves brasilieras. *Mem. Inst. Oswaldo Cruz* 36: 405–44.

Moreau, R E (1939a) Numerical data on African birds' behaviour at the nest: *Hirundo s. smithii* Leach, the Wire-tailed Swallow. *Proc. Zool. Soc. Lond.* 109A: 109–25.

—— (1939b) Parental care by some African swallows and swifts. *Bull. Brit. Orn. Club* 59: 145–9.

—— (1940) Numerical data on African birds' behaviour at the nest II: *Psalidoprocne holomelaena massaica* Neum, the Roughwing Bank Martin. *Ibis* XIV(4): 234–48.

—— (1947) Relations between number in brood, feeding rate and nestling period in nine species of birds in Tanganyika territory. *J. Anim. Ecol.* 16: 205–9.

—— (1972) *The Palearctic African Bird Migration Systems.* Academic Press, London.

——, **and Moreau, W M** (1940) Incubation and fledging periods of African birds. *Auk* 57: 313–25.

Morgan, R A (1979) Sand Martin nest record cards. *Bird Study* 26: 129–32.

Morioka, H (1974) Jaw musculature of swifts (Aves: Apodidae). *Bull. Nat. Sci. Mus. Tokyo* 17: 1–16.

Morrison, A (1939) Birds of the Department of Huancavelica, Peru. *Ibis* 111: 457–86.

Morton, E S (1987) Variation in mate guarding intensity by male Purple Martins. *Behaviour* 101: 211–24.

—— (1988) Dawnsong of the Purple Martin. *Atlantic Nat.* 38: 38–48.

——, **Forman, L, and Braun, M** (ms) Extrapair copulation and the evolution of colonial breeding in Purple Martins.

Moss, W W, and Camin, J H (1970) Nest parasitism, productivity and clutch size in Purple Martins. *Science* 168: 1000–2.

Muldal, A, Gibbs, H L, and Robertson, R J (1985) Preferred nest spacing of an obligate cavity-nesting bird, the Tree Swallow. *Condor* 87: 356–63.

Myres, M T (1957) Clutch size and laying dates in Cliff Swallows. *Condor* 59: 311–16.

Naumberg, E M B (1930) *The Birds of Matto Grosso, Brazil.* American Museum of Natural History, New York.

Nevill, A (1984) Fairy and Tree Martins in Otago. *Notornis* 31: 173–5.

Newman, J R (1979) Effects of industrial air pollution on wildlife. *Biol. Conserv.* 15: 181–90.

Niethammer, G (1956) Zur Vogelwelt Boliviens (Teil II: Passeres). *Bonn. Zool. Beitr.* 1–3: 84–150.

Niles, D M (1972) Molt cycles of Purple Martins. *Condor* 74: 61–71.

Nyandoro, R (1987) Comments on territorial behaviour and weights of Wire-tailed Swallows. *Honeyguide* 33: 62–3.

Ogle, D (1986) The status and seasonality of birds in Nakhon Sawan Province, Thailand. *Nat. Hist. Bull. Siam. Soc.* 34: 115–43.

Oliver, D W (1975) A cause of decline in farmyard House Martin colonies. *Scot. Birds* 8: 325–7.

Oliver, W R B (1930) *New Zealand Birds.* Fine Arts (NZ), Wellington . (2nd edn. 1955)

Olrog, C Ch (1965) Contenidos estomacales de aves del noroeste Argentina. *Hornero* 10: 158–63.

Oo-u-kijo (1936) *Riparia paludicola brevicaudata* in Taiwan, Formosa. *Bot. Zool. Tokyo* 4: 2065–75.

Osburn, W (1869) Notes on the mountain birds of Jamaica. *Zoologist* 208: 6709–22, 6833–41.

Ouellet, H (1970) Changes in the bird fauna of the Montreal Region, Canada. *Can. Field Nat.* 84: 27–34.

Packenham, R H W (1979) *The Birds of Zanzibar and Pemba.* British Ornithologists' Union, London.

Palmer, R S (1972) Patterns of molting. In: *Avian Biology, Vol. II* (Ed. by D S Farner, J R King and K C Parkes), pp. 65–155. Academic Press, New York.

Park, P (1981a) A colour banding study of Welcome Swallows breeding in southern Tasmania. *Corella* 5: 37–41.

—— (1981b) Results from a nesting study of Welcome Swallows in southern Tasmania. *Corella* 5: 85–90.

Parker, T A, III, and O'Neill, J P (1980) Notes on little known birds of the upper Urubamba valley, southern Peru. *Auk* 97: 167–76.

——, **Parker, S A, and Plenge, M A** (1982) *An Annotated Checklist of Peruvian Birds.* Buteo, Vermillion, South Dakota.

——, **and Remsen, J V, Jr** (1987) Fifty-two Amazonian bird species new to Bolivia. *Bull. Brit. Orn. Club* 107: 94–107.

——, **and Rowlett, R A** (1984) Some noteworthy records of birds from Bolivia. *Bull. Brit. Orn. Club* 104: 110–13.

Parker, T A, III, Schulenberg, T S, Graves, G R, and Braun, M J (1985) The avifauna of the Huancabamba region, northern Peru, *Orn. Monogr.* 36: 169–97.

Parkes, K C (1970) On the validity of some supposed 'first state records' from Yucatan. *Wilson Bull.* 82: 92–5.

—— (1987) Was the 'Chinese' White-eyed River Martin an Oriental Pratincole? *Forktail* 3: 68–9.

Paterson, A (1972) *Birds of the Bahamas.* Durrell Publications, Brattleboro, Vermont.

Pavlova, N R (1962) Characteristics of reproduction and the diet of the Sand Martin in the Oka Reserve. *Ornitologiya* 4: 122–31.

Paynter, R A, Jr (1957) Rough-winged Swallow of the race *stuarti* in Chiapas and British Honduras. *Condor* 59: 212–3.

Paz, U (1987) *The Birds of Israel.* Christopher Helm, London.

Persson, C (1978) Dispersion of Sand Martins in Skåne, southern Sweden. *Anser.* Suppl. 3: 199–212.

Pescott, T (1978) Tree Martins as cave nesters. *Aust. Bird-Watcher* 7: 273–6.

Peters, J L (1960) *Checklist of the Birds of the World. Vol. 9.* Harvard University Press, Cambridge, Massachusetts.

Petersen, A J (1955) The breeding cycle in the Bank Swallow. *Wilson Bull.* 67: 235–86.

——, **and Mueller, P C** (1979) Longevity and colony loyalty in Bank Swallows. *Bird-Banding* 50: 69–70.

Peterson, W R, Nikula, B J, and Holt, D W (1986) First record of Brown-chested Martin for North America. *Am. Birds* 40: 192–3.

Fereyra, J A (1969) Avifauna Argentina. Familia Hirundinidae: Golondrinas. *Hornero* 11: 1–19.

Phillips, A R (1986) *The Known Birds of North and Middle America: Distribution and Variation, Migrations, Changes, Hybrids, etc. Part I Hirundinidae to Mimidae.* Private, Denver.

——, **Marshall, A J, and Monson, G** (1964) *The Birds of Arizona.* University of Arizona Press.

Phillips, W W A (1950) Nests and eggs of Ceylon birds. *Ceylon J. Sci. (B),* XXIV, part 1: 63–83.

Pinchon, R A (1963) *Faune des Antilles Françaises.* Fort-de-France.

Pitman, C R S (1931) The breeding habits and eggs of *Hirundo senegalensis senegalensis* – the Mosque Swallow in Uganda. *Ool. Rec.* 11: 14–16.

Plowes, D C H (1944) A brief survey of the birds of Bloemhof District. *Ostrich* 15: 81–103.

Prenn, F (1929) Ueber das Vorkommen von Felsenschwalbe und Zwergfliegenfanger usw in der Umgebung von Kufstein (Nordkrol). *Orn. Monatsber.* XXXVII/2.

—— (1937) Beobachtungen zur Lebensweise der Felsenschwalbe *Riparia rupestris* (Scop). *J. für Orn.* 85: 577–86.

Priest, C D (1935) *Birds of Southern Rhodesia. Vol. 3.* Clowes & Sons, London.

Pringle, V L (1948) Unusual nesting sites. *Ostrich* 19: 157.

Prinzinger, R, and Siedle, K (1986) Experimental procf of torpidity in young House Martins, *Delichon urbica. J. für Orn.* 127: 95–6.

——, and Siedle, K (1988) Ontogeny of metabolism, thermoregulation and torpor in the House Martin (*Delichon urbica urbica* (L.) and its ecological significance. *Oecologia* 761: 307–12.

Prodon, R (1982) Sur la nidification, le régime alimentaire et les vocalisations de l'Hirondelle rousseline en France. *Alauda* 50: 176–92.

Quinney, T E (1983) Tree Swallows cross a polygyny threshold. *Auk* 100: 750–4.

—— (1986) Male and female parental care in Tree Swallows. *Wilson Bull.* 98: 147–50.

——, and Ankney, C D (1985) Prey size selection by Tree Swallows. *Auk* 102: 245–50.

Rand, A L (1936) The distribution and habitats of Madagascar birds. *Bull. Am. Mus. Nat. Hist.* 72: 142–499.

——, Friedmann, H, and Traylor, M A, Jr (1959) Birds from Gabon and Moyen Congo. *Fieldiana Zool.* 41 No. 2.

Reilly, P N, Brooker, M G, and Johnstone, G W (1975) Birds of the southwest Nullarbor Plain. *Emu* 75: 73–6.

——, and Garrett, W J (1973) Nesting of Fairy Martins in culverts. *Emu* 73: 188–9.

Remsen, J V, Jr (1985) Community organization and ecology of birds of high-elevation humid forest of the Bolivian Andes. *Orn. Monogr.* 36: 233–56.

Rheinwald, G, Gutscher, H, and Hörmeyer, K (1976) Einfluss des Alters der Mehlschwalbe auf ihre Brut. *Vogelwarte* 28: 190–206.

Ricklefs, R E (1968) Weight recession in nestling birds. *Auk* 85: 30–5.

—— (1971) Foraging behavior of Mangrove Swallows at Barro Colorado Island. *Auk* 88: 635–51.

—— (1976) Growth rates of birds in the humid New World Tropics. *Ibis* 118: 179–207.

Riddell, D, and Taylor, A (1984) Fairy Martin at Cape Reinga. *Notornis* 31: 224.

Ridgway, R (1904) Birds of North and Middle America. *Bull. US Nat. Mus.* 50: 23–103.

Riley, J H (1905) List of birds collected or observed during the Bahama expedition of the Geographic Society of Baltimore. *Auk* 22: 349–60.

Robbins, C S, Bystrak, D, and Geissler, P H (1986) *The Breeding Bird Survey: its First 15* years 1965–1979. USDI Fish & Wildlife Service, Washington D.C.

Roberts, A (1922) Review of the nomenclature of South African birds. *Ann. Trans. Mus.* 8: 188–272.

—— (1939) Swifts and other birds nesting in buildings. *Ostrich* 10: 85–99.

Robertson, R J, and Gibbs, H L (1982) Superterritoriality in Tree Swallows: a re-examination. *Condor* 84: 313–6.

——, and Stutchbury, B J (1988) Experimental evidence for sexually selected infanticide in Tree Swallows. *Anim. Behav.* 36: 749–53.

Robertson, W B, Jr, and Kushlan, J A (1974) *The Southern Florida Avifauna.* Memoir 2. Miami Geological Society, Miami.

Rogers, K, Rogers, A, and Rogers, O (1986) *Bander's Aid: A Guide to Ageing and Sexing Bush Birds.* Private, St Andrews, Victoria.

Rohwer, S, and Niles, D M (1977) An historical analysis of spring arrival times in Purple Martins: a test of two hypotheses. *Bird Banding* 48: 162–7.

——, and Niles, D M (1979) The subadult plumage of male Purple Martins: variability, female mimicry and recent evolution. *Z. Tierpsychol.* 51: 282–300.

Rowan, M K (1968) The origins of European Swallows 'wintering' in South Africa. *Ostrich* 39: 76–84.

Russell, S M (1964) A distributional study of the birds of British Honduras. *Orn. Monogr.* 1: 1–195.

——, and Lamm, D W (1978) Notes on the distribution of birds in Sonora, Mexico. *Wilson Bull.* 90: 123–31.

Rydzewski, W (1978) The longevity of ringed birds. *Ring* 96–7: 218–62.

Salter, B E (1960) At home with the swallows. *Aust. Bird Watcher* 1: 63–5.

Salvan, J (1969) Contribution à l'étude des oiseaux du Tchad. *L'Oiseau* 39: 38–69.

Samuel, D E (1971a) Vocal repertoire of sympatric Barn and Cliff Swallows. *Auk* 88: 839–55.

—— (1971b) The breeding biology of Barn and Cliff Swallows in West Virginia. *Wilson Bull.* 83: 284–301.

Schaeffer, F S (1970) Observation of 'billing' in courtship behaviour of the Tree Swallow. *Bird Banding* 41: 242.

Schmidt, R K (1959) Notes on the Pearl-breasted Swallow *Hirundo dimidiata* in the south-western Cape. *Ostrich* 30: 155–8.

—— (1962) Breeding of the Larger Striped

Swallow *Cecropis cucullata* in the south-west Cape. *Ostrich* 33: 3–8.

—— (1964) Incubation period of Rock Martins (*Ptyonoprogne fuligula* (Lichtenstein)). *Ostrich* 35: 122.

Schmitt, C G, Schmitt, D C, Remsen, J V, Jr, and Glick, D D (1986) New bird records for Departamento Santa Cruz, Bolivia. *Hornero* 12: 307–11.

Schönwetter, M (1979) *Handbuch der Oologie*. Vol. 2. Ed. by W Meise. Akademie Verlag, Berlin.

Schouteden, H (1957) Faune du Congo Belge et du Ruanda-Urundi. Vol. IV. Oiseaux passereaux I. *Ann. Mus. Roy. Congo Belge, Tervuren, Sci. Zool.* 57.

Schrader, N W (1976) Breeding of the Welcome Swallow at Ivanhoe in western New South Wales. *Aust. Birds* 111: 1–17.

Schulenberg, T S, and Remsen, J V, Jr (1982) Eleven bird species new to Bolivia. *Bull. Brit. Orn. Club* 102: 52–7.

——, **and Parker, T A III** (1981) Status and distribution of some northwest Peruvian birds. *Condor* 83: 209–16.

Sclater, P L, and Hudson, W H (1888) *Argentine Ornithology*. Vol. 1. Porter, London.

——, **and Salvin, O** (1879) On the birds collected by T. K. Salmon in the State of Antioquia, United States of Colombia. *Proc. Zool. Soc. Lond.* 1879: 486–550.

Sclater, W L, and Moreau, R E (1933) Taxonomic and field notes on some birds of Northeastern Tanganyika Territory. Part IV. *Ibis* XIII(3): 187–91.

Scott, D, and Brooke, M (1985) The endangered avifauna of south-eastern Brazil; a report on the BOU/WWF expeditions of 1980/81 and 1981/82. *ICBP Tech. Publ.* 4: 115–39.

Sealy, S G (1983) Rough-winged Swallow scavenging adult midges. *Wilson Bull.* 94: 368–9.

Sedgwick, E H (1949) Tree Martin (*Hylochelidon nigricans*) nesting on wooden buildings. *West. Aust. Nat.* 1: 154–5.

—— (1958) Fairy Martins in southwestern Australia. *West. Aust. Nat.* 6: 100–5.

Selander, R K, and Baker, J K (1957) The Cave Swallow in Texas. *Condor* 59: 345–63

Serle, W (1940) Field observations on some northern Nigerian birds. Part II. *Ibis* XIV(4): 1–47.

—— (1943) Further field observations on northern Nigerian birds. *Ibis* 85: 413–37.

—— (1949) Birds of Sierra Leone III. *Ostrich* 20: 70–91.

—— (1950a) Notes on the birds of south-western Nigeria. *Ibis* 84–94.

—— (1950b) A contribution to the ornithology of British Cameroon. *Ibis* 92: 602–38.

—— (1954) A second contribution to the ornithology of British Cameroon. *Ibis* 96: 47–80.

—— (1957) A contribution to the ornithology of the eastern region of Nigeria. *Ibis* 99: 371–418.

—— (1965) A third contribution to the ornithology of British Cameroon. *Ibis* 107: 60–94, 230–46.

—— (1981) The breeding season of birds in the lowland rainforest and in the mountain forest of West Cameroon. *Ibis* 123: 62–74.

Serventy, D L (1958) Bird notes from the Dumbleyung Camp-out. *Emu* 58: 5–20.

—— (1970) Torpidity in the White-backed Swallow. *Emu* 70: 27–8.

——, **and Whittell, H M** (1962) *Birds of Western Australia.* 3rd edn. Paterson, Perth.

Sharland, M S R (1943) Nesting habits of the Tree Martin. *Emu* 43: 75.

Sharpe, R B (1870) On the Hirundinidae of the Ethiopian region. *Proc. Zool. Soc. Lond.* 1870: 286–326.

——, **and Wyatt, C W** (1885–1894) *A Monograph of the Hirundinidae or Family of Swallows.* Sotheran, London.

Sharrock, J T R (1976) *The Atlas of Breeding Birds in Britain and Ireland.* BTO, Tring.

Shaw, G G (1983) Organochlorine pesticide and PCB residues in eggs and nestlings of Tree Swallows, *Tachycineta bicolor*, in Central Alberta. *Can. Field Nat.* 98: 258–60.

Shaw, J R (1979) Some notes on the fledging of Wire-tailed Swallows. *Honeyguide* 98: 35–7.

Shelley, L O (1934) Two pairs of Tree Swallows mated during two successive seasons. *Bird-banding* 5: 91.

Shields, W M (1984) Barn Swallow mobbing: self defence, collateral kin defence, group defence or parental care? *Anim. Behav.* 32: 132–48.

—— (1984b) Factors affecting nest and site fidelity in Adirondack Barn Swallows (*Hirundo rustica*). *Auk* 101: 780–9.

Shields, W M, and Crook, J R (1987) Barn Swallow coloniality: a net cost for group breeding in the Adirondacks? *Ecology* 68: 1373–86.

——, **Crook, J R, Hebblethwaite, M L, and Wiles-Ehmann, S S** (1988) Ideal free coloniality in the swallows. In: *The Ecology of*

Social Behaviour (Ed. by C N Slobodchikoff), pp. 189–228. Academic Press, San Diego.

Shillingford, N F (1965) Unusual nesting of the Larger Striped Swallow. *Bokmakierie* 17: 21.

Shirling, A E (1935) Observations on the Violet-green Swallow. *Wilson Bull.* 47: 192–4.

Short, L L (1975) A zoogeographic analysis of the South American Chaco avifauna. *Bull. Am. Mus. Nat. Hist.* 154: 1–352.

Show Tsen-Hwang (1930) Notes on some summer birds of Chafoo, China. *Auk*: 542–5.

Sibley, C G, and Ahlquist, J E (1982) The relationships of the swallows (Hirundinidae). *J. Yamashina Inst. Orn.* 14: 122–30.

——, —— (1985) The phylogeny of the Australo-Papuan passerine birds. *Emu* 85: 1–14.

Sieber, O (1980) Kausale und funktionelle Aspekte der Verteilung von Uferschwalben-bruten. *Z. Tierpsychol.* 52: 19–56.

—— (1985) Individual recognition of parental calls by Bank Swallow chicks (*Riparia riparia*). *Anim. Behav.* 33: 107–16.

Sikes, P J, and Arnold, K A (1984) Movement and mortality estimates of Cliff Swallows in Texas. *Wilson Bull.* 96: 419–25.

Simeonow, S D (1968) Über die Nistweise der Rötelschwalbe in Bulgarien. *J. für Orn.* 109: 57–61.

Simmons, K (1987) *The Sunning Behaviour of Birds*. Bristol Ornithologists' Club, Bristol.

Skead, D M (1964) Birds of the Aniatol forests, King William's Town and Stutterheim, C.P. *Ostrich* 35: 142–59.

—— (1966) Birds frequenting the intertidal zone of the Cape Peninsula. *Ostrich* 37: 10–6.

—— (1979) Feeding associations of *Hirundo spilodera* with other animals. *Bokmakierie* 31: 63.

——, and Skead, C J (1970) Hirundinid mortality during adverse weather, November 1968. *Ostrich* 41: 247–51.

Skutch, A F (1952) Life history of the Blue-and-white Swallow. *Auk* 69: 392–406.

—— (1960) Life histories of Central American birds. II. *Pac. Coast Avif.* no. 34.

—— (1981) *New Studies of Tropical American Birds*. Nuttall Ornithological Club, Cambridge, Massachusetts.

Slud, P (1964) The birds of Costa Rica: distribution and ecology. *Bull. Am. Mus. Nat. Hist.* 128: 1–430.

Smirensky, S M, and Mishchenko, A L (1981) Taxonomical status and history of formation of the range of *Hirundo rustica* in the Amur territory. *Zool. Zh.* 60: 1533–41.

Smith, K D (1957) An annotated checklist of the birds of Eritrea. *Ibis* 99: 307–37.

Smythies, B E (1953) *The Birds of Burma. 2nd edn.* Oliver & Boyd, Edinburgh.

—— (1968) *The Birds of Borneo. 2nd edn.* Oliver & Boyd, Edinburgh.

Snapp, B D (1976) Colonial breeding in the Barn Swallow (*Hirundo rustica*) and its adaptive significance. *Condor* 78: 471–80.

Snell, M L (1963) A study of the Blue Swallow. *Bokmakierie* 31: 74–8.

—— (1969) Notes on the breeding of the Blue Swallow. *Ostrich* 40: 65–74.

—— (1970) Nesting behaviour of a pair of blue Swallows. *Bokmakierie* 22: 27–9.

—— (1979) The vulnerable Blue Swallow. *Bokmakerie* 31: 74–8.

Snow, D W, and Snow, B K (1964) Breeding seasons and annual cycles of Trinidad land-birds. *Zoologica* 49: 1–39.

Snyder (1966) *Birds of Guyana*. Peabody Museum, Salem, Massachusetts.

Sophason, S, and Dobias, Q (1984) The fate of the 'Princess Bird' or White-eyed River Martin (*Pseudochelidon sirintarae*). *Nat. Hist. Bull. Siam Soc.* 32: 1–10.

Speich, S M, Jones, H L, and Benedict, E M (1985) Review of the natural nesting of the Barn Swallow in North America. *Am. Midl. Nat.* 115: 248–54.

Stadler, H (1928) Die Stimme der Felsenschwalbe (*Ptyonoprogne rupestris*). *Orn. Beob.* 25: 53–6.

Stake, J D, and Stake, P D (1983) Apparent torpidity in Tree Swallows. *Conn. Warbler* 3: 36–7.

Stanford, J K, and Mayr, E (1941) The Vernay-Cutting Expedition to Northern Burma. *Ibis* 1941: 365–72.

Staub, J J F (1973) *Oiseaux de l'Ile Maurice et de Rodrigue*. Mauritius Printing Company, Port Louis, Mauritius.

Stepanyan, L S, and Vasil'chenko, A A (1980) The Eastern Martin *Delichon dasypus* (Bonaparte 1850) in the fauna of the USSR. *Byull. Mosk. Obshch. Ispyt. Prirody* 87: 32–8.

Stewart, R M (1972) Nestling mortality in swallows due to inclement weather. *Calif. Birds* 3: 69–70.

Stiles, F G (1981) The taxonomy of rough-winged swallows in southern Central America. *Auk* 98: 282–93.

Stoddard, P K (1988) The 'bugs' call of the Cliff Swallow: a rare food signal in a colonially nesting bird species. *Condor* 90: 714–15.

——, and Beecher, M D (1983) Parental recognition of offspring in the Cliff Swallow. *Auk* 100: 795–9.

Stoner, D (1936) Studies on the Bank Swallow in the Oneida Lake Region. *Roosevelt Wildl. Ann. 4. Bull. NY State Coll. Forestry, Syracuse Univ.* 9: 126–233.

Storer, R W (1971) Classification of birds. In: *Avian Biology. Vol. 1.* Ed. by D S Farner, J R King, and K C Parker. Pp. 1–18. Academic Press, New York.

Storr, G M (1965) The avifauna of Rottnest Island, Western Australia. III. Land birds. *Emu* 64: 172–80.

Strahm, J (1953) Über Standort und Anlage des Nestes bei Felsenschwalben. *Orn. Beob.* 50: 41–8.

—— (1954) Observations sur la reproduction de l'Hirondelle de rochers. *Nos Oiseaux* 22: 187–96.

—— (1956) Nouvelles observations sur la reproduction des hirondelles. *Nos Oiseaux* 23: 257–65.

—— (1963) Notes sur le territoire de nidification chez l'hirondelle de rocher. *Nos Oiseaux* 27: 61–6.

Stresemann, E, and Stresemann, V (1969) Die Mauser von *Ptyonoprogne rupestris* und *Delichon nipalensis. J. für Orn.* 110: 39–52.

Stuart, S N (1986) *Conservation of Cameroon Montane Forests.* ICBP, Cambridge.

Stutchbury, B J, and Robertson, R J (1985) Floating populations of female Tree Swallows. *Auk* 102: 651–4.

——, —— (1987a) Behavioral tactics of subadult female floaters in the Tree Swallow. *Behav. Ecol. Sociobiol.* 20: 413–9.

——, —— (1987b) Two methods of sexing adult Tree Swallows before they begin breeding. *J. Field Orn.* 58: 236–42.

——, —— (1987c) Signaling subordinate and female status: two hypotheses for the adaptive significance of subadult plumage in Tree Swallows. *Auk* 104: 717–23.

——, —— (1987d) Do nest building and first egg dates reflect settlement patterns of females? *Condor* 89: 587–93.

——, —— (1988) Within season and age-related patterns of reproductive performance in female Tree Swallows (*Tachycineta bicolor*). *Can. J. Zool.* 66: 827–41.

Summers, R W (1975) On the ecology of *Craterina hirundis (Diptera: Hippoboscidae)* in Scotland. *J. Zool. Lond.* 175: 557–70.

Svensson, S (1969) Häckningsbiologiska studier i en koloni av backsvala vid Ammärnås ar 1968. *Vår Fågelvärld* 28: 236–40.

Swarth, H S (1931) *The Avifauna of the Galapagos Islands.* California Academy of Science, San Francisco.

Tate, P (1981) *Swallows.* Witherby, London.

Tatner, P (1978) A survey of House Martins in part of south Manchester 1975. *Naturalist* 103: 59–68.

Taylor, P B (1979) Palaearctic and intra-African migrant birds in Zambia: a report for the period May 1971 to December 1976. *Zambian Orn. Soc. Occ. Pap.* 1: 1–169.

Taylor, J S (1942) Notes on the martins, swallows and swifts: Graaf-Reinet. *Ostrich* 13: 148–56.

—— (1949) Notes on the martins, swallows and swifts of Fort Beaufort C.P. *Ostrich* 20: 26–8.

Thiollay, J M (1985) The birds of the Ivory Coast: status and distribution. *Malimbus* 7: 1–59.

Todd, W E C, and Worthington, N W (1911) A contribution to the ornithology of the Bahama Islands. *Annals Carnegie Mus.* 7: 388–464.

Took, J M E (1967) Grey-rumped Swallows at sea. *Ostrich* 38: 199.

Tostain, D (1979) Nidification sur un bateau de l'Hirondelle à Ailes Blanches, *Tachycineta albiventer*, en Guyana Française. *Gerfaut* 69: 393–5.

Traylor, M A, and Parelius, D (1967) A collection of birds from the Ivory Coast. *Fieldiana Zool.* 51: 91–117.

Tree, A J (1976) Movements of the Grey-rumped Swallow. *Honeyguide* 87: 35.

—— (1986a) The European Sand Martin in Zimbabwe. *Honeyguide* 32: 5–9.

—— (1986b) The Banded Sand Martin in Zimbabwe. *Honeyguide,* 32: 10–2.

——, and Earlé, R A (1984) The Brown Sand Martin – a potential national ringing project. *Safring News* 13: 71–4.

Turner, A K (1980) The use of time and energy by aerial-feeding birds. Ph.D. thesis. University of Stirling.

—— (1981) Lepidopteran larvae in the diet of the Swallow. *Bird Study* 28: 65.

—— (1982a) Counts of aerial-feeding birds in relation to pollution levels. *Bird Study* 29: 221–6.

—— (1982b) Timing of laying by Swallows (*Hirundo rustica*) and Sand Martins (*Riparia riparia*). *J. Anim. Ecol.* 51: 29–46.

—— (1983a) Time and energy constraints on the brood size of Swallows *Hirundo rustica* and Sand Martins *Riparia riparia*. *Oecologia* 59: 331–8.

—— (1983b) Food selection and the timing of breeding of the Blue-and-White Swallow *Notiochelidon cyanoleuca* in Venezuela. *Ibis* 125: 450–62.

—— (1984) Nesting and feeding habits of Brown-chested Martins in relation to weather conditions. *Condor* 86: 30–5.

——, and Bryant, D M (1979) Growth of nestling Sand Martins. *Bird Study* 26: 117–22.

Tye, A (1985) Preuss's Cliff Swallow *Hirundo preussi* breeding in Sierra Leone. *Malimbus* 7: 95–6.

——, and Tye, H (1986) Nepal House Martin *Delichon nipalensis* new to Thailand. *Forktail* 1: 83–5.

Uchida, S (1932) Studies of Swallows by the banding method. *Bird Banding* 3: 1–11.

Urban, E K (1959) Birds from Coahuila, Mexico. *Univ. Kans. Publ. Mus. Nat. Hist.* 11: 443–516.

——, and Brown, L H (1971) *A Checklist of the Birds of Ethiopia.* Haile Selassie I University Press, Addis Ababa.

Valverde, J A (1957) *Aves del Saharo Español.* Madrid.

Van Someren, V G L (1916) A list of birds collected in Uganda and British East Africa with notes on their nesting and other habits. *Ibis* XII(1): 373–472.

—— (1958) *A Birdwatcher in Kenya.* Oliver & Boyd, Edinburgh.

——, and Van Someren, G R C (1949) *The Birds of Bwamba.* The Uganda Society, Kampala.

Vasil'chenko, A A (1987) *The Birds of Khamar-Daban.* Nauka, Novosibirsk.

Vaurie, C (1951) Notes on some Asiatic swallows. *Am. Mus. Novit.* No. 1529: 1–47.

—— (1954) Systematic notes on Palearctic birds. No. 12. Muscicapinae, Hirundinidae and Sturnidae. *Am. Mus. Novit.* No. 1694: 1–18.

Verhayen, R (1954) Exploration du Parc National Upemba. *Miss. Q.F. de Witte* 19: 538–47.

Vincent, A W (1949) On the breeding habits of some African birds. *Ibis* 91: 111–6.

Vincent, R T (1972) Fairy Martin in southern Tasmania. *Emu* 72: 115–6.

von Gunten, K (1961) Zur Ernährungsbiologie der Mehlschwalbe *Delichon urbica*. Die qualitative Zusammensetzung der Nahrung. *Orn. Beob.* 58: 13–34.

—— (1963) Untersuchungen an einer Dorfgemeinschaft von Mehlschwalben. *Orn. Beob.* 60: 1–11.

von Vietinghoff-Riesch, A (1955) *Die Rauchschwalbe.* Duncher and Humblot, Berlin.

von Wicht, U (1978) Zur Arealausweitung der Rötelschwalbe in Europa. *Anz. orn. Ges. Bayern* 17: 79–98.

Voous, K H (1977) List of recent Holarctic bird species. *Ibis* 119: 223–56.

Vowles, R S, and Vowles, G A (1985) Some notes on the birds of Borneo. *Bull. Brit. Orn. Club* 105: 71–3.

Wagner, H O (1951) Zugbeobachtungen an der Schwalbe *Stelgidopteryx ruficollis* in Mexico. *Vogelwarte* 16: 59–62.

Walsh, H (1978) Food of nestling Purple Martins. *Wilson Bull.* 90:248–60.

Wang (1959) Preliminary studies on the life-history of the House Swallow. *Acta Zool. Sinica* 11: 138–44.

Watson, I M (1955) Some species seen at the Laverton Saltworks, Victoria, 1950–53, with notes on seasonal changes. *Emu* 55: 224–8.

Waugh, D R (1978) Predation strategies in aerial-feeding birds. Ph.D. thesis, University of Stirling.

—— (1979) The diet of Sand Martins during the breeding season. *Bird Study* 26: 123–8.

——, and Hails, C J (1983) Feeding ecology of a tropical aerial-feeding bird guild. *Ibis* 125: 200–17.

Weatherhead, P J, Sealy, S G, and Barclay, R M R (1985) Risks of clustering in thermally-stressed swallows. *Condor* 87: 443–4.

Wells, D R (1968) Zonation of bird communities on Fernando Po. *Bull. Nigerian Orn. Soc.* 5: 71–87.

—— (1984) Bird report. 1978 and 1979. *Malay Nat. J.* 38: 111–50.

Wendelken, P W, and Martin, R F (1986) Recent data on the distribution of birds in Guatemala. *Bull. Brit. Orn. Club* 106: 16–22.

Weston, F M (1965) A survey of the birdlife of northwestern Florida. *Bull. Tall Timbers Res. Sta.* 5: 1–147.

Wetmore, A (1916) Birds of Porto Rico. *USDA Bull.* 326: 1–140.

—— (1926) Observations on the birds of Argentina, Paraguay, Uruguay and Chile. *US Natn Mus. Bull.* 133: 1–448.

—— (1941) Notes on birds of the Guatemalan highlands. *Proc. US Nat. Mus.* 89: 523–81.

——, **and Lincoln, F C** (1933) Additional notes on the birds of Haiti and the Dominican Republic. *Proc. US Nat. Mus.* 82: 1–68.

——, **Pasquier, R F, and Olson, S L** (1984) *Birds of the Republic of Panama.* Smithsonian Institution, Washington D.C.

——, **and Swales, B H** (1931) The birds of Haiti and the Dominican Republic. *US Natn. Mus. Bull.* 155.

Weydemeyer, W. (1934) Tree Swallows at home in Montana. *Bird-lore* 36: 100–5.

—— (1973) The spring migration pattern at Fortune, Montana. *Condor* 75: 400–13.

White, C M (1961) *A Revised Checklist of African Broadbills, Pittas, Larks, Swallows, Wagtails and Pipits.* Government Printer, Lusaka.

——, **and Bruce, M D** (1986) *The Birds of Wallacea.* British Ornithologists' Union, London.

White, G (1789) *The Natural History of Selbourne.*

Williams, J G (1966) A new species of swallow from Kenya. *Bull. Brit. Orn. Club* 86: 40.

Willis, E O, and Oniki, Y (1985) Bird specimens new for the state of Sao Paulo, Brazil. *Rev. Brazil Biol.* 45: 105–8.

Wilson, A S (1926) Lista de aves del sur de Santa Fe. *Hornero* 3: 349–63.

Windsor, D, and Emlen, S T (1975) Predator and prey interactions of adult and prefledgling Bank Swallows and Sparrow Hawks. *Condor* 77: 359–61.

Winterbottom, J M (1939) Miscellaneous notes on some birds of northern Rhodesia. *Ibis* XIV(3): 712–34.

—— (1942) A contribution to the ornithology of Barotseland. *Ibis* XIV(6): 337–89.

—— (1962) Some manuscript notes of S. F. Townsend for the period 1878–1925. *Ostrich* 52: 66–71.

Wolf, L L (1976) Avifauna of the Cerro de la Muerte Region, Costa Rica. *Am. Mus. Novit.* 2606: 1–37.

Wolters, H E (1952) Die Gattungen der westpalaerktischen Sperlingsvogel (Ordn Passeriformes). *Bonn. Zool. Beitr.* 3: 231–88.

—— (1971) Probleme der Gattungsabrenzung in der Ornithologie. *Bonn. Zool. Beitr.* 22: 210–9.

Wood, M (1973) Nesting behaviour of the Welcome Swallow. *Aust. Bird Watcher* 4: 270–1.

Young, C G (1946) Birds of Cameroon Mountain District. *Ibis* 88: 348–82.

Zach, R (1982) Hatching asynchrony, egg size, growth and fledging in Tree Swallows. *Auk* 99: 695–700.

Zimmer, J J (1955) Studies on Peruvian birds. No. 66. The swallows. *Am. Mus. Novit.* 1723: 1–35.

Zimmerman, D A (1978) Mascarene Martins in Kenya. *Scopus* 2: 74–5.

Zink, G (1970) The migrations of European Swallows to Africa from data obtained through ringing in Europe. *Ostrich Suppl.* 8: 211–22.

Zotta, A R (1936) Sobre el contenido estomacal de aves argentinas. *Hornero* 6: 261–70.

—— (1940) Lista sobre el contenido estomacal de las aves argentinas. *Hornero* 7: 402–11.

Zusi, R L (1978) Remarks on the generic allocation of *Pseudochelidon sirintarae. Bull. Brit. Orn. Club* 98: 13–5.

INDEX